W9-CQB-156

World Civilization Sources

Edited by

THEODORE KALLMAN

San Joaquin Delta College

KENDALL/HUNT PUBLISHING COMPANY

4050 Westmark Drive Dubuque, Iowa 52002

Cover photo by Joe Bisson

Copyright © 2005 by Theodore Kallman

ISBN 978-0-7575-2139-3

Kendall/Hunt Publishing Company has the exclusive rights to reproduce this work, to prepare derivative works from this work, to publicly distribute this work, to publicly perform this work and to publicly display this work.

All rights reserved. No part of this publication may be reproduced, stored in a retrieval system, or transmitted, in any form or by any means, electronic, mechanical, photocopying, recording, or otherwise, without the prior written permission of Kendall/Hunt Publishing Company.

Printed in the United States of America
10 9 8 7 6 5 4 3 2

Contents

CHAPTER 1: ORIGINS OF CIVILIZATIONS — 1

1.1 The Babylonian Creation Epic (ca. 2000 B.C.E.) 2
1.2 The Epic of Gilgamesh 9
1.3 Law Code, *Hammurabi* 15
1.4 A Hymn to the Nile 20
1.5 Hymn to the One Universal God 22

CHAPTER 2: KINGDOMS AND EMPIRES IN THE NEAR EAST — 29

2.1 Annals of Nubian Kings (593 B.C.E.) 30
2.2 Genesis: The Hebrew Creation and Flood Stories 33
2.3 Deuteronomy 43
2.4 Inscription of Tiglath-Pileser I, King of Assyria (1120 B.C.E.) 48
2.5 The Gathas, *Zarathustra* 50

CHAPTER 3: THE FOUNDATION OF INDIAN SOCIETY, TO 300 C.E. — 53

3.1 Rig Veda, The Creation Hymn 54
3.2 The Upanishads 56
3.3 The Life of the Buddha 59

CHAPTER 4: CHINA'S CLASSICAL AGE, TO 256 B.C.E. — 63

4.1 Analects, *Confucius* 64
4.2 The Mandate of Heaven 71

CHAPTER 5: THE GREEK EXPERIENCE — 73

5.1 Crito, *Plato* 74
5.2 The Politics, *Aristotle* 78

Chapter 6: The Glory of Rome 87

6.1 The Epistle to the Romans, *Paul of Tarsus (Saint Paul)* 88

Chapter 7: East Asia, ca. 200 B.C.E.-800 C.E. 95

7.1 Records of the Grand Historian, *Sima Qian* 96
7.2 Chronicles of Japan 98

Chapter 8: The Making of Europe 101

8.1 The Enchiridion, *St. Augustine* 102
8.2 The Institutes of Justinian 110

Chapter 9: The Islamic World, ca. 600-1400 113

9.1 The Holy Qur'an 114
9.2 The Pact of Ibn Muslama and The Pact of Umar 121

Chapter 10: African Societies and Kingdoms, ca. 400-1450 125

10.1 The Chronicle of Guinea, *Gomes Eannes de Azurara* 126
10.2 Description of the Coasts of East Africa and Malabar, *Duarte Barbosa* 129

Chapter 11: Southern and Central Asia, ca. 300-1400 135

11.1 Description of India, *Abu'l Raihan al-Biruni* 136

Chapter 12: East Asia, ca. 800-1400 141

12.1 Letter to Changchun, *Chinggis Khan* 142
12.2 Travels, *Marco Polo* 144
12.3 The Tale of the Genji, *Lady Murasaki Shikibu* 147

Chapter 13: Europe in the Middle Ages 153

13.1 A Letter to Pope Leo III and The Capitulary on the Missi, *Charlemagne* 154
13.2 Call for a Crusade, *Pope Urban II* 158

Chapter 14: Civilization in the Americas, ca. 400-1500 161

14.1 Memoirs: The Aztecs, *Bernal Diaz del Castillo* 162
14.2 The Chronicle of Peru: The Incas 164

CHAPTER 15: EUROPE IN THE RENAISSANCE AND REFORMATION **167**

15.1 The Spark for the Reformation: Indulgences, *Johann Tetzel* 168
15.2 Ninety-five Theses, *Martin Luther* 170
15.3 Condemnation of Peasant Revolt, *Martin Luther* 176

CHAPTER 16: GLOBAL INTERACTION **179**

16.1 Journal (1492), *Christopher Columbus* 180

CHAPTER 17: CONSTITUTIONALISM IN EUROPE **201**

17.1 The Divine Right of Kings, *James I* 202
17.2 English Bill of Rights (1689) 207

CHAPTER 18: NEW WESTERN WORLD-VIEW **209**

18.1 On Patriotism and Toleration, *Voltaire* 210
18.2 The Social Contract (1762), *Jean-Jacques Rousseau* 216

CHAPTER 19: AFRICA, 1400-1800 **221**

19.1 The Life of Olaudah Equiano, *Olaudah Equiano* 222

CHAPTER 20: ISLAMIC WORLD, 1450-1800 **227**

20.1 Turkish Letters (1589), *Ogier Ghiselin de Busbecq* 228
20.2 Akbarnama (1602), *Abul Fazl* 232

CHAPTER 21: EAST ASIA, 1400-1800 **237**

21.1 Letter from China (1683), *Ferdinand Verbiest* 238
21.2 A Secret Plan for Managing the Country (1798), *Honda Toshiaki* 243

CHAPTER 22: WESTERN POLITICAL REVOLUTIONS **253**

22.1 Declaration of the Rights of Man and of the Citizen (1789) 254
22.2 Declaration of the Rights of Woman and Citizen (1791), *Olympe de Gouges* 257

CHAPTER 23: EUROPEAN INDUSTRIAL REVOLUTION **261**

23.1 Condition of the Working Class in England in 1844, *Friedrich Engels* 262

Chapter 24: Isms and Upheaval 269

24.1 An Inquiry into the Nature and Causes of the Wealth of Nations (1776), *Adam Smith* 270
24.2 The Communist Manifesto (1848), *Karl Marx* and *Friedrich Engels* 276

Chapter 25: European Life: Late Nineteenth Century 283

25.1 The Origin of Species by Means of Natural Selection (1859), *Charles Darwin* 284
25.2 Social Darwinism: Poor Laws and The Coming Slavery (1884), *Herbert Spencer* 288

Chapter 26: Western Imperialism, 1800-1914 297

26.1 The White Man's Burden (1899), *Rudyard Kipling* 298
26.2 Standard Treaty (1886), *Royal Niger Company* 300

Chapter 27: Imperialism in Asia 303

27.1 Letter of Advice to Queen Victoria, *Lin Tse-Hsü* 304
27.2 Advice about the Policy of Isolation, *Ii Naosuke* 308
27.3 A Japanese Plan for a Modern Army, *Aritomo Yamagata* 311

Chapter 28: Nation Building 317

28.1 Monroe Doctrine (1823), *James Monroe* 318
28.2 Thirteenth Amendment (1865) 321
28.3 Slavery in the Yucatan (1909), *Arnold Channing* and *Frederick J. Tabor Frost* 322

Chapter 29: War and Revolution 325

29.1 What Is to Be Done?, *V. I. Lenin* 326
29.2 Fourteen Points (1918), *Woodrow Wilson* 334

Chapter 30: Asian Nationalism 337

30.1 Sykes-Picot Agreement (1916) 338
30.2 Balfour Declaration (1917), *Arthur Balfour* 340
30.3 Indian Home Rule, *Mohandas Gandhi* 342
30.4 Revolutionary Ideology, *Mao Zedong* 347

Chapter 31: Age of Anxiety 353

31.1 Beyond Good and Evil, *Friedrich Nietzsche* 354

Chapter 32: Dictatorships and World War II **373**

32.1 Mein Kampf (1925), *Adolf Hitler* 374

Chapter 33: Recovery and Crisis **379**

33.1 Truman Doctrine, *Harry S. Truman* 380

Chapter 34: Contemporary Asia and Africa **383**

34.1 United Nations Resolution 242 (1967) 384
34.2 Islamic Revival, Reform, and Nationalism (1940), *Muhammad Ali Jinnah* 385

Chapter 35: Developing Countries **389**

35.1 Disease Factor in Africa, *K. David Patterson* and *Gerald W. Hartwig* 390

Chapter 36: One World **401**

36.1 Charter of the United Nations (1945) 402

Study Questions **415**

CHAPTER 1

Origins of Civilizations

1.1

The Babylonian Creation Epic (ca. 2000 B.C.E.)

The climate and geography in Mesopotamia made life hazardous and unpredictable. There was little continuity or order in the land. Compared to Egypt, which was isolated and dependent on the predictable flooding of the Nile River, the Mesopotamians lived with uncertainty. Their religion reflected these environmental conditions. The Tigris and Euphrates Rivers and their vulnerable location meant that change in Mesopotamia was often rapid and violent. In response, the Mesopotamians explained their social reality through the capriciousness of their gods.

The Babylonian Creation Epic reflected the creation myths of much of Mesopotamia and was echoed in Genesis, the first book of the Bible. The goddess Tiamat, who represented the primeval sea, was the oldest of the gods. She was the patron of primeval chaos and gave birth to the other gods. Tiamat tried to destroy those gods, but Marduk, the warrior god of the Babylonians, brought order by killing her in a bitter conflict and dividing her body into the sky and earth. The world that emerged maintained precarious stability and was always subject to the whims of its inexplicable divinities.

This myth is an early attempt to answer the question, "How did it all begin?" The Mesopotamians thought about these matters in human terms, i.e., their gods were anthropomorphic. They never organized their beliefs into a philosophy, but their myths provided understandable explanations of natural phenomena. They were appealing because they were emotionally satisfying.

Source: Morris Jastrow, *The Civilization of Babylonia and Assyria* (Philadelphia: J. B. Lippincott, 1915), pp. 428-441, passim.

The First Tablet

When in the height heaven was not named,
And the earth beneath did not yet bear a name,
And the primeval Apsu, who begat them,
And chaos, Tiamut, the mother of them both—
Their waters were mingled together,
And no field was formed, no marsh was to be seen;
When of the gods none had been called into being,
And none bore a name, and no destinies were ordained;
Then were created the gods in the midst of heaven,

Lahmu and Lahamu were called into being . . .
Ages increased, . . .
Then Ansar and Kisar were created, and over them. . . .
Long were the days, then there came forth . . .
Anu, their son, . . .
Ansar and Anu . . .
And the god Anu . . .
Nudimmud, whom his fathers, his begetters . . .
Abounding in all wisdom, . . .
He was exceeding strong . . .
He had no rival . . .
Thus were established and were . . . the great gods.
But Tiamat and Apsu were still in confusion . . .
They were troubled and . . .
In disorder . . .
Apsu was not diminished in might . . .
And Tiamat roared . . .
She smote, and their deeds . . .
Their way was evil . . .
Then Apsu, the begetter of the great gods,
Cried unto Mummu, his minister, and said unto him:
"O Mummu, thou minister that rejoicest my spirit,
Come, unto Tiamut let us go!"
So they went and before Tiamat they lay down,
They consulted on a plan with regard to the gods, their sons.
Apsu opened his mouth and spake,
And unto Tiamut, the glistening one, he addressed the word:
". . . their way . . .,
By day I can not rest, by night I can not lie down in peace.
But I will destroy their way, I will . . .
Let there be lamentation, and let us lie down again in peace."
When Tiamat heard these words,
She raged and cried aloud . . .
She . . . grievously . . .,
She uttered a curse, and unto Apsu she spake:
"What then shall we do?
Let their way be made difficult, and let us lie down again in peace."
Mummu answered, and gave counsel unto Apsu,
. . . and hostile to the gods was the counsel Mummu gave:
"Come, their way is strong, but thou shalt destroy it;
Then by day shalt thou have rest, by night shalt thou lie down in peace."
Apsu harkened unto him and his countenance grew bright,
Since he (Mummu) planned evil against the gods his sons.

. . . he was afraid . . .,
His knees became weak; they gave way beneath him,
Because of the evil which their first-born had planned.
. . . their . . . they altered.
. . . they . . .,
Lamentation . . . they sat in sorrow
. . . .
Then Ea, who knoweth all that is, went up and he beheld their muttering.

. . . he spake:
". . . thy . . . he hath conquered and
. . . he weepeth and sitteth in tribulation.
. . . of fear,
. . . we shall not lie down in peace.
. . . Apsu is laid waste,
. . . and Mummu, who were taken captive, in . . .
. . . thou didst . . .
. . . let us lie down in peace.
. . . they will smite. . . .
. . . let us lie down in peace.
. . . thou shalt take vengeance for them,
. . . unto the tempest shalt thou . . . !"
And Tiamat harkened unto the word of the bright god, and said:
". . . shalt thou entrust! Let us wage war!"
. . . the gods in the midst of . . .
. . . for the gods did she create.
They banded themselves together and at the side of Tiamat they advanced;
They were furious; they devised mischief without resting night and day.
They prepared for battle, fuming and raging;
They joined their forces and made war,
Ummu-Hubur, who formed all things,
Made in addition weapons invincible; she spawned monster-serpents,
Sharp of tooth, and merciless of fang;
With poison, instead of blood, she filled their bodies.
Fierce monster-vipers she clothed with terror,
With splendor she decked them, she made them of lofty stature.
Whoever beheld them, terror overcame him,
Their bodies reared up and none could withstand their attack.
She set up vipers and dragons, and the monster Lahamu,
And hurricanes, and raging hounds, and scorpion-men,
And mighty tempests, and fish-men, and rams;
They bore cruel weapons, without fear of the fight.
Her commands were mighty, none could resist them;

After this fashion, huge of stature, she made eleven monsters.
Among the gods who were her sons, inasmuch as he had given her support,
She exalted Kingu; in their midst she raised him to power.
To march before the forces, to lead the host,
To give the battle-signal, to advance to the attack,
To direct the battle, to control the fight,
Unto him she entrusted; in costly raiment she made him sit, saying:
"I have uttered thy spell, in the assembly of the gods I have raised thee to power.
The dominion over all the gods have I entrusted unto him.
Be thou exalted, thou my chosen spouse,
May they magnify thy name over all of them . . . the Anunnaki."
She gave him the Tablets of Destiny, on his breast she laid them, saying:
"Thy command shall not be without avail, and the word of thy mouth shall be established."
Now Kingu, thus exalted, having received the power of Anu,
Decreed the fate among the gods his sons, saying:
"Let the opening of your mouth quench the Fire-god;
Whoso is exalted in the battle, let him display his might!"

The Second Tablet

Tiamat made weighty her handiwork,
Evil she wrought against the gods her children.
To avenge Apsu, Tiamat planned evil,
But how she had collected her forces, the god . . . to Ea divulged.
Ea harkened to this thing, and
He was grievously afflicted and he sat in so
The days went by, and his anger was appease
And to the place of Ansar his father he took his
He went and, standing before Ansar, the father w
All that Tiamat had plotted he repeated unto him,
Saying, "Tiamat our mother hath conceived a hatred
With all her force she rageth, full of wrath.
All the gods have turned to her,
With those, whom ye created, they go at her side.
They are banded together and at the side of Tiamat they ad
They are furious, they devise mischief without resting night
They prepare for battle, fuming and raging;
They have joined their forces and are making war.
Ummu-Hubur, who formed all things,
Hath made in addition weapons invincible; she hath spawned mons serpents,
Sharp of tooth, and merciless of fang.
With poison, instead of blood, she hath filled their bodies.
Fierce monster-vipers she hath clothed with terror,

With splendor she hath decked them; she hath made them of lofty stature.
Whoever beholdeth them is overcome by terror,
Their bodies rear up and none can withstand their attack.
She hath set up vipers, and dragons, and the monster Lahamu,
And hurricanes and raging hounds, and scorpion-men,
And mighty tempests, and fish-men and rams;
They bear cruel weapons, without fear of the fight.
Her commands are mighty; none can resist them;
After this fashion, huge of stature, hath she made eleven monsters.
Among the gods who are her sons, inasmuch as he hath given her support,
She hath exalted Kingu; in their midst she hath raised him to power.
To march before the forces, to lead the host,
To give the battle-signal, to advance to the attack.
To direct the battle, to control the fight,
Unto him hath she entrusted; in costly raiment she hath made him sit, saying:
'I have uttered thy spell; in the assembly of the gods I have raised thee to power,
The dominion over all the gods have I entrusted unto thee.
Be thou exalted, thou my chosen spouse,
May they magnify they name over all of them . . .'
She hath given him the Tablets of Destiny, on his breast she laid them, saying:
'Thy command shall not be without avail, and the word of they mouth shall be established.'
Now Kingu, thus exalted, having received the power of Anu,
Decreed the fate for the gods, her sons, saying:
'Let the opening of your mouth quench the Fire-god;
Whoso is exalted in the battle, let him display his might!'"
When Ansar heard how Tiamat was mightily in revolt,
. . ., he bit his lips,
. . ., his mind was not at peace,
His . . ., he made a bitter lamentation:
". . . battle,
. . . thou . . .
Mummu and Apsu thou hast smitten,
But Tiamat hath exalted Kingu, and where is one who can oppose her?"
. . . deliberation
. . . the . . . of the gods, Nudimmud.

Ansar unto his son addressed the word:
". . . my mighty hero,
Whose strength is great and whose onslaught can not be withstood,
Go and stand before Tiamat,
That her spirit may be appeased, that her heart may be merciful.
But if she will not harken unto they word,
Our word shalt thou speak unto her, that she may be pacified."

He heard the word of his father Ansar
And he directed his path to her, toward her he took the way.
Anu drew nigh, he beheld the muttering of Tiamat,
But he could not withstand her, and he turned back.
. . . Ansar
. . . he spake unto him:

. . . an avenger . . .
. . . valiant
. . . in the place of his decision
. . . he spake unto him:
. . . thy father
"Thou art my son, who maketh merciful his heart.
. . . to the battle shalt thou draw nigh,
. . . he that shall behold thee shall have peace."
And the lord rejoiced at the word of his father,
And he drew nigh and stood before Ansar.
Ansar beheld him and his heart was filled with joy,
He kissed him on the lips and his fear departed from him.
"O my father, let not the word of thy lips be overcome,
Let me go, that I may accomplish all that is in thy heart.
O Ansar, let not the word of thy lips be overcome,
Let me go, that I may accomplish all that is in thy heart."
"What man is it, who hath brought thee forth to battle?
. . . Tiamat, who is a woman, is armed and attacketh thee.
. . . rejoice and be glad;
The neck of Tiamat shalt thou swiftly trample under foot.
. . . rejoice and be glad;
The neck of Tiamat shalt thou swiftly trample under foot.
O my son, who knoweth all wisdom,
Pacify Tiamat with thy pure incantation.
Speedily set out upon thy way,
For thy blood shall not be poured out; thou shalt return again."
The lord rejoiced at the word of his father,
His heart exulted, and unto his father he spake:
"O Lord of the gods, Destiny of the great gods,
If I, your avenger,
Conquer Tiamat and give you life,
Appoint an assembly, make my fate preeminent and proclaim it.
In Upsukkinaku seat yourself joyfully together,
With my word in place of you will I decree fate.
May whatsoever I do remain unaltered,
May the word of my lips never be changed nor made of no avail."

The Third Tablet

Ansar opened his mouth, and
Unto Gaga, his minister, spake the word:
"O Gaga, thou minister that rejoicest my spirit,
Unto Lahmu and Lahamu will I send thee.
. . . thou canst attain,
. . . thou shalt cause to be brought before thee.
. . . let the gods, all of them,
Make ready for a feast, at a banquet let them sit,
Let them eat bread, let them mix wine,
That for Marduk, their avenger, they may decree the fate.
Go, Gaga, stand before them,
And all that I tell thee, repeat unto them, and say:
'Ansar, your son, hath sent me,
The purpose of his heart he hath made known unto me.
The purpose of his heart he hath made known unto me.
He saith that Tiamat our mother hath conceived a hatred for us,
With all her force she rageth, full of wrath.
All the gods have turned to her,
With those, whom ye created, they go at her side.
They are banded together, and at the side of Tiamat they advance;
They are furious, they devise mischief without resting night and day.
They prepare for battle, fuming and raging;
They have joined their forces and are making war.
Ummu-Hubur, who formed all things,
Hath made in addition weapons invincible; she hath spawned monster-serpents,
Sharp of tooth and merciless of fang.
With poison, instead of blood, she hath filled their bodies.
Fierce monster-vipers she hath clothed with terror,
With splendor she hath decked them; she hath made them of lofty stature.
Whoever beholdeth them, terror overcometh him,
Their bodies rear up and none can withstand their attack.
She hath set up vipers, and dragons, and the monster Lahamu,
And hurricanes, and raging hounds, and scorpion-men,
And mighty tempests, and fish-men, and rams;
They bear merciless weapons, without fear of the fight.
Her commands are mighty; none can resist them;
After this fashion, huge of stature, hath she made eleven monsters.
Among the gods who are her sons, inasmuch as he hath given her support,
She hath exalted Kingu; in their midst she hath raised him to power.
To march before the forces, to lead the host,
To give the battle-signal, to advance to the attack,
To direct the battle, to control the fight,

1.2

The Epic of Gilgamesh

The *Epic of Gilgamesh* is the first epic poem in human history. An epic poem is a narration of the achievements, labors, and sometimes the failures of heroes that embodies a people's conception of its own past. Produced by the Sumerians, the *Epic* evolved from five earlier myths, the oldest of which goes back to the third millennium B.C.E. Gilgamesh was the semi-historical king of Uruk whom the Sumerians, Babylonians, and Assyrians considered a hero and a god. The poem recounts the wanderings of Gilgamesh and his companion Enkidu as they pursue immortality and a place among the gods. They attempt to do so by performing wondrous feats against fearsome agents of the gods, who are determined to thwart them. They meet the goddess Ishtar, after which Enkidu dies, and Gilgamesh decides to continue the search for immortality. He seeks out anyone who might tell him how to do so. His journey involves the effort not only to escape from death but also to reach an understanding of the meaning of life.

The human desire to escape the grip of death—to achieve immortality—is one of the oldest wishes of all peoples. The *Epic of Gilgamesh* is the earliest recorded treatment of this topic.

During his search, Gilgamesh learns that life after death is so dreary that he returns to Uruk, where he becomes a good king and ends his life happily. The *Epic of Gilgamesh* is an excellent literary work and an impressive intellectual triumph. It shows the Sumerians grappling with such enduring questions as life and death, humankind and deity, and immortality. Despite its great antiquity, it addresses questions important to people today.

This selection describes Gilgamesh's encounter with Utnapishtim whose story has a remarkable resemblance to that of Noah in the Book of Genesis.

SOURCE: Charles F. Horne, ed., *The Sacred Books and Early Literature of the East, Vol. I, Babylonia* (New York: Parke, Austin, and Lipscomb, 1917), pp. 208-214.

"I will reveal to thee, Gilgamesh, a secret story,
And the decision of the gods I will tell thee.
The city of Shuruppak, a city which thou knowest,
The one that lies on the Euphrates,
That city was old, and the gods thereof
Induced the great gods to bring a cyclone over it;
It was planned by their father Anu,
By their counselor, the warrior Enlil,
By their herald Ninib,
By their leader En-nugi.

The lord of brilliant vision, Ea, was with them.
He repeated their decision to the reed-hut.
'Reed-hut, reed-hut, wall, wall,
Reed-hut, hear! Wall, give ear!
O man of Shuruppak, son of Ubara-tutu,
Break up the house, build a ship,
Abandon your property, seek life!
Throw aside your possession and preserve life!
Bring into the ship seed of all living things!
The ship that thou shalt build,
Let its dimensions be measured, so that
Its breadth and length be made to correspond.
On a level with the deep, provide it with a covering.'"

In another version the name of the hero of the deluge is given as Atrakhasis, signifying "the very clever one." This alternate name is introduced also at the end of our version of the tale, where Ea says that he sent Atrakhasis a dream which the latter correctly understood. Evidently two traditions of the manner in which the hero of the deluge was warned of the coming destruction were current. Both were embodied in our tale, which thus is revealed as itself a composite production. Ut-napishtim continues his narrative:

"I understood and spoke to Ea, my lord:
'The command of my lord which thou hast commanded,
As I have understood it, I will carry out.
But what shall I answer the city, the people, and the elders?'
Ea opened his mouth and spoke:
Spoke to me, his servant.
'As answer thus speak to them:
Know that Enlil has conceived hatred toward me,
So that I can no longer dwell in your city.
On Enlil's territory I dare no longer set my face.
Therefore, I go to the "deep" to dwell with Ea, my lord.
Over you he will cause blessing to rain down.
Catch of bird, catch of fish,'
And . . . rich crops."

At this point the tablet is defective. Ut-napishtim must have told Gilgamesh how he completed the ship, first drawing a plan and building according to it. Thereupon the text proceeds:

"On the fifth day, I designed its outline.
According to the plan, the walls were to be ten *gar* high.
Corresponding, ten *gar* the measure of its width.

I determined upon its shape and drew it.
I weighted it sixfold.
I divided the superstructure into seven parts.
Its interior I divided into nine parts.
Water-plugs I constructed in the interior.
I selected a pole and added accessories.
Six *sar* of asphalt I poured on the outer wall.
Three *sar* of pitch I poured on the inner wall.
Three *sar* the workmen carried away in their baskets. Of oil,
Besides one *sar* of oil which was used for the sacrifices,
The boatman secreted two *sar* of oil."

Ut-napishtim then proceeds:

"All that I had I loaded on her.
All that I had of silver I loaded on her.
All that I had of gold I loaded on her.
All that I had of living beings of all kinds I loaded on her.
I brought to the ship all my family and household;
Cattle of the field, beasts of the field, all the workmen I brought on board."

The ship draws water to two-thirds of its bulk.

The description of the storm which now follows is one of the finest passages in the narrative:

"Shamash had fixed the time,
'When the rulers of darkness at evening-time shall cause a terrific rain-storm,
Step into the ship and close the door!'
The fixed time approached,
When the rulers of darkness at evening-time were to cause a terrific rain-storm.
I recognized the symptoms of such a day,
A day, for the appearance of which I was in terror.
I entered the ship and closed the door.
To steer the ship, to Puzur-Kurgal, the boatman,
I entrusted the palace, together with its cargo.
As morning dawned,
There arose on the firmament of heaven black clouds,
Adad thundered therein;
Nabu and Lugal marched in advance,
Ira tears out the ship's pole.
Ninib marches, commanding the attack,
The Anunnaki lift torches,

Illuminating the land with their sheen,
Adad's roar reaches to heaven,
All light is changed to darkness.

■ ■ ■

One day the hurricane raged . . .
Storming furiously . . .
Coming like a combat over men.
Brother sees not brother:
Those in heaven do not know one another.
The gods are terrified at the cyclone,
They flee and mount to the heaven of Anu;
The gods crouch like dogs in an enclosure.
Ishtar cries aloud like one in birth-throes,
The mistress of the gods howls aloud:
'That day be turned to clay,
When I in the assembly of the gods decreed evil;
That I should have decreed evil in the assembly of the gods!
For the destruction of my people should have ordered a combat!
Did I bring forth my people,
That like fish they should fill the sea?'
All of the Anunnaki weep with her.
The gods sit down, depressed and weeping.
Their lips are closed . . .
Six days and nights
The storm, cyclone, and hurricane continued to sweep over the land.
When the seventh day approached, the hurricane and cyclone ceased the combat,
After having fought like warriors.
The sea grew quiet, the evil storm abated, the cyclone was restrained.
I looked at the day and the roar had quieted down.
And all mankind had turned to clay.
Like an enclosure . . . had become.
I opened a window and light fell on my face,
I bowed down and sat down and wept,
Tears flowed over my face.
I looked in all directions of the sea.
At a distance of twelve miles an island appeared.
At mount Nisir the ship stood still.
Mount Nisir took hold of the ship so that it could not move.
One day, two days, Mount Nisir, etc.
Three days, four days, Mount Nisir, etc.
Five days, six days, Mount Nisir, etc.
When the seventh day arrived,

I sent forth a dove, letting it free.
The dove went hither and thither;
Not finding a resting-place, it came back.
I sent forth a swallow, letting it free.
The swallow went hither and thither.
Not finding a resting-place, it came back.
I sent forth a raven, letting it free.
The raven went and saw the decrease of the waters.
It ate, croaked, but did not turn back.
Then I let all out to the four regions and brought an offering.
I brought a sacrifice on the mountain top.
Seven and seven *adagur* jars I arranged.
Beneath them I strewed reeds, cedar-wood and myrtle.
The gods smelled the odor,
The gods smelled the sweet odor.
The gods, like flies, gathered around the sacrificer."

The gods now realize what havoc had been wrought by their decision and begin to regret it. Ishtar, more particularly as the mother goddess, bitterly laments the destruction of mankind.

"As soon as the mistress of the gods arrived,
She raised on high the large necklace which Anu had made according to his art.
'Ye gods, as surely as I will not forget these precious stones at my neck,
So I will remember these days—never to forget them.
Let the gods come to the sacrifice,
But let Enlil not come to the sacrifice.
Because without reflection he brought on the cyclone,
And decreed destruction for my people.'
As soon as Enlil arrived,
He saw the ship, and Enlil was enraged.
Filled with anger at the Igigi.
'Who now has escaped with his life?
No man was to survive the destruction!'
Ninib opened his mouth and spoke,
Spoke to the warrior Enlil,
'Who except Ea can plan any affair?
Ea indeed knows every order.'
Ea opened his mouth and spoke,
Spoke to the warrior Enlil:
'Thou art the leader and warrior of the gods.
But why didst thou, without reflection, bring on the cyclone?
On the sinner impose his sin,

On the evil-doer impose his evil,
But be merciful not to root out completely; be considerate not to destroy altogether!
Instead of bringing on a cyclone,
Lions might have come and diminished mankind.
Instead of bringing on a cyclone,
Jackals might have come and diminished mankind.
Instead of bringing on a cyclone,
Famine might have come and overwhelmed the land.
Instead of bringing on a cyclone,
Ira might have come and destroyed the land.
I did not reveal the oracle of the great gods,
I sent Atrakhasis a dream and he understood the oracle of the gods.
Now take counsel for him.'"

Enlil is moved by this eloquent appeal and is reconciled. He himself accords immortal life to Ut-napishtim and his wife, and with this act the story ends.

"Enlil mounted the ship,
Took hold of my hand and took me aboard,
Took me and caused my wife to kneel at my side,
Touched our foreheads, stepped between us and blessed us.
'Hitherto Ut-napishtim was a man;
Now Ut-napishtim and his wife shall be on a level with the gods.
Ut-napishtim shall dwell in the distance, at the confluence of the streams.'
Then they took me and placed me at the confluence of the streams."

It is evident that the entire deluge episode has no connection whatsoever with Gilgamesh. It is introduced in accordance with the trait of epics everywhere to embellish the stories of the adventures of the popular hero and to bring him into association with as many of the popular tales and myths as possible. At the close of Ut-napishtim's long recital and thread of the story is again taken up. Ut-napishtim, moved by pity for Gilgamesh, feels inclined to make an effort to secure immortality for Gilgamesh, and this despite the entirely hopeless outlook conveyed by Ut-napishtim's first address. He tells Gilgamesh that if he can ward off sleep for six days and seven nights the secret of immortal life will be revealed to him. Gilgamesh, however, is unable to endure the ordeal, and falls asleep. Ut-napishtim says to his wife:

"Behold the strong one who longed for life;
Sleep has blown upon him like a hurricane."

His wife says to Ut-napishtim, the one dwelling in the distance:

"Touch him, that the man may awake;
May he return safely on the way on which he came;

1.3

Law Code, Hammurabi

Much information about the Mesopotamians comes from compilations of laws, prescriptions, and decisions written as early as the twenty-third century B.C.E. The best known of these are the Laws (Code) of Hammurabi. The Code is the most remarkable and complete code of ancient law on record before the legislation recorded in the Pentateuch.

Hammurabi was an eighteenth-century B.C.E. Babylonian king who had won victories over neighboring states, and who some scholars have tried to identify with Amraphel in the Bible (Genesis 14). He then issued his code likely using older Sumerian and Akkadian laws.

The laws refer to almost all aspects of life in Babylonia. They are sufficiently elaborate to meet the needs of a distinctly complex society and depict the degree of civilization existing in the Tigris-Euphrates valley.

The following selections are taken from this code, which originally had about 282 articles and included a lengthy prologue and epilogue. One can make an interesting study by comparing this code with Mosaic law and noting the similarities and dissimilarities.

SOURCES:

1. William Stearns Davis, *Readings in Ancient History. Vol. I: Greece and the East* (Boston: Allyn and Bacon, 1912), 35-38.
2. C. H. Johns, *Babylonian and Assyrian Laws, Contracts and Letters* [Library of Ancient Inscriptions] (New York: Charles Scribner's Sons, 1904), 33-35.
3. Chilperic Edwards, *The Hammurabi Code* (1904), 23-80, passim.

1: If a seignior accused a(nother) seignior and brought a charge of murder against him, but has not proved it, his accuser shall be put to death.

■ ■ ■

3: If a seignior came forward with false testimony in a case, and has not proved the word which he spoke, if that case was a case involving life, that seignior shall be put to death.
4: If he came forward with (false) testimony concerning gain or money, he shall bear the penalty of that case.

■ ■ ■

6: If a seignior stole the property of church or state, that seignior shall be put to death; also the one who received the stolen goods from his hand shall be put to death.

■ ■ ■

17: If a seignior caught a fugitive male or female slave in the open and has taken him to his owner, the owner of the slave shall pay him two shekels of silver.

18: If that slave will not name his owner, he shall take him to the palace in order that his record may be investigated, and they shall return him to his owner.

19: If he has kept that slave in his house (and) later the slave has been found in his possession, that seignior shall be put to death.

■ ■ ■

22: If a seignior committed robbery and has been caught, that seignior shall be put to death.

23: If the robber has not been caught, the robbed seignior shall set forth the particulars regarding his lost property in the presence of god, and the city and governor, in whose territory and district the robbery was committed, shall make good to him his lost property.

■ ■ ■

48: If a debt is outstanding against a seignior and Adad has inundated his field or a flood has ravaged (it) or through lack of water grain has not been produced in the field, he shall not make any return of grain to his creditor in that year; he shall cancel his contract-tablet and he shall pay no interest for that year.

■ ■ ■

53: If a seignior was too lazy to make [the dike of] his field strong and did not make his dike strong and a break has opened up in his dike and he has accordingly let the water ravage the farmland, the seignior in whose dike the break was opened shall make good the grain that he let get destroyed.

54: If he is not able to make good the grain, they shall sell him and his goods, and the farmers whose grain the water carried off shall divide (the proceeds).

141: If a seignior's wife, who was living in the house of the seignior, has made up her mind to leave in order that she may engage in business, thus neglecting her house (and) humiliating her husband, they shall prove it against her; and if her husband has then decided on her divorce, he may divorce her, with nothing to be given her as her divorce-settlement upon her departure. If her husband has not decided on her divorce, her husband may marry another woman, with the former woman living in the house of her husband like a maidservant.

142: If a woman so hated her husband that she has declared, "You may not have me," her record shall be investigated at her city council, and if she was careful and was not at fault, even though her husband has been going out and disparaging her greatly, that woman, without incurring any blame at all, may take her dowry and go off to her father's house.

■ ■ ■

195: If a son has struck his father, they shall cut off his hand.

196: If a seignior has destroyed the eye of a member of the aristocracy, they shall destroy his eye.

197: If he has broken a(nother) seignior's bone, they shall break his bone.

198: If he has destroyed the eye of a commoner or broken the bone of a commoner, he shall pay one mina of silver.

199: If he has destroyed the eye of a seignior's slave or broken the bone of a seignior's slave, he shall pay one-half his value.

200: If a seignior has knocked out a tooth of a seignior of his own rank, they shall knock out his tooth.

201: If he has knocked out a commoner's tooth, he shall pay one-third mina of silver.

202:If a seignior has struck the cheek of a seignior who is superior to him, he shall be beaten sixty (times) with an oxtail whip in the assembly.

■ ■ ■

209: If a seignior struck a(nother) seignior's daughter and has caused her to have a miscarriage, he shall pay ten shekels of silver for her fetus.

210: If that woman has died, they shall put his daughter to death.

211: If by a blow he has caused a commoner's daughter to have a miscarriage, he shall pay five shekels of silver.

212: If that woman has died, he shall pay one-half mina of silver.

224. If a cow doctor or an ass doctor has treated a cow or an ass for a severe wound, and affected a cure, the owner thereof shall give the healer one sixth of a silver shekel as his fee.

If any one hire a working ox for one year, he shall pay for its hire four *gur* of corn.

If any one hire an ox or an ass, and a lion kill it in the open field, the owner must stand the loss.

[But] if any one hire an ox, and through negligence or his beatings it die, then he must render back ox for ox to the owner.

225. If he has treated an ox, or an ass, for a severe injury, and caused it to die, he shall pay one-quarter of its value to the owner of the ox, or the ass.

226. If brander has cut out a mark on a slave, without the consent of his owner, that brander shall have his hands cut off.

229. If a builder has built a house for a man, and his work is not strong, and if the house he has built falls in and kills the householder, that builder shall be slain.

230. If the child of the householder is killed, the child of that builder shall be slain.

231. If the slave of the householder is killed, he shall give slave for slave to the householder.

232. If goods have been destroyed, he shall replace all that has been destroyed; and because the house that he built was not made strong, and it has fallen in, he shall restore the fallen house out of his own personal property.

233. If a builder has built a house for a man, and his work is not done properly, and a wall shifts, then that builder shall make that wall good with his own silver. . . .

236. If a man has let his boat to a boatman, and the boatman has been careless and the boat has been sunk or lost, the boatman shall restore a boat to the owner.

237. If a man has hired a boat and boatman, and loaded it with corn, wool, oil or dates, or whatever it be, and the boatman has been careless, and sunk the boat, or lost what is in it, the boatman shall restore the boat which he sank, and whatever he lost that was in it.

■ ■ ■

244. If a man has hired an ox, or an ass, and a lion has killed it in the open field, the loss falls on its owner.

245. If a man has hired an ox and has caused its death, by carelessness, or blows, he shall restore ox for ox, to the owner of the ox.

■ ■ ■

249. If a man has hired an ox, and God has struck it, and it has died, the man that hired the ox shall make affidavit and go free.

250. If a bull has gone wild and gored a man, and caused his death, there can be no suit against the owner.

251. If a man's ox be a gorer, and has revealed its evil propensity as a gorer, and he has not blunted its horn, or shut up the ox, and then that ox has gored a free man, and caused his death, the owner shall pay half a mina of silver.

■ ■ ■

265. If a herdsman, to whom oxen or sheep have been given, has defaulted, has altered the price, or sold them, he shall be prosecuted, and shall restore oxen, or sheep, tenfold, or their owner.

266. If lightning has struck a fold, or a lion has made a slaughter, the herdsman shall purge himself by oath, and the owner of the fold shall bear the loss of the fold.

267. If the herdsman has been careless, and a loss has occurred in the fold, the herdsman shall make good the loss of the fold; he shall repay the oxen, or sheep, to their owner.

■ ■ ■

278. If a man has bought a male or female slave and the slave has not fulfilled his month, but the *bennu* disease has fallen upon him, he shall return the slave to the seller and the buyer shall take back the money he paid.

279. If a man has bought a male or female slave and a claim has been raised, the seller shall answer the claim.

280. If a man, in a foreign land, has bought a male, or female, slave of another, and if when he has come home the owner of the male or female slave has recognized his slave, and if the slave be a native of the land, he shall grant him his liberty without money.

281. If the slave was a native of another country, the buyer shall declare on oath the amount of money he paid, and the owner of the slave shall repay the merchant what he paid and keep his slave.

282. If a slave has said to his master, "You are not my master," he shall be brought to account as his slave, and his master shall cut off his ear.

The oppressed, who has a lawsuit, shall come before my image as king of justice. He shall read the writing on my pillar, he shall perceive my precious words. The word of my pillar shall explain to him his cause, and he shall find his right. His heart shall be glad [and he shall say,] "The Lord Hammurabi has risen up as a true father to his people; the will of Marduk, his god, he has made to be feared; he has achieved victory for Marduk above and below. He has rejoiced the heart of Marduk, his lord, and gladdened the flesh of his people for ever. And the land he has placed in order." . . .

In after days and for all time, the king who is in the land shall observe the words of justice which are written upon my pillar. He shall not alter the law of the land which I have formulated, or the statutes of the country that I have enacted. . . . If that man has wisdom, and desires to keep his land in order, he will heed the words which are written upon my pillar. . . . The . . . people he shall govern; their laws he shall pronounce, their statutes he shall decide. He shall root out of the land the perverse and the wicked; and the flesh of his people he shall delight.

Hammurabi, the king of justice, am I, to whom Shamash has granted rectitude. My words are well weighed: my deeds have no equal, leveling the exalted, humbling the proud, expelling the haughty. If that man heeds my words that I have engraved upon my pillar, departs not from the laws, alters not my words, changes not my sculptures, then may Shamash make the scepter of that man to endure as long as I, the king of justice, and to lead his people with justice.

These judgments of righteousness did Hammurabi the mighty king confirm, and caused the land to take on a sure government and a beneficent rule.

1.4

A Hymn to the Nile

Egypt, as Herodotus the Greek historian says, "is the gift of the Nile." Without its annual and predictable flooding, Egypt would be an unproductive desert like the land around it. The Egyptians acknowledged their debt to the Nile, the bounty of which was even more marvelous because they were neither aware of its source nor the cause of its flooding. This feeling of gratitude is expressed in the very ancient hymn included here.

SOURCE: William Stearns Davis, *Readings in Ancient History. Vol. I: Greece and the East* (Boston: Allyn and Bacon, 1912), 1-3.

Adoration to the Nile!
Hail to thee, O Nile!
Who manifestest thyself over this land,
Who cometh to give life to Egypt!
Mysterious is thy issuing forth from the darkness,
On this day whereon it is celebrated!
Watering the orchards created by Ra
To cause all the cattle to live
Thou givest the earth to drink, O inexhaustible one!
Loving the fruits of Seb
And the first fruits of Nepera
Thou causest the workshops of Ptah to prosper.

    Lord of the fish, during the inundation,
    No bird alights on the crops!

Thou createst corn, thou bringest forth the barley,
Assuring perpetuity to the temples.
If thou ceasest thy toil and thy work,
Then all that exists is in anguish.
If the gods suffer in heaven,
Then the faces of men waste away. . . .
If the Nile smiles the earth is joyous,
Every stomach is full of rejoicing,
Every spine is happy,

Every jawbone crushes its food. . . .
A festal song is raised for thee on the harp,
With the accompaniment of the hand.
The young men and thy children acclaim thee
And prepare their long exercises.

Thou art the august ornament of the earth,
Letting thy bark advance before men,
Lifting up the heart of women in labor,
And loving the multitude of the flocks.

When thou shinest in the royal city,
The rich man is sated with good things,
The poor man even disdains the lotus,
All that is produced is of the choicest,
All the plants exist for thy children.

If thou hast refused to grant nourishment,
The dwelling is silent, devoid of all that is good,
The country falls exhausted.

O inundation of the Nile,
Offerings are made unto thee,
Oxen are immolated to thee,
Great festivals are instituted for thee,
Birds are sacrificed to thee,
Gazelles are taken for thee in the mountain,
Pure flames are prepared for thee. . . .

O Nile, come and prosper!
O thou who makest men to live through his flocks,
Likewise his flocks through his orchards,

Come and prosper, come,
O Nile, come and prosper!

1.5

Hymn to the One Universal God

In Egypt, man evolved two great religious ideas, without the slightest evidence of aid from any supernatural power, or what is called revelation. These two remarkable ideas were: first, the faith in immortality and, secondly, the wholly separate conception of a single, universal, omnipotent deity.

This second idea burst upon Egypt in full splendor during the New Kingdom (1570-1075 B.C.E.). We can trace the slow growth of the belief from earlier times. It was, apparently, the natural outcome of the nation's experience. In the old days, Egypt was made up of many smaller states. Each group of people had its own particular god or gods, and each recognized the existence of the rival deities of its neighbors. When one sovereign, with a court of ranked officials, reigned over the entire Nile valley, a similar hierarchy gradually evolved among the many gods. None was rejected, but they were loosely arranged in various ranks and duties, with Re (Ra) and Osiris as the chief gods. There was even a glimmering sense that these two were really one—the source of life—the Sun-god.

Through the Middle Kingdom, even when they were conceived most broadly, these gods remained, merely Egyptian gods. The seafarers and desert-wanderers who visited Egypt from afar had other sovereigns than Pharaoh, and their gods were accepted as different from those of Pharaoh.

When, however, the New Kingdom began, and Thutmose III, and other conquerors extended their power far beyond Egypt's natural borders, there sprang up the idea of world dominion. Following upon this came the stupendous idea of a world-god—a Pharaoh among gods—an omnipotent deity who swayed the universe. Logically, to be omnipotent, he must also be eternal, and if he had existed before all things, then he must have created them. Therefore he was the Creator, alone in power. Other gods, if they existed, were as much his creations as were the beings of the visible world. This splendid view of the deity is expressed in the following hymn. However, there is no evidence that Egyptian thought took the next step and saw that, if this sole Deity were omnipotent, he must also be omniscient and omnipresent.

Even the view of a single omnipotent god did not find ready acceptance throughout Egypt. The mass of people probably never grasped it, and the priesthood was slow in granting it approval. The last sovereign of the mighty Eighteenth Dynasty, Amen-hotep IV, was the great kingly advocate of the new idea. He attempted violently to establish the worship of the "one god," whom he called Aton and identified anew as the sun. In his reforming enthusiasm Amen-hotep even changed his own name, which meant "worshiper of the god Amen," to Akhenaten, or "worshiper of Aton." The opening hymn in this section is his, or at least the voice of his period.

Stupendous as was the dominating power of an Egyptian monarch, Akhenaten's utmost effort could not dethrone the long-established older gods. Both he and his dynasty perished in the religious struggle that followed, and the nation forcibly rejected "one god, Aton." Yet the monarch's great spiritual idea did not perish with its embodiment. The solemn realization of its vastness gradually permeated the Egyptian priesthood. Frequently it thought of all its thousand deities as mere outward manifestations of the One. Whether addressing one god or another, Re, Osiris, or the Nile, it hailed the divinity as universal and all-powerful. This hymn marks the highest development, both of religion and poetry, that Egypt ever reached.

Source: Charles F. Horne, ed., *The Sacred Books and Early Literature of the East, Volume II: Egypt* (New York: Parke, Austin, and Lipscomb, 1917), pp. 289-295.

Hymn to Aton, the Creator

Splendor and Power of Aton

Thy dawning is beautiful in the horizon of the sky,
O living Aton, Beginning of life!
When thou risest in the eastern horizon
Thou fillest every land with thy beauty.
Thou art beautiful, great, glittering, high above every land,
Thy rays, they encompass the lands, even all that thou hast made.
Thou art Re, and thou carriest them all away captive;
Thou bindest them by thy love.
Though thou art far away, thy rays are upon earth;
Though thou art on high, thy footprints are the day.

Night

When thou settest in the western horizon of the sky,
The earth is in darkness like the dead;
They sleep in their chambers,
Their heads are wrapped up,
Their nostrils are stopped,
And none seeth the other,
While all their things are stolen
Which are under their heads,
And they know it not.
Every lion cometh forth from his den,
All serpents, they sting.
Darkness . . .
The world is in silence,
He that made them resteth in his horizon.

Day and Man

Bright is the earth when thou risest in the horizon.
When thou shinest as Aton by day
Thou drivest away the darkness.
When thou sendest forth thy rays,
The Two Lands (Egypt) are in daily festivity,
Awake and standing upon their feet
When thou hast raised them up.
Their limbs bathed, they take their clothing,
Their arms uplifted in adoration to thy dawning.
Then in all the world they do their work.

Day and the Animals and Plants

All cattle rest upon their pasturage,
The trees and the plants flourish,
The birds flutter in their marshes,
Their wings uplifted in adoration to thee.
All the sheep dance upon their feet,
All winged things fly,
They live when thou hast shone upon them.

Day and the Waters

The barks sail up-stream and down-stream alike.
Every highway is open because thou dawnest.
The fish in the river leap up before thee.
Thy rays are in the midst of the great green sea.

Creation of Man

Creator of the germ in woman,
Maker of seed in man,
Giving life to the son in the body of his mother,
Soothing him that he may not weep,
Nurse even in the womb,
Giver of breath to animate every one that he maketh!
When he cometh forth from the body . . . on the day of his birth,
Thou openest his mouth in speech,
Thou suppliest his necessities.

Creation of Animals

When the fledgling in the egg chirps in the shell,
Thou givest him breath therein to preserve him alive.
When thou hast brought him together,

To the point of bursting it in the egg,
He cometh forth from the egg
To chirp with all his might.
He goeth about upon his two feet
When he hath come forth therefrom.

The Whole Creation

How manifold are thy works!
They are hidden from before us,
O sole God, whose powers no other possesseth.
Thou didst create the earth according to thy heart
While thou wast alone:
Men, all cattle large and small,
All that are upon the earth,
That go about upon their feet;
All that are on high,
That fly with their wings.
The foreign countries, Syria and Kush,
The land of Egypt;
Thou settest every man into his place,
Thou suppliest his necessities.
Every one has his possessions,
And his days are reckoned.
The tongues are divers in speech,
Their forms likewise and their skins are distinguished.
For thou makest different the strangers.

Watering the Earth in Egypt and Abroad

Thou makest the Nile in the Netherworld,
Thou bringest it as thou desirest,
To preserve alive the people.
For thou hast made them for thyself,
The lord of them all, resting among them;
Thou lord of every land, who risest for them.
Thou Sun of day, great in majesty.
All the distant countries,
Thou makest also their life,
Thou hast set a Nile in the sky;
When it falleth for them,
It maketh waves upon the mountains,
Like the great green sea,
Watering their fields in their town.

How excellent are thy designs, O lord of eternity!
There is a Nile in the sky for the strangers
And for the cattle of every country that go upon their feet.
But the Nile, it cometh from the Netherworld for Egypt.

The Seasons

Thy rays nourish every garden;
When thou risest they live,
They grow by thee.
Thou makest the seasons
In order to create all thy work:
Winter to bring them coolness,
And heat that they may taste thee.
Thou didst make the distant sky to rise therein,
In order to behold all that thou hast made,
Thou alone, shining in thy form as living Aton,
Dawning, glittering, going afar and returning.
Thou makest millions of forms
Through thyself alone;
Cities, towns, and tribes, highways and rivers.
All eyes see thee before them,
For thou art Aton of the day over the earth.

■ ■ ■

Revelation to the King

Thou art in my heart,
There is no other that knoweth thee
Save thy son Ikhn-aton.
Thou hast made him wise
In thy designs and in thy might.
The world is in thy hand,
Even as thou hast made them.
When thou hast risen they live,
When thou settest they die;
For thou art length of life of thyself,
Men live through thee,
While their eyes are upon thy beauty
Until thou settest.
All labor is put away
When thou settest in the west.

■ ■ ■

Thou didst establish the world,
And raise them up for thy son,
Who came forth from thy limbs,
The King of Upper and Lower Egypt,
Living in Truth, Lord of the Two Lands,
Nefer-khepru-Re, Wan-Re (Ikhn-aton),
Son of Re, living in Truth, lord of diadems,
Ikhn-aton, whose life is long;
And for the chief royal wife, his beloved,
Mistress of the Two Lands, Nefer-nefru-Aton, Nofretete,
Living and flourishing forever and ever.

CHAPTER 2

Kingdoms and Empires in the Near East

2.1

Annals of Nubian Kings (593 B.C.E.)

The invasions of the Sea Peoples ushered in a decline in Egypt known as the Third Intermediate Period (eleventh to seventh centuries B.C.E.). In southern Egypt, the pharaoh's decline opened the way for the Nubians, who extended northward into the Nile Valley. They had already adopted some features of Egyptian culture during the Eighteenth Dynasty when they had briefly been incorporated into the Egyptian empire. Now they adopted Egyptian culture wholesale, repeating a Near Eastern pattern of the conqueror assimilating into the conquered culture.

The Kushites were an independent African people who established a kingdom in modern Sudan around 2000 B.C.E. The Kushites also adopted Egyptian culture. In the eighth century B.C.E., the Kushites swept into the Nile valley and briefly reunited Egypt.

This selection describes the accession of King Aspalta (r. 593-568 B.C.E.) through a system called "uterine descent," in which succession passed from the king to one of his sister's sons.

Source: E. A. Wallis Budge, *Egyptian Literature. Volume II: Annals of Nubian Kings* (London: Kegan Paul, Trench, Trübner, 1912), 89-104.

Behold now, the whole army of His Majesty was in the city, the name whereof is Tu-āb, and the god who dwells there is Tetun, the Governor of Ta-Sti [Northern Nubia] the god of Kesh [Kush], after the Hawk had arrived upon his tomb.

Behold now, there were there six generals who filled the heart of the military assembly of His Majesty; and there were there six officials who were favourites of the Overseer of the Seal. And behold, there were there six Overseers of Books who were favourites of the Chief Overseer of Books; and behold, there were there six Princes and Overseers of the Seal of the House of the king. And they said unto the whole army, "Come, let us crown our Lord over us, who shall be like a young bull, which the herdsmen cannot subdue." And these soldiers meditated upon the matter most carefully, and they said, "Our Lord is standing among us, though we know him not.

But we must know who he is, and we will enter his service and we will serve him, even as the Two Lands served Horus, the son of Isis, after he had seated himself upon the throne of his father Osiris, and we will ascribe praise unto his two Uatchti serpents."

And one said to his fellow among them, "No person whatsoever know who he is except Rā himself; may the god drive away from him evil of every kind in every place wheresoever he may be." And one said to his fellow among them, "Rā has set in Ānkhtet, but his crown is in our midst." And one said to his fellow among them, "This is truth. It is the decree of Rā, from the time when the heavens came into being, and from the time when the crown of the king was created, and he made him to be his beloved son, because the king is the image of Rā among the living. Behold, Rā has set him in this land, wishing him to be the overlord of this land."

And one said to his fellow among them, "Has not Rā entered into the sky? His throne is empty of a Ruler. His noble deeds remain perfected by his two hands. Rā has made him to be his beloved son because he knew him, saying, 'He made laws which were good while he was on his throne.'"

And all these soldiers meditated upon the matter most carefully, and said, "Our Lord is standing among us, though we know not who he is."

Then all the soldiers of His Majesty spoke with one voice (or, mouth) saying, "Surely there exists this god, Ȧmen-Rā, the Lord of the Throne of the Two Lands, Dweller in the Holy Mountain, the god of Kesh.

Come and let us go before him. Let us not do anything without his knowledge, for that thing which is done without his knowledge is not good. Come and place the matter with the god, who has been the god of the kings of Kesh since the time of Rā, for it is he who shall guide us.

The kings of Kesh are in his hands, and he gives the country to his beloved son. Let us give praises to his face, and let us smell the earth upon our bellies. Let us say before him, 'We have come before you, O Ȧmen, give to us a Lord over us, who shall make us to live, who shall build the temples of all the gods and goddesses of the Land of the South and the Land of the North, and who shall establish their offerings. We will do nothing without your knowledge, you shall be our leader (or, guide) and we will do nothing in the matter without your knowledge.'" And the whole army said, "This is a good saying in very truth, a million times over." Then the generals of His Majesty and the high officials of the House of the king went into the god-house of Ȧmen, and they found the servants of the god (i.e., priests) and the chief libationers standing round about the temple. And they said to them, "We have come before the god Ȧmen-Rā, the Dweller within the Holy Mountain, so that he may give us a Lord to be over us who shall make us to live, who shall build the temples of all the gods and goddesses of the Land of the South and the Land of the North, and shall establish their offerings. We will do nothing without the knowledge of this god, for he is our leader (or, guide)."

And the servants of the god and the chief libationers made an entrance into the temple, and they performed all the rites which had to be performed, and they sprinkled water therein and censed it. And the generals of His Majesty and the princes of the House of the king made an entrance into the temple, and they placed themselves on their bellies in the presence of this god, and they said, "We have come to you, Ȧmen-Rā, Lord of the Throne of the Two Lands, Dweller within the Holy Mountain. Give to us a Lord to make us to live, to build the temples of the gods of the Land of the South and the Land of the North, and to establish the offering in them. The exalted estate of kingship rests wholly in your hands: grant it to your beloved son."

Then they placed the royal brethren before this god, but he did not lead out any one of them. And next, on the second occasion, when they set before this god the royal brother, the son of Ȧmen, born of the goddess Nut, the Lady of heaven, the son of Rā, [Ȧspelta], the ever-living, this god Ȧmen-Rā, Lord of the Throne of the Two Lands, spoke, saying: "This is the

King, your Lord, this is he who shall make you to live, this is he who shall build every temple of the Land of the South and the Land of the North, this is he who shall establish their offerings; for his father was Keb, the son of Rā, whose word is law, and his mother was the royal sister, royal mother, Queen of Kesh, daughter of Rā, [NENSELSA], the everliving; and her mother was the royal sister, the high-priestess of Ȧmen-Rā, the king of the gods of Thebes, whose word is law; and her mother was the royal sister, whose word is law; and her mother was the royal sister, whose word is law; and her mother was the royal sister, whose word is law; and her mother was the royal sister, whose word is law; and her mother was the royal sister and Queen of Kesh, whose word is law. He is your Lord."

And the generals of His Majesty and the high officials of the House of the king threw themselves down on their bellies before this god, and they made the most humble obeisance, and they gave praise unto this god because of the strength (or, dominion) which he had made for his beloved son, the king of the South and North, [Ȧspelta], the everliving.

And His Majesty entered into the temple to be crowned before his divine Father, Ȧmen-Rā, the Lord of the Throne of the Two Lands, and he found every crown of the kings of Kesh and their scepters laid before this god, saying: "I have come, Ȧmen-Rā, the Lord of the Throne of the Two Lands, the Dweller within the Holy Mountain; grant to me the exalted dignity which shall remain permanent, which it was not in my heart [to aspire to], through the greatness of thy love, and grant to me the crown, through thy heart's love, and the scepter." And this god said: "The crown of your divine brother, the King of the South and North, whose word is law, is yours, and it shall be established on your head even as the . . . is stablished on your head. His scepter is in your grasp, and it shall overthrow for you all your enemies."

Then His Majesty placed on his head the crown of his divine brother, the King of the South and North, whose word is law, and took his scepter in his grasp. And His Majesty placed himself on his belly before this god, and, making the most humble obeisance, said: "I have come unto you Ȧmen-Rā, the Lord of the Throne of the Two Lands, the Dweller within the Holy Mountain, god of olden time, whose love is sweet, who hears him that makes a petition unto him straightaway, . . . grant to me life, stability, serenity of every kind, health, joy of heart of every kind, like Rā for ever, and a happy old age.

Grant to me the perception . . . in the time of Rā. Let not lie down. . . . Grant that the love of me shall be in the country of Kesh, and awe of me in the land of Kenset. . . . Grant that the love of me shall be. . . ." And this god said: "I have given unto you all these things, and you shall never, never have need to say, 'Would that I had them.'"

Then His Majesty made a coming forth (or, appearance) from the temple into the midst of his soldiers like the rising [of Rā], and his soldiers rejoiced in him and uttered loud cries of gladness. And the hearts of the high officers of the House of the king were exceedingly happy, and they ascribed praises unto His Majesty, and said: "Come in peace, O our Lord . . . like the years of Horus in the midst of thy soldiers. You rise (or, are crowned) upon the throne of Horus, like Rā, for ever."

And in this first year of the coronation of His Majesty he established festivals.

. . . and he gave to the priests of the temple of Ȧmen-Rā, the Lord of the Throne of the Two Lands, the Dweller within the Holy Mountain . . . one hundred vessels of beer, and forty *shu,* in all one hundred and forty vessels of beer.

2.2

Genesis: The Hebrew Creation and Flood Stories

The Hebrew version of the creation of the world and its subsequent destruction by flood is found in the book of Genesis, the first book of the Hebrew Scriptures, and part of the Torah or the Law. The books of the Torah are also called the Pentateuch. These books tell the history of the Jews from the Creation through the death of Moses, and they contain the Ten Commandments and the basic laws of Judaism.

For many centuries, the first five books of the Hebrew Scriptures were attributed to Moses as the sole author. Modern textual analysis, however, has revealed a variety of writing styles (including five different names for God), a lack of sequence, and many repetitions and variations in the narrative. Thus, these books were no doubt written by several authors and at different times. Anachronistic historical references help date the writing of different passages. For example, Genesis 11:31 describes the Hebrew patriarch Abraham as he leaves "Ur of the Chaldaeans" to go to Canaan circa 1800 B.C.E.; but one could only identify the city of Ur as Chaldaean between 612 and 539, the period of the short-lived Chaldaean Empire. Thus, the existing version of the Torah could not have been written earlier than the seventh century B.C.E. Earlier writings probably existed, but Hebrew priests did not preserve them after combining them into one sacred and comprehensive religious text.

Source: The Holy Bible (New York: American Bible Society, n.d.).

Chapter 1

In the beginning God created the heaven and the earth.
2 And the earth was without form, and void; and darkness *was* upon the face of the deep.
And the Spirit of God moved upon the face of the waters.
3 And God said, Let there be light: and there was light.
4 And God saw the light, that *it was* good: and God divided the light from the darkness.
5 And God called the light Day, and the darkness he called Night. And the evening and
the morning were the first day.
6 ¶ And God said, Let there be a firmament in the midst of the waters, and let it divide the
waters from the waters.
7 And God made the firmament, and divided the waters which *were* under the firmament
from the waters which *were* above the firmament: and it was so.

8 And God called the firmament Heaven. And the evening and the morning were the second day.

9 ¶ And God said, Let the waters under the heaven be gathered together unto one place, and let the dry *land* appear: and it was so.

10 And God called the dry *land* Earth; and the gathering together of the waters called he Seas: and God saw that *it was* good.

11 And God said, Let the earth bring forth grass, the herb yielding seed, *and* the fruit tree yielding fruit after his kind, whose seed *is* in itself, upon the earth: and it was so.

12 And the earth brought forth grass, *and* herb yielding seed after his kind, and the tree yielding fruit, whose seed *was* in itself, after his kind: and God saw that *it was* good.

13 And the evening and the morning were the third day.

14 ¶ And God said, Let there be lights in the firmament of the heaven to divide the day from the night; and let them be for signs, and for seasons, and for days, and years:

15 And let them be for lights in the firmament of the heaven to give light upon the earth: and it was so.

16 And God made two great lights; the greater light to rule the day, and the lesser light to rule the night: *he made* the stars also.

17 And God set them in the firmament of the heaven to give light upon the earth,

18 And to rule over the day and over the night, and to divide the light from the darkness: and God saw that *it was* good.

19 And the evening and the morning were the fourth day.

20 And God said, Let the waters bring forth abundantly the moving creature that hath life, and fowl *that* may fly above the earth in the open firmament of heaven.

21 And God created great whales, and every living creature that moveth, which the waters brought forth abundantly after their kind, and every winged fowl after his kind: and God saw that *it was* good.

22 And God blessed them, saying, Be fruitful, and multiply, and fill the waters in the seas, and let fowl multiply in the earth.

23And the evening and the morning were the fifth day.

24 ¶ And God said, Let the earth bring forth the living creature after his kind, cattle, and creeping thing, and beast of the earth after his kind: and it was so.

25 And God made the beast of the earth after his kind, and cattle after their kind, and every thing that creepeth upon the earth after his kind: and God saw that *it was* good.

26 ¶ And God said, Let us make man in our image, after our likeness: and let them have dominion over the fish of the sea, and over the fowl of the air, and over the cattle, and over all the earth, and over every creeping thing that creepeth upon the earth.

27 So God created man in his *own* image, in the image of God created he him; male and female created he them.

28 And God blessed them, and God said unto them, Be fruitful, and multiply, and replenish the earth, and subdue it: and have dominion over the fish of the sea, and over the fowl of the air, and over every living thing that moveth upon the earth.

29 ¶ And God said, Behold, I have given you every herb bearing seed, which *is* upon the face of all the earth, and every tree, in the which *is* the fruit of a tree yielding seed; to you it shall be for meat.

30 And to every beast of the earth, and to every fowl of the air, and to every thing that creepeth upon the earth, wherein *there is* life, *I have given* every green herb for meat: and it was so.

31 And God saw every thing that he had made, and, behold, *it was* very good. And the evening and the morning were the sixth day.

CHAPTER 2

Thus the heavens and the earth were finished, and all the host of them.

2 And on the seventh day God ended his work which he had made; and he rested on the seventh day from all his work which he had made.

3 And God blessed the seventh day, and sanctified it: because that in it he had rested from all his work which God created and made.

4 ¶ These *are* the generations of the heavens and of the earth when they were created, in the day that the LORD God made the earth and the heavens,

5 And every plant of the field before it was in the earth, and every herb of the field before it grew: for the LORD God had not caused it to rain upon the earth, and *there was* not a man to till the ground.

6 But there went up a mist from the earth, and watered the whole face of the ground.

7 And the LORD God formed man *of* the dust of the ground, and breathed into his nostrils the breath of life; and man became a living soul.

8 ¶ And the LORD God planted a garden eastward in Ē'den; and there he put the man whom he had formed.

9 And out of the ground made the LORD God to grow every tree that is pleasant to the sight, and good for food; and tree of life also in the midst of the garden, and the tree of knowledge of good and evil.

10 And a river went out of Ē'den to water the garden; and from thence it was parted, and became into four heads.

11 The name of the first is Pī'sŏn: that *is* it which compasseth the whole land of Hăv'ĭ-läh, where *there is* gold;

12 And the gold of that land *is* good: there *is* bdellium and the onyx stone.

13 And the name of the second river *is* Gī'hŏn: the same *is* it that compasseth the whole land of Ethiopia.

14 And the name of the third river *is* Hĭd'dē-kĕl: that *is* it which goeth toward the east of Assyria. And the fourth river *is* Eū-phrā'tēs.

15 And the LORD God took the man, and put him into the garden of Ē'den to dress it and to keep it.

16 And the LORD God commanded the man, saying, Of every tree of the garden thou mayest freely eat:

17 But of the tree of the knowledge of good and evil, thou shalt not eat of it: for in the day that thou eatest thereof thou shalt surely die.

18 ¶ And the LORD God said, *It is* not good that the man should be alone; I will make him a help meet for him.

19 And out of the ground the LORD God formed every beast of the field, and every fowl of the air; and brought *them* unto Adam to see what he would call them: and whatsoever Adam called every living creature, that *was* the name thereof.

20 And Adam gave names to all cattle, and to the fowl of the air, and to every beast of the field; but for Adam there was not found a help meet for him.

21 And the LORD God caused a deep sleep to fall upon Adam, and he slept; and he took one of his ribs, and closed up the flesh instead thereof.

22 And the rib, which the LORD God had taken from man, made he a woman, and brought her unto the man.

23 And Adam said, This *is* now bone of my bones, and flesh of my flesh: she shall be called Woman, because she was taken out of man.

24 Therefore shall a man leave his father and his mother, and shall cleave unto his wife: and they shall be one flesh.

25 And they were both naked, the man and his wife, and were not ashamed.

CHAPTER 3

Now the serpent was more subtile than any beast of the field which the LORD God had made. And he said unto the woman, Yea, hath God said, Ye shall not eat of every tree of the garden?

2 And the woman said unto the serpent, We may eat of the fruit of the trees of the garden:

3 But of the fruit of the tree which *is* in the midst of the garden, God hath said, Ye shall not eat of it, neither shall ye touch it, lest ye die.

4 And the serpent said unto the woman, Ye shall not surely die:

5 For God doth know that in the day ye eat thereof, then your eyes shall be opened, and ye shall be as gods, knowing good and evil.

6 And when the woman saw that the tree *was* good for food, and that it *was* pleasant to the eyes, and a tree to be desired to make *one* wise, she took of the fruit thereof, and did eat, and gave also unto her husband with her; and he did eat.

7 And the eyes of them both were opened, and they knew that they *were* naked; and they sewed fig leaves together, and made themselves aprons.

8 And they heard the voice of the LORD God walking in the garden in the cool of the day: and Adam and his wife hid themselves from the presence of the LORD God amongst the trees of the garden.

9 And the LORD God called unto Adam, and said unto him, Where *art* thou?

10 And he said, I heard thy voice in the garden, and I was afraid, because I *was* naked; and I hid myself.

11 And he said, Who told thee that thou *wast* naked? Hast thou eaten of the tree, whereof I commanded thee that thou shouldest not eat?

12 And the man said, The woman whom thou gavest *to be* with me, she gave me of the tree, and I did eat.

13 And the LORD God said unto the woman, What *is* this *that* thou has done? And the woman said, The serpent beguiled me, and I did eat.

14 And the LORD God said unto the serpent, Because thou has done this, thou *art* cursed above all cattle, and above every beast of the field; upon thy belly shalt thou go, and dust shalt thou eat all the days of thy life:

15 And I will put enmity between thee and the woman, and between thy seed and her seed; it shall bruise thy head, and thou shalt bruise his heel.

16 Unto the woman he said, I will greatly multiply thy sorrow and thy conception; in sorrow thou shalt bring forth children; and thy desire *shall be* to thy husband, and he shall rule over thee.

17 And unto Adam he said, Because thou hast hearkened unto the voice of thy wife, and hast eaten of the tree, of which I commanded thee, saying, Thou shalt not eat of it: cursed *is* the ground for thy sake; in sorrow shalt thou eat *of* it all the days of thy life;

18 Thorns also and thistles shall it bring forth to thee; and thou shalt eat the herb of the field:

19 In the sweat of thy face shalt thou eat bread, till thou return unto the ground; for out of it wast thou taken: for dust thou *art,* and unto dust shalt thou return.

20 And Adam called his wife's name Eve; because she was the mother of all living.

21 Unto Adam also and to his wife did the LORD God make coats of skins, and clothed them.

22 ¶ And the LORD God said, Behold, the man is become as one of us, to know good and evil: and now, lest he put forth his hand, and take also of the tree of life, and eat, and live for ever:

23 Therefore the LORD God sent him forth from the garden of Ē′den, to till the ground from whence he was taken.

24 So he drove out the man: and he placed at the east of the garden of Ē′den cherubim, and a flaming sword which turned every way, to keep the way of the tree of life.

CHAPTER 6

And it came to pass, when men began to multiply on the face of the earth, and daughters were born unto them,

2 That the sons of God saw the daughters of men that they *were* fair; and they took them wives of all which they chose.

3 And the LORD said, My Spirit shall not always strive with man, for that he also *is* flesh: yet his days shall be a hundred and twenty years.

5 ¶ And GOD saw that the wickedness of man *was* great in the earth, and *that* every imagination of the thoughts of his heart *was* only evil continually.

6 And it repented the LORD that he had made man on the earth, and it grieved him at his heart.

7 And the LORD said, I will destroy man whom I have created from the face of the earth; both man, and beast, and the creeping thing, and the fowls of the air; for it repenteth me that I have made them.

8 But Noah found grace in the eyes of the LORD.

11 The earth also was corrupt before God; and the earth was filled with violence.

12 And God looked upon the earth, and, behold, it was corrupt; for all flesh had corrupted his way upon the earth.

13 And God said unto Noah, The end of all flesh is come before me; for the earth is filled with violence through them; and, behold, I will destroy them with the earth.

14 ¶ Make thee an ark of gopher wood; rooms shalt thou make in the ark, and shalt pitch it within and without with pitch.

15 And this *is the fashion* which thou shalt make it *of:* The length of the ark *shall be* three hundred cubits, the breadth of it fifty cubits, and the height of it thirty cubits.

16 A window shalt thou make to the ark, and in a cubit shalt thou finish it above; and the door of the ark shalt thou set in the side thereof; *with* lower, second, and third *stories* shalt thou make it.

17 And, behold, I, even I, do bring a flood of waters upon the earth, to destroy all flesh, wherein *is* the breath of life, from under heaven; *and* every thing that *is* in the earth shall die.

18 But with thee will I establish my covenant; and thou shalt come into the ark, thou, and thy sons, and thy wife, and thy sons' wives with thee.

19 And of every living thing of all flesh, two of every *sort* shalt thou bring into the ark, to keep *them* alive with thee; they shall be male and female.

20 Of fowls after their kind, and of cattle after their kind, of every creeping thing of the earth after his kind; two of every *sort* shall come unto thee, to keep *them* alive.

21 And take thou unto thee of all food that is eaten, and thou shalt gather *it* to thee; and it shall be for food for thee, and for them.

22 Thus did Noah; according to all that God commanded him, so did he.

CHAPTER 7

And the LORD said unto Noah, Come thou and all thy house into the ark; for thee have I seen righteous before me in this generation.

2 Of every clean beast thou shalt take to thee by sevens, the male and his female: and of beasts that *are* not clean by two, the male and his female.

3 Of fowls also of the air by sevens, the male and the female; to keep seed alive upon the face of all the earth.

4 For yet seven days, and I will cause it to rain upon the earth forty days and forty nights; and every living substance that I have made will I destroy from off the face of the earth.

5 And Noah did according unto all that the LORD commanded him.

6 And Noah *was* six hundred years old when the flood of waters was upon the earth.

7 ¶ And Noah went in, and his sons, and his wife, and his sons' wives with him, into the ark, because of the waters of the flood.

8 Of clean beasts, and of beasts that *are* not clean, and of fowls, and of every thing that creepeth upon the earth,

9 There went in two and two unto Noah into the ark, the male and the female, as God had commanded Noah.

10 And it came to pass after seven days, that the waters of the flood were upon the earth.

11 ¶ In the six hundredth year of Noah's life, in the second month, the seventeenth day of the month, the same day were all the fountains of the great deep broken up, and the windows of heaven were opened.

12 And the rain was upon the earth forty days and forty nights.

13 In the selfsame day entered Noah, and Shĕm, and Ham, and Jā'phĕth, the sons of Noah, and Noah's wife, and the three wives of his sons with them, into the ark;

14 They, and every beast after his kind, and all the cattle after their kind, and every creeping thing that creepeth upon the earth after his kind, and every fowl after his kind, every bird of every sort.

15 And they went in unto Noah into the ark, two and two of all flesh, wherein *is* the breath of life.

16 And they that went in, went in male and female of all flesh, as God had commanded him: and the LORD shut him in.

17 And the flood was forty days upon the earth; and the waters increased, and bare up the ark, and it was lifted up above the earth.

18 And the waters prevailed and were increased greatly upon the earth; and the ark went upon the face of the waters.

19 And the waters prevailed exceedingly upon the earth; and all the high hills, that *were* under the whole heaven, were covered.

20 Fifteen cubits upward did the waters prevail; and the mountains were covered.

21 And all flesh died that moved upon the earth, both of fowl, and of cattle, and of beast, and of every creeping thing that creepeth upon the earth, and every man:

22 All in whose nostrils *was* the breath of life, of all that *was* in the dry *land,* died.

23 And every living substance was destroyed which was upon the face of the ground, both man, and cattle, and the creeping things, and the fowl of the heaven; and they were destroyed from the earth: and Noah only remained *alive,* and they that *were* with him in the ark.

24 And the waters prevailed upon the earth a hundred and fifty days.

CHAPTER 8

And God remembered Noah, and every living thing, and all the cattle that *was* with him in the ark: and God made a wind to pass over the earth, and the waters assuaged.

2 The fountains also of the deep and the windows of heaven were stopped, and the rain from heaven was restrained.

3 And the waters returned from off the earth continually: and after the end of the hundred and fifty days the waters were abated.

4 And the ark rested in the seventh month, on the seventeenth day of the month, upon the mountains of Ar'ȧ-răt.

5 And the waters decreased continually until the tenth month: in the tenth *month,* on the first *day* of the month, were the tops of the mountains seen.

6 ¶ And it came to pass at the end of forty days, that Noah opened the window of the ark which he had made:

7 And he sent forth a raven, which went forth to and fro, until the waters were dried up from off the earth.

8 Also he sent forth a dove from him, to see if the waters were abated from off the face of the ground.

9 But the dove found no rest for the sole of her foot, and she returned unto him into the ark; for the waters *were* on the face of the whole earth. Then he put forth his hand, and took her, and pulled her in unto him into the ark.

10 And he stayed yet other seven days; and again he sent forth the dove out of the ark.

11 And the dove came in to him in the evening, and, lo, in her mouth *was* an olive leaf plucked off: so Noah knew that the waters were abated from off the earth.

12 And he stayed yet other seven days, and sent forth the dove, which returned not again unto him any more.

13 ¶ And it came to pass in the six hundredth and first year, in the first *month,* the first *day* of the month, the waters were dried up from off the earth: and Noah removed the covering of the ark, and looked, and, behold, the face of the ground was dry.

14 And in the second month, on the seven and twentieth day of the month, was the earth dried.

15 ¶ And God spake unto Noah, saying,

16 Go forth of the ark, thou, and thy wife, and thy sons, and thy sons' wives with thee.

17 Bring forth with thee every living thing that *is* with thee, of all flesh, *both* of fowl, and of cattle, and of every creeping thing that creepeth upon the earth; that they may breed abundantly in the earth, and be fruitful, and multiply upon the earth.

18 And Noah went forth, and his sons, and his wife, and his sons' wives with him:

19 Every beast, every creeping thing, and every fowl, *and* whatsoever creepeth upon the earth, after their kinds, went forth out of the ark.

20 ¶ And Noah builded an alter unto the LORD; and took of every clean beast, and of every clean fowl, and offered burnt offerings on the altar.

21 And the LORD smelled a sweet savor; and the LORD said in his heart, I will not again curse the ground any more for man's sake; for the imagination of man's heart *is* evil from his youth: neither will I again smite any more every thing living, as I have done.

22 While the earth remaineth, seedtime and harvest, and cold and heat, and summer and winter, and day and night shall not cease.

CHAPTER 9

And God blessed Noah and his sons, and said unto them, Be fruitful, and multiply, and replenish the earth.

9 And I, behold, I establish my covenant with you, and with your seed after you;

10 And with every living creature that *is* with you, of the fowl, of the cattle, and of every beast of the earth with you; from all that go out of the ark, to every beast of the earth.

11 And I will establish my covenant with you; neither shall all flesh be cut off any more by the waters of a flood; neither shall there any more be a flood to destroy the earth.

12 And God said, This *is* the token of the covenant which I make between me and you, and every living creature that *is* with you, for perpetual generations:

13 I do set my bow in the cloud, and it shall be for a token of a covenant between me and the earth.

20 And Noah began *to be* a husband-man, and he planted a vineyard:

21 And he drank of the wine, and was drunken; and he was uncovered within his tent.

22 And Ham, the father of Cā'năan, saw the nakedness of his father, and told his two brethren without.

23 And Shĕm and Jā'phĕth took a garment, and laid *it* upon both their shoulders, and went backward, and covered the nakedness of their father; and their faces *were* backward, and they saw not their father's nakedness.

24 And Noah awoke from his wine, and knew what his younger son had done unto him.

25 And he said, Cursed *be* Cā'năan; a servant of servants shall he be unto his brethren.

26 And he said, Blessed *be* the LORD God of Shĕm; and Cā'năan shall be his servant.

27 God shall enlarge Jā'phĕth, and he shall dwell in the tents of Shĕm; and Cā'năan shall be his servant.

CHAPTER 17

And when Abram was ninety years old and nine, the LORD appeared to Abram, and said unto him, I *am* the Almighty God; walk before me, and be thou perfect.

2 And I will make my covenant between me and thee, and will multiply thee exceedingly.

3 And Abram fell on his face: and God talked with him, saying,

4 As for me, behold, my covenant *is* with thee, and thou shalt be a father of many nations.

5 Neither shall thy name any more be called Abram, but thy name shall be Abraham; for a father of many nations have I made thee.

6 And I will make thee exceeding fruitful, and I will make nations of thee, and kings shall come out of thee.

7 And I will establish my covenant between me and thee and thy seed after thee in their generations, for an everlasting covenant, to be a God unto thee and to thy seed after thee.

8 And I will give unto thee, and to thy seed after thee, the land wherein thou art a stranger, all the land of Cā'năan, for an everlasting possession; and I will be their God.

9 ¶ And God said unto Abraham, Thou shalt keep my covenant therefore, thou, and thy seed after thee in their generations.

10 This *is* my covenant, which ye shall keep, between me and you and thy seed after thee; Every man child among you shall be circumcised.

11 And ye shall circumcise the flesh of your foreskin; and it shall be a token of the covenant betwixt me and you.

12 And he that is eight days old shall be circumcised among you, every man child in your generations, he that is born in the house, or bought with money of any stranger, which *is* not of thy seed.

13 He that is born in thy house, and he that is bought with thy money, must needs be circumcised: and my covenant shall be in your flesh for an everlasting covenant.

14 And the uncircumcised man child whose flesh of his foreskin is not circumcised, that soul shall be cut off from his people; he hath broken my covenant.

2.3

Deuteronomy

During the migration out of Egypt, Moses molded the Hebrews into a people and wedded them to his god. No longer a loose band of nomads, they were now the Israelites—descendants of Abraham, Isaac, and Jacob.

The Biblical book, *Deuteronomy,* which achieved its final form in the seventh century B.C.E., contains one version of this transformation. Deuteronomy was revised during a time of religious reformation when the king of Jerusalem was trying to abolish all pagan worship, especially that of the Assyrians. Nevertheless, the sources on which Deuteronomy is based date from the time of Moses.

After forty years of wandering, the Israelites have reached the frontier of Canaan. Moses delivers a final message, knowing that he will die before his people reach the promised land.

SOURCE: The Holy Bible (New York: American Bible Society, n.d.).

CHAPTER 5

And Moses called all Ĭş′rā-ĕl, and said unto them, Hear, O Ĭş′rā-ĕl, the statutes and judgments which I speak in your ears this day, that ye may learn them, and keep and do them.

2 The LORD our God made a covenant with us in Hō′rĕb.

3 The LORD made not this covenant with our fathers, but with us, *even* us, who *are* all of us here alive this day.

4 The LORD talked with you face to face in the mount out of the midst of the fire,

5 (I stood between the LORD and you at that time, to show you the word of the LORD: for ye were afraid by reason of the fire, and went not up into the mount,) saying,

6 ¶ I *am* the LORD thy God, which brought thee out of the land of Egypt, from the house of bondage.

7 Thou shalt have none other gods before me.

8 Thou shalt not make thee *any* graven image, *or* any likeness *of any thing* that *is* in heaven above, or that *is* in the earth beneath, or that *is* in the waters beneath the earth:

9 Thou shalt not bow down thyself unto them, nor serve them: for I the LORD thy God *am* a jealous God, visiting the iniquity of the fathers upon the children unto the third and fourth *generation* of them that hate me,

10 And showing mercy unto thousands of them that love me and keep my commandments.

11 Thou shalt not take the name of the LORD thy God in vain: for the LORD will not hold *him* guiltless that taketh his name in vain.

12 Keep the Sabbath day to sanctify it, and the LORD thy God hath commanded thee.

13 Six days thou shalt labor, and do all thy work:

14 But the seventh day *is* the sabbath of the LORD thy God: *in it* thou shalt not do any work, thou, nor thy son, nor thy daughter, nor thy manservant, nor thy maidservant, nor thine ox, nor thine ass, nor any of thy cattle, nor thy stranger that *is* within thy gates; that thy manservant and thy maidservant may rest as well as thou.

15 And remember that thou wast a servant in the land of Egypt, and *that* the LORD thy God brought thee out thence through a mighty hand and by a stretched out arm: therefore the LORD thy God commanded thee to keep the sabbath day.

16 ¶ Honor thy father and thy mother, as the LORD thy God hath commanded thee; that thy days may be prolonged, and that it may go well with thee, in the land which the LORD thy God giveth thee.

17 Thou shalt not kill.

18 Neither shalt thou commit adultery.

19 Neither shalt thou steal.

20 Neither shalt thou bear false witness against thy neighbor.

21 Neither shalt thou desire thy neighbor's wife, neither shalt thou covet thy neighbor's house, his field, or his manservant, or his maidservant, his ox, or his ass, or any *thing* that *is* thy neighbor's.

22 ¶ These words the LORD spake unto all your assembly in the mount out of the midst of the fire, of the cloud, and of the thick darkness, with a great voice; and he added no more. And he wrote them in two tables of stone, and delivered them unto me.

23 And it came to pass, when ye heard the voice out of the midst of the darkness, (for the mountain did burn with fire,) that ye came near unto me, *even* all the heads of your tribes, and your elders;

24 And ye said, Behold, the LORD our God hath showed us his glory and his greatness, and we have heard his voice out of the midst of the fire: we have seen this day that God doth talk with man, and he liveth.

25 Now therefore why should we die? for this great fire will consume us: if we hear the voice of the LORD our God any more, then we shall die.

26 For who *is there of* all flesh, that hath heard the voice of the living God speaking out of the midst of the fire, as we *have,* and lived?

27 Go thou near, and hear all that the LORD our God shall say; and speak thou unto us all that the LORD our God shall speak unto thee; and we will hear *it,* and do *it.*

28 And the LORD heard the voice of your words, when ye spake unto me; and the LORD said unto me, I have heard the voice of the words of this people, which they have spoken unto thee: they have well said all that they have spoken.

29 Oh that there were such a heart in them, that they would fear me, and keep all my commandments always, that it might be well with them, and with their children for ever!

30 Go say to them, Get you into your tents again.

31 But as for thee, stand thou here by me, and I will speak unto thee all the commandments, and the statutes, and the judgments, which thou shalt teach them, that they may do *them* in the land which I give them to possess it.

32 Ye shall observe to do therefore as the LORD your God hath commanded you: ye shall not turn aside to the right hand or to the left.

33 Ye shall walk in all the ways which the LORD your God hath commanded you, that ye may live, and *that it may be* well with you, and *that* ye may prolong *your* days in the land which ye shall possess.

CHAPTER 6

Now these *are* the commandments, the statutes, and the judgments, which the LORD your God commanded to teach you, that ye might do *them* in the land whither ye go to possess it:

2 That thou mightest fear the LORD thy God, to keep all his statutes and his commandments, which I command thee, thou, and thy son, and thy son's son, all the days of thy life; and that thy days may be prolonged.

3 ¶ Hear therefore, O Ĭş'rā-ĕl, and observe to do *it;* that it may be well with thee, and that ye may increase mightily, as the LORD God of thy fathers hath promised thee, in the land that floweth with milk and honey.

4 Hear, O Ĭş'rā-ĕl: The LORD our God *is* one LORD:

5 And thou shalt love the LORD thy God with all thine heart, and with all thy soul, and with all thy might.

6 And these words, which I command thee this day, shall be in thine heart:

7 And thou shalt teach them diligently unto thy children, and shalt talk of them when thou sittest in thine house, and when thou walkest by the say, and when thou liest down, and when thou risest up.

8 And thou shalt bind them for a sign upon thine hand, and they shall be as frontlets between thine eyes.

9 And thou shalt write them upon the posts of thy house, and on thy gates.

10 And it shall be, when the LORD thy God shall have brought thee into the land which he sware unto thy fathers, to Abraham, to Isaac, and to Jacob, to give thee great and goodly cities, which thou buildedst not,

11 And houses full of all good *things,* which thou filledst not, and wells digged, which thou diggedst not, vineyards and olive trees, which thou plantedst not; when thou shalt have eaten and be full;

12 *Then* beware lest thou forget the LORD, which brought thee forth out of the land of Egypt, from the house of bondage.

13 Thou shalt fear the LORD thy God, and serve him, and shalt swear by his name.

14 Ye shall not go after other gods, of the gods of the people which *are* round about you;

15 (For the LORD thy God *is* a jealous God among you;) lest the anger of the LORD thy God be kindled against thee, and destroy thee from off the face of the earth.

16 ¶ Ye shall not tempt the LORD your God, as ye tempted *him* in Măs'sȧh.

17 Ye shall diligently keep the commandments of the LORD your God, and his testimonies, and his statutes, which he hath commanded thee.

18 And thou shalt do *that which is* right and good in the sight of the LORD; that it may be well with thee, and that thou mayest go in and possess the good land which the LORD sware unto thy fathers,

19 To cast out all thine enemies from before thee, as the LORD hath spoken.

20 *And* when thy son asketh thee in time to come, saying, What *mean* the testimonies, and the statutes, and the judgments, which the LORD our God hath commanded you?

21 Then thou shalt say unto thy son, We were Phā′raōh's bondmen in Egypt; and the LORD brought us out of Egypt with a mighty hand:

22 And the LORD showed signs and wonders, great and sore, upon Egypt, upon Phā′raōh, and upon all his household, before our eyes:

23 And he brought us out from thence, that he might bring us in, to give us the land which he sware unto our fathers.

24 And the LORD commanded us to do all these statutes, to fear the LORD our God, for our good always, that he might preserve us alive, as *it is* at this day.

25 And it shall be our righteousness, if we observe to do all these commandments before the LORD our God, as he hath commanded us.

CHAPTER 7

When the LORD thy God shall bring thee into the land whither thou goest to possess it, and hath cast out many nations before thee, the Hĭt′-tītes, and the Gĭr′gȧ-shītes, and the Ăm′ō-rītes, and the Cā′năan-ītes, and the Pĕr′ĭz-zītes, and the Hī′vītes, and the Jĕb′ū-sītes, seven nations greater and mightier than thou;

2 And when the LORD thy God shall deliver them before thee; thou shalt smite them, *and* utterly destroy them; thou shalt make no covenant with them, nor show mercy unto them:

3 Neither shalt thou make marriages with them; thy daughter thou shalt not give unto his son, nor his daughter shalt thou take unto thy son.

4 For they will turn away thy son from following me, that they may serve other gods: so will the anger of the LORD be kindled against you, and destroy thee suddenly.

5 But thus shall ye deal with them; ye shall destroy their altars, and break down their images, and cut down their groves, and burn their graven images with fire.

6 For thou *art* a holy people unto the LORD thy God: the LORD thy God hath chosen thee to be a special people unto himself, above all people that *are* upon the face of the earth.

7 The LORD did not set his love upon you, nor choose you, because ye were more in number than any people; for ye *were* the fewest of all people:

8 But because the LORD loved you, and because he would keep the oath which he had sworn unto your fathers, hath the LORD brought you out with a mighty hand, and redeemed you out of the house of bondmen, from the hand of Phā′raōh king of Egypt.

9 Know therefore that the LORD thy God, he *is* God, the faithful God, which keepeth covenant and mercy with them that love him and keep his commandments to a thousand generations;

10 And repayeth them that hate him to their face, to destroy them: he will not be slack to him that hateth him, he will repay him to his face.

11 Thou shalt therefore keep the commandments, and the statutes, and the judgments, which I command thee this day, to do them.

12 ¶ Wherefore it shall come to pass, if ye hearken to these judgments, and keep and do them, that the LORD thy God shall keep unto thee the covenant and the mercy which he sware unto thy fathers:

13 And he will love thee, and bless thee, and multiply thee: he will also bless the fruit of thy womb, and the fruit of thy land, thy corn, and thy wine, and thine oil, the increase of thy kine, and the flocks of thy sheep, in the land which he sware unto thy fathers to give thee.

14 Thou shalt be blessed above all people: there shall not be male or female barren among you, or among your cattle.

15 And the LORD will take away from thee all sickness, and will put none of the evil diseases of Egypt, which thou knowest, upon thee; but will lay them upon all *them* that hate thee.

16 And thou shalt consume all the people which the LORD thy God shall deliver thee; thine eye shall have no pity upon them: neither shalt thou serve their gods; for that *will be* a snare unto thee.

17 If thou shalt say in thine heart, These nations *are* more than I; how can I dispossess them?

18 Thou shalt not be afraid of them: *but* shalt well remember what the LORD thy God did unto Phā'raōh, and unto all Egypt;

19 The great temptations which thine eyes saw, and the signs, and the wonders, and the mighty hand, and the stretched out arm, whereby the LORD thy God brought thee out: so shall the LORD thy God do unto all the people of whom thou art afraid.

20 Moreover the LORD thy God will send the hornet among them, until they that are left, and hide themselves from thee, be destroyed.

21 Thou shalt not be affrighted at them: for the LORD thy God *is* among you, a mighty God and terrible.

22 And the LORD thy God will put out those nations before thee by little and little: thou mayest not consume them at once, lest the beasts of the field increase upon thee.

23 But the LORD thy God shall deliver them unto thee, and shall destroy them with a mighty destruction, until they be destroyed.

24 And he shall deliver their kings into thine hand, and thou shalt destroy their name from under heaven: there shall no man be able to stand before thee, until thou have destroyed them.

25 The graven images of their gods shall ye burn with fire: thou shalt not desire the silver or gold *that is* on them, nor take *it* unto thee, lest thou be snared therein: for it *is* an abomination to the LORD thy God.

26 Neither shalt thou bring an abomination into thine house, lest thou be a cursed thing like it: *but* thou shalt utterly detest it, and thou shalt utterly abhor it; for it *is* a cursed thing.

2.4

Inscription of Tiglath-Pileser I, King of Assyria (1120 B.C.E.)

Tiglath-Pileser I was the first king of Assyria who made extensive conquests. This inscription recording his victories was found on four large octagonal cylinders buried under the foundation of the great temple at Assur, the oldest of the Assyrian capitals.

In this inscription we find the regular earmarks of an Assyrian royal chronicle: constant invocations of the gods, endless self-praise, and continued glorification of acts of cruelty. Assyria was a great success as a military monarchy; her kings were bold leaders of a brave and battle-loving people, but they had no genius for organizing peaceful government. They were content to force a defeated nation to pay tribute and submit to general spoliation while leaving the kings and laws to the conquered natives. The result was ceaseless revolts whenever the Assyrian terror abated, followed by ruthless conquests repeated often.

Source: William Stearns Davis, *Readings in Ancient History. Vol. I: Greece and the East* (Boston: Allyn and Bacon, 1912), 20-23.

Assur the great lord, director of the hosts of the gods, the giver of the scepter and the crown, the stablisher of the kingdom; *Bel* the Lord, king of all the spirits of the earth, the father of the gods, the lord of the world, [and all ye other] great gods, guiders of heaven and earth, whose onset is opposition and combat, who have magnified the kingdom of Tiglath-Pileser, the prince, the chosen of the desire of your hearts, the exalted shepherd . . . with a crown supreme, you have clothed him: to rule over the land of Bel mightily you have established him. . . .

Tiglath-Pileser, the powerful king, the king of hosts who has no rival, the king of the four zones, the king of all the kinglets, the lord of lords, the shepherd prince, the king of kings, the exalted prophet, to whom by proclamation of Samas [the Sun-God] the illustrious scepter has been given as a gift . . . the illustrious prince whose glory has overwhelmed all regions, the mighty destroyer, who like the rush of a flood is made strong against the hostile land, *he* has destroyed the foemen of Assur [*i.e.* Assyria].

Countries, mountains, fortresses and kinglets, the enemies of Assur I have conquered and their territories I have made to submit. With sixty kings I have contended furiously, and power and rivalry over them I displayed. A rival in the combat, a confronter in the battle, I have not. To the land of Assyria I have added land, to its men I have added men: the boundary of my own land I have enlarged, and all their lands I have conquered.

At the beginning of my reign 20,000 men of the Muskaya and their five kings to their strength trusted and came down: the land of Kummukh [along the upper Euphrates] they seized.

Trusting in Assur my lord I assembled my chariots and armies. There upon I delayed not. The mountains of Kasiyara, a difficult region, I crossed. With their 20,000 fighting men, and their five kings in the land of Kummukh I contended. A destruction of them I made. The bodies of their warriors in destructive battle like the Inundator [the god Rimmon] I overthrew. Their corpses I spread over the valleys and the high places of the mountains. *Their heads I cut off: at the sides of their cities I heaped them like mounds.* Their spoil, their property, their goods, to a countless number I brought forth. Six thousand men, the relics of their armies, which before my weapons had fled, and took my feet. I laid hold upon them and counted them among the men of my own country.

[After telling at great length about his numerous conquests, rebels crushed, cities taken, kings reduced and general slaughter of the enemy, Tiglath-Pileser boasts of his feats as a royal hunter: a matter wherein an Assyrian king would take almost as much pride as in his conquests.]

Under the protection of [the god] Uras, who loves me, from young wild bulls, powerful and large in the deserts, with my mighty bow, a lasso of iron and my pointed spear, their lives I ended. Their hides and their horns to my city of Assur I brought.

Ten powerful male elephants . . . I slew. Four elephants alive I captured. Their hides and their teeth along with the live elephants I brought to my city of Assur.

One hundred twenty lions, with my stout heart in the conflict of my heroism on my feet I slew, and 800 lions in my chariot with javelins (?) I slaughtered.

2.5

The Gathas, Zarathustra

The *Gathas* are short devotional hymns contained in the *Avesta,* the fundamental text of Zoroastrianism. Most of the *Avesta* dates from well after Zarathustra's time, but either Zarathustra or one of his early disciples composed the *Gathas.* Their archaic language and often unclear references make them difficult to interpret with full confidence but they are our only credible sources from the original teachings of the Persian prophet. As such, they illustrate, however ambiguously, his vision and message.

SOURCES:

1. Charles F. Horne, ed., *The Sacred Books and Early Literature of the East, Volume VII: Ancient Persia* (New York: Parke, Austin, and Lipscomb, 1917), pp. 11-13, 32-38.
2. James Hope Moulton, *Early Zoroastrianism* (London: Williams & Norgate, 1913), 364-370, passim.

THE GATHA USTAVAITI

Yasna XLIII

4. Then shall I recognize thee as strong and holy, Mazda, when by the hand in which thou thyself dost hold the destinies that thou wilt assign to the Liar and the Righteous, by the glow of thy Fire whose power is Right, the might of Good Thought shall come to me.

5. As the holy one I recognized thee, Mazda Ahura, when I saw thee in the beginning at the birth of Life, when thou madest actions and words to have their need—evil for the evil, a good Destiny for the good—through thy wisdom when creation shall reach its goal.

6. At which goal thou wilt come with thy holy Spirit, O Mazda, with Dominion, at the same with Good Thought, by whose action the settlements will prosper through Right. Their judgments shall Piety proclaim, even those of thy wisdom which none can deceive.

7. As the holy one I recognized thee, Mazda Ahura, when Good Thought came to me and asked me, "Who art thou? To whom dost thou belong? By what sign wilt thou appoint the days for questioning about thy possessions and thyself?"

8. Then I said to him: "To the first question, Zarathushtra am I, a true foe to the Liar, to the utmost of my power, but a powerful support would I be to the Righteous, that I may attain the future things of the infinite Dominion, according as I praise and sing thee, Mazda.

15. As the holy one I recognized thee, Mazda Ahura, when Good Thought came to me, when the still mind taught me to declare what is best: "Let not a man seek again and again to please the Liars, for they make all the righteous enemies."

16. And thus Zarathushtra himself, O Ahura, chooses that spirit of thine that is holiest, Mazda. May Right be embodied, full of life and strength! May Piety abide in the Dominion where the sun shines! May Good Thought give destiny to men according to their works!

Yasna XLIV

3. This I ask thee, tell me truly, Ahura. Who is by generation the Father of Right, at the first? Who determined the path of sun and stars? Who is it by whom the moon waxes and wanes again? This, O Mazda, and yet more, I am fain to know.

4. This I ask thee, tell me truly, Ahura. Who upheld the earth beneath and the firmament from falling? Who the waters and the plants? Who yoked swiftness to winds and clouds? Who is, O Mazda, creator of Good Thought?

5. This I ask thee, tell me truly, Ahura. What artist made light and darkness? What artist made sleep and waking? Who made morning, noon, and night, that call the understanding man to his duty?

7. This I ask thee, tell me truly, Ahura. Who created together with Dominion the precious Piety? Who made by wisdom the son obedient to his father? I strive to recognize by these things thee, O Mazda, creator of all things through the holy spirit.

10. This I ask thee, tell me truly, Ahura. The Religion which is the best for all that are, which in union with Right should prosper all that is mine, will they duly observe it, the religion of my creed, with the words and action of Piety, in desire for thy future good things, O Mazda?

11. This I ask thee, tell me truly, Ahura—whether Piety will extend to those to whom thy Religion shall be proclaimed? I was ordained at the first by thee: all others I look upon with hatred of spirit.

12. This I ask thee, tell me truly, Ahura. Who among those with whom I would speak is a righteous man, and who a liar? On which side is the enemy?

13. This I ask thee, tell me truly, Ahura—whether we shall drive the Lie away from us to those who being full of disobedience will not strive after fellowship with Right, nor trouble themselves with counsel of Good Thought.

17. This I ask thee, tell my truly, Ahura—whether through you I shall attain my goal, O Mazda, even attachment unto you, and that my voice may be effectual, that Welfare and Immortality may be ready to unite according to that promise with him who joins himself with Right.

18. This I ask thee, tell me truly, Ahura—whether I shall indeed, O Right, earn that reward, even ten mares with a stallion and a camel, which was promised to me, O Mazda, as well as through thee the future gift of Welfare and Immortality.

Yasna XLV

3. I will speak of that which Mazda Ahura, the all-knowing, revealed to me first in this earthly life. Those of you that put not in practise this word as I think and utter it, to them shall be woe at the end of life.

5. I will speak of that which the Holiest declared to me as the word that is best for mortals to obey: he, Mazda Ahura, said, "They who at my bidding render him obedience, shall all attain unto Welfare and Immortality by the actions of the Good Spirit."

7. In immortality shall the soul of the righteous be joyful, in perpetuity shall be the torments of the Liars. All this doth Mazda Ahura appoint by his Dominion.

CHAPTER 3

The Foundation of Indian Society, to 300 C.E.

3.1

Rig Veda, The Creation Hymn

Most religions contain creation "myths." In this case, "myth" does not refer to "fairy stories" as much as to fundamental attempts to answer the most profound questions we can ask: How did the universe come into being? How and when were humans created?

The name "Rig" means a song of praise, and "Veda" means holy knowledge; so the Rig Veda is a book of holy knowledge made up of hymns. There are other Hymn Vedas, but the Rig is the oldest and most important. A Hindu tradition represents the Vedas as being as old as creation and the authors are reputed to have "seen" each hymn, not composed it; thus, it was a revelation.

The Hindus have no records of ancient chronology, yet some modern scholars claim that the Rig Veda is eight to twelve thousand years old. It was handed down by oral tradition long before it was written. The earliest evidence only dates from 1200 B.C.E., and other scholars set 2000 B.C.E. as the earliest beginnings.

The Rig consists of more than a thousand hymns, divided into ten mandalas, or books. The Creation Hymn is in the tenth mandala which contains many of the most celebrated hymns. It is interesting in its resemblance to the Biblical account of creation.

Source: Charles F. Horne, ed., *The Sacred Books and Early Literature of the East. Vol. IX: India and Brahmanism* (New York: Parke, Austin, and Lipscomb, 1917), 48.

Book X.—Hymn 129

1. Then was not non-existent nor existent: there was no realm of air, no sky beyond it.

What covered in, and where and what gave shelter? Was water there, unfathomed depth of water?

2. Death was not then, nor was there aught immortal: no sign was there, the day's and night's divider.

That One Thing, breathless, breathed by its own nature: apart from it was nothing whatsoever.

3. Darkness there was: at first concealed in darkness this All was indiscriminated chaos.

All that existed then was void and formless: by the great power of Warmth was born that Unit.

4. Thereafter rose Desire in the beginning—Desire, the primal seed and germ of Spirit.

Sages who searched with their heart's thought discovered the existent's kinship in the non-existent.

5. Transversely was their severing line extended: what was above it then, and what below it?

There were begetters, there were mighty forces, free action here and energy up yonder.

6. Who verily knows and who can here declare it, whence it was born and whence comes this creation?

The Gods are later than this world's production. Who knows then whence it first came into being?

7. He, the first origin of this creation, whether he formed it all or did not form it,

Whose eye controls this world in highest heaven, he verily knows its, or perhaps he knows not.

3.2

The Upanishads

The development of a religion is a slow and continuous process. Thus, it was with Hinduism. The whole of the Vedic literature consisted of four *Vedas*, several commentaries on the *Vedas*, and various philosophical investigations collected in the *Upanishads*. The *Upanishads* were critical to the development of modern Hinduism. They explored and explained the mystical aspects of the religion; most important, they addressed the nature of the human soul—the part of us that transcends the physical body.

One important idea in the *Upanishads* is the transmigration of souls, a process of death and rebirth that lasts until the human soul attains a level of absolute purity. At that point, one surrenders his individuality and the soul becomes one with the *Brahman*, a state of existence associated with the chief god of the Hindu pantheon *(Brahma)*. It refers to a state of absolute perfection instead of an ascension to the godhead. Rebirth is tied directly to the caste system and the idea of good *karma*—the obeying of *dharma*, or religious law. At each level of Hindu castes, *dharma* assumes increasing strictness. When a soul is reborn, good *karma* in its past existence allows its new physical body to be that of a higher caste. This progression eventually allows every soul the opportunity to transcend human existence and reach *Brahman*.

Source: F. Max Mueller, trans., *The Upanishads*, in Mueller, ed., *The Sacred Books of the East*, 50vols. (Oxford: Clarendon Press, 1879-1910), vol. I, pp. 92, 104-105; vol. 15, pp. 168-169, 173, 175-177, passim.

The Chandogya Upanishad

There lived once Svetaketu. . . . To him his father Uddalaka . . . said: "Svetaketu, go to school; for no one belonging to our race, dear son, who, not having studied, is, as it were, a Brahmin by birth only."

Having begun his apprenticeship when he was twelve years of age, Svetaketu returned to his father, when he was twenty-four, having then studied all the Vedas,—conceited, considering himself well-read, and stern.

His father said to him: "Svetaketu, as you are so conceited, considering yourself so well-read, and so stern, my dear, have you ever asked for that instruction by which we hear what cannot be heard, by which we perceive what cannot be perceived, by which we know what cannot be known?"

"What is that instruction, Sir?" he asked. . . .

"Fetch me . . . a fruit of the Nyagrodha tree."

"Here is one, Sir."

"Break it."

"It is broken, Sir."

"What do you see there?"

"These seeds, almost infinitesimal."

"Break one of them."

"It is broken, Sir."

"What do you see there?"

"Not anything, Sir."

The father said: "My son, that subtle essence which you do not perceive there, of that very essence this great Nyagrodha tree exists.

"Believe it, my son. That which is the subtle essence, in it all that exists has its self. It is the True. It is the Self, and you, . . . Svetaketu, are it."

"Please, Sir, inform me still more," said the son.

"Be it so, my child," the father replied.

"Place this salt in water, and then wait on me in the morning."

The son did as he was commanded.

The father said to him: "Bring me the salt, which you placed in the water last night."

The son having looked for it, found it not, for, of course, it was melted.

The father said: "Taste it from the surface of the water. How is it?"

The son replied: "It is salt."

"Taste it from the middle. How is it?"

The son replied: "It is salt."

"Taste it from the bottom. How is it?"

The son replied: "It is salt."

The father said: "Throw it away and then wait on me."

He did so; but the salt exists forever.

Then the father said: "Here also, in this body, . . . you do not perceive the True, my son; but there indeed it is.

"That which is the subtle essence, in it all that exists has its self. It is the True. It is the Self, and you, Svetaketu, are it."

The Brihadaranyaka Upanishad

"And when the body grows weak through old age, or becomes weak through illness, at that time that person, after separating himself from his members, as a mango, or fig, or pippala-fruit is separated from the stalk, hastens back again as he came, to the place from which he started, to new life. . . .

"Then both his knowledge and his work take hold of him and his acquaintance with former things.

"And as a caterpillar, after having reached the end of a blade of grass, and after having made another approach to another blade, draws itself together towards it, thus does this Self, after having thrown off this body and dispelled all ignorance, and after making another approach to another body, draw himself together towards it.

"And as a goldsmith, taking a piece of gold, turns it into another, newer and more beautiful shape, so does this Self, after having thrown off this body and dispelled all ignorance, make unto himself another, newer and more beautiful shape. . . .

"Now as a man is like this or like that, according as he acts and according as he behaves, so will he be:—a man of good acts will become good, a man of bad acts, bad. He becomes pure by pure deeds, bad by bad deeds.

"And here they say that a person consists of desires. And as is his desire, so is his will; and as is his will, so is his deed; and whatever deed he does, that he will reap.

"And here there is this verse: 'To whatever object a man's own mind is attached, to that he goes strenuously together with his deed; and having obtained the consequences of whatever deed he does here on earth, he returns again from that world . . . to this world of action.'

"So much for the man who desires. But as to the man who does not desire, who, not desiring, freed from desires, is satisfied in his desires, or desires the Self only, his vital spirits do not depart elsewhere,—being Brahman, he goes to Brahman.

"On this there is this verse: 'When all desires which once entered his heart are undone, then does the mortal become immortal, then he obtains Brahman.'"

■ ■ ■

"Now as a man, when embraced by a beloved wife, knows nothing that is without, nothing that is within, thus this person, when embraced by the intelligent Self, knows nothing that is without, nothing that is within. This indeed is his true form, in which his wishes are fulfilled, in which the Self only is his wish, in which no wish is left,—free from any sorrow.

"Then a father is not a father, a mother not a mother, the worlds not worlds, the gods not gods, the Vedas not Vedas. Then a thief is not a thief, a murderer not a murderer, a Kandala not a Kandala, a Sramana not a Sramana, a Tapasa not a Tapasa. He is not followed by good, not followed by evil, for he has then overcome all the sorrows of the heart."

3.3

The Life of the Buddha

The following selection reveals some of the major precepts of Buddhism. It is from a Sanskrit text, *The Life of Buddha*, by Asvaghosha (ca. 420 C.E.) and concerns teachings all Buddhists accept. It refers to a time when the Buddha, upon attaining enlightenment, described how others could do so as well.

SOURCE: Paul Carus, *The Gospel of Buddha* (Chicago: The Open Court Publishing Co., 1915), 39-43.

ENLIGHTENMENT

The Bodhisattva, having put Mara to flight, gave himself up to meditation. All the miseries of the world, the evils produced by evil deeds and the sufferings arising therefrom, passed before his mental eye, and he thought:

"Surely if living creatures saw the results of all their evil deeds, they would turn away from them in disgust. But selfhood blinds them, and they cling to their obnoxious desires. They crave pleasure for themselves and they cause pain to others; when death destroys their individuality, they find no peace; their thirst for existence abides and their selfhood reappears in new births. Thus they continue to move in the coil and can find no escape from the hell of their own making. And how empty are their pleasures, how vain are their endeavors! Hollow like the plantain-tree and without contents like the bubble. The world is full of evil and sorrow, because it is full of lust. Men go astray because they think that delusion is better than truth. Rather than truth they follow error, which is pleasant to look at in the beginning but in the end causes anxiety, tribulation, and misery."

And the Bodhisattva began to expound the Dharma. The Dharma is the truth. The Dharma is the scared law. The Dharma is religion. The Dharma alone can deliver us from error, from wrong and from sorrow.

Pondering on the origin of birth and death, the Enlightened One recognized that ignorance was the root of all evil; and these are the links in the development of life, called the twelve nidanas: In the beginning there is existence blind and without knowledge; and in this sea of ignorance there are stirrings formative and organizing. From stirrings, formative and organizing, rises awareness or feelings. Feelings beget organisms that live as individual beings. These organisms develop the six fields, that is, the five senses and the mind. The six fields come in contact with things. Contact begets sensation. Sensation creates the thirst of individualized being. The thirst of being creates a cleaving to things. The cleaving produces the growth and continuation of selfhood. Selfhood continues in renewed birth. The renewed births of selfhood are the causes of sufferings, old age, sickness, and death. They produce lamentation, anxiety, and despair.

The cause of all sorrow lies at the very beginning; it is hidden in the ignorance from which life grows. Remove ignorance and you will destroy the wrong desires that rise from ignorance; destroy these desires and you will wipe out the wrong perception that rises from them. Destroy wrong perception and there is an end of errors in individualized beings. Destroy the errors in individualized beings and the illusions of the six fields will disappear. Destroy illusions and the contact with things will cease to beget misconception. Destroy misconception and you do away with thirst. Destroy thirst and you will be free of all morbid cleaving. Remove the cleaving and you destroy the selfishness of selfhood. If the selfishness of selfhood is destroyed you will be above birth, old age, disease, and death, and you will escape all suffering.

The Enlightened One saw the four noble truths which point out the path that leads to Nirvana or the extinction of self: The first noble truth is the existence of sorrow. The second noble truth is the cause of suffering. The third noble truth is the cessation of sorrow. The fourth noble truth is the eightfold path that leads to the cessation of sorrow.

This is the Dharma. This is the truth. This is religion. And the Enlightened One uttered this stanza:

"Through many births I sought in vain
The Builder of this House of Pain.
Now, Builder, You are plain to see,
And from this House at last I'm free;
I burst the rafters, roof and wall,
And dwell in the Peace beyond them all."

There is self and there is truth. Where self is, truth is not. Where truth is, self is not. Self is the fleeting error of samsara; it is individual separateness and that egotism which begets envy and hatred. Self is the yearning for pleasure and the lust after vanity. Truth is the correct comprehension of things; it is the permanent and everlasting, the real in all existence, the bliss of righteousness.

The existence of self is an illusion, and there is no wrong in this world, no vice, no evil, except what flows from the assertion of self. The attainment of truth is possible only when self is recognized as an illusion. Righteousness can be practiced only when we have freed our mind from passions of egotism. Perfect peace can dwell only where all vanity has disappeared.

Blessed is he who has understood the Dharma. Blessed is he who does no harm to his fellow-beings. Blessed is he who overcomes wrong and is free from passion. To the highest bliss has he attained who has conquered all selfishness and vanity. He has become the Buddha, the Perfect One.

THE FIRST CONVERTS

The Blessed One tarried in solitude seven times seven days, enjoying the bliss of emancipation. At that time Tapussa and Bhallika, two merchants, came traveling on the road near by, and when they saw the great samana, majestic and full of peace, they approached him respectfully and offered him rice cakes and honey.

This was the first food that the Enlightened One ate after he attained Buddhahood.

And the Buddha addressed them and pointed out to them the way of salvation. The two merchants, seeing the holiness of the conqueror of Mara, bowed down in reverence and said: "We take our refuge, Lord, in the Blessed One and in the Dharma." Tapussa and Bhallika were the first that became followers of the Buddha and they were lay disciples.

"Let us, then, abandon the heresy of worshiping Isvara and of praying to him; let us no longer lose ourselves in vain speculations or profitless subtleties; let us surrender self and all selfishness, and as all things are fixed by causation, let us practice good so that good may result from our actions."

And Anathapindika said: "I see that thou art the Buddha, the Blessed One, the Tathagata, and I wish to open to thee my whole mind. Having listened to my words advise me what I shall do. My life is full of work, and having acquired great wealth, I am surrounded with cares. Yet I enjoy my work, and apply myself to it with all diligence. Many people are in my employ and depend upon the success of my enterprises.

"Now, I have heard thy disciples praise the bliss of the hermit and denounce the unrest of the world. 'The Holy One,' they say, 'has given up his kingdom and his inheritance, and has found the path of righteousness, thus setting an example to all the world how to attain Nirvana:' My heart yearns to do what is right and to be a blessing unto my fellows. Let me then ask thee, Must I give up my wealth, my home, and my business enterprises, and, like thyself, go into homelessness in order to attain the bliss of a religious life?"

And the Buddha replied: "The bliss of a religious life is attainable by every one who walks in the noble eightfold path. He that cleaves to wealth had better cast it away than allow his heart to be poisoned by it; but he who does not cleave to wealth, and possessing riches, uses them rightly, will be a blessing unto his fellows. It is not life and wealth and power that enslave men, but the cleaving to life and wealth and power. The bhikkhu who retires from the world in order to lead a life of leisure will have no gain, for a life of indolence is an abomination, and lack of energy is to be despised. The Dharma of the Tathagata does not require a man to go into homelessness or to resign the world, unless he to despise him, is wicked. The Tathagata," the Buddha continued, "does not seek salvation in austerities, but neither does he for that reason indulge in worldly pleasures, nor live in abundance. The Tathagata has found the middle path.

"There are two extremes, O bhikkhus, which the man who has given up the world ought not to follow—the habitual practice, on the one hand, of self-indulgence which is unworthy, vain and fit only for the worldly-minded—and the habitual practice, on the other hand, of self-mortification, which is painful, useless and unprofitable.

"Neither abstinence from fish and flesh, nor going naked, nor shaving the head, nor wearing matted hair, nor dressing in a rough garment, nor covering oneself with dirt, nor sacrificing to Agni, will cleanse a man who is not free from delusions. Reading the Vedas, making offerings to priests, or sacrifices to the gods, self-mortification by heat or cold, and many such penances performed for the sake of immortality, these do not cleanse the man who is not free from delusions. Anger, drunkenness, obstinacy, bigotry, deception, envy, self-praise, disparaging others, superciliousness and evil intentions constitute uncleanness; not verily the eating of flesh.

"A middle path, O bhikkhus, avoiding the two extremes, has been discovered by the Tathagata—a path which opens the eyes, and bestows understanding, which leads to peace of mind, to the higher wisdom, to full enlightenment, to Nirvana! What is that middle path, O bhikkhus, avoiding these two extremes, discovered by the Tathagata—that path which opens the eyes, and bestows understanding, which leads to peace of mind, to the higher wisdom, to full enlightenment, to Nirvana? Let me teach you, O bhikkhus, the middle path, which keeps aloof from both extremes. By suffering, the emaciated devotee produces confusion and sickly thoughts in his mind. Mortification is not conducive even to worldly knowledge; how much less to a triumph over the senses!

The Dharma of the Tathagata requires every man to free himself from the illusion of self, to cleanse his heart, to give up his thirst for pleasure, and lead a life of righteousness. And whatever men do, whether they remain in the world as artisans, merchants, and officers of the king, or retire from the world and devote themselves to a life of religious meditation, let them put their whole heart into their task; let them be diligent and energetic, and, if they are like the lotus, which, although it grows in the water, yet remains untouched by the water, if they struggle in life without cherishing envy or hatred, if they live in the world not a life of self but a life of truth, then surely joy, peace, and bliss will dwell in their minds."

CHAPTER 4

China's Classical Age, to 256 B.C.E.

4.1

Analects, Confucius

Confucius (ca. 551-479 B.C.E.) taught that clear thinking and self-discipline lead the superior man to correct action in all his relationships. Through moral influence and education, he should lead the common herd with kindliness and justice. Confucius advocated paternalism based on the golden rule. Having failed as minister of justice in Lu (500-496 B.C.E.) to secure cooperation of his prince, he edited the *Annals* of that state to illustrate his monarchical doctrine of political morality. His precepts, or *Analects,* were gathered a century later.

During the Western Han dynasty (202 B.C.E.-9 C.E.), training in Confucian philosophy became a requirement for civil service, and the *Analects* remained a key component of Chinese morality.

SOURCES:

1. Charles F. Horne, *The Sacred Books and Early Literature of the East, Volume XI: Ancient China* (Parke, Austin, and Lipscomb, 1917), pp. 276-277, 350-353.
2. Epiphanus Wilson, ed., *Oriental Literature: The Literature of China,* Rev. ed., Vol. IV (New York: The Colonial Press, 1900), pp. 8-10.
3. *Confucianism Analects, the Great Learning, and the Doctrine of the Mean* in *Chinese Classics Series of the Clarendon Press,* Vol. I, trans. James Legge (Oxford: U.K.: Clarendon Press, 1893).

BOOK II

Good Government—Filial Piety—The Superior Man

Sayings of the Master:—

"Let a ruler base his government upon virtuous principles, and he will be like the pole-star, which remains steadfast in its place, while all the host of stars turn towards it.

"The 'Book of Odes' contains three hundred pieces, but one expression in it may be taken as covering the purport of all, viz., Unswerving mindfulness.

"To govern simply by statute, and to reduce all to order by means of pains and penalties, is to render the people evasive, and devoid of any sense of shame.

"To govern upon principles of virtue, and to reduce them to order by the Rules of Propriety, would not only create in them the sense of shame, but would moreover reach them in all their errors.

"When I attained the age of fifteen, I became bent upon study. At thirty, I was a confirmed student. At forty, nought could move me from my course. At fifty, I comprehended the will and decrees of Heaven. At sixty, my ears were attuned to them. At seventy, I could follow my heart's desires, without overstepping the lines of rectitude."

To a question of Mang-i, as to what filial piety consisted in, the master replied, "In not being perverse." Afterwards, when Fan Ch'i was driving him, the Master informed him of this question and answer, and Fan Ch'i asked, "What was your meaning?" The Master replied, "I meant that the Rules of Propriety should always be adhered to in regard to those who brought us into the world: in ministering to them while living, in burying them when dead, and afterwards in the offering to them of sacrificial gifts."

To a query of Mang Wu respecting filial piety, the Master replied, "Parents ought to bear but one trouble—that of their own sickness."

To a like question put by Tsz-yu, his reply was this: "The filial piety of the present day simply means the being able to support one's parents—which extends even to the case of dogs and horses, all of which may have something to give in the way of support. If there be no reverential feeling in the matter, what is there to distinguish between the cases?"

To a like question of Tsz-hiá, he replied: "The manner is the difficulty. If, in the case of work to be done, the younger folks simply take upon themselves the toil of it; or if, in the matter of meat and drink, they simply set these before their elders—is this to be taken as filial piety?"

Once the Master remarked, "I have conversed with Hwúi the whole day long, and he has controverted nothing that I have said, as if he were without wits. But when his back was turned, and I looked attentively at his conduct apart from me, I found it satisfactory in all its issues. No, indeed! Hwúi is not without his wits."

Other observations of the Master:—

"If you observe what things people (usually) take in hand, watch their motives, and note particularly what it is that gives them satisfaction, shall they be able to conceal from you what they are? Conceal themselves, indeed!

"Be versed in ancient lore, and familiarize yourself with the modern; then may you become teachers.

"The great man is not a mere receptacle."

In reply to Tsz-kung respecting the great man:—

"What he first says, as a result of his experience, he afterwards follows up.

"The great man is catholic-minded, and not one-sided. The common man is the reverse.

"Learning, without thought, is a snare; thought, without learning, is a danger.

"Where the mind is set much upon heterodox principles—there truly and indeed is harm."

To the disciple Tsz-lu the Master said, "Shall I give you a lesson about knowledge? When you know a thing, maintain that you know it; and when you do not, acknowledge your ignorance. This is characteristic of knowledge."

Tsz-chang was studying with an eye to official income. The Master addressed him thus: "Of the many things you hear, hold aloof from those that are doubtful, and speak guardedly with reference to the rest; your mistakes will then be few. Also, of the many courses you see adopted, hold aloof from those that are risky, and carefully follow the others; you will then seldom have occasion for regret. Thus, being seldom mistaken in your utterances, and having few occasions for regret in the line you take, you are on the high road to your preferment."

To a question put to him by Duke Ngai as to what should be done in order to render the people submissive to authority, Confucius replied, "Promote the straightforward, and reject those whose courses are crooked, and the thing will be effected. Promote the crooked and reject the straightforward, and the effect will be the reverse."

When Ki K'ang asked of him how the people could be induced to show respect, loyalty, and willingness to be led, the Master answered, "Let there be grave dignity in him who has the oversight of them, and they will show him respect; let him be seen to be good to his own parents, and kindly in disposition, and they will be loyal to him; let him promote those who have ability, and see to the instruction of those who have it not, and they will be willing to be led."

Some one, speaking to Confucius, inquired, "Why, sir, are you not an administrator of government?" The Master rejoined, "What says the 'Book of the Annals,' with reference to filial duty?—'Make it a point to be dutiful to your parents and amicable with your brethren; the same duties extend to an administrator.' If these, then, also make an administrator, how am I to take your words about being an administrator?"

On one occasion the Master remarked, "I know not what men are good for, on whose word no reliance can be placed. How should your carriages, large or little, get along without your whipple-trees or swing-trees?"

Tsze-chang asked if it were possible to forecast the state of the country ten generations hence. The Master replied in this manner: "The Yin Dynasty adopted the rules and manners of the Hsia line of kings, and it is possible to tell whether it retrograded or advanced. The Chau line has followed the Yin, adopting its ways, and whether there has been deterioration or improvement may also be determined. Some other line may take up in turn those of Chau; and supposing even this process to go on for a hundred generations, the result may be known."

Other sayings of the Master:

"It is but flattery to make sacrificial offerings to the departed spirits not belonging to one's own family.

"It is moral cowardice to leave undone what one perceives to be right to do."

Book III—Abuse of Properties

"Let young people," said he, "show filial piety at home, respectfulness towards their elders when away from home; let them be circumspect, be truthful; their love going out freely towards all, cultivating good-will to men. And if, in such a walk, there be time or energy left for other things, let them employ it in the acquisition of literary or artistic accomplishments."

The disciple Tsz-hiá said, "The appreciation of worth in men of worth, thus diverting the mind from lascivious desires—ministering to parents while one is the most capable of so doing—serving one's ruler when one is able to devote himself entirely to that object—being sincere in one's language in intercourse with friends: this I certainly must call evidence of learning, though others may say there has been 'no learning.'"

Sayings of the Master:—

"If the great man be not grave, he will not be revered, neither can his learning be solid.

"Give prominent place to loyalty and sincerity.

"Have no associates in study who are not advanced somewhat like yourself.

"When you have erred, be not afraid to correct yourself."

A saying of the Scholar Tsang:—

"The virtue of the people is renewed and enriched when attention is seen to be paid to the departed, and the remembrance of distant ancestors kept and cherished."

Tsz-k'in put this query to his fellow disciple Tsz-kung: said he, "When our Master comes to this or that State, he learns without fail how it is being governed. Does he investigate matters? or are the facts given him?"

Tsz-kung answered, "Our Master is a man of pleasant manners, and of probity, courteous, moderate, and unassuming: it is by his being such that he arrives at the facts. Is not his way of arriving at things different from that of others?"

A saying of the Master:—

"He who, after three years' observation of the will of his father when alive, or of his past conduct if dead, does not deviate from that father's ways, is entitled to be called 'a dutiful son.'"

Sayings of the Scholar Yu:

"For the practice of the Rules of Propriety, one excellent way is to be natural. This naturalness became a great grace in the practice of kings of former times; let everyone, small or great, follow their example.

"It is not, however, always practicable; and it is not so in the case of a person who does things naturally, knowing that he should act so, and yet who neglects to regulate his acts according to the Rules.

"When truth and right are hand in hand, a statement will bear repetition. When respectfulness and propriety go hand in hand, disgrace and shame are kept afar-off. Remove all occasion for alienating those to whom you are bound by close ties, and you have them still to resort to."

A saying of the Master:—

"The man of greater mind who, when he is eating, craves not to eat to the full; who has a home, but craves not for comforts in it; who is active and earnest in his work and careful in his words; who makes towards men of high principle, and so maintains his own rectitude—that man may be styled a devoted student."

Tsz-kung asked, "What say you, sir, of the poor who do not cringe and fawn; and what of the rich who are without pride and haughtiness?" "They are passable," the Master replied; "yet they are scarcely in the same category as the poor who are happy, and the rich who love propriety."

"In the 'Book of the Odes,'" Tsz-kung went on to say, "we read of one

Polished, as by the knife and file,
The graving-tool, the smoothing-stone.

Does that coincide with your remark?"

"Ah! such as you," replied the Master, "may well commence a discussion on the Odes. If one tell you how a thing goes, you know what ought to come."

"It does not greatly concern me," said the Master, "that men do not know me; my great concern is, my not knowing them."

BOOK XIX.—TEACHINGS OF VARIOUS DISCIPLES

"The learned official," said Tsze-chang, "who when he sees danger ahead will risk his very life, who when he sees a chance of success is mindful of what is just and proper, who in his religious acts is mindful of the duty of reverence, and when in mourning thinks of his loss, is indeed a fit and proper person for his place."

Again he said, "If a person hold to virtue but never advance in it, and if he have faith in right principles and do not build himself up in them, how can he be regarded either as having such, or as being without them?"

Tsze-hia's disciples asked Tsze-chang his views about intercourse with others. "What says your Master?" he rejoined. "He says," they replied, "'Associate with those who are qualified, and repel from you such as are not.'" Tsze-chang then said, "That is different from what I have learnt. A superior man esteems the worthy and wise, and bears them all. He makes much of the good and capable, and pities the incapable. Am I eminently worthy and wise?—who is there then among men whom I will not bear with? Am I not worthy and wise?—others will be minded to repel me: I have nothing to do with repelling them."

Sayings of Tsze-hia:

"Even in inferior pursuits there must be something worthy of contemplation, but if carried to an extreme there is danger of fanaticism; hence the superior man does not engage in them.

"The student who daily recognizes how much he yet lacks, and as the months pass forgets not what he has succeeded in learning, may undoubtedly be called a lover of learning.

"Wide research and steadfast purpose, eager questioning and close reflection—all this tends to humanize a man.

"As workmen spend their time in their workshops for the perfecting of their work, so superior men apply their minds to study in order to make themselves thoroughly conversant with their subjects.

"When an inferior man does a wrong thing, he is sure to gloss it over.

"The superior man is seen in three different aspects: look at him from a distance, he is imposing in appearance; approach him, he is gentle and warm-hearted; hear him speak, he is acute and strict.

"Let such a man have the people's confidence, and he will get much work out of them; so long, however, as he does not possess their confidence they will regard him as grinding them down.

"When confidence is reposed in him, he may then with impunity administer reproof; so long as it is not, he will be regarded as a detractor.

"Where there is no over-stepping of barriers in the practise of the higher virtues, there may be freedom to pass in and out in the practise of the lower ones."

Tsze-yu had said, "The pupils in the school of Tsze-hia are good enough at such things as sprinkling and scrubbing floors, answering calls and replying to questions from superiors, and advancing and retiring to and from such; but these things are only offshoots—as to the root of things they are nowhere. What is the use of all that?"

When this came to the ears of Tsze-hia, he said, "Ah! there he is mistaken. What does a master, in his methods of teaching, consider first in his precepts? And what does he account next, as that about which he may be indifferent? It is like as in the study of plants—classification by *differentiæ*. How may a master play fast and loose in his methods of instruction? Would they not indeed be sages, who could take in at once the first principles and the final developments of things?"

Further observations of Tsze-hia:

"In the public service devote what energy and time remain to study. After study devote what energy and time remain to the public service.

"As to the duties of mourning, let them cease when the grief is past.

"My friend Tsze-chang, although he has the ability to tackle hard things, has not yet the virtue of philanthropy."

The learned Tsang observed, "How loftily Tsze-chang bears himself! Difficult indeed along with him to practise philanthropy!"

Again he said, "I have heard this said by the Master, that 'though men may not exert themselves to the utmost in other duties, yet surely in the duty of mourning for their parents they will do so!'"

Again, "This also I have heard said by the Master: 'The filial piety of Mang Chwang in other respects might be equaled, but as manifested in his making no changes among his father's ministers, nor in his father's mode of government—that aspect of it could not easily be equaled.'"

Yang Fu, having been made senior Criminal Judge by the Chief of the Mang clan, consulted with the learned Tsang. The latter advised him as follows: "For a long time the Chiefs have failed in their government, and the people have become unsettled. When you arrive at the facts of their cases, do not rejoice at your success in that, but rather be sorry for them, and have pity upon them."

Tsze-kung once observed, "We speak of 'the iniquity of Chau,'—but 'twas not so great as this. And so it is that the superior man is averse from settling in this sink, into which everything runs that is foul in the empire."

Again he said, "Faults in a superior man are like eclipses of the sun or moon: when he is guilty of a trespass men all see it; and when he is himself again, all look up to him."

Kung-sun Ch'au of Wei inquired of Tsze-kung how Confucius acquired his learning.

Tsze-kung replied, "The teachings of Wan and Wu have not yet fallen to the ground. They exist in men. Worthy and wise men have the more important of these stored up in their minds; and others, who are not such, store up the less important of them; and as no one is thus without the teachings of Wan and Wu, how should our Master not have learned? And moreover what permanent preceptor could he have?"

Shuh-sun Wu-shuh, addressing the high officials at the Court, remarked that Tsze-kung was a greater worthy than Confucius.

Tsze-fuh King-pih went and informed Tsze-kung of this remark.

Tsze-kung said, "Take by way of comparison the walls outside our houses. My wall is shoulder-high, and you may look over it and see what the house and its contents are worth. My Master's wall is tens of feet high, and unless you should effect an entrance by the door, you would fail to behold the beauty of the ancestral hall and the rich array of all its officers. And they who effect an entrance by the door, methinks, are few! Was it not, however, just like him—that remark of the Chief?"

Shuh-sun Wu-shuh had been casting a slur on the character of Confucius.

"No use doing that," said Tsze-kung; "he is irreproachable. The wisdom and worth of other men are little hills and mounds of earth: traversible. He is the sun, or the moon, impossible to reach and pass. And what harm, I ask, can a man do to the sun or the moon, by wishing to intercept himself from either? It all shows that he knows not how to gauge capacity."

Tsze-k'in, addressing Tsze-kung, said, "You depreciate yourself. Confucius is surely not a greater worthy than yourself."

Tsze-kung replied, "In the use of words one ought never to be incautious; because a gentleman for one single utterance of his is apt to be considered a wise man, and for a single utterance may be accounted unwise. No more might one think of attaining to the Master's perfections than think of going upstairs to Heaven! Were it ever his fortune to be at the head of the government of a country, then that which is spoken of as 'establishing the country' would be establishment indeed; he would be its guide and it would follow him, he would tranquillize it and it would render its willing homage: he would give forward impulses to it to which it would harmoniously respond.

4.2

The Mandate of Heaven

The Mandate of Heaven was a political-social philosophy that served as the basic Chinese explanation for the success and failure of monarchs and states until the empire collapsed in 1912. The idea first appeared in the *Book of Documents,* one of the first written texts in Chinese history, dating from the early Zhou period.

According to China's sages, whenever a dynasty fell, it had lost the moral right to rule, a right that only Heaven can grant. Heaven did not mean a personal god, but a cosmic, all-pervading power. The Zhou rulers may have created the theory of the Mandate of Heaven to justify their overthrow of the Shang. Remember the king was the father of his people, and paternal authority was the basic cement of Chinese society from earliest times. Rebellion against the father, therefore, needed extraordinary justification.

Source: James Legge, trans., *The Sacred Books of China: The Texts of Confucianism,* in F. Max Mueller, ed., *The Sacred Books of the East,* Vol. 3 (Oxford: Clarendon Press, 1879-1910), 92-95.

In the twelfth month of the first year . . . Yi Yin sacrificed to the former king, and presented the heir-king reverently before the shrine of his grandfather. All the princes from the domain of the nobles and the royal domain were present; all the officers also, each continuing to discharge his particular duties, were there to receive the orders of the chief minister. Yi Yin then clearly described the complete virtue of the Meritorious Ancestor for the instruction of the young king.

He said, "Oh! of old the former kings of Xia cultivated earnestly their virtue, and then there were no calamities from Heaven. The spirits of the hills and rivers likewise were all in tranquility; and the birds and beasts, the fishes and tortoises, all enjoyed their existence according to their nature. But their descendant did not follow their example, and great Heaven sent down calamities, employing the agency of our ruler who was in possession of its favoring appointment. The attack on Xia may be traced to the orgies in Ming Tiao. . . . Our king of Shang brilliantly displayed his sagely prowess; for oppression he substituted his generous gentleness; and the millions of the people gave him their hearts. Now your Majesty is entering on the inheritance of his virtue;—all depends on how you commence your reign. To set up love, it is for you to love your relations; to set up respect, it is for you to respect your elders. The commencement is in the family and the state. . . .

"Oh! the former king began with careful attention to the bonds that hold men together. He listened to expostulation, and did not seek to resist it; he conformed to the wisdom of the ancients; occupying the highest position, he displayed intelligence; occupying an inferior position, he displayed his loyalty; he allowed the good qualities of the men whom he employed and did not seek that they should have every talent. . . .

"He extensively sought out wise men, who should be helpful to you, his descendant and heir. He laid down the punishments for officers, and warned those who were in authority, saying, 'If you dare to have constant dancing in your palaces, and drunken singing in your chambers,—that is called the fashion of sorcerers; if you dare to set your hearts on wealth and women, and abandon yourselves to wandering about or to the chase,—that is called the fashion of extravagance; if you dare to despise sage words, to resist the loyal and upright, to put far from you the aged and virtuous, and to seek the company of . . . youths,—that is called the fashion of disorder. Now if a high noble or officer be addicted to one of these three fashions with their ten evil ways, his family will surely come to ruin; if the prince of a country be so addicted, his state will surely come to ruin. The minister who does not try to correct such vices in the sovereign shall be punished with branding.' . . .

"Oh! do you, who now succeed to the throne, revere these warnings in your person. Think of them!—sacred counsels of vast importance, admirable words forcibly set forth! The ways of Heaven are not invariable:—on the good-doer it sends down all blessings, and on the evil-doer it sends down all miseries. Do you but be virtuous, be it in small things or in large, and the myriad regions will have cause for rejoicing. If you not be virtuous, be it in large things or in small, it will bring the ruin of your ancestral temple."

CHAPTER 5

The Greek Experience

5.1

Crito, Plato

Socrates was the first of the great Greek philosophical triumvirate. His uncompromising search for truth led him to expose hypocrisy wherever he found it. He earned the enmity of many who were targets of his exposés or of his unrelenting logic. Athens tolerated Socrates for seventy years but in the aftermath of Athens' defeat in the Peloponnesian War, he found himself under attack. In 399 B.C.E., a conservative politician accused him of introducing strange gods and corrupting the youth of Athens. After being found guilty, Socrates chose death over exile.

Much of what we know about him comes from the *Dialogues* of Plato (427-348 B.C.E.), one of Socrates' students. The *Dialogues* consist of a series of conversations that Socrates had on ethical, political, and social issues. But it is not always clear if the thoughts expressed are those of Socrates or of Plato.

The selection here is from the *Crito*. An old friend, Crito, offers Socrates an escape plan. He refuses, and in doing so, delivers what is known as "The Speech of the Laws of Athens," in which he addresses the obligations of citizenship.

Sources:

1. Benjamin Jowett, trans., *Dialogues of Plato,* Rev. ed. (New York: The Colonial Press, 1899), pp. 48-53.
2. B. Jowett, trans., *The Dialogues of Plato,* 3rd ed., 5 vols. (Oxford University Press, 1892), Vol. 2, pp. 151-156.

Dialogues of Plato

Soc. In leaving the prison against the will of the Athenians, do I wrong any? or rather do I not wrong those whom I ought least to wrong? Do I not desert the principles which were acknowledged by us to be just? What do you say?

Cr. I cannot tell, Socrates, for I do not know.

Soc. Then consider the matter in this way: Imagine that I am about to play truant (you may call the proceeding by any name which you like), and the laws and the government come and interrogate me: "Tell me, Socrates," they say; "what are you about? are you going by an act of yours to overturn us—the laws and the whole State, as far as in you lies? Do you imagine that a State can subsist and not be overthrown, in which the decisions of law have no power, but are set aside and overthrown by individuals?" What will be our answer, Crito, to these and the like words? Anyone, and especially a clever rhetorician, will have a good deal to urge about the evil of setting aside the law which requires a sentence to be carried out; and we might reply, "Yes; but the State has injured us and given an unjust sentence." Suppose I say that?

Cr. Very good, Socrates.

Soc. "And was that our agreement with you?" the law would say; "or were you to abide by the sentence of the State?" And if I were to express astonishment at their saying this, the law would probably add: "Answer, Socrates, instead of opening your eyes: you are in the habit of asking and answering questions. Tell us what complaint you have to make against us which justifies you in attempting to destroy us and the State? In the first place did we not bring you into existence? Your father married your mother by our aid and begat you. Say whether you have any objection to urge against those of us who regulate marriage?" None, I should reply. "Or against those of us who regulate the system of nurture and education of children in which you were trained? Were not the laws, who have the charge of this, right in commanding your father to train you in music and gymnastic?" Right, I should reply. "Well, then, since you were brought into the world and nurtured and educated by us, can you deny in the first place that you are our child and slave, as your fathers were before you? And if this is true you are not on equal terms with us; nor can you think that you have a right to do to us what we are doing to you. Would you have any right to strike or revile or do any other evil to a father or to your master, if you had one, when you have been struck or reviled by him, or received some other evil at his hands?—you would not say this? And because we think right to destroy you, do you think that you have any right to destroy us in return, and your country as far as in you lies? And will you, O professor of true virtue, say that you are justified in this? Has a philosopher like you failed to discover that our country is more to be valued and higher and holier far than mother or father or any ancestor, and more to be regarded in the eyes of the gods and of men of understanding? also to be soothed, and gently and reverently entreated when angry, even more than a father, and if not persuaded, obeyed? And when we are punished by her, whether with imprisonment or stripes, the punishment is to be endured in silence; and if she leads us to wounds or death in battle, thither we follow as is right; neither may anyone yield or retreat or leave his rank, but whether in battle or in a court of law, or in any other place, he must do what his city and his country order him; or he must change their view of what is just: and if he may do no violence to his father or mother, much less may he do violence to his country." What answer shall we make to this, Crito? Do the laws speak truly, or do they not?

Cr. I think that they do.

Soc. Then the laws will say: "Consider, Socrates, if this is true, that in your present attempt you are going to do us wrong. For, after having brought you into the world, and nurtured and educated you, and given you and every other citizen a share in every good that we had to give, we further proclaim and give the right to every Athenian, that if he does not like us when he has come of age and has seen the ways of the city, and made our acquaintance, he may go where he pleases and take his goods with him; and none of us laws will forbid him or interfere with him. Any of you who does not like us and the city, and who wants to go to a colony or to any other city, may go where he likes, and take his goods with him. But he who has experience of the manner in which we order justice and administer the State, and still remains, has entered into an implied contract that he will do as we command him. And he who disobeys us is, as we maintain, thrice wrong: first, because in disobeying us he is disobeying his parents; secondly, because we are the authors of his education; thirdly, because he has made an agreement with us that he will duly obey our commands; and he neither obeys them nor convinces us that our commands are wrong; and we do not rudely impose them, but give him the alternative of obeying or convincing us; that is what we offer, and he does neither. These are the sort of accusations to which, as we were saying, you, Socrates, will be exposed if you accomplish your intentions; you, above all other Athenians." Suppose I ask, why is this? they will justly retort upon me that I above all other men have acknowledged the agreement. "There is clear proof," they will say, "Socrates, that we and the city were not displeasing to you. Of all Athenians you have been the most constant resident in the city, which, as you never leave, you may be supposed to love. For you never went out of the city either to see the games, except once when you went to the Isthmus, or to any other place unless when you were on military service; nor did you travel as other men do. Nor had you any curiosity to know other States or their laws: your affections did not go beyond us and our State; we were your special favorites, and you acquiesced in our government of you; and this is the State in which you begat your children, which is a proof of your satisfaction. Moreover, you might, if you had liked, have fixed the penalty at banishment in the course of the trial—the State which refuses to let you go now would have let you go then. But you pretended that you preferred death to exile, and that you were not grieved at death. And now you have forgotten these fine sentiments, and pay no respect to us, the laws, of whom you are the destroyer; and are doing what only a miserable slave would do, running away and turning your back upon the compacts and agreements which you made as a citizen. And first of all answer this very question: Are we right in saying that you agreed to be governed according to us in deed, and not in word only? Is that true or not?" How shall we answer that, Crito? Must we not agree?

Cr. There is no help, Socrates.

Soc. Then will they not say: "You, Socrates, are breaking the covenants and agreements which you made with us at your leisure, not in any haste or under any compulsion or deception, but having had seventy years to think of them, during which time you were at liberty to leave the city, if we were not to your mind, or if our covenants appeared to you to be unfair. You had your choice, and might have gone either to Lacedæmon or Crete, which you often praise for their good government, or to some other Hellenic or foreign State. Whereas you, above all other Athenians, seemed to be so fond of the State, or, in other words, of us her laws (for who would like a State that has no laws), that you never stirred out of her: the halt, the blind, the maimed, were not more stationary in her than you were. And now you run away and forsake your agreements. Not so, Socrates, if you will take our advice; do not make yourself ridiculous by escaping out of the city.

"For just consider, if you transgress and err in this sort of way, what good will you do, either to yourself or to your friends? That your friends will be driven into exile and deprived of citizenship, or will lose their property, is tolerably certain; and you yourself, if you fly to one of the neighboring cities, as, for example, Thebes or Megara, both of which are well-governed cities, will come to them as an enemy, Socrates, and their government will be against you, and all patriotic citizens will cast an evil eye upon you as a subverter of the laws, and you will confirm in the minds of the judges the justice of their own condemnation of you.

For he who is a corrupter of the laws is more than likely to be corrupter of the young and foolish portion of mankind. Will you then flee from well-ordered cities and virtuous men? and is existence worth having on these terms? Or will you go to them without shame, and talk to them, Socrates? And what will you say to them? What you say here about virtue and justice and institutions and laws being the best things among men? Would that be decent of you? Surely not. But if you go away from well-governed States to Crito's friends in Thessaly, where there is great disorder and license, they will be charmed to have the tale of your escape from prison, set off with ludicrous particulars of the manner in which you were wrapped in a goatskin or some other disguise, and metamorphosed as the fashion of runaways is—that is very likely; but will there be no one to remind you that in your old age you violated the most sacred laws from a miserable desire of a little more life? Perhaps not, if you keep them in a good temper; but if they are out of temper you will hear many degrading things; you will live, but how?—as the flatterer of all men, and the servant of all men; and doing what?—eating and drinking in Thessaly, having gone abroad in order that you may get a dinner. And where will be your fine sentiments about justice and virtue then? Say that you wish to live for the sake of your children, that you may bring them up and educate them—will you take them into Thessaly and deprive them of Athenian citizenship? Is that the benefit which you would confer upon them? Or are you under the impression that they will be better cared for and educated here if you are still alive, although absent from them; for that your friends will take care of them? Do you fancy that if you are an inhabitant of Thessaly they will take care of them, and if you are an inhabitant of the other world they will not take care of them? Nay; but if they who call themselves friends are truly friends, they surely will.

"Listen, then, Socrates, to us who have brought you up. Think not of life and children first, and of justice afterwards, but of justice first, that you may be justified before the princes of the world below. For neither will you nor any that belong to you be happier or holier or juster in this life, or happier in another, if you do as Crito bids. Now you depart in innocence, a sufferer and not a doer of evil; a victim, not of the laws, but of men. But if you go forth, returning evil for evil, and injury for injury, breaking the covenants and agreements which you have made with us, and wronging those whom you ought least to wrong, that is to say, yourself, your friends, your country, and us, we shall be angry with you while you live, and our brethren, the laws in the world below, will receive you as an enemy; for they will know that you have done your best to destroy us. Listen, then, to us and not to Crito."

This is the voice which I seem to hear murmuring in my ears, like the sound of the flute in the ears of the mystic; that voice, I say, is humming in my ears, and prevents me from hearing any other. And I know that anything more which you may say will be in vain. Yet speak, if you have anything to say.

Cr. I have nothing to say, Socrates.

Soc. Then let me follow the intimations of the will of God.

5.2

The Politics, Aristotle

Aristotle (384-322 B.C.E.) was the pupil of Plato and the tutor to Alexander. He founded the Peripatetic (walking about) school or Lyceum, in the grove of the hero Lycus.

Source: Aristotle, *The Politics*. In *The Politics and Economics of Aristotle*, translated by Edward Walford. (London: Bell & Daldy, 1866), pp. 239-243, 245-250.

Book I

Every state is a community of some kind, and every community is established with a view to some good; for mankind always act in order to obtain that which they think good. But, if all communities aim at some good, the state or political community, which is the highest of all, and which embraces all the rest, aims, and in a greater degree than any other, at the highest good.

Now there is an erroneous opinion that a statesman, king, householder, and master are the same, and that they differ, not in kind, but only in the number of their subjects. For example, the ruler over a few is called a master; over more, the manager of a household; over a still larger number, a statesman or king, as if there were no difference between a great household and a small state. The distinction which is made between the king and the statesman is as follows: When the government is personal, the ruler is a king; when, according to the principles of the political science, the citizens rule and are ruled in turn, then he is called a statesman.

But all this is a mistake; for governments differ in kind, as will be evident to any one who considers the matter according to the method which has hitherto guided us. As in other departments of science, so in politics, the compound should always be resolved into the simple elements or least parts of the whole. We must therefore look at the elements of which the state is composed, in order that we may see in what they differ from one another, and whether any scientific distinction can be drawn between the different kinds of rule.

He who thus considers things in their first growth and origin, whether a state or anything else, will obtain the clearest view of them. In the first place (1) there must be a union of those who cannot exist without each other; for example, of male and female, that the race may continue; and this is a union which is formed, not of deliberate purpose, but because, in common with other animals and with plants, mankind have a natural desire to leave behind them an image of themselves. And (2) there must be a union of natural ruler and subject, that both may be preserved. For he who can foresee with his mind is by nature intended to be lord and master, and he who can work with his body is a subject, and by nature a slave; hence master and slave have the same interest. Nature, however, has distinguished between the female and the slave. For she is not niggardly, like the smith who fashions the Delphian knife for many uses; she makes each thing for a single use, and every instrument is best made when intended for one and not for many uses. But among barbarians no distinction is made between women and slaves, because there is no natural ruler among them: they are a community of slaves, male and female. Wherefore the poets say—

> "It is meet that Hellenes should rule over barbarians;"

as if they thought that the barbarian and the slave were by nature one.

Out of these two relationships between man and woman, master and slave, the family first arises, and Hesiod is right when he says—

> "First house and wife and an ox for the plough,"

for the ox is the poor man's slave. The family is the association established by nature for the supply of men's every day wants, and the members of it are called by Charondas "companions of the cupboard," and by Epimenides the Cretan, "companions of the manger." But when several families are united, and the association aims at something more than the supply of daily needs, then comes into existence the village. And the most natural form of the village appears to be that of a colony from the family, composed of the children and grandchildren, who are said to be "suckled with the same milk." And this is the reason why Hellenic states were originally governed by kings; because the Hellenes were under royal rule before they came together, as the barbarians still are. Every family is ruled by the eldest, and therefore in the colonies of the family the kingly form of government prevailed because they were of the same blood. As Homer says [of the Cyclopes]:—

> "Each one gives law to his children and to his wives."

For they lived dispersedly, as was the manner in ancient times. Wherefore men say that the Gods have a king, because they themselves either are or were in ancient times under the rule of a king. For they imagine, not only the forms of the Gods, but their ways of life to be like their own.

When several villages are united in a single community, perfect and large enough to be nearly or quite self-sufficing, the state comes into existence, originating in the bare needs of life, and continuing in existence for the sake of a good life. And therefore, if the earlier forms of society are natural, so is the state, for it is the end of them, and the completed nature is the end. For what each thing is when fully developed, we call its nature, whether we are speaking of a man, a horse, or a family. Besides, the final cause and end of a thing is the best, and to be self-sufficing is the end and the best.

Hence it is evident that the state is a creation of nature, and that man is by nature a political animal. And he who by nature and not by mere accident is without a state, is either above humanity, or below it; he is the

"Tribeless, lawless, heartless one,"

whom Homer denounces—the outcast who is a lover of war; he may be compared to a bird which flies alone.

Now the reason why man is more of a political animal than bees or any other gregarious animals is evident. Nature, as we often say, makes nothing in vain, and man is the only animal whom she has endowed with the gift of speech. And whereas mere sound is but an indication of pleasure or pain, and is therefore found in other animals (for their nature attains to the perception of pleasure and pain and the intimation of them to one another, and no further), the power of speech is intended to set forth the expedient and inexpedient, and likewise the just and the unjust. And it is a characteristic of man that he alone has any sense of good and evil, of just and unjust, and the association of living beings who have this sense makes a family and a state.

Thus the state is by nature clearly prior to the family and to the individual, since the whole is of necessity prior to the part; for example, if the whole body be destroyed, there will be no foot or hand, except in an equivocal sense, as we might speak of a stone hand; for when destroyed the hand will be no better. But things are defined by their working and power; and we ought not to say that they are the same when they are no longer the same, but only that they have the same name. The proof that the state is a creation of nature and prior to the individual is that the individual, when isolated, is not self-sufficing; and therefore he is like a part in relation to the whole. But he who is unable to live in society, or who has no need because he is sufficient for himself, must be either a beast or a god: he is no part of a state. A social instinct is implanted in all men by nature, and yet he who first founded the state was the greatest of benefactors. For man, when perfected, is the best of animals, but, when separated from law and justice, he is the worst of all; since armed injustice is the more dangerous, and he is equipped at birth with the arms of intelligence and with moral qualities which he may use for the worst ends. Wherefore, if he have not virtue, he is the most unholy and the most savage of animals, and the most full of lust and gluttony. But justice is the bond of men in states, and the administration of justice, which is the determination of what is just, is the principle of order in political society.

Book III

Having determined these questions, we have next to consider whether there is only one form of government or many, and if many, what they are, and how many, and what are the differences between them.

A constitution is the arrangement of magistracies in a State, especially of the highest of all. The government is everywhere sovereign in the State, and the constitution is in fact the government. For example, in democracies the people are supreme, but in oligarchies, the few; and, therefore, we say that these two forms of government are different: and so in other cases.

First, let us consider what is the purpose of a State, and how many forms of government there are by which human society is regulated. We have already said, in the former part of this treatise, when drawing a distinction between household management and the rule of a master, that man is by nature a political animal. And therefore, men, even when they do not require one another's help, desire to live together all the same, and are in fact brought together by their common interests in proportion as they severally attain to any measure of well-being. This is certainly the chief end, both of individuals and of States. And also for the sake of mere life (in which there is possibly some noble element) mankind meet together and maintain the political community, so long as the evils of existence do not greatly overbalance the good. And we all see that men cling to life even in the midst of misfortune, seeming to find in it a natural sweetness and happiness.

There is no difficulty in distinguishing the various kinds of authority; they have been often defined already in popular works. The rule of a master, although the slave by nature and the master by nature have in reality the same interests, is nevertheless exercised primarily with a view to the interest of the master, but accidentally considers the slave, since, if the slave perish, the rule of the master perishes with him. On the other hand, the government of a wife and children and of a household, which we have called household management, is exercised in the first instance for the good of the governed or for the common good of both parties, but essentially for the good of the governed, as we see to be the case in medicine, gymnastic, and the arts in general, which are only accidentally concerned with the good of the artists themselves. (For there is no reason why the trainer may not sometimes practise gymnastics, and the pilot is always one of the crew.) The trainer or the pilot considers the good of those committed to his care. But, when he is one of the persons taken care of, he accidentally participates in the advantage, for the pilot is also a sailor, and the trainer becomes one of those in training. And so in politics: when the State is framed upon the principle of equality and likeness, the citizens think that they ought to hold office by turns. In the order of nature everyone would take his turn of service; and then again, somebody else would look after his interest, just as he, while in office, had looked after theirs. But nowadays, for the sake of the advantage which is to be gained from the public revenues and from office, men want to be always in office. One might imagine that the rulers, being sickly, were only kept in health while they continued in office; in that case we may be sure that they would be hunting after places. The conclusion is evident: that governments, which have a regard to the common interest, are constituted in accordance with strict principles of justice, and are therefore true forms; but those which regard only the interest of the rulers are all defective and perverted forms, for they are despotic, whereas a State is a community of freemen.

Having determined these points, we have next to consider how many forms of government there are, and what they are; and in the first place what are the true forms, for when they are determined the perversions of them will at once be apparent. The words "constitution" and "government" have the same meaning, and the government, which is the supreme authority in States, must be in the hands of one, or of a few, or of many. The true forms of government, therefore, are those in which the one, or the few, or the many, govern with a view to the common interest; but governments which rule with a view to the private interest, whether of the one, or of the few, or of the many, are perversions. For citizens, if they are truly citizens, ought to participate in the advantages of a State. Of forms of government in which one rules, we call that which regards the common interests, kingship or royalty; that in which more than one, but not many, rule, aristocracy [the rule of the best]; and it is so called, either because the rulers are the best men, or because they have at heart the best interests of the State and of the citizens. But when the citizens at large administer the State for the common interest, the government is called by the generic name—a constitution. And there is a reason for this use of language. One man or a few may excel in virtue; but of virtue there are many kinds: and as the number increases it becomes more difficult for them to attain perfection in every kind, though they may in military virtue, for this is found in the masses. Hence, in a constitutional government the fighting-men have the supreme power, and those who possess arms are the citizens.

Of the above mentioned forms, the perversions are as follows:—of royalty, tyranny; of aristocracy, oligarchy; of constitutional government, democracy. For tyranny is a kind of monarchy which has in view the interest of the monarch only; oligarchy has in view the interest of the wealthy democracy, of the needy: none of them the common good of all.

Tyranny, as I was saying, is monarchy exercising the rule of a master over political society; oligarchy is when men of property have the government in their hands; democracy, the opposite, when the indigent, and not the men of property, are the rulers.

But a State exists for the sake of a good life, and not for the sake of life only: if life only were the object, slaves and brute animals might form a State, but they cannot, for they have no share in happiness or in a life of free choice. Nor does a State exist for the sake of alliance and security from injustice, nor yet for the sake of exchange and mutual intercourse; for then the Tyrrhenians and the Carthaginians, and all who have commercial treaties with one another, would be the citizens of one State. True, they have agreements about imports, and engagements that they will do no wrong to one another, and written articles of alliance. But there are no magistracies common to the contracting parties who will enforce their engagements; different States have each their own magistracies. Nor does one State take care that the citizens of the other are such as they ought to be, nor see that those who come under the terms of the treaty do no wrong or wickedness at all, but only that they do no injustice to one another. Whereas, those who care for good government take into consideration [the larger question of] virtue and vice in States. Whence it may be further inferred that virtue must be the serious care of a State which truly deserves the name: for [without this ethical end] the community becomes a mere alliance which differs only in place from alliances of which the members live apart; and law is only a convention, "a surety to one another of justice," as the sophist Lycophron says, and has no real power to make the citizens good and just.

This is obvious; for suppose distinct places, such as Corinth and Megara, to be united by a wall, still they would not be one city, not even if the citizens had the right to intermarry, which is one of the rights peculiarly characteristic of States. Again, if men dwelt at a distance from one another, but not so far off as to have no intercourse, and there were laws among them that they should not wrong each other in their exchanges, neither would this be a State. Let us suppose that one man is a carpenter, another a husband-man, another a shoemaker, and so on, and that their number is ten thousand: nevertheless, if they have nothing in common but exchange, alliance, and the like, that would not constitute a State. Why is this? Surely not because they are at a distance from one another: for even supposing that such a community were to meet in one place, and that each man had a house of his own, which was in a manner his State, and that they made alliance with one another, but only against evil-doers; still an accurate thinker would not deem this to be a State, if their intercourse with one another was of the same character after as before their union. It is clear then that a State is not a mere society, having a common place, established for the prevention of crime and for the sake of exchange. These are conditions without which a State cannot exist; but all of them together do not constitute a State, which is a community of well-being in families and aggregations of families, for the sake of a perfect and self-sufficing life. Such a community can only be established among those who live in the same place and intermarry. Hence arise in cities family connections, brotherhoods, common sacrifices, amusements which draw men together. They are created by friendship, for friendship is the motive of society. The end is the good life, and these are the means towards it. And the State is the union of families and villages having for an end a perfect and self-sufficing life, by which we mean a happy and honorable life.

Our conclusion, then, is that political society exists for the sake of noble actions, and not of mere companionship. And they who contribute most to such a society have a greater share in it than those who have the same or a greater freedom or nobility of birth but are inferior to them in political virtue; or than those who exceed them in wealth but are surpassed by them in virtue.

From what has been said it will be clearly seen that all the partisans of different forms of government speak of a part of justice only.

There is also a doubt as to what is to be the supreme power in the State:—Is it the multitude? Or the wealthy? Or the good? Or the one best man? Or a tyrant? Any of these alternatives seems to involve disagreeable consequences. If the poor, for example, because they are more in number, divide among themselves the property of the rich—is not this unjust? No, by heaven (will be the reply), for the lawful authority [i.e., the people] willed it. But if this is not injustice, pray what is? Again, when [in the first division] all has been taken, and the majority divide anew the property of the minority, is it not evident, if this goes on, that they will ruin the State? Yet surely, virtue is not the ruin of those who possess her, nor is justice destructive of a State; and therefore this law of confiscation clearly cannot be just. If it were, all the acts of a tyrant must of necessity be just; for he only coerces other men by superior power, just as the multitude coerce the rich. But is it just then that the few and the wealthy should be the rulers? And what if they, in like manner, rob and plunder the people—is this just? If so, the other case [i.e., the case of the majority plundering the minority] will likewise be just. But there can be no doubt that all these things are wrong and unjust.

Then ought the good to rule and have supreme power? But in that case everybody else, being excluded from power, will be dishonored. For the offices of a State are posts of honor; and if one set of men always hold them, the rest must be deprived of them. Then will it be well that the one best man should rule? Nay, that is still more oligarchical, for the number of those who are dishonored is thereby increased. Some one may say that it is bad for a man, subject as he is to all the accidents of human passion, to have the supreme power, rather than the law. But what if the law itself be democratical or oligarchical, how will that help us out of our difficulties? Not at all; the same consequences will follow.

Most of these questions may be reserved for another occasion. The principle that the multitude ought to be supreme rather than the few best is capable of a satisfactory explanation, and, though not free from difficulty, yet seems to contain an element of truth. For the many, of whom each individual is but an ordinary person, when they meet together may very likely be better than the few good, if regarded not individually but collectively, just as a feast to which many contribute is better than a dinner provided out of a single purse. For each individual among the many has a share of virtue and prudence, and when they meet together they become in a manner one man, who has many feet, and hands, and senses; that is a figure of their mind and disposition. Hence the many are better judges than a single man of music and poetry; for some understand one part, and some another, and among them, they understand the whole. There is a similar combination of qualities in good men, who differ from any individual of the many, as the beautiful are said to differ from those who are not beautiful, and works of art from realities, because in them the scattered elements are combined, although, if taken separately, the eye of one person or some other feature in another person would be fairer than in the picture.

In all sciences and arts the end is a good, and especially and above all in the highest of all—this is the political science of which the good is justice, in other words, the common interest. All men think justice to be a sort of equality; and to a certain extent they agree in the philosophical distinctions which have been laid down by us about ethics. For they admit that justice is a thing having relation to persons, and that equals ought to have equality. But there still remains a question; equality or inequality of what? here is a difficulty which the political philosopher has to resolve. For very likely some persons will say that offices of State ought to be unequally distributed according to superior excellence, in whatever respect, of the citizen, although there is no other difference between him and the rest of the community; for that those who differ in any one respect have different rights and claims. But, surely, if this is true, the complexion or height of a man, or any other advantage, will be a reason for his obtaining a greater share of political rights. The error here lies upon the surface, and may be illustrated from the other arts and sciences. When a number of flute-players are equal in their art, there is no reason why those of them who are better born should have better flutes given to them; for they will not play any better on the flute, and the superior instrument should be reserved for him who is the superior artist. If what I am saying is still obscure, it will be made clearer as we proceed. For if there were a superior flute-player who was far inferior in birth and beauty, although either of these may be a greater good than the art of flute-playing, and persons gifted with these qualities may excel the flute-player in a greater ratio than he excels them in his art, still he ought to have the best flutes given to him, unless the advantages of wealth and birth contribute to excellence in flute-playing, which they do not. Moreover upon this principle any good may be compared with any other. For if a given height, then height in general may be measured either against height or against freedom. Thus if A excels in height more than B in virtue, and height in general is more excellent than virtue, all things will be commensurable [which is absurd]; for if a certain magnitude is greater than some other, it is clear that some other will be equal. But since no such comparison can be made, it is evident that there is good reason why in politics men do not ground their claim to office on every sort of inequality any more than in the arts. For if some be slow, and others swift, that is no reason why the one should have little and the others much; it is in gymnastic contests that such excellence is rewarded. Whereas the rival claims of candidates for office can only be based on the possession of elements which enter into the composition of a State [such as wealth, virtue, etc.]. And therefore the noble, or free-born, or rich, may with good reason claim office; for holders of offices must be freemen and taxpayers: a State can be no more composed entirely of poor men than entirely of slaves. But if wealth and freedom are necessary elements, justice and valor are equally so; for without the former a State cannot exist at all, without the latter not well.

If the existence of the State is alone to be considered, then it would seem that all, or some at least, of these claims are just; but, if we take into account a good life, as I have already said, education and virtue have superior claims. As, however, those who are equal in one thing ought not to be equal in all, nor those who are unequal in one thing to be unequal in all, it is certain that all forms of government which rest on either of these principles are perversions. All men have a claim in a certain sense, as I have already admitted, but they have not an absolute claim. The rich claim because they have a greater share in the land, and land is the common element of the State; also they are generally more trustworthy in contracts. The free claim under the same title as the noble; for they are nearly akin. And the noble are citizens in a truer sense than the ignoble, since good birth is always valued in a man's own home and country. Another reason is, that those who are sprung from better ancestors are likely to be better men, for nobility is excellence of race. Virtue, too, may be truly said to have a claim, for justice has been acknowledged by us to be a social virtue, and it implies all others. Again, the many urge their claim against the few; for, when taken collectively, and compared with the few, they are stronger and richer and better. But, what if the good, the rich, the noble, and the other classes who make up a State, are all living together in the same city, will there, or will there not, be any doubt who shall rule?—No doubt at all in determining who ought to rule in each of the above-mentioned forms of government. For States are characterized by differences in their governing bodies—one of them has a government of the rich, another of the virtuous, and so on. But a difficulty arises when all these elements coexist. How are we to decide? Suppose the virtuous to be very few in number; may we consider their numbers in relation to their duties, and ask whether they are enough to administer a State, or must they be so many as will make up a State? Objections may be urged against all the aspirants to political power. For those who found their claims on wealth or family have no basis of justice; on this principle, if any one person were richer than all the rest, it is clear that he ought to be the ruler of them. In like manner he who is very distinguished by his birth ought to have the superiority over all those who claim on the ground that they are freeborn. In an aristocracy, or government of the best, a like difficulty occurs about virtue; for if one citizen be better than the other members of the government, however good they may be, he too, upon the same principle of justice, should rule over them. And if the people are to be supreme because they are stronger than the few, then if one man, or more than one, but not a majority, is stronger than the many, they ought to rule, and not the many.

Book IV

We have now to inquire what is the best constitution for most States, and the best life for most men, neither assuming a standard of virtue which is above ordinary persons, nor an education which is exceptionally favored by nature and circumstances, nor yet an ideal State which is an aspiration only, but having regard to the life in which the majority are able to share, and to the form of government which States in general can attain. As to those aristocracies, as they are called, of which we were just now speaking, they either lie beyond the possibilities of the greater number of States, or they approximate to the so-called constitutional government, and therefore need no separate discussion. And in fact the conclusion at which we arrive respecting all these forms rests upon the same grounds. For if it has been truly said in the "Ethics" that the happy life is the life according to unimpeded virtue, and that virtue is a mean, then the life which is in a mean, and in a mean attainable by everyone, must be the best. And the same principles of virtue and vice are characteristic of cities and of constitutions; for the constitution is in a figure the life of a city.

Now in all States there are three elements; one class is very rich, another very poor, and a third in a mean. It is admitted that moderation and the mean are best, and therefore it will clearly be best to possess the gifts of fortune in moderation; for in that condition of life men are most ready to listen to reason. But he who greatly excels in beauty, strength, birth or wealth, or on the other hand who is very poor, or very weak, or very much disgraced, finds it difficult to follow reason. Of these two the one sort grow into violent and great criminals, the others into rogues and petty rascals. And two sorts of offences correspond to them, the one committed from violence, the other from roguery. The petty rogues are disinclined to hold office, whether military or civil, and their aversion to these two duties is as great an injury to the State as their tendency to crime. Again, those who have too much of the goods of fortune, strength, wealth, friends, and the like, are neither willing nor able to submit to authority. The evil begins at home: for when they are boys, by reason of the luxury in which they are brought up, they never learn, even at school, the habit of obedience. On the other hand, the very poor, who are in the opposite extreme, are too degraded. So that the one class cannot obey, and can only rule despotically; the other knows not how to command and must be ruled like slaves. Thus arises a city, not of freemen, but of masters and slaves, the one despising, the other envying; and nothing can be more fatal to friendship and good-fellowship in States than this: for good-fellowship tends to friendship; when men are at enmity with one another, they would rather not even share the same path. But a city ought to be composed, as far as possible, of equals and similars; and these are generally the middle classes. Wherefore the city which is composed of middle-class citizens is necessarily best governed; they are, as we say, the natural elements of a State. And this is the class of citizens which is most secure in a State, for they do not, like the poor, covet their neighbors' goods; nor do others covet theirs, as the poor covet the goods of the rich; and as they neither plot against others, nor are themselves plotted against, they pass through life safely. Wisely then did Phocylides pray, "Many things are best in the mean; I desire to be of a middle condition in my city."

CHAPTER 6

The Glory of Rome

6.1

The Epistle to the Romans, Paul of Tarsus (Saint Paul)

Paul of Tarsus was a Hellenized Jew who helped form the Christian Church. Initially he persecuted Christians, but, after his conversion on the road to Damascus, he became a catalyst in the spread of Jesus' teachings. His most important accomplishment was changing Christianity from a Jewish sect into a distinct religion.

Paul wrote the *Epistle to the Romans* to the Christians in Rome to inform them of his plans for a mission in Spain and to instruct them in the faith. It is the most fully articulated expression of Paul's theology of salvation.

Source: *The Holy Bible* (New York: American Bible Society, n. d.).

Chapter 1

Paul, a servant of Jesus Christ, called *to be* an apostle, separated unto the gospel of God,

2 (Which he had promised afore by his prophets in the holy Scriptures,)

3 Concerning his Son Jesus Christ our Lord, which was made of the seed of David according to the flesh;

4 And declared *to be* the Son of God with power, according to the Spirit of holiness, by the resurrection from the dead:

5 By whom we have received grace and apostleship, for obedience to the faith among all nations, for his name:

6 Among whom are ye also the called of Jesus Christ:

7 To all that be in Rome, beloved of God, called *to be* saints: Grace to you, and peace, from God our Father and the Lord Jesus Christ.

15 So, as much as in me, I am ready to preach the gospel to you that are at Rome also.

16 For I am not ashamed of the gospel of Christ: for it is the power of God unto salvation to every one that believeth; to the Jew first, and also to the Greek.

17 For therein is the righteousness of God revealed from faith to faith: as it is written, The just shall live by faith.

28 Therefore we conclude that a man is justified by faith without the deeds of the law.

29 *Is he* the God of the Jews only? *is he* not also of the Ġĕn'tīleş? Yes of the Ġĕn'tīleş also:

30 Seeing *it is* one God, which shall justify the circumcision by faith, and uncircumcision through faith.

CHAPTER 4

13 For the promise, that he should be the heir of the world, *was* not to Abraham, or to his seed, through the law, but through the righteousness of faith.

14 For if they which are of the law *be* heirs, faith is made void, and the promise made of none effect:

15 Because the law worketh wrath: for where no law is, *there is* no transgression.

16 Therefore *it is* of faith, that *it might be* by grace; to the end the promise might be sure to all the seed; not to that only which is of the law, but to that also which is of the faith of Abraham; who is the father of us all,

17 (As it is written, I have made thee a father of many nations).

CHAPTER 5

Therefore being justified by faith, we have peace with God through our Lord Jesus Christ:

2 By whom also we have access by faith into this grace wherein we stand, and rejoice in hope of the glory of God.

5 And hope maketh not ashamed; because the love of God is shed abroad in our hearts by the Holy Ghost which is given unto us.

6 For when we were yet without strength, in due time Christ died for the ungodly.

9 Much more then, being now justified by his blood, we shall be saved from wrath through him.

10 For if, when we were enemies, we were reconciled to God by the death of his Son; much more, being reconciled, we shall be saved by his life.

CHAPTER 8

There *is* therefore now no condemnation to them which are in Christ Jesus, who walk not after the flesh, but after the Spirit.

2 For the law of the Spirit of life in Christ Jesus hath made me free from the law of sin and death.

5 For they that are after the flesh do mind the things of the flesh; but they that are after the Spirit, the things of the Spirit.

6 For to be carnally minded *is* death; but to be spiritually minded *is* life and peace.

7 Because the carnal mind *is* enmity against God: for it is not subject to the law of God, neither indeed can be.

8 So then they that are in the flesh cannot please God.

9 But ye are not in the flesh, but in the Spirit, if so be that the Spirit of God dwell in you. Now if any man have not the Spirit of Christ, he is none of his.

10 And if Christ *be* in you, the body *is* dead because of sin; but the Spirit *is* life because of righteousness.

11 But if the Spirit of him that raised up Jesus from the dead dwell in you, he that raised up Christ from the dead shall also quicken your mortal bodies by his Spirit that dwelleth in you.

12 Therefore, brethren, we are debtors, not to the flesh, to live after the flesh.

13 For if ye live after the flesh, ye shall die: but if ye through the Spirit do mortify the deeds of the body, ye shall live.

14 For as many as are led by the Spirit of God, they are the sons of God.

15 For ye have not received the spirit of bondage again to fear; but ye have received the Spirit of adoption, whereby we cry, Abba, Father.

16 The Spirit itself beareth witness with our spirit, that we are the children of God:

17 And if children, then heirs; heirs of God, and joint-heirs with Christ, if so be that we suffer with *him,* that we may be also glorified together.

18 For I reckon that the sufferings of this present time *are* not worthy *to be compared* with the glory which shall be revealed in us.

19 For the earnest expectation of the creature waiteth for the manifestation of the sons of God.

20 For the creature was made subject to vanity, not willingly, but by reason of him who hath subjected *the same* in hope;

21 Because the creature itself also shall be delivered from the bondage of corruption into the glorious liberty of the children of God.

22 For we know that the whole creation groaneth and travaileth in pain together until now.

23 And not only *they,* but ourselves also, which have the firstfruits of the Spirit, even we ourselves groan within ourselves, waiting for the adoption, *to wit,* the redemption of our body.

24 For we are saved by hope: but hope that is seen is not hope: for what a man seeth, why doth he yet hope for?

25 But if we hope for that we see not, *then* do we with patience wait for *it.*

26 Likewise the Spirit also helpeth our infirmities: for we know not what we should pray for as we ought: but the Spirit itself maketh intercession for us with groanings which cannot be uttered.

27 And he that searcheth the hearts knoweth what *is* the mind of the Spirit, because he maketh intercession for the saints according to *the will of* God.

28 And we know that all things work together for good to them that love God, to them who are the called according to *his* purpose.

29 For whom he did foreknow, he also did predestinate *to be* conformed to the image of his Son, that he might be the firstborn among many brethren.

30 Moreover, whom he did predestinate, them he also called: and whom he called, them he also justified: and whom he justified, them he also glorified.

31 What shall we then say to these things? If God *be* for us, who *can be* against us?

32 He that spared not his own Son, but delivered him up for us all, how shall he not with him also freely give us all things?

33 Who shall lay any thing to the charge of God's elect? *It is* God that justifieth.

34 Who *is* he that condemneth? *It is* Christ that died, yea rather, that is risen again, who is even at the right hand of God, who also maketh intercession for us.

35 Who shall separate us from the love of Christ? *shall* tribulation, or distress, or persecution, or famine, or nakedness, or peril, or sword?

36 As it is written, For thy sake we are killed all the day long; we are accounted as sheep for the slaughter.

37 Nay, in all these things we are more than conquerors through him that loved us.

38 For I am persuaded, that neither death, nor life, nor angels, nor principalities, nor powers, nor things present, nor things to come,

39 Nor height, nor depth, nor any other creature, shall be able to separate us from the love of God, which is in Christ Jesus our Lord.

Chapter 9

I say the truth in Christ, I lie not, my conscience also bearing me witness in the Holy Ghost,

2 That I have great heaviness and continual sorrow in my heart.

3 For I could wish that myself were accursed from Christ for my brethren, my kinsmen according to the flesh:

4 Who are Ĭş′rā-ĕl-ītes; to whom *pertaineth* the adoption, and the glory, and the covenants, and the giving of the law, the service *of God,* and the promises;

5 Whose *are* the fathers, and of whom as concerning the flesh Christ *came,* who is over all, God blessed for ever. Amen.

6 Not as though the word of God hath taken none effect. For they *are* not all Ĭş′rā-ĕl, which are of Ĭş′rā-ĕl:

7 Neither, because they are the seed of Abraham, *are they* all children: but, In Isaac shall thy seed be called.

8 That is, They which are the children of the flesh, these *are* not the children of God: but the children of the promise are counted for the seed.

9 For this *is* the word of promise, At this time will I come, and Sarah shall have a son.

10 And not only *this;* but when Rē-bĕc′cȧ also had conceived by one, *even* by our father Isaac,

11 (For *the children* being not yet born, neither having done any good or evil, that the purpose of God according to election might stand, not of works, but of him that calleth;)

12 It was said unto her, The elder shall serve the younger.

13 As it is written, Jacob have I loved, but Ē′sāū have I hated.

14 What shall we say then? *Is there* unrighteousness with God? God forbid.

15 For he saith to Moses, I will have mercy on whom I will have mercy, and I will have compassion on whom I will have compassion.

16 So then *it is* not of him that willeth, nor of him that runneth, but of God that showeth mercy.

17 For the Scripture saith unto Phā′-raōh, Even for this same purpose have I raised thee up, that I might show my power in thee, and that my name might be declared throughout all the earth.

18 Therefore hath he mercy on whom he will *have mercy,* and whom he will he hardeneth.

19 Thou wilt say then unto me, Why doth he yet find fault? For who hath resisted his will?

20 Nay but, O man, who art thou that repliest against God? Shall the thing formed say to him that formed *it,* Why hast thou made me thus?

21 Hath not the potter power over the clay, of the same lump to make one vessel unto honor, and another unto dishonor?

22 *What* if God, willing to show *his* wrath, and to make his power known, endured with much long-suffering the vessels of wrath fitted to destruction:

23 And that he might make known the riches of his glory on the vessels of mercy, which he had afore prepared unto glory,

24 Even us, whom he hath called, not of the Jews only, but also of the Ġĕn′-tīleş?

25 As he saith, also in Ō′şēe, I will call them my people, which were not my people; and her beloved, which was not beloved.

26 And it shall come to pass, *that* in the place where it was said unto them, Ye *are* not my people; there shall they be called the children of the living God.

27 Ē-şā′ịăs also crieth concerning Ĭş′rā-ĕl, Though the number of the children of Ĭş′rā-ĕl be as the sand of the sea, a remnant shall be saved:

28 For he will finish the work, and cut *it* short in righteousness: because a short work will the Lord make upon the earth.

29 And as Ē-şā′ịăs said before, Except the Lord of Săb′ā-ŏth had left us a seed, we had been as Sŏd′ō-mȧ, and been made like unto Gō-mŏr′rȧh.

30 What shall we say then? That the Ġĕn′tīleş, which followed not after righteousness, have attained to righteousness, even the righteousness which is of faith.

CHAPTER 10

9 That if thou shalt confess with thy mouth the Lord Jesus, and shalt believe in thine heart that God hath raised him from the dead, thou shalt be saved.

10 For with the heart man believeth unto righteousness; and with the mouth confession is made unto salvation.

11 For the Scripture saith, Whosoever believeth on him shall not be ashamed.

12 For there is no difference between the Jew and the Greek: for the same Lord over all is rich unto all that call upon him.

13 For whosoever shall call upon the name of the Lord shall be saved.

CHAPTER 12

9 *Let* love be without dissimulation. Abhor that which is evil; cleave to that which is good.

10 *Be* kindly affectioned one to another with brotherly love; in honor preferring one another;

11 Not slothful in business; fervent in spirit; serving the Lord;

12 Rejoicing in hope; patient in tribulation; continuing instant in prayer;

13 Distributing to the necessity of saints; given to hospitality.

14 Bless them which persecute you: bless, and curse not.

15 Rejoice with them that do rejoice, and weep with them that weep.

16 *Be* of the same mind one toward another. Mind not high things, but condescend to men of low estate. Be not wise in your own conceits.

17 Recompense to no man evil for evil. Provide things honest in the sight of all men.

18 If it be possible, as much as lieth in you, live peaceably with all men.

19 Dearly beloved, avenge not yourselves, but *rather* give place unto wrath: for it is written, Vengenance *is* mine; I will repay, saith the Lord.

20 Therefore if thine enemy hunger, feed him; if he thirst, give him drink: for in so doing thou shalt heap coals of fire on his head.

21 Be not overcome of evil, but overcome evil with good.

Chapter 13

8 Owe no man any thing, but to love one another: for he that loveth another hath fulfilled the law.

9 For this, Thou shalt not commit adultery, Thou shalt not kill, Thou shalt not steal, Thou shalt not bear false witness, Thou shalt not covet; and if *there be* any other commandment, it is briefly comprehended in this saying, namely, Thou shalt love thy neighbor as thyself.

10 Love worketh no ill to his neighbor: therefore love *is* the fulfilling of the law.

Chapter 16

I commend unto you Phē′bē our sister, which is a servant of the church which is at Çĕn-chrē′à:

2 That ye receive her in the Lord, as becometh saints, and that ye assist her in whatsoever business she hath need of you: for she hath been a succorer of many, and of myself also.

3 Greet Priscilla and Ăq′uĭ-là, my helpers in Christ Jesus:

4 Who have for my life laid down their own necks: unto whom not only I give thanks, but also all the churches of the Ġĕn′tīleş.

5 Likewise *greet* the church that is in their house.

CHAPTER 7

East Asia, ca. 200 B.C.E. -800 C.E.

7.1

Records of the Grand Historian, Sima Qian

Sima Qian (145-ca 85 B.C.E.) was a Chinese historian who was responsible for the development of Chinese historical writing during the Han Dynasty. He wrote a comprehensive history of China from the ancient mythical sage-kings to his own day. He divided his account into a chronology recounting political events, biographies of key individuals, and treatises on subjects such as geography, taxation, and court rituals. Like the Greek Thucydides, Sima Qian believed fervently in visiting the sites where history was made, examining artifacts, and questioning people about events. He was also interested in China's geographical variations, local customs, and local history. As an official of the emperor, he had access to important people and documents and to the imperial library. The result of his research, ten years in the making, was *Records of the Grand Historian.*

Sima Qian's work set the standard for Chinese historical writing. His records of Lao-Tze and the other sages approach near enough to their originals in time to preserve some resemblance to the living men. But one cannot accept his anecdotes entirely or literally.

Source: Charles F. Horne, ed. *The Sacred Books and Early Literature of the East* (New York: Parke, Austin, and Lipscomb, 1917), pp. 396-398.

Sima Qian

Lao-Tze said to Confucius, "The men about whom you talk are dead, and their bones are moldered to dust; only their words are left. Moreover, when the superior man gets his opportunity, he mounts aloft; but when the time is against him, he is carried along by the force of circumstances. I have heard that a good merchant, though he have rich treasures safely stored, appears as if he were poor; and that the superior man, though his virtue be complete, is yet to outward seeming stupid. Put away your proud air and many desires, your insinuating habit and wild will. They are of no advantage to you—this is all I have to tell you." Confucius said to his disciples after the interview: "I know how birds can fly, fishes swim, and animals run. But the runner may be snared, the swimmer hooked, and the flyer shot by the arrow. But there is the dragon: I can not tell how he mounts on the wind through the clouds, and rises to heaven. To-day I have seen Lao-Tze, and can only compare him to the dragon."

■ ■ ■

Lao-Tze cultivated the Tao and its attributes, the chief aim of his studies being how to keep himself concealed and remain unknown. He continued to reside at the capital of Chau, but after a long time, seeing the decay of the dynasty, he left it and went away to the barrier-gate, leading out of the kingdom on the northwest. Yin Hsi, the warden of the gate, said to him, "You are about to withdraw yourself out of sight. Let me insist on your first composing for me a book." On this, Lao-Tze wrote a book in two parts, setting forth his views on the Tao and its attributes, in more than 5000 characters. He then went away, and it is not known where he died. He was a superior man, who liked to keep himself unknown.

■ ■ ■

Those who attach themselves to the doctrine of Lao-Tze condemn that of the Literati, and the Literati on their part condemn Lao-Tze, verifying the saying, "Parties whose principles are different can not take counsel together." Lao-Tze taught that by doing nothing others are as a matter of course transformed, and that rectification in the same way ensues from being pure and still.

■ ■ ■

Chuang-Tze had made himself well acquainted with all the literature of his time, but preferred the views of Lao-Tze, and ranked himself among his followers, so that of the more than ten myriads of characters contained in his published writings the greater part are occupied with metaphorical illustrations of Lao's doctrines. He made "The Old Fisherman," "The Robber Chih," and "The Cutting open Satchels," to satirize and expose the disciples of Confucius, and clearly exhibit the sentiments of Lao. Such names and characters as "Wei-lei Hsu" and "Khang-sang Tze" are fictitious, and the pieces where they occur are not to be understood as narratives of real events.

But Chuang was an admirable writer and skilful composer, and by his instances and truthful descriptions hit and exposed the Mohists and Literati. The ablest scholars of his day could not escape his satire nor reply to it, while he allowed and enjoyed himself with his sparkling, dashing style; and thus it was that the greatest men, even kings and princes, could not use him for their purposes.

King Wei of Chu, having heard of the ability of Chuang Chau, sent messengers with large gifts to bring him to his court, and promising also that he would make him his chief minister. Chuang-Tze, however, only laughed and said to them, "A thousand ounces of silver are a great gain to me, and to be a high noble and minister is a most honorable position. But have you not seen the victim-ox for the border sacrifice? It is carefully fed for several years, and robed with rich embroidery that it may be fit to enter the Grand Temple. When the time comes for it to do so, it would prefer to be a little pig, but it can not get to be so. Go away quickly, and do not soil me with your presence. I had rather amuse and enjoy myself in the midst of a filthy ditch than be subject to the rules and restrictions in the court of a sovereign. I have determined never to take office, but prefer the enjoyment of my own free will."

7.2

Chronicles of Japan

In the sixth century, a Korean king sent Buddhist images and scriptures into Japan. Buddhism immediately became a political football. One faction of the ruling clan favored its adoption, and other factions opposed it. The turmoil ended in 587 when the pro-Buddhist group defeated its opponents.

The pro-Buddhist faction undertook reforms of the state, designed to strengthen Yamato rule by introducing Chinese practices. Prince Shotoku (574-622), the author of the *Seventeen Article Constitution,* led this effort. Issued in 604, this document upheld the rights of the ruler and commanded his subjects to obey him. It recommended a bureaucracy similar to China's, admonished the nobility to avoid conflict, and urged adherence to Buddhism.

Prince Shotoku was a patron of Buddhist temples, sponsoring the Horyuji Temple and staffing it with clergy from Korea. He opened direct relations with China, recently unified by the Sui. Japan sent four missions to China during the short-lived Sui Dynasty.

Even after his death, Prince Shotoku's policies were pursued. In 645 his supporters gained supremacy, and proclaimed the Taika Reforms, an effort to create an imperial and bureaucratic system like that of the Tang Empire. The reforms included outlawing private land ownership and introducing the equal-field system and per capita taxes.

SOURCE: "Chronicles of Japan," in W. G. Aston, trans., *Nihongi: Chronicles of Japan from the Earliest Times to A.D. 697,* 2 vols. (London: Kegan, Paul, Trench, Truebner, 1896), vol. 2, pp. 128-133, passim.

The Prince Imperial in person prepared for the first time laws. There were seventeen clauses as follows:—

1. Harmony is to be valued, and an avoidance of wanton opposition to be honored. All men are influenced by class-feelings, and there are few who are intelligent. Hence there are some who disobey their lords and fathers, or who maintain feuds with the neighboring villages. But when those above are harmonious and those below are friendly, and there is concord in the discussion of business, right views of things spontaneously gain acceptance. Then what is there which cannot be accomplished!

2. Sincerely reverence the three treasures. The three treasures: the Buddha, the Law, and the Priesthood, are the final refuge . . . . and are the supreme objects of faith in all countries. What man in what age can fail to reverence this law? Few men are utterly bad. They may be taught to follow it. But if they do not go to the three treasures, how shall their crookedness be made straight?

3. When you receive the Imperial commands, fail not scrupulously to obey them. The lord is Heaven, the vassal is Earth. Heaven overspreads, and Earth upbears. When this is so, the four seasons follow their due course, and the powers of Nature obtain their efficacy. If the Earth attempted to overspread, Heaven would simply fall in ruin. Therefore is it that when the lord speaks, the vassal listens; when the superior acts, the inferior yields compliance. Consequently when you receive the Imperial commands, fail not to carry them out scrupulously. Let there be a want of care in this matter, and ruin is the natural consequence.

4. The Ministers and functionaries should make decorous behavior their leading principle, for the leading principle of the government of the people consists in decorous behavior. If the superiors do not behave with decorum, the inferiors are disorderly: if inferiors are wanting in proper behavior, there must necessarily be offenses. Therefore it is that when lord and vassal behave with propriety, the distinctions of rank are not confused: when the people behave with propriety, the Government of the Commonwealth proceeds of itself. . . .

6. Chastise that which is evil and encourage that which is good. This was the excellent rule of antiquity. Conceal not, therefore, the good qualities of others, and fail not to correct that which is wrong when you see it. Flatterers and deceivers are a sharp weapon for the overthrow of the State, and a pointed sword for the destruction of the people. Sycophants are also fond, when they meet, of speaking at length to their superiors on the errors of their inferiors; to their inferiors, they censure the faults of their superiors. Men of this kind are all wanting in fidelity to their lord, and in benevolence toward the people. From such an origin great civil disturbances arise.

7. Let every man have his own charge, and let not the spheres of duty be confused. When wise men are entrusted with office, the sound of praise arises. If unprincipled men hold office, disasters and tumults are multiplied. In this world, few are born with knowledge: wisdom is the product of earnest meditation. In all things, whether great or small, find the right man, and they will surely be well managed: on all occasions, be they urgent or the reverse, meet but with a wise man, and they will of themselves be amenable. In this way will the State be lasting and the Temples of the Earth and of Grain will be free from danger. Therefore did the wise sovereigns of antiquity seek the man to fill the office, and not the office for the sake of the man. . . .

10. Let us cease from wrath, and refrain from angry looks. Nor let us be resentful when others differ from us. For all men have hearts, and each heart has its own leanings. Their right is our wrong, and our right is their wrong. We are not unquestionably sages, nor are they unquestionably fools. Both of us are simply ordinary men. How can any one lay down a rule by which to distinguish right from wrong? For we are all, one with another, wise and foolish, like a ring which has no end. Therefore, although others give way to anger, let us on the contrary dread our own faults, and though we alone may be in the right, let us follow the multitude and act like them.

11. Give clear appreciation to merit and demerit, and deal out to each its sure reward or punishment. In these days, reward does not attend upon merit, nor punishment upon crime. You high functionaries who have charge of public affairs, let it be your task to make clear rewards and punishments. . . .

15. To turn away from that which is private, and to set our faces toward that which is public—this is the path of a Minister. Now if a man is influenced by private motives, he will assuredly feel resentments, and if he is influenced by resentful feelings, he will assuredly fail to act harmoniously with others. If he fails to act harmoniously with others, he will assuredly sacrifice the public interest to his private feelings. When resentment arises, it interferes with order, and is subversive of law. . . .

16. Let the people be employed [in forced labor] at seasonable times. This is an ancient and excellent rule. Let them be employed, therefore, in the winter months, when they are at leisure. But from Spring to Autumn, when they are engaged in agriculture or with the mulberry trees, the people should not be so employed. For if they do not attend to agriculture, what will they have to eat? If they do not attend to the mulberry trees, what will they do for clothing?

17. Decisions on important matters should not be made by one person alone. They should be discussed with many. But small matters are of less consequence. It is unnecessary to consult a number of people. It is only in the case of the discussion of weighty affairs, when there is a suspicion that they may miscarry, that one should arrange matters in concert with others, so as to arrive at the right conclusion.

CHAPTER 8

The Making of Europe

8.1

The Enchiridion, St. Augustine

St. Augustine of Hippo (354-430) is the finest representative of the blending of classical and Christian ideas and a brilliant thinker in the history of the West. Other than the Biblical authors, no one else had a greater impact on Christian thought. Augustine was born in what is now Algeria in North Africa. His father was a pagan, his mother a devout Christian.

Augustine received a basic Roman education, memorizing the works of Virgil, Cicero, and Sallust. At the age of seventeen, Augustine went to Carthage to further his education. He also took a mistress. At Carthage, Augustine began an intellectual and spiritual pilgrimage through several philosophies and heretical Christian sects.

In 383 he traveled to Rome where he failed as a teacher. Four years later, in Milan, Augustine received Christian baptism. He later became a bishop of Hippo Regius in North Africa. He became a renowned preacher to Christians, a vigorous defender of Christianity, and the author of more than ninety-three books.

The Enchiridion ("Manual") contains Augustine's conception of true Christian doctrine. The central idea is original sin. Once he had worked out his doctrine, he devoted his life to purging Christian theology of all heretical elements. As a result, orthodox Christianity has remained Augustinian.

SOURCE: J. F. Shaw, trans., *The Enchiridion* in *The Works of Aurelius Augustine, Bishop of Hippo*, vol. 9 (Edinburgh: T. & T. Clark, 1877).

God's Judgments Upon Fallen Men and Angels. The Death of the Body is Man's Peculiar Punishment

. . . Now the evils I have mentioned are common to all who for their wickedness have been justly condemned by God, whether they be men or angels. But there is one form of punishment peculiar to man—the death of the body. God had threatened him with this punishment of death if he should sin, leaving him indeed to the freedom of his own will, but yet commanding his obedience under pain of death; and He placed him amid the happiness of Eden, as it were in a protected nook of life, with the intention that, if he preserved his righteousness, he should thence ascend to a better place.

Through Adam's Sin His Whole Posterity were Corrupted, and were Born Under the Penalty of Death, which He had Incurred

Thence, after his sin, he was driven into exile, and by his sin the whole race of which he was the root was corrupted in him, and thereby subjected to the penalty of death. And so it happens that all descended from him, and from the woman who had led him into sin, and was condemned at the same time with him,—being the offspring of carnal lust on which the same punishment of disobedience was visited,—were tainted with the original sin, and were by it drawn through divers errors and sufferings into that last and endless punishment which they suffer in common with the fallen angels, their corrupters and masters, and the partakers of their doom. And thus "by one man sin entered into the world, and death by sin; and so death passed upon all men, for that all have sinned." By "the world" the apostle, of course, means in this place the whole human race.

The State of Misery to Which Adam's Sin Reduced Mankind, and the Restoration Effected through the Mercy of God

Thus, then, matters stood. The whole mass of the human race was under condemnation, was lying steeped and wallowing in misery, and was being tossed from one form of evil to another, and, having joined the faction of the fallen angels, was paying the well-merited penalty of that impious rebellion. For whatever the wicked freely do through blind and unbridled lust, and whatever they suffer against their will in the way of open punishment, this all evidently pertains to the just wrath of God. But the goodness of the Creator never fails either to supply life and vital power to the wicked angels (without which their existence would soon come to an end); or, in the case of mankind, who spring from a condemned and corrupt stock, to impart form and life to their seed, to fashion their members, and through the various seasons of their life, and in the different parts of the earth, to quicken their senses, and bestow upon them the nourishment they need. For He judged it better to bring good out of evil, than not to permit any evil to exist. And if He had determined that in the case of men, as in the case of the fallen angels, there should be no restoration to happiness, would it not have been quite just, that the being who rebelled against God, who in the abuse of his freedom spurned and transgressed the command of his Creator when he could so easily have kept it, who defaced in himself the image of his Creator by stubbornly turning away from His light, who by an evil use of his free-will broke away from his wholesome bondage to the Creator's laws,—would it not have been just that such a being should have been wholly and to all eternity deserted by God, and left to suffer the everlasting punishment he had so richly earned? Certainly so God would have done, had He been only just and not also merciful, and had He not designed that His unmerited mercy should shine forth the more brightly in contrast with the unworthiness of its objects.

Men Are Not Saved by Good Works, nor by the Free Determination of Their Own Will, but by the Grace of God through Faith

But this part of the human race to which God has promised pardon and a share in His eternal kingdom, can they be restored through the merit of their own works? God forbid. For what good work can a lost man perform, except so far as he has been delivered from perdition? Can they do anything by the free determination of their own will? Again I say, God forbid. For it was by the evil use of his free-will that man destroyed both it and himself. For, as a man who kills himself must, of course, be alive when he kills himself, but after he has killed himself ceases to live, and cannot restore himself to life; so, when man by his own free-will sinned, then sin being victorious over him, the freedom of his will was lost. "For of whom a man is overcome, of the same is he brought in bondage." This is the judgment of the Apostle Peter. And as it is certainly true, what kind of liberty, I ask, can the bond-slave possess, except when it pleases him to sin? For he is freely in bondage who does with pleasure the will of his master. Accordingly, he who is the servant of sin is free to sin. And hence he will not be free to do right, until, being freed from sin, he shall begin to be the servant of righteousness. And this is true liberty, for he has pleasure in the righteous deed; and it is at the same time a holy bondage, for he is obedient to the will of God. But whence comes this liberty to do right to the man who is in bondage and sold under sin, except he be redeemed by Him who has said, "If the Son shall make you free, ye shall be free indeed"? And before this redemption is wrought in a man, when he is not yet free to do what is right, how can he talk of the freedom of his will and his good works, except he be inflated by that foolish pride of boasting which the apostle restrains when he says, "By grace are ye saved, through faith"?

Faith Itself is the Gift of God; and Good Works will not be Wanting in Those Who Believe

And lest men should arrogate to themselves the merit of their own faith at least, not understanding that this too is the gift of God, this same apostle, who says in another place that he had "obtained mercy of the Lord to be faithful," here also adds: "and that not of yourselves; it is the gift of God: not of works, lest any man should boast." And lest it should be thought that good works will be wanting in those who believe, he adds further: "For we are His workmanship, created in Christ Jesus unto good works, which God hath before ordained that we should walk in them." We shall be made truly free, then, when God fashions us, that is, forms and creates us anew, not as men—for He has done that already—but as good men, which His grace is now doing, that we may be a new creation in Christ Jesus, according as it is said: "Create in me a clean heart, O God." For God had already created his heart, so far as the physical structure of the human heart is concerned; but the psalmist prays for the renewal of the life which is still lingering in his heart.

The Freedom of the Will is Also the Gift of God, for God Worketh in Us Both to Will and to do

And further, should any one be inclined to boast, not indeed of his works, but of the freedom of his will, as if that first merit belong to him, this very liberty of good action being given to him as a reward he had earned, let him listen to this same preacher of grace, when he says: "For it is God which worketh in you, both to will and to do of His own good pleasure"; and in another place: "So, then, it is not of him that willeth, nor of him that runneth, but of God that showeth mercy." Now as, undoubtedly, if a man is of the age to use his reason, he cannot believe, hope, love, unless he will to do so, nor obtain the prize of the high calling of God unless he voluntarily run for it; in what sense is it "not of him that willeth, nor of him that runneth, but of God that showeth mercy," except that, as it is written, "The preparation of the heart is from the Lord"? Otherwise, if it is said, "it is not of him that willeth nor of him that runneth, but of God that showeth mercy," because it is of both, that is, both of the will of man and of the mercy of God, so that we are to understand the saying, "It is not of him that willeth, nor of him that runneth, but of God that showeth mercy," as if it meant the will of man alone is not sufficient, if the mercy of God go not with it—then it will follow that the mercy of God alone is not sufficient, if the will of man go not with it; and therefore, if we may rightly say, "it is not of man that willeth, but of God that showeth mercy," because the will of man by itself is not enough, why may we not also rightly put it in the converse way: "It is not of God that showeth mercy, but of man that willeth," because the mercy of God by itself does not suffice? Surely, if no Christian will dare to say this, "It is not of God that showeth mercy, but of man that willeth," lest he should openly contradict the apostle, it follows that the true interpretation of the saying, "It is not of him that willeth, nor of him that runneth, but of God that showeth mercy," is that the whole work belongs to God, who both makes the will of man righteous, and thus prepares it for assistance, and assists it when it is prepared. For the man's righteousness of will precedes many of God's gifts, but not all and it must itself be included among those which it does not precede. We read in Holy Scripture, both that God's mercy "shall prevent me," and that His mercy "shall follow me." It prevents the unwilling to make him willing; it follows the willing to make his will effectual. Why are we taught to pray for our enemies, who are plainly unwilling to lead a holy life, unless that God may work willingness in them? And why are we ourselves taught to ask that we may receive, unless that He who has created in us the wish, may Himself satisfy the wish? We pray, then, for our enemies, that the mercy of God may prevent them, as it has prevented us: we pray for ourselves that His mercy may follow us.

Men, Being by Nature the Children of Wrath, Needed a Mediator. In What Sense God is Said to be Angry

And so the human race was lying under a just condemnation, and all men were the children of wrath. Of which wrath it is written: "All our days are passed away in Thy wrath; we spend our years as a tale that is told." Of which wrath also Job says: "Man that is born of a woman is of few days, and full of trouble." Of which wrath also the Lord Jesus says: "He that believeth on the Son hath everlasting life: and he that believeth not the Son shall not see life; but the wrath of God abideth on him." He does not say it will come, but it "abideth on him." For every man is born with it; wherefore the apostle says: "We were by nature the children of wrath, even as others." Now, as men were lying under this wrath by reason of their original sin, and as this original sin was the more heavy and deadly in proportion to the number and magnitude of the actual sins which were added to it, there was need for a Mediator, that is, for a reconciler, who, by the offering of one sacrifice, of which all the sacrifices of the law and the prophets were types, should take away this wrath. Wherefore the apostle says: "For if, when we were enemies, we were reconciled to God by the death of His Son, much more, being reconciled, we shall be saved by His life." Now when God is said to be angry, we do not attribute to Him such a disturbed feeling as exists in the mind of an angry man; but we call His just displeasure against sin by the name "anger," a word transferred by analogy from human emotions. But our being reconciled to God through a Mediator, and receiving the Holy Spirit, so that we who were enemies are made sons ("For as many as are led by the Spirit of God, they are the sons of God"): this is the grace of God through Jesus Christ our Lord.

Christ, who was Himself Free From Sin, was made Sin for Us, that We might be Reconciled to God

Begotten and conceived, then, without any indulgence of carnal lust, and therefore bringing with Him no original sin, and by the grace of God joined and united in a wonderful and unspeakable way in one person with the Word, the Only-begotten of the Father, a son by nature, not by grace, and therefore having no sin of His own; nevertheless, on account of the likeness of sinful flesh in which He came, He was called sin, that He might be sacrificed to wash away sin. For, under the Old Covenant, sacrifices for sin were called sins. And He, of whom all these sacrifices were types and shadows, was Himself truly made sin. Hence the apostle, after saying, "We pray you in Christ's stead, be ye reconciled to God," forthwith adds: "for He hath made Him to be sin for us who knew no sin; that we might be made the righteousness of God in Him." He does not say, as some incorrect copies read, "He who knew no sin did sin for us," as if Christ had Himself sinned for our sakes; but he says, "Him who knew no sin," that is, Christ God, to whom we are to be reconciled, "hath made to be sin for us," that is, hath made Him a sacrifice for our sins, by which we might be reconciled to God. He, then being made sin, just as we are made righteousness (our righteousness being not our own, but God's, not in ourselves, but in Him); He being made sin, not His own, but ours, not in Himself, but in us, showed, by the likeness of sinful flesh in which He was crucified, that though sin was not in Him, yet that in a certain sense He died to sin, by dying in the flesh which was the likeness of sin; and that although He himself had never lived the old life of sin, yet by His resurrection He typified our new life springing up out of the old death in sin.

By the Sacrifice of Christ All Things are Restored, and Peace is Made Between Earth and Heaven

And, of course, the holy angels, taught by God, in the eternal contemplation of whose truth their happiness consists, know how great a number of the human race are to supplement their ranks, and fill up the full tale of their citizenship. Wherefore the apostle says, that "all things are gathered together in one in Christ, both which are in heaven and which are on earth." The things which are in heaven are gathered together when what was lost thereform in the fall of the angels is restored from among men; and the things which are on earth are gathered together, when those who are predestined to eternal life are redeemed from their old corruption. And thus, through that single sacrifice in which the Mediator was offered up, the one sacrifice of which the many victims under the law were types, heavenly things are brought into peace with earthly things, and earthly things with heavenly. Wherefore, as the same apostle says: "For it pleased the Father that in Him should all fullness dwell: and, having made peace through the blood of His cross, by Him to reconcile all things to Himself: by Him, I say, whether they be things in earth or things in heaven."

Predestination to Eternal Life is Wholly of God's Free Grace

And, moreover, who will be so foolish and blasphemous as to say that God cannot change the evil wills of men, whichever, whenever and wheresoever He chooses, and direct them to what is good? But when He does this, He does it of mercy; when He does it not, it is of justice that He does it not; for "He hath mercy on whom He will have mercy, and whom He will He hardeneth." And when the apostle said this, he was illustrating the grace of God, in connection with which he had just spoken of the twins in the womb of Rebecca, "who being not yet born, neither having done any good or evil, that the purpose of God according to election might stand, not of works, but of Him that calleth, it was said unto her, 'The elder shall serve the younger.'" And in reference to this matter he quotes another prophetic testimony: "Jacob have I loved, but Esau have I hated." But perceiving how what he had said might affect those who could not penetrate by their understanding the depth of this grace: "What shall we say then?" he says: "Is there unrighteousness with God? God forbid." For it seems unjust that, in the absence of any merit or demerit from good or evil works, God should love the one and hate the other. Now, if the apostle had wished us to understand that there were future good works of the one, and evil works of the other, which of course God foreknew, he would never have said, "not of works," but, "of future works," and in that way would have solved the difficulty, or rather there would then have been no difficulty to solve. As it is, however, after answering, "God forbid"; that is, God forbid that there should be unrighteousness with God; he goes on to prove that there is no unrighteousness in God's doing this, and says: "For he saith to Moses, I will have mercy on whom I will have mercy, and I will have compassion on whom I will have compassion." Now who but a fool would think that God was unrighteous, either in inflicting penal justice on those who earned it, or in extending mercy to the unworthy? Then he draws his conclusion: "So then it is not of him that willeth, nor of him that runneth, but of God that showeth mercy." Thus both the twins were born children of wrath, not on account of any works of their own, but because they were bound in the fetters of that original condemnation which came through Adam. But He who said, "I will have mercy on whom I will have mercy," loved Jacob of His undeserved grace, and hated Esau of His deserved judgement. And as this judgment was due to both, the former learnt from the case of the latter that the fact of the same punishment not falling upon himself gave him no room to glory in any merit of his own, but only in the riches of the divine grace; because "it is not of him that willeth, nor of him that runneth, but of God that showeth mercy." And indeed the whole face, and, if I may use the expression, every lineament of the countenance of Scripture conveys by a very profound analogy this wholesome warning to every one who looks carefully into it, that he who glories should glory in the Lord.

As God's Mercy is Free, So His Judgments are Just, and Cannot be Gainsaid

Now after commending the mercy of God, saying, "So it is not of him that willeth, nor of him that runneth, but of God that showeth mercy," that he might commend His Justice also (for the man who does not obtain mercy finds, not iniquity, but justice, there being no iniquity with God), he immediately adds: "For the scripture saith unto Pharaoh, 'Even for this same purpose have I raised thee up, that I might show my power in thee, and that my name might be declared throughout all the earth.'" And then he draws a conclusion that applies to both, that is, both to His mercy and His justice: "Therefore hath He mercy on whom He will have mercy, and whom He will He hardeneth." "He hath mercy" of His great goodness, "He hardeneth" without any injustice; so that neither can he that is pardoned glory in any merit of his own, nor he that is condemned complain of anything but his own demerit. For it is grace alone that separates the redeemed from the lost, all having been involved in one common perdition through their common origin. Now if any one, on hearing this, should say, "Why doth He yet find fault? For who hath resisted His will?" as if a man ought not to be blamed for being bad, because God hath mercy on whom He will have mercy, and whom He will He hardeneth, God forbid that we should be ashamed to answer as we see the apostle answered: "Nay, but, O man, who are thou that repliest against God? Shall the thing formed say to Him that formed it, Why hast Thou made me thus? Hath not the potter power over the clay, of the same lump to make one vessel unto honour, and another unto dishonour?" Now some foolish people think that in this place the apostle had no answer to give; and for want of a reason to render, rebuked the presumption of his interrogator. But there is great weight in this saying: "Nay, but, O man, who are thou?" and in such a matter as this it suggests to a man in a single word the limits of his capacity, and at the same time does in reality convey an important reason. For if a man does not understand these matters, who is he that he should reply against God? And if he does understand them, he finds no further room for reply. For then he perceives that the whole human race was condemned in its rebellious head by a divine judgment so just, that if not a single member of the race had been redeemed, no one could justly have questioned the justice of God; and that it was right that those who are redeemed should be redeemed in such a way as to show, by the greater number who are unredeemed and left in their just condemnation, what the whole race deserved, and whether the deserved judgment of God would lead even the redeemed, did not His undeserved mercy interpose, so that every mouth might be stopped of those who wish to glory in their own merits, and that he that glorieth might glory in the Lord.

There is No Ground in Scripture for the Opinion of Those Who Deny the Eternity of Future Punishments

It is in vain, then, that some, indeed very many, make moan over the eternal punishment, and perpetual, unintermitted torments of the lost, and say they do not believe it shall be so; not, indeed, that they directly oppose themselves to Holy Scripture, but, at the suggestion of their own feelings, they soften down everything that seems hard, and give a milder turn to statements which they think are rather designed to terrify than to be received as literally true. For "Hath God," they say, "forgotten to be gracious? hath He in anger shut up His tender mercies?" Now, they read this in one of the holy psalms. But without doubt we are to understand it as spoken of those who are elsewhere called "vessels of mercy," because even they are freed from misery not on account of any merit of their own, but solely through the pity of God. Or, if the men we speak of insist that this passage applies to all mankind, there is no reason why they should therefore suppose that there will be an end to the punishment of those of whom it is said, "These shall go away into everlasting punishment"; for this shall end in the same manner and at the same time as the happiness of those of whom it is said, "but the righteous unto life eternal." But let them suppose, if the thought gives them pleasure, that the pains of the damned are, at certain intervals, in some degree assuaged. For even in this case the wrath of God, that is, their condemnation (for it is this, and not any disturbed feeling in the mind of God that is called his wrath), abideth upon them; that is, His wrath, though it still remains, does not shut up His tender mercies; though His tender mercies are exhibited, not in putting an end to their eternal punishment, but in mitigating, or in granting them a respite from, their torments; for the psalm does not say, "to put an end to His anger," or, "when His anger is passed by," but "in His anger." Now, if this anger stood alone, or if it exited in the smallest conceivable degree, yet to be lost out of the kingdom of God, to be an exile from the city of God, to be alienated from the life of God, to have no share in that great goodness which God hath laid up for them that fear Him, and hath wrought out for them that trust in Him, would be a punishment so great, that, supposing it to be eternal, no torments that we know of, continued through as many ages as man's imagination can conceive, could be compared with it.

The Death of the Wicked Shall be Eternal in the Same Sense As the Life of The Saints

This perpetual death of the wicked, then, that is, their alienation from the life of God, shall abide for ever, and shall be common to them all, whatever men, prompted by their human affections, may conjecture as to a variety of punishments, or as to a mitigation or intermission of their woes; just as the eternal life of the saints shall abide for ever, and shall be common to them all, whatever grades of rank and honour there may be among those who shine with an harmonious effulgence.

8.2

The Institutes of Justinian

Compared to western Europe, the Byzantine Empire to the east and south was a pillar of stability and continuity. A principal means of maintaining continuity between the Byzantine Empire and its predecessor, the Roman empire, was through the use of the Justinian Code. Initiated in 528 during the reign of Emperor Justinian (r. 527-565), this code contained a compilation of Roman laws, a growing collection of new laws, and a manual for students (the *Institutes*).

Source: The Institutes of Justinian, trans. Thomas C. Sandars (London: Longmans, Green, 1874), pp. 1-7.

The Institutes of Justinian: Byzantium and the Legacy of Roman Law

Preamble

In the Name Of Our Lord Jesus Christ.

The Emperor Cæsar Flavius Justinianus, vanquisher of the Alamani, Goths, Francs, Germans, Antes, Alani, Vandals, Africans, pious, happy, glorious, triumphant conqueror, ever August, to the youth desirous of studying the law, greeting.

The imperial majesty should be not only made glorious by arms, but also strengthened by laws, that, alike in time of peace and in time of war, the state may be well governed, and that the emperor may not only be victorious in the field of battle, but also may by every legal means repel the iniquities of men who abuse the laws, and may at once religiously uphold justice and triumph over his conquered enemies.

1. By our incessant labours and great care, with the blessing of God, we have attained this double end. The barbarian nations reduced under our yoke know our efforts in war; to which also Africa and very many other provinces bear witness, which, after so long an interval, have been restored to the dominion of Rome and our empire, by our victories gained through the favour of heaven. All nations moreover are governed by laws which we have either promulgated or arranged.

2. When we had arranged and brought into perfect harmony the hitherto confused mass of imperial constitutions, we then extended our care to the endless volumes of ancient law; and sailing as it were across the mid ocean, have now completed, through the favour of heaven, a work we once despaired of.

3. When by the blessing of God this task was accomplished, we summoned the most eminent Tribonian, master and ex-quæstor of our palace, together with the illustrious Theophilus and Dorotheus, professors of law, all of whom have on many occasions proved to us their ability, legal knowledge, and obedience to our orders; and we specially charged them to compose, under our authority and advice, Institutes, so that you may no more learn the first elements of law from old and erroneous sources, but apprehend them by the clear light of imperial wisdom; and that your minds and ears may receive nothing that is useless or misplaced, but only what obtains in actual practice. So that, whereas, formerly, the foremost among you could scarcely, after four years' study, read the imperial constitutions, you may now commence your studies by reading them, you who have been thought worthy of an honour and a happiness so great as that the first and last lessons in the knowledge of the law should issue for you from the mouth of the emperor.

4. When therefore, by the assistance of the same eminent person Tribonian and that of other illustrious and learned men, we had compiled the fifty books, called Digests or Pandects, in which is collected the whole ancient law, we directed that these Institutes should be divided into four books, which might serve as the first elements of the whole science of law.

5. In these books a brief exposition is given of the ancient laws, and of those also, which, overshadowed by disuse, have been again brought to light by our imperial authority.

6. These four books of Institutes thus compiled, from all the Institutes left us by the ancients, and chiefly from the commentaries of our Gaius, both from his Institutes and his Journal, and also from many other commentaries, were presented to us by the three learned men we have above named. We read and examined them, and have accorded to them all the force of our constitutions.

7. Receive, therefore, with eagerness, and study with cheerful diligence, these our laws, and show yourselves persons of such learning that you may conceive the flattering hope of yourselves being able, when your course of legal study is completed, to govern our empire in the different portions that may be entrusted to your care.

Given at Constantinople on the eleventh day of the calends of December, in the third consulate of the Emperor Justinian, ever August.

Book One

Justice is the constant and perpetual wish to render every one his due.

1. Jurisprudence is the knowledge of things divine and human; the science of the just and the unjust.

2. Having explained these general terms, we think we shall commence our exposition of the law of the Roman people most advantageously, if we pursue at first a plain and easy path, and then proceed to explain particular details with the utmost care and exactness. For, if at the outset we overload the mind of the student, while yet new to the subject and unable to bear much, with a multitude and variety of topics, one of two things will happen—we shall either cause him wholly to abandon his studies, or, after great toil, and often after great distrust of himself (the most frequent stumbling-block in the way of youth), we shall at last conduct him to the point, to which, if he had been led by an easier road, he might, without great labour, and without any distrust of his own powers, have been sooner conducted.

3. The maxims of law are these: to live honestly, to hurt no one, to give every one his due.

4. The study of law is divided into two branches; that of public and that of private law. Public law regards the government of the Roman Empire; private law, the interests of individuals. We are now to treat of the latter, which is composed of thee elements, and consists of precepts belonging to natural law, to the law of nations, and to the civil law.

CHAPTER 9

The Islamic World, ca. 600-1400

9.1

The Holy Qur'an

The religion of Islam was revealed to an Arabian merchant named Muhammad in 610 C.E. Within about twenty years, by the time of Muhammad's death in 632, the peoples of the Arabian Peninsula had widely accepted the religion. The next few decades would see Islam spread quickly into Egypt, North Africa, and the Middle East.

In the 650s, shortly after Muhammad's death, an "official" version of God's words to Muhammad and Muhammad's sayings was written down. The Qur'an is a document much like the Judeo-Christian Old Testament, containing the myths of the religion, and its basic tenets and practices. Not surprisingly, given the influence of both Judaism and Christianity on the Arabian peninsula, there are many things that the three religions share in common. The following excerpt not only discusses some basic beliefs of Islam, but also illustrates some similarities between these three monotheistic religions.

Sources:

1. Stanley Lane-Poole, *The Speech and Table-Talk of the Prophet Mohammed* (London: Macmillan, 1882), pp. 15, 32, 83, 133-137.
2. J. M. Rodwell, trans., *The Koran* (London: J. M. Dent, 1871), pp. 411, 415.

SAY: HE IS ONE GOD;
God the Eternal.
He begetteth not, nor is begotten;
Nor is there one like unto Him.

■ ■ ■

MAGNIFY the name of thy LORD, THE MOST HIGH,
Who created, and fashioned,
And decreed, and guided,
Who bringeth forth the pasturage,
Then turneth it dry and brown.

■ ■ ■

It is not righteousness that ye turn your face towards the east or the west, but righteousness is [in] him who believeth in God and the Last Day, and the Angels, and the Scripture, and the Prophets, and who giveth wealth for the love of God to his kinsfolk and to orphans and the needy and the son of the road and them that ask and for the freeing of slaves, and who is instant in prayer, and giveth the alms; and those who fulfil their covenant when they covenant, and the patient in adversity and affliction and in time of violence, these are they who are true, and these are they who fear God.

SAY: We believe in God, and what hath been sent down to thee, and what was sent down to Abraham, and Ishmael, and Isaac, and Jacob, and the tribes, and what was given to Moses, and to Jesus, and the prophets from their Lord,—we make no distinction between any of them,—and to Him are we resigned: and whoso desireth other than Resignation [Islām] for a religion, it shall certainly not be accepted from him, and in the life to come he shall be among the losers.

■ ■ ■

Fight in the path of God with those who fight with you;—but exceed not; verily God loveth not those who exceed.—And kill them wheresoever ye find them, and thrust them out from whence they thrust you out; for dissent is worse than slaughter; but fight them not at the Sacred Mosque, unless they fight you there: but if they fight you, then kill them: such is the reward of the infidels! But if they desist, then verily God is forgiving and merciful.—But fight them till there be no dissent, and the worship be only to God;—but, if they desist, then let there be no hostility save against the transgressors.

■ ■ ■

Men are superior to women on account of the qualities with which God hath gifted the one above the other, and on account of the outlay they make from their substance for them. Virtuous women are obedient, careful, during *the husband's* absence, because God hath of them been careful. . . . *other* women who seem good in your eyes, marry *but* two, or three, or four; and if ye *still* fear that ye shall not act equitably, then one only; or the slaves whom ye have acquired: this will make justice on your part easier.

Those unbelievers of the People of the Book
and the idolaters wish not that any good
should be sent down upon you from your Lord;
but God singles out for His mercy whom he will;
God is of bounty abounding. . . .

Many of the People of the Book wish they might
restore you as unbelievers, after you have believed,
in the jealousy of their souls, after the truth
has become clear to them; yet do you pardon
and be forgiving, till God brings His command;
truly God is powerful over everything.
And perform the prayer, and pay the alms;
whatever good you shall forward to your souls' account,
you shall find it with God; assuredly God
sees the things you do.

And they say, "None shall enter Paradise
except that they be Jews or Christians."
Such are their fancies. Say: "Produce your
proof, if you speak truly."
Nay, but whosoever submits his will to God,
being a good-doer, his wage is with his Lord,
and no fear shall be on them, neither shall
they sorrow.

The Jews say, "The Christians stand not on
anything";
the Christians say, "The Jews stand not on
anything";
yet they recite the Book. So too the ignorant
say the like of them. God shall decide
between them on the Day of Resurrection
touching their differences.
And who does greater evil than he who bars
God's places of worship, so that His Name
be not rehearsed in them, and strives to
destroy them?
Such men might never enter them, save in
fear; for them is degradation in the present world,
and in the world to come a mighty
chastisement.

To God belong the East and the West;
whithersoever you turn, there is the
Face of God;
God is All-embracing, All-knowing. . . .
Children of Israel, remember My blessing
wherewith I blessed you, and that I have
preferred you above all beings. . . .

And when his Lord tested Abraham
with certain words, and he fulfilled them.
He said, "Behold, I make you a leader
for the people." Said he, "And of my seed?"
He said, "My covenant shall not reach
the evildoers."
And when We appointed the House to be
a place of visitation for the people,
and a sanctuary,

and: "Take to yourselves Abraham's station
for a place of prayer." And We made covenant
with Abraham and Ishmael, "Purify
My House for those that shall go about it
and those that cleave to it, to those who bow
and prostrate themselves." . . .

When his Lord said to him, "Surrender,"
he said, "I have surrendered me to
the Lord of all Being."
And Abraham charged his sons with this
and Jacob likewise: My sons, God has
chosen for you the religion;
see that you die not
save in surrender."

Why, were you witnesses, when death came
to Jacob? When he said to his sons,
"What will you serve after me?" They said,
"We will serve thy God and the God of thy
fathers
Abraham, Ishmael, and Isaac, One God;
to Him we surrender."
That is a nation that has passed away;
there awaits them that they have earned,
and there awaits you that you have earned;
you shall not be questioned concerning
the things they did.

And they say, "Be Jew or Christians and
you shall be guided." Say thou: "Nay, rather
the creed of Abraham, a man of pure faith;
he was no idolater."
Say you: "We believe in God, and
in that which has been sent down on us
and sent down on Abraham, Ishmael,
Isaac and Jacob, and the Tribes,
and that which was given to Moses and Jesus
and the Prophets, of their Lord; we
make no division between any of them, and
to Him we surrender."
And if they believe in the like of that you
believe in, then they are truly guided; but if

they turn away, then they are clearly in
schism,
God will suffice you for them; He is
the All-hearing, the All-knowing;
the baptism of God; and who is there
that baptizes fairer than God?
Him we are serving.
Say: "Would you then dispute with us
concerning God, who is our Lord
and your Lord? Our deeds belong to us,
and to you belong your deeds; Him
we serve sincerely. . . ."

It is not piety, that you turn your faces
to the East and to the West.
True piety is this:
to believe in God, and the Last Day,
the angels, the Book, and the Prophets,
to give of one's substance, however cherished,
to kinsmen, and orphans,
the needy, the traveler, beggars,
and to ransom the slave,
to perform the prayer, to pay the alms.
And they who fulfill their covenant
when they have engaged in a covenant,
and endure with fortitude
misfortune, hardship, and peril,
these are they who are true in their faith,
these are the truly godfearing. . . .

O believers, prescribed for you is
the Fast, even as it was prescribed for
those that were before you—haply you
will be godfearing—
for days numbered; and if any of you
be sick, or if he be on a journey,
then a number of other days. . . .

And fight in the way of God with those
who fight with you, but aggress not: God
loves not the aggressors.
And slay them wherever you come upon them,

and expel them from where they expelled you;
persecution is more grievous than slaying.
But fight them not by the Holy Mosque
until they should fight you there;
then, if they fight you, slay them—
such is the recompense of unbelievers—
but if they give over, surely God is
All-forgiving, All-compassionate.
Fight them, till there is no persecution
and the religion is God's; then if they
give over, there shall be no enmity
save for evildoers.
The holy month for the holy month;
holy things demand retaliation.
Whoso commits aggression against you,
do you commit aggression against him
like as he has committed against you;
and fear you God, and know that God is
with the godfearing.

And expend in the way of God;
and cast not yourselves by your own hands
into destruction, but be good-doers; God
loves the good-doers.

Fulfill the Pilgrimage and the Visitation
unto God; but if you are prevented,
then such offering as may be feasible. . . .
And when you have performed your holy rites
remember God, as you remember your fathers
or yet more devoutly. . . .
God
there is no god but He, the
Living, the Everlasting.
Slumber seizes Him not, neither sleep;
to Him belongs
all that is in the heavens and the earth.
Who is there that shall intercede with Him
save by his leave?
He knows what lies before them and
what is after them,
and they comprehend not anything of

His knowledge save such as He
wills.
His Throne comprises the heavens and earth;
The preserving of them
Oppresses Him not;
He is the All-high, the All-glorious.
No compulsion is there in religion.
Rectitude has become clear from error.
So whosoever disbelieves in idols
and believes in God, has laid hold of
the most firm handle, unbreaking; God is
All-hearing, All-knowing.

God is the Protector of the believers;
He brings them forth from the shadows
into the light. . . .
Those who believe and do deeds of
righteousness,
and perform the prayer, and pay the alms—
their wage awaits them with their Lord,
and no fear shall be on them, neither shall
they sorrow. . . .

God charges no soul save to its capacity;
standing to its account is what it has earned,
and against its account what it has merited.

Our Lord,
take us not to task
if we forget, or make mistake.
Our Lord,
charge us not with a load such
as Thou didst lay upon those before us.
Our Lord,
do Thou not burden us
beyond what we have the strength to bear.
And pardon us,
and forgive us,
and have mercy on us;
Thou art our Protector.
And help us against the people
of the unbelievers.

9.2

The Pact of Ibn Muslama and The Pact of Umar

One question that faced conquering Islamic armies was how to deal with the non-Muslim subjects, particularly Jews and Christians. Contrary to one popular image, the Muslim conquerors of the seventh and eighth centuries did not, as a general policy, force their non-Arab subjects to convert to Islam.

There is some evidence of forced conversions and massacres of non-Muslim populations during this first age of expansion. The Qur'an expressly forbids forced conversion, and the Prophet's own actions underscored that prohibition.

In 628 Muhammad entered into a contract, or *dhimma*, with an Arabic Jewish tribe. He guaranteed to defend them and to respect their religious practices in return for their submission, assistance, and payment of tribute. This contract of protection became the paradigm for Islam's leaders as Arab armies exploded out of the peninsula; however, the manner in which Muslims applied the *dhimma* differed depending on the circumstances. The following two documents show us two varieties of the *dhimma* and reflect some ways that the pact tended to change over time.

Our first document records a peace pact Habib ibn Muslama (617-662) offered to the Christians in Tiflis around 653. He was the military commander who conquered Armenia and Georgia in the region between the Black and Caspian seas. Ibn Muslama's pact with the Christians of Tiflis is a good example of the earliest form of the *dhimma*.

The second document purports to be the pact of peace offered by Caliph Umar I (r. 634-644) to the Christians of Syria around 637. Most scholars agree it came later—in the ninth century when crushing local revolts occupied the Abassid Dynasty (r. 750-1258) and they needed historical support for policies that were more repressive than those of their Umayyad predecessors (r. 661-750).

However their pacts of protection might differ, the non-Muslims who lived under these compacts were known as *dhimmis* and paid a *jizya*, or poll tax (tax levied on persons rather than property), as a token of their submission to the authority of Islam.

SOURCES:

1. Al-Baladhuri, *Kitah Futah al-Buldan (The Origin of the Islamic State)*, P. K. Hitti, trans. (New York, 1916), pp. 316-317.
2. T. W. Arnold, trans., *The Preaching of Islam*, 2nd ed. (London, 1913), pp. 57-59.

The Pact of Ibn Muslama

In the name of Allah, the compassionate, the merciful. This is a statement from Habib ibn-Muslama to the inhabitants of Tiflis, . . . securing them safety for their lives, churches, convents, religious services and faith, provided they acknowledge their humiliation and pay tax to the amount of one *dinar* on every household. You are not to combine more than one household into one in order the reduce the tax, nor are we to divide the same household into more than one in order to increase it. You owe us counsel and support against the enemies of Allah and his Prophet to the utmost of your ability, and are bound to entertain the needy Muslim for one night and provide him with that food used by "the people of the Book" and which it is legal for us to partake of. If a Muslim is cut off from his companions and falls into your hands, you are bound to deliver him to the nearest body of the "Believers," unless something stands in the way. If you return to the obedience of Allah and observe prayer, you are our brethren in faith, otherwise poll-tax is incumbent on you. In case an enemy of yours attacks and subjugates you while the Muslims are too busy to come to your aid, the Muslims are not held responsible, nor is it a violation of the covenant with you. The above are your rights and obligations to which Allah and his angels are witness and it is sufficient to have Allah for witness.

The Pact of Umar

In the name of God, the Merciful, the Compassionate! This is a writing to Umar from the Christians of *such and such a city.* When you marched against us, we asked of you protection for ourselves, our posterity, and our co-religionists; and we made this stipulation with you that we will not erect in our city or the suburbs any new monastery, church, cell, or hermitage; that we will not repair any of such buildings that might fall into ruins, or renew those that might be situated in the Muslim quarters of the town; that we will not refuse the Muslims entry into our churches either by night or by day; that we will open the gates wide to passengers and travelers; that we will receive any Muslim traveler into our houses and give him food and lodging for three nights; that we will not harbor any spy in our churches or houses or conceal any enemy of the Muslims.

That we will not teach our children the Qur'an; that we will not make a show of the Christian religion or invite anyone to embrace it; that we will not prevent any of our kinsmen from embracing Islam, if they so desire. That we will honor the Muslims and rise up in our assemblies when they wish to take their seats; that we will not imitate them in our dress, either in the cap, turban, sandals, or parting of the hair; that we will not make use of their expressions of speech or adopt their surnames; that we will not ride on saddles or gird on swords or take to ourselves arms or wear them or engrave Arabic inscriptions on our rings; that we will not sell wine; that we will shave the front of our heads; that we will keep to our own style of dress, wherever we might be; that we will wear belts around our waists.

That we will not display the cross upon our churches or display our crosses or our sacred books in the streets of the Muslims or in their marketplaces; that we will strike the clappers in our churches lightly; that we will not recite our services in a loud voice when a Muslim is present; that we will not carry palm-branches or our images in procession in the streets; that at the burial of our dead we will not chant loudly or carry lighted candles in the streets of the Muslims or their marketplaces; that we will not take any slaves who have already been in the possession of Muslims or spy into their houses; and that we will not strike any Muslim.

All this we promise to observe, on behalf of ourselves and our co-religionists, and receive protection from you in exchange; and if we violate any of the conditions of this agreement, then we forfeit your protection and you are at liberty to treat us as enemies and rebels.

CHAPTER 10

African Societies and Kingdoms, ca. 400-1450

10.1

The Chronicle of Guinea, Gomes Eannes de Azurara

Simultaneously with Zheng He's fleets sailing the western seas and Muslim sailors dominating the coastal traffic of virtually every land washed by the Indian Ocean, the Portuguese were inching down the west coast of Africa.

From 1419 on, Prince Henry (1394-1460) almost annually sent out ships in an attempt to push toward the sub-Saharan land the Portuguese called *Guinea.* In 1434, one of his caravels rounded the feared Cape Bojador, along the western Saharan coast. Once this psychological and navigational barrier had been broken, the pace of exploration quickened. By 1460 Portuguese sailors had ventured as far south as modern Sierra Leone. Finally, Bartholomew Dias rounded the southern tip of Africa in 1488, and Vasco da Gama, seeking "Christians and spices," landed in Calicut in May 1498. Da Gama lost two of his four ships and many of his crew, but the profits from this small enterprise were astounding. Portugal was in the Indian Ocean to stay.

Portugal's commercial empire was still half a century in the future when, in 1452, Gomes Eannes de Azurara (ca. 1400-ca. 1472) began to compose a history of the life and work of Prince Henry "the Navigator." Azurara's history details Portuguese explorations along the coast of West Africa until 1448. He promised a sequel because Henry was still alive and actively promoting voyages to Africa when *The Chronicle of Guinea* was completed in 1453. Azurara's other duties apparently intervened, and he never returned to the topic. Still, the chronicle he managed to write is a revealing picture of the spirit behind Portugal's first generation of oceanic exploration and colonialism.

In the following excerpts Azurara explains why Prince Henry sponsored the expeditions and defends the consequent enslavement of West Africans. Trade in Guinean slaves became an integral part of Portuguese imperialism. It began in 1441 with the capture of ten Africans, and Azurara estimated that, by 1448, 927 African slaves had come to Portugal. This exploitation disturbed Azurara, a humane man, and he could not foresee that between 1450 and 1500, 150,000 more Africans would enter Portugal as slaves, and over the next four centuries, European and Euro-American slavers would transport untold millions of so-called heathens out of Africa.

Source: Gomes Eannes de Azurara, *The Chronicle of Discovery and Conquest of Guinea,* trans. Charles Raymond Beazely and Edgar Prestage, 2 vols. (London: Hakluyt Society, 1896), vol. 1, pp. 27-29, 83-85.

We imagine that we know a matter when we are acquainted with the doer of it and the end for which he did it. And since in former chapters we have set forth the Lord Infant as the chief actor in these things, giving as clear an understanding of him as we could, it is meet that in this present chapter we should know his purpose in doing them. And you should note well that the noble spirit of this Prince, by a sort of natural constraint, was ever urging him both to begin and to carry out very great deeds. For which reason, after the taking of Ceuta he always kept ships well armed against the Infidel, both for war, and because he had also a wish to know the land that lay beyond the isles of Canary and that Cape called Bojador, for that up to his time, neither by writings, nor by the memory of man, was known with any certainty the nature of the land beyond that Cape. Some said indeed that Saint Brendan had passed that way; and there was another tale of two galleys rounding the Cape, which never returned. But this does not appear at all likely to be true, for it is not to be presumed that if the said galleys went there, some other ships would not have endeavored to learn what voyage they had made. And because the said Lord Infant wished to know the truth of this—since it seemed to him that if he or some other lord did not endeavor to gain that knowledge, no mariners or merchants would ever dare to attempt it—(for it is clear that none of them ever trouble themselves to sail to a place where there is not a sure and certain hope of profit)—and seeing also that no other prince took any pains in this matter, he sent out his own ships against those parts, to have manifest certainty of them all. And to this he was stirred up by his zeal for the service of God and of the King Edward his Lord and brother, who then reigned. And this was the first reason of his action.

The second reason was that if there chanced to be in those lands some population of Christians, or some havens, into which it would be possible to sail without peril, many kinds of merchandise might be brought to this realm, which would find a ready market, and reasonably so, because no other people of these parts traded with them, nor yet people of any other that were known; and also the products of this realm might be taken there, which traffic would bring great profit to our countrymen.

The third reason was that, as it was said that the power of the Moors in that land of Africa was very much greater than was commonly supposed, and that there were no Christians among them, nor any other race of men; and because every wise man is obliged by natural prudence to wish for a knowledge of the power of his enemy; therefore the said Lord Infant exerted himself to cause this to be fully discovered, and to make it known determinately how far the power of those infidels extended.

The fourth reason was because during the one and thirty years that he had warred against the Moors, he had never found a Christian king, nor a lord outside this land, who for the love of our Lord Jesus Christ would aid him in the said war. Therefore he sought to know if there were in those parts any Christian princes, in whom the charity and the love of Christ was so ingrained that they would aid him against those enemies of the faith.

The fifth reason was his great desire to make increase in the faith of our Lord Jesus Christ and to bring to him all the souls that should be saved,—understanding that all the mystery of the Incarnation, Death, and Passion of our Lord Jesus Christ was for this sole end—namely the salvation of lost souls—whom the said Lord Infant by his travail and spending would fain bring into the true path. For he perceived that no better offering could be made unto the Lord than this; for if God promised to return one hundred goods for one, we may justly believe that for such great benefits, that is to say for so many souls as were saved by the efforts of this Lord, he will have so many hundreds of rewards in the kingdom of God, by which his spirit may be glorified after this life in the celestial realm. For I who wrote this history saw so many men and women of those parts turned to the holy faith, that even if the Infant had been a heathen, their prayers would have been enough to have obtained his salvation. And not only did I see the first captives, but their children and grandchildren as true Christians as if the Divine grace breathed in them and imparted to them a clear knowledge of itself.

10.2

Description of the Coasts of East Africa and Malabar, Duarte Barbosa

Duarte Barbosa was a Portuguese linguist who made two voyages to India in the early 1500s. From his personal observations during his travels through the Indian Ocean, Barbosa wrote *Libro des Coisas da India.* It was a geographical and ethnographic survey of peoples, lands, and commerce from Africa to China.

Journeys from Europe to India regularly included stops on the coast of East Africa. Among the people Barbosa encountered were Africans (he calls them Gentiles), Moors (Muslims), Christians, and Indians. His descriptions of their towns provide a unique view of the commercial vitality of the peoples living there at the beginning of the sixteenth century.

With no regrets, Barbosa describes the destruction of many Muslim towns along the coast and the slaughter that befell the inhabitants if they resisted. The Portuguese captured these people and took their gold, silver, and other resources. His description of "Benamatapa" in South Africa is one of the few descriptions we have of the great wealth and power emanating from the gold-bearing regions in the interior and their trade relations with the coast.

Source: Duarte Barbosa, *Description of Coasts of East Africa and Malabar in the Beginning of the 16th Century* (London: Hakluyt Society, 1866), 4-15.

Sofala

Whereon is a town of the Moors called Sofala, close to which town the King of Portugal has a fort. These Moors established themselves there a long time ago on account of the great trade in gold which they carry on with the Gentiles of the mainland: these speak somewhat of bad Arabic (garabia), and have got a king over them, who is at present subject to the King of Portugal. And the mode of their trade is that they come by sea in small barks which they call zanbucs (sambuk), from the kingdoms of Quiloa, and Mombaza, and Melindi; and they bring much cotton cloth of many colours, and white and blue, and some of silk; and grey, and red, and yellow beads, which come to the said kingdoms in other larger ships from the great kingdom of Cambay, which merchandise these Moors buy and collect from other Moors who bring them there, and they pay for them in gold by weight, and for a price which satisfies them; and the said Moors keep them and sell these cloths to the Gentiles of the kingdom of

Benamatapa who come there laden with gold, which gold they give in exchange for the before mentioned cloths without weighing, and so much in quantity that these Moors usually gain one hundred for one. They also collect a large quantity of ivory, which is found all round Sofala, which they likewise sell in the great kingdom of Cambay at five or six ducats the hundred weight, and so also some amber, which these Moors of Sofala bring them from the Vciques. They are black men, and men of colour—some speak Arabic, and the rest make use of the language of the Gentiles of the country. They wrap themselves from the waist downwards with cloths of cotton and silk, and they wear other silk cloths above named, such as cloaks and wraps for the head, and some of them wear hoods of scarlet, and of other coloured woolen stuffs and camelets, and of other silks. And their victuals are millet, and rice, and meat, and fish. . . . The Moors have now recently begun to produce much fine cotton in this country, and they weave it into white stuff because they do not know how to dye it, or because they have not got any colours; and they take the blue or coloured stuffs of Cambay and unravel them, and again weave the threads with their white thread, and in this manner they make coloured stuffs, by means of which they get much gold.

Kingdom of Benamatapa

On entering within this country of Sofala, there is the kingdom of Benamatapa, which is very large and peopled by Gentiles, whom the Moors call Cafers. These are brown men, who go bare, but covered from the waist downwards, with coloured stuffs, or skins of wild animals; and the persons most in honour among them wear some of the tails of the skin behind them, which go trailing on the ground for state and show. . . . They carry swords in scabbards of wood bound with gold or other metals, and they wear them on the left hand side as we do, in sashes of coloured stuffs, which they make for this purpose with four or five knots, and their tassels hanging down, like gentlemen; and in their hands azagayes, and others carry bows and arrows: it must be mentioned that the bows are of middle size, and the iron points of the arrows are very large and well wrought. They are men of war, and some of them are merchants: their women go naked as long as they are girls, only covering their middles with cotton cloths, and when they are married and have children, they wear other cloths over their breasts.

Zinbaoch

Leaving Sofala for the interior of the country, at XV days journey from it, there is a large town of Gentiles, which is called Zinbaoch; and it has houses of wood and straw, in which town the King of Benamatapa frequently dwells, and from there to the city of Benamatapa there are six days journey, and the road goes from Sofala, inland, towards the Cape of Good Hope. And in the said Benamatapa, which is a very large town, the king is used to make his longest residence; and it is thence that the merchants bring to Sofala the gold which they sell to the Moors without weighing it, for coloured stuffs and beads of Cambay, which are much used and valued amongst them; and the people of this city of Benamatapa say that this gold comes from still further off towards the Cape of Good Hope, from another kingdom subject to this king of Benamatapa, who is a great lord, and holds many other kings as his subjects, and many other lands, which extend far inland, both towards the Cape of Good Hope and towards Mozambich. . . .

This king constantly takes with him into the field a captain, whom they call Sono, with a great quantity of men-at-arms, and amongst them they bring six thousand women, who also bear arms and fight. With these forces he goes about subduing and pacifying whatever kings rise up or desire to revolt. The said king of Benamatapa sends, each year, many honourable persons throughout his kingdoms to all the towns and lordships, to give them new regulations, so that all may do them obeisance. . . .

Angoy

After passing this river of Zuama, at XI leagues from it, there is a town of the Moors on the sea coast, which is called Angoy, and has a king, and the Moors who live there are all merchants, and deal in gold, ivory, silk, and cotton stuffs, and beads of Cambay, the same as do those of Sofala. And the Moors bring these goods from Quiloa, and Monbaza, and Melynde, in small vessels hidden from the Portuguese ships; and they carry from there a great quantity of ivory, and much gold. And in this town of Angoy there are plenty of provisions of millet, rice, and some kinds of meat. These men are very brown and copper coloured; they go naked from the waist upwards, and from thence downwards, they wrap themselves with cloths of cotton and silk, and wear other cloths folded after the fashion of cloaks, and some wear caps and others hoods, worked with stuffs and silks; and they speak the language belonging to the country, which is that of the Pagans, and some of them speak Arabic. These people are sometimes in obedience to the king of Portugal, and at times they throw it off, for they are a long way off from the Portuguese forts.

Mozambique Island

Mozambique . . . has a very good port, and all the Moors touch there who are sailing to Sofala, Zuama, or Anguox. Amongst these Moors there is a sheriff, who governs them, and does justice. These are of the language and customs of the Moors of Anguox, in which island the King of Portugal now holds a fort, and keeps the said Moors under his orders and government. At this island the Portuguese ships provide themselves with water and wood, fish and other kinds of provisions; and at this place they refit those ships which stand in need of repair. And from this island likewise the Portuguese fort in Sofala draws its supplies, both of Portuguese goods and of the produce of India, on account of the road being longer by the mainland. . . .

Island of Quiloa

There is another island close to the mainland, called Quiloa, in which there is a town of the Moors, built of handsome houses of stone and lime, and very lofty, with their windows like those of the Christians; in the same way it has streets, and these houses have got their terraces, and the wood worked in with the masonry, with plenty of gardens, in which there are many fruit trees and much water. This island has got a king over it, and from hence there is trade with Sofala with ships, which carry much gold, which is dispersed thence through all Arabia Felix, for henceforward all this country is thus named on account of the short of the sea being peopled with many towns and cities of the Moors; and when the King of Portugal discovered this land, the Moors of Sofala, and Zuama, and Anguox, and Mozambique, were all under obedience to the King of Quiloa, who was a great king amongst them. And there is much gold in this town, because all the ships which go to Sofala touch at this island, both in going and coming back. These people are Moors, of a dusky colour, and some of them are black and some white; they are very well dressed with rich cloths of gold, and silk, and cotton, and the women also go very well dressed out with much gold and silver in chains and bracelets on their arms, and legs, and ears. The speech of these people is Arabic, and they have got books of the Alcoran, and honour greatly their prophet Muhamad. This King, for his great pride, and for not being willing to obey the King of Portugal, had this town taken from him by force, and in it they killed and captured many people, and the King fled from the island, in which the King of Portugal ordered a fortress to be built, and thus he holds under his command and government those who continued to dwell there.

Island of Mombaza

A city of the Moors, called Bombaza, [is] very large and beautiful, and built of high and handsome houses of stone and whitewash, and with very good streets, in the manner of those of Quiloa. And it also had a king over it. The people are of dusky white, and brown complexions, and likewise the women, who are much adorned with silk and gold stuffs. It is a town of great trade in goods, and has a good port, where there are always many ships, both of those that sail for Sofala and those that come from Cambay and Melinde, and others which sail to the islands of Zanzibar, Manfia, and Penda, which will be spoken of further on. This Mombaza is a country well supplied with plenty of provisions. . . . The inhabitants at times are at war with the people of the continent, and at other times at peace, and trade with them, and obtain much honey and wax, and ivory. This King, for his pride and unwillingness to obey the King of Portugal, lost his city, and the Portuguese took it from him by force, and the King fled, and they killed and made captives many of his people, and the country was ravaged, and much plunder was carried off from it of gold and silver, copper, ivory, rich stuffs of gold and silk, and much other valuable merchandize.

Melinde

This town has fine houses of stone and whitewash, of several stories, with their windows and terraces, and good streets. The inhabitants are dusky and black, and go naked from the waist upwards, and from that downwards they cover themselves with cloths of cotton and silk, and others wear wraps like cloaks, and handsome caps on their heads. The trade is great which they carry on in cloth, gold, ivory, copper, quicksilver, and much other merchandise, with both Moors and Gentiles of the kingdom of Cambay, who come to their port with ships laden with cloth, which they buy in exchange for gold, ivory, and wax. Both parties find great profit in this. . . . This King and people have always been very friendly and obedient to the King of Portugal, and the Portuguese have always met with much friendship and good reception amongst them.

Penda, Manfia, and Zanzibar

Between this island of San Lorenzo and the continent, not very far from it, are three islands, which are called one Manfia, another Zanzibar, and the other Penda; these are inhabited by Moors; they are very fertile islands, with plenty of provisions. . . . They produce many sugar canes, but do not know how to make sugar. These islands have their kings. The inhabitants trade with the mainland with their provisions and fruits; they have small vessels, very loosely and badly made, without decks, and with a single mast; all their planks are sewn together with cords of reed or matting, and the sails are of palm mats. They are very feeble people, with very few and despicable weapons. In these islands they live in great luxury, and abundance; they dress in very good cloths of silk and cotton, which they buy in Mombaza of the merchants from Cambay, who reside there. Their wives adorn themselves with many jewels of gold from Sofala, and silver, in chains, ear-rings, bracelets, and ankle rings, and are dressed in silk stuffs: and they have many mosques, and hold the Alcoran of Mahomed.

CHAPTER 11

Southern and Central Asia, ca. 300-1400

11.1

Description of India, Abu'l Raihan al-Biruni

At the end of the tenth century, Sultan Mahmud of Ghazana (r. 998-1030), who bore the titles the *Sword of Islam* and the *Image Breaker,* began a series of seventeen raids into India from his base south of Kabul in modern Afghanistan. This Turkish lord did not attempt to conquer all of India, but he did take control of the subcontinent's northwestern region of Punjab (part of the modern Islamic state of Pakistan). For a century and a half after Mahmud's death, Islam penetrated no farther into India, but the Muslims did establish the precedent of Islamic jihads against infidel Hindus.

The riches that Mahmud accumulated from his plunder and destruction of Hindu temples (he carried off six and one-half tons of gold from one expedition alone) enabled him to turn his remote capital of Ghazana into a center of Islamic culture. Scholars and artists from all over Southwest Asia gathered at Mahmud's court. Many came willingly; others were forced to come. In 1017 Mahmud conquered the Central Asian Islamic state of Khwarazm, located west of Ghazana and just south of the Aral Sea. The conqueror brought back many of Khwarazm's intellectuals and artisans to his capital, including the Iranian scholar, Abu'l Raihan al-Biruni (973-ca. 1050).

Known to subsequent generations as *al-Ustadh* (the Master), al-Biruni was primarily an astronomer, mathematician, and linguist, but his wide-ranging interests and intellect involved him in many other fields of inquiry. For thirteen years following his capture, al-Biruni served Mahmud, probably as court astrologer, and traveled with him into India's Punjab region. Here, al-Biruni spent the bulk of his period of service to Mahmud. Shortly after his lord's death in 1030, al-Biruni completed his *Description of India,* an encyclopedic account of Indian civilization, especially Hindu science. The following excerpts come from the book's opening pages, in which the author deals with the essential differences that separate Hindus from Muslims.

Source: Edward C. Sachau, trans., *Alberuni's India* (Delhi, 1910), pp. 17-25, passim.

On the Hindus in General, as an Introduction to Our Account of Them

Before entering on our exposition, we must form an adequate idea of that which renders it so particularly difficult to penetrate to the essential nature of any Indian subject. The knowledge of these difficulties will either facilitate the progress of our work, or serve as an apology for any shortcomings of ours. For the reader must always bear in mind that the Hindus entirely differ from us in every respect, many a subject appearing intricate and obscure which would be perfectly clear if there were more connection between us. The barriers which separate Muslims and Hindus rest on different causes.

First, they differ from us in everything which other nations have in common. And here we first mention the language, although the difference of language also exists between other nations. . . .

Secondly, they totally differ from us in religion, as we believe in nothing in which they believe, and *vice versa.* On the whole, there is very little disputing about theological topics among themselves; at the utmost, they fight with words, but they will never stake their soul or body or their property on religious controversy. On the contrary, all their fanaticism is directed against those who do not belong to them—against all foreigners. They call them *mleccha, i.e.* impure, and forbid having any connection with them, be it by intermarriage or any other kind of relationship, or by sitting, eating, and drinking with them, because thereby, they think, they would be polluted. They consider as impure anything which touches the fire and the water of a foreigner; and no household can exist without these two elements. Besides, they never desire that a thing which once has been polluted should be purified and thus recovered, as, under ordinary circumstances, if anybody or anything has become unclean, he or it would strive to regain the state of purity. They are not allowed to receive anybody who does not belong to them, even if he wished it, or was inclined to their religion. This, too, renders any connection with them quite impossible, and constitutes the widest gulf between us and them.

In the third place, in all manners and usages they differ from us to such a degree as to frighten their children with us, with our dress, and our ways and customs, and as to declare us to be devil's breed, and our doings as the very opposite of all that is good and proper. By the way, we must confess, in order to be just, that a similar depreciation of foreigners not only prevails among us and the Hindus, but is common to all nations towards each other. I recollect a Hindu who wreaked his vengeance on us for the following reason: —

Some Hindu king had perished at the hand of an enemy of his who had marched against him from our country. After his death there was born a child to him, which succeeded him, by the name of Sagara. On coming of age, the young man asked his mother about his father, and then she told him what had happened. Now he was inflamed with hatred, marched out of his country into the country of the enemy, and plentifully satiated his thirst of vengeance upon them. After having become tired of slaughtering, he compelled the survivors to dress in our dress, which was meant as an ignominious punishment for them. When I heard of it, I felt thankful that he was gracious enough not to compel us to Indianise ourselves and to adopt Hindu dress and manners. . . .

But then came Islam; the Persian empire perished, and the repugnance of the Hindus against foreigners increased more and more when the Muslims began to make their inroads into their country; for Muhammad Ibn Al-Qasim entered Sind . . . and conquered the cities of Bahmanwa and Mulasthana, the former of which he called *Al-mansura,* the latter *Al-ma'mura.* He entered India proper, and penetrated even as far as Kanauj, marched through the country of Gandhara, and on his way back, through the confines of Kashmir, sometimes fighting sword in hand, sometimes gaining his ends by treaties, leaving to the people their ancient belief, except in the case of those who wanted to become Muslims. All these events planted a deeply rooted hatred in their hearts.

Now in the following times no Muslim conqueror passed beyond the frontier of Kabul and the river Sind until the days of the Turks, when they seized the power in Ghazna under the Samani dynasty, and the supreme power fell to the lot of Sabuktagin. This prince chose the holy war as his calling, and therefore called himself *al-Ghazi.* In the interest of his successors he constructed, in order to weaken the Indian frontier, those roads on which afterwards his son Mahmud marched into India during a period of thirty years and more. God be merciful to both father and son! Mahmud utterly ruined the prosperity of the country, and performed there wonderful exploits, by which the Hindus became like atoms of dust scattered in all directions, and like a tale of old in the mouth of the people. Their scattered remains cherish, of course, the most inveterate aversion towards all Muslims. This is the reason, too, why Hindu sciences have retired far away from those parts of the country conquered by us, and have fled to places which our hand cannot yet reach, to Kashmir, Benares, and other places. And there the antagonism between them and all foreigners receives more and more nourishment both from political and religious sources.

In the fifth place, there are other causes, the mentioning of which sounds like satire—peculiarities of their national character, deeply rooted in them, but manifest to everybody. We can only say, folly is an illness for which there is no medicine, and the Hindus believe that there is no country but theirs, no nation like theirs, no kings like theirs, no religion like theirs, no science like theirs. They are haughty, foolishly vain, self-conceited, and stolid. They are by nature niggardly in communicating that which they know, and they take the greatest possible care to withhold it from men of another caste among their own people, still much more, of course, from any foreigner. According to their belief, there is no other country on earth but theirs, no other race of man but theirs, and no created beings besides them have any knowledge of science whatsoever. . . . If they traveled and mixed with other nations, they would soon change their mind, for their ancestors were not as narrow-minded as the present generation is. One of their scholars, Varahamihira, in a passage where he calls on the people to honor the Brahmins, says: *"The Greeks, though impure, must be honored, since they were trained in sciences and therein excelled others. What, then, are we to say of a Brahmin, if he combines with his purity the height of science?"* In former times, the Hindus used to acknowledge that the progress of science due to the Greeks is much more important than that which is due to themselves. But from this passage of Varahamihira alone you see what a self-lauding man he is, while he gives himself airs as doing justice to others. . . .

The heathen Greeks, before the rise of Christianity, held much the same opinions as the Hindus; their educated classes thought much the same as those of the Hindus; their common people held the same idolatrous views as those of the Hindus. Therefore I like to confront the theories of the one nation with those of the other simply on account of their close relationship, not in order to correct them. For that which is not *the truth* does not admit of any correction and all heathenism, whether Greek or Indian, is in its heart and soul one and the same belief, because it is only a deviation *from the truth.* The Greeks, however, had philosophers who, living in their country, discovered and worked out for them the elements of science, not of popular superstition, for it is the object of the upper classes to be guided by the results of science, while the common crowd will always be inclined to plunge into wrong-headed wrangling, as long as they are not kept down by fear of punishment. Think of Socrates when he opposed the crowd of his nation as to their idolatry and did not want to call the stars gods! At once eleven of the twelve judges of the Athenians agreed on a sentence of death, and Socrates died faithful to the truth.

The Hindus had no men of this stamp both capable and willing to bring sciences to a classical perfection. Therefore you mostly find that even the so-called scientific theorems of the Hindus are in a state of utter confusion, devoid of any logical order, and in the last instance always mixed up with the silly notions of the crowd, *e.g.* immense numbers, enormous spaces of time, and all kinds of religious dogmas, which the vulgar belief does not admit of being called into question. . . . I can only compare their mathematical and astronomical literature, as far as I know it, to a mixture of pearl shells and sour dates, or of pearls and dung, or of costly crystals and common pebbles. Both kinds of things are equal in their eyes, since they cannot raise themselves to the methods of a strictly scientific deduction.

CHAPTER 12

East Asia, ca. 800-1400

12.1

Letter to Changchun, Chinggis Khan

In 1210 Chinggis Khan's armies captured *Zhongdu* (modern *Beijing*), the capital of the *Jin Empire*, which the *Ruzhen*, a Manchu steppe-people, had established in China a century earlier. Nine years later Chinggis Khan commissioned a letter to the Daoist monk *Changchun* (1148-1227), bidding him to travel to the court of the Great Khan to instruct him in the Way. Evidence shows that Chinggis Khan wanted instruction not in the Dao of saintly wisdom but in the way of achieving physical immortality. Changchun was the thirteenth century's most famous master of the *Golden Lotus* sect of Daoism. Its members devoted themselves to searching in the spiritual world for the *dan*, a magical entity that contained the secret to everlasting life.

Despite his advanced age, Changchun traveled to Zhongdu in 1220, accompanied by nineteen disciples. When he arrived at his destination, Changchun discovered that the Great Khan had left to campaign in the west. Changchun and his disciples set out to catch up with Chinggis Khan, finally reaching him in Afghanistan in May 1222. After instructing the Great Khan in "the ways of preserving life," Changchun received leave to return to China in April 1223, arriving back in Zhongdu in January 1224. He settled down in a monastery provided by the Mongol khan and passed away on July 23, 1227, the same month and year in which Chinggis Khan died.

Chinggis Khan, who was illiterate, did not write the letter that initiated this series of adventures for Changchun. In all likelihood, one of the khan's Chinese advisors composed it, using traditional Chinese modes of expression and thought to express the Mongol leader's general ideas.

SOURCE: Chinggis Khan, *Letter to Changchun*, from E. Bretschneider, *Medieval Researches from Eastern Asiatic Sources* (London, 1875), pp. 37-39.

Heaven has abandoned China owing to its arrogance and extravagant luxury. But I, living in the northern wilderness, do not have inordinate passions. I have only one coat and one food. I eat the same food and am dressed in the same rags as my humble herdsmen. I consider the people my children and take an interest in talented men as though they were my brothers. We always agree in our principles, and we are always united by mutual affection. At military exercises I am always in the forefront, and in battle I am never in the rear. In the space of seven years I have accomplished a great work, uniting the whole world in one empire. I do not myself possess extraordinary qualities. However, the regime of the Jin is inconstant, and therefore Heaven assists me in obtaining the Jin throne. The Song to the south, . . . the Xi-Xia to the east and the barbarians in the west, have all acknowledged my supremacy. It seems to me that such a vast empire has not been seen since the remote time of our ancestral khans.

But insofar as my calling is high, the obligations incumbent upon me are also heavy, and I fear that in my governance there might be something lacking. To cross a river we construct boats and rudders. Likewise we invite sage men, and choose assistants, to keep an empire in good order. Ever since I came to the throne, I have constantly taken to heart the ruling of my people, but I could not find worthy individuals to occupy the offices of the three and nine. With respect to these circumstances, I inquired and heard that you, Master, have penetrated the truth, and that you walk in the way of right. Deeply learned and well experienced, you have greatly explored the laws. Your holiness is evident. You have conserved the rigorous rules of the ancient sages. You are endowed with the eminent talents of celebrated men. For a long time you have lived in rocky caverns and have retired from the world. Yet people who have themselves acquired sanctity flock to you in innumerable multitudes, like clouds on the paths of the immortals. I knew that after the war you had continued to live in Shandong, at the same place, and I constantly thought of you. I know the stories of returning from the Wei River in the same cart and of the thrice-repeated invitations in the reed hut. But what shall I do? We are separated by mountains and plains of great extent, and I cannot meet you. I can only descend from the throne and stand to the side. I have fasted and washed. I have ordered my adjutant, Liu Zhonglu, to prepare an escort and cart for you. Do not be afraid of the 1,000 *li*. I implore you to move your sainted steps. Do not think of the extent of the sandy desert. Show pity for the people in the present state of affairs, or have pity on me, and communicate to me the means of preserving life. I shall personally serve you. I hope that you will at least leave me a trifle of your wisdom. Say but a single word to me and I will be happy.

In this letter I have briefly expressed my thoughts, and hope also that you, having penetrated the principles of the Great Dao, are in sympathy with all that is right and will not resist the wishes of the people. Dated: the first day of the fifth month (May 15, 1219).

12.2

Travels, Marco Polo

Marco Polo was the son of an Italian merchant who traveled the Silk Road to Mongol China in 1275. Emperor Kublai Khan appointed Marco Polo, a gifted linguist and master of four languages, as an official in the Privy Council in 1277. For three years he was a tax inspector in Yanzhou, a city on the Grand Canal near the northeastern coast. He also visited Karakorum, the old capital of the original Mongol empire. Marco Polo stayed in the Khan's court for seventeen years, getting great wealth in gold and jewelry.

Reportedly, Marco Polo kept a detailed diary about his travels and his experiences in China. He recalled in great detail when he and other members of his family first met the Emperor Kublai Khan: "They knelt before him and made obeisance with the utmost humility. The Great Khan bade them to rise and received them honorably and entertained them with good cheer. He asked many questions about their condition and how they fared after their departure. . . . Then they presented the privileges and letters which the Pope had sent, with which he was greatly pleased, and handed over the holy oil, which he received with joy and prized very highly."

Marco Polo's account of his life under the Mongols, and his personal experiences in China's Yuan Dynasty caused both curiosity and doubts among Westerners. Many questioned the validity of his records, wondering if he had ever reached China. The controversy led to a book in 1995 entitled *Did Marco Polo Go to China?* by Frances Wood, head of Chinese Studies at the British Library. Wood argued that Marco Polo probably only went as far as Constantinople, where he gathered information on China from Arabs and Persians who had returned from a trip to China.

Source: Thomas Wright, ed., *The Travels of Marco Polo, the Venetian* (London: G. Bell & Sons, 1912).

It is their custom that the bodies of all deceased grand khans and other great lords from the family of Chinggis Khan are carried for internment to a great mountain called Altai. No matter where they might die, even if it is a hundred days' journey away, they nevertheless are brought here for burial. It is also their custom that, in the process of conveying the bodies of these princes, the escort party sacrifices whatever persons they happen to meet along the route, saying to them: "Depart for the next world and there serve your deceased master." They believe that all whom they kill in this manner will become his servants in the next life. They do the same with horses, killing all the best, so that the dead lord might use them in the next world. When the corpse of Mongke Khan was transported to this mountain, the horsemen who accompanied it slew upward of 20,000 people along the way.

Now that I have begun speaking about the Tartars, I will tell you more about them. They never remain fixed in one location. As winter approaches they move to the plains of a warmer region in order to find sufficient pasturage for their animals. In summer they inhabit cool regions in the mountains where there is water and grass and their animals are free of the annoyance of gad-flies and other biting insects. They spend two or three months progressively climbing higher and grazing as they ascend, because the grass is not sufficient in any one spot to feed their extensive herds.

Their huts, or tents, are circular and formed by covering a wooden frame with felt. These they transport on four-wheeled carts wherever they travel, since the framework is so well put together that it is light to carry. Whenever they set their huts up, the entrance always faces south. They also have excellent two-wheeled vehicles so well covered with black felt that, no matter how long it rains, rain never penetrates. These are drawn by oxen and camels and serve to carry their wives, children, and all necessary utensils and provisions.

It is the women who tend to their commercial concerns, buying and selling, and who tend to all the needs of their husbands and households. The men devote their time totally to hunting, hawking, and warfare. They have the best falcons in the world, as well as the best dogs. They subsist totally on meat and milk, eating the produce of their hunting, especially a certain small animal, somewhat like a hare, which our people call Pharaoh's rats, which are abundant on the steppes in summer. They likewise eat every manner of animal: horses, camels, even dogs, provided they are fat. They drink mare's milk, which they prepare in such a way that it has the qualities and taste of white wine. In their language they call it *kemurs*.

Their women are unexcelled in the world so far as their chastity and decency of conduct are concerned, and also in regard to their love and devotion toward their husbands. They regard marital infidelity as a vice which is not simply dishonorable but odious by its very nature. Even if there are ten or twenty women in a household, they live in harmony and highly praiseworthy concord, so that no offensive word is ever spoken. They devote full attention to their tasks and domestic duties, such as preparing the family's food, managing the servants, and caring for the children, whom they raise in common. The wives' virtues of modesty and chastity are all the more praiseworthy because the men are allowed to wed as many women as they please. The expense to the husband for his wives is not that great, but the benefit he derives from their trading and from the work in which they are constantly employed is considerable. For this reason, when he marries he pays a dowry to his wife's parents. The first wife holds the primary place in the household and is reckoned to be the husband's most legitimate wife, and this status extends to her children. Because of their unlimited number of wives, their offspring is more numerous than that of any other people. When a father dies, his son may take all of his deceased father's wives, with the exception of his own mother. They also cannot marry their sisters, but upon a brother's death they may marry their sisters-in-law. Every marriage is solemnized with great ceremony.

This is what they believe. They believe in an exalted god of heaven, to whom they burn incense and offer up prayers for sound mind and body. They also worship a god called Natigay, whose image, covered with felt or other cloth, is kept in everyone's house. They associate a wife and children with this god, placing the wife on his left side and the children before him. . . . They consider Natigay as the god who presides over their earthly concerns, protecting their children, their cattle, and their grain. They show him great respect. Before eating they always take a fat portion of meat and smear the idol's mouth with it, as well as the mouths of his wife and children. Then they take some of the broth in which the meat has been cooked and pour it outside, as an offering. When this has been done they believe that their god and his family have had their proper share. The Tartars then proceed to eat and drink without further ceremony.

The rich among these people dress in gold cloth and silks and the furs of sable, ermine, and other animals. All their accouterments are expensive.

Their weapons are bows, iron maces, and in some instances, spears. The bow, however, is the weapon at which they are the most expert, being accustomed to use it in their sports from childhood. They wear armor made from the hides of buffalo and other beasts, fire-dried and thus hard and strong.

They are brave warriors, almost to the point of desperation, placing little value on their lives, and exposing themselves without hesitation to every sort of danger. They are cruel by nature. They are capable of undergoing every manner of privation, and when it is necessary, they can live for a month on the milk of their mares and the wild animals they catch. Their horses feed on grass alone and do not require barley or other grain. The men are trained to remain on horseback for two days and two nights without dismounting, sleeping in the saddle while the horse grazes. No people on the earth can surpass them in their ability to endure hardships, and no other people shows greater patience in the face of every sort of deprivation. They are most obedient to their chiefs, and are maintained at small expense. These qualities, which are so essential to a soldier's formation, make them fit to subdue the world, which in fact they have largely done.

When one of the great Tartar chiefs goes to war, he puts himself at the head of an army of 100,000 horsemen and organizes them in the following manner. He appoints an officer to command every ten men and others to command groups of 100, 1,000, and 10,000 men respectively. Thus ten of the officers who command ten men take their orders from an officer who commands 100; ten of these captains of a 100 take their orders from an officer in charge of a 1,000; and ten of these officers make orders from one who commands 10,000. By this arrangement, each officer has to manage only ten men or ten bodies of men. . . . When the army goes into the field, a body of 200 men is sent two days' march in advance, and parties are stationed on each flank and in the rear, to prevent surprise attack.

When they are setting out on a long expedition, they carry little with them. . . . They subsist for the most part on mare's milk, as has been said. . . . Should circumstances require speed, they can ride for ten days without lighting a fire or taking a hot meal. During this time they subsist on the blood drawn from their horses, each man opening a vein and drinking the blood. They also have dried milk. . . . When setting off on an expedition, each man takes about ten pounds. Every morning they put about half a pound of this into a leather flask, with as much water as necessary. As they ride, the motion violently shakes the contents, producing a thin porridge which they take as dinner. . . .

All that I have told you here concerns the original customs of the Tartar lords. Today, however, they are corrupted. Those who live in China have adopted the customs of the idol worshippers, and those who inhabit the eastern provinces have adopted the ways of the Muslims.

12.3

The Tale of the Genji, Lady Murasaki Shikibu

The Tale of the Genji, although quoted by Japanese critics as the standard example of classic Japanese prose, is little ahead of similar narratives of its period. Its author was a lady of the Japanese Court, who died around 1025 C.E., so that the story was probably written a few years earlier. We know the author only by her court-name of Murasaki Shikibu, which means literally, the "purple violet of the *Shikibu* or ceremonial staff." Each person was known in court by the official department in which they served or were ranked, and to this was added an individual name, usually fanciful or poetic. So that this lady was called the "Ceremonial Staff's Violet." She was married, and lived long in retirement as a widow; she had a daughter, also an authoress, and kept a diary that is still preserved. The tomb of Murasaki Shikibu is today a shrine in a Buddhist temple in Kyoto, the scene of her narrative.

The Tale of the Genji traces the various love experiences of Genji, a young noble who flits, as was the fashion of the time, from one lady to another. The character of each of these ladies is carefully depicted. Modern Japanese critics theorize that the purpose of the piece was to satirically contrast the loyalty of woman with the shallowness and selfishness of man. The original narrative is very long, containing more than forty chapters, of which only an excerpt is here, as the shifting love affairs of Genji make it an easy matter to drop the rambling tale at any point. The original work passes on from Genji to his sons, and was probably completed by another and less artistic hand than that of the admired Murasaki.

Source: Charles F. Horne, ed. *The Sacred Books and Early Literature of the East, Vol. XIII: Japan* (New York: Parke, Austin, and Lipscomb, 1917), pp. 231, 252-259.

"I have only just now discovered," continued he, "how difficult it is to meet with a fair creature, of whom one can say, 'This is, indeed, *the* one; here is, at last, perfection.' There are, indeed, many who fascinate; many who are ready with their pens, and who, when occasion may require, are quick at repartee. But how often such girls as these are conceited about their own accomplishments, and endeavor unduly to disparage those of others! There are again some who are special pets of their parents, and most jealously watched over at home. Often, no doubt, they are pretty, often graceful; and frequently they will apply themselves with effect to music and to poetry, in which they may even attain to special excellence. But then, their friends will keep their drawbacks in the dark, and eulogize their merits to the utmost. If we were to give full credence to this exaggerated praise we could not but fail in every single instance to be more or less disappointed."

So saying Tô-no-Chiûjiô paused, and appeared as if he were ashamed of having such an experience, when Genji smilingly remarked, "Can any one of them, however, exist without at least one good point?"

"Nay, were there any so little favored as that, no one would ever be misled at all!" replied Tô-no-Chiûjiô, and he continued, "In my opinion, the most and the least favored are in the same proportion. I mean, they are both not many. Their birth, also, divides them into three classes. Those, however, who are especially well born are often too jealously guarded, and are, for the most part, kept secluded from the outside gaze, which frequently tends to make their deportment shy and timid. It is those of the middle class, who are much more frequently seen by us, who afford us most chance of studying their character. As for the lower class, it would be almost useless to trouble ourselves with them."

Thus Tô-no-Chiûjiô appeared to be thoroughly at home in his description of the merits of the fair sex, which made Genji amused, and he said: "But how do you define the classes you have referred to, and classify them into three? Those who are of high birth sink sometimes in the social scale until the distinction of their rank is forgotten in the abjectness of their present position. Others, again, of low origin, rise to a high position, and, with self-important faces and in ostentatious residences, regard themselves as inferior to none. Into what class will you allot *these?*"

Just at this moment the Sama-no-Kami and Tô Shikib-no-Jiô joined the party. They came to pay their respects to Genji, and both of them were gay and light-hearted talkers. So Tô-no-Chiûjiô now made over the discussion to them, and it was carried to rather questionable lengths.

"However exalted a lady's position may be," said Sama-no-Kami, "if her origin is an unenviable one, the estimation of the public for her would be widely different from that which it shows to those who are naturally entitled to it. If, again, adverse fortune assails one whose birth is high, so that she becomes friendless and helpless, degradation here will meet our eyes, though her heart may still remain as noble as ever. Examples of both of these are very common. After much reflection, I can only come to the conclusion that both of them should be included in the middle class. In this class, too, must be included many daughters of the Duriô, who occupy themselves with local administration. These ladies are often very attractive, and are not seldom introduced at Court and enjoy high favor."

"And successes depend pretty much upon the state of one's fortune, I fancy," interrupted Genji, with a placid smile.

"That is a remark very unlikely to fall from the lips of a champion of romance," chimed in Tô-no-Chiûjiô.

"There may be some," resumed Sama-no-Kami, "who are of high birth, and to whom public respect is duly paid, yet whose domestic education has been much neglected. Of a lady such as this we may simply remark, 'Why, and how, is it that she is so brought up?' and she would only cause discredit to her class. There are, of course, some who combine in themselves every perfection befitting their position. These best of the best are, however, not within every one's reach. But, listen! Within an old dilapidated gateway, almost unknown to the world, and overgrown with wild vegetation, perchance we might find, shut up, a maiden charming beyond imagination. Her father might be an aged man, corpulent in person, and stern in mien, and her brothers of repulsive countenance; but there, in an uninviting room, she lives, full of delicacy and sentiment, and fairly skilled in the arts of poetry or music, which she may have acquired by her own exertions alone, unaided. If there were such a case, surely she deserves our attention, save that of those of us who themselves are highly exalted in position."

So saying, Sama-no-Kami winked slyly at Shikib-no-Jiô. The latter was silent: perhaps he fancied that Sama-no-Kami was speaking in the above strain, with a hidden reference to his (Shikib's) sisters, who, he imagined, answered the description.

Meantime, Genji may have thought, "If it is so difficult to choose one even from the best class, how can—Ah!" and he began to close his eyes and doze. His dress was of soft white silk, partly covered by the *naoshi,* worn carelessly, with its cord left loose and untied. His appearance and bearing formed quite a picture.

Meanwhile, the conversation went on about different persons and characters, and Sama-no-Kami proceeded: "It is unquestionable that though at first glance many women appear to be without defects, yet when we come to the actual selection of any one of them, we should seriously hesitate in our choice.

"Let me illustrate my meaning by reference to the numerous public men who may be aspiring to fulfil the duties of several important posts. You will at once recognize the great difficulty there would be in fixing upon the individual statesman under whose guardianship the empire could best repose. And supposing that, if at last, by good fortune, the most able man were designated, even then we must bear in mind that it is not in the power of one or two individuals, however gifted they may be, to carry on the whole administration of the kingdom alone. Public business can only be tranquilly conducted when the superior receives the assistance of subordinates, and when the subordinate yields a becoming respect and loyalty to his superior, and affairs are thus conducted in a spirit of mutual conciliation. So, too, it is in the narrow range of the domestic circle. To make a good mistress of that circle, one must possess, if our ideal is to be fully realized, many important qualifications. Were we to be constantly indulging in the severity of criticism, always objecting to this or that, a perfect character would be almost unattainable. Men should therefore bear with patience any trifling dissatisfaction which they may feel, and strive constantly to keep alive, to augment, and to cherish the warmth of their early love. Only such a man as this can be called faithful, and the partner of such a man alone can enjoy the real happiness of affection. How unsatisfactory to us, however, seems the actual world if we look round upon it. Still more difficult must it be to satisfy such as you who seek your companions but from among the best!

"How varied are the characters and the dispositions of women! Some who are youthful and favored by Nature strive almost selfishly to keep themselves with the utmost reserve. If they write, they write harmlessly and innocently; yet, at the same time, they are choice in their expressions, which have delicate touches of bewitching sentiment. This might possibly make us entertain a suddenly conceived fancy for them; yet they would give us but slight encouragement. They may allow us just to hear their voices, but when we approach them they will speak with subdued breath, and almost inaudibly. Beware, however, lest among these you chance to encounter some astute artiste, who, under a surface that is smooth, conceals a current that is deep. This sort of lady, it is true, generally appears quite modest; but often proves, when we come closer, to be of a very different temperament from what we anticipated. Here is one drawback to be guarded against.

"Among characters differing from the above, some are too full of sentimental sweetness—whenever occasion offers them romance they become spoilt. Such would be decidedly better if they had less sentiment, and more sense.

"Others, again, are singularly earnest—too earnest, indeed—in the performance of their domestic duty; and such, with their hair pushed back, devote themselves like household drudges to household affairs. Man, whose duties generally call him from home all the day, naturally hears and sees the social movements both of public and private life, and notices different things, both good and bad. Of such things he would not like to talk freely with strangers, but only with some one closely allied to him. Indeed, a man may have many things in his mind which cause him to smile or to grieve. Occasionally something of a political nature may irritate him beyond endurance. These matters he would like to talk over with his fair companion, that she might soothe him, and sympathize with him. But a woman as above described is often unable to understand him, or does not endeavor to do so; and this only makes him more miserable. At another time he may brood over his hopes and aspirations; but he has no hope of solace. She is not only incapable of sharing these with him, but might carelessly remark, 'What ails you?' How severely would this try the temper of a man!

"If, then, we clearly see all these, the only suggestion I can make is that the best thing to do is to choose one who is gentle and modest, and strive to guide and educate her according to the best ideal we may think of. This is the best plan; and why should we not do so? Our efforts would not be surely all in vain. But no! A girl whom we thus educate, and who proves to be competent to bear us company, often disappoints us when she is left alone. She may then show her incapability, and her occasional actions may be done in such an unbecoming manner that both good and bad are equally displeasing. Are not all these against us men?—Remember, however, that there are some who may not be very agreeable at ordinary times, yet who flash occasionally upon us with a potent and almost irresistible charm."

Thus Sama-no-Kami, though eloquent, not having come to one point or another, remained thoughtful for some minutes, and again resumed:

"After all, as I have once observed, I can only make this suggestion: That we should not too much consider either birth or beauty, but select one who is gentle and tranquil, and consider her to be best suited for our last haven of rest. If, in addition, she is of fair position, and is blessed with sweetness of temper, we should be delighted with her, and not trouble ourselves to search or notice any trifling deficiency. And the more so as, if her conscience is clear and pure, calmness and serenity of features can naturally be looked for.

"There are women who are too diffident, and too reserved, and carry their generosity to such an extent as to pretend not to be aware even of such annoyances as afford them just grounds of complaint. A time arrives when their sorrows and anxieties become greater than they can bear. Even then, however, they can not resort to plain speaking, and complain. But, instead thereof, they will fly away to some remote retreat among the mountain hamlets, or to some secluded spot by the seaside, leaving behind them some painful letter or despairing verses, and making themselves mere sad memories of the past. Often when a boy I heard such stories read by ladies, and the sad pathos of them even caused my tears to flow; but now I can only declare such deeds to be acts of mere folly. For what does it all amount to? Simply to this: That the woman, in spite of the pain which it causes her, and discarding a heart which may be still lingering toward her, takes to flight, regardless of the feelings of others—of the anguish, and of the anxiety, which those who are dearest to her suffer with her. Nay, this act of folly may even be committed simply to test the sincerity of her lover's affection for her. What pitiable subtlety!

"Worse than this, the woman thus led astray, perhaps by ill advice, may even be beguiled into more serious errors. In the depth of her despairing melancholy she will become a nun. Her conscience, when she takes the fatal vow, may be pure and unsullied, and nothing may seem able to call her back again to the world which she forsook. But, as time rolls on, some household servant or aged nurse brings her tidings of the lover who has been unable to cast her out of his heart, and whose tears drop silently when he hears aught about her. Then, when she hears of his affections still living, and his heart still yearning, and thinks of the uselessness of the sacrifice she has made voluntarily, she touches the hair on her forehead, and she becomes regretful. She may, indeed, do her best to persevere in her resolve, but if one single tear bedews her cheek, she is no longer strong in the sanctity of her vow. Weakness of this kind would be in the eyes of Buddha more sinful than those offenses which are committed by those who never leave the lay circle at all, and she would eventually wander about in the 'wrong passage.'

"But there are also women, who are too self-confident and obtrusive. These, if they discover some slight inconsistency in men, fiercely betray their indignation and behave with arrogance. A man may show a little inconsistency occasionally, but yet his affection may remain; then matters will in time become right again, and they will pass their lives happily together. If, therefore, the woman can not show a tolerable amount of patience, this will but add to her unhappiness. She should, above all things, strive not to give way to excitement; and when she experiences any unpleasantness, she should speak of it frankly but with moderation. And if there should be anything worse than unpleasantness she should even then complain of it in such a way as not to irritate the men. If she guides her conduct on principles such as these, even her very words, her very demeanor, may in all probability increase his sympathy and consideration for her. One's self-denial and the restraint which one imposes upon one's self, often depend on the way in which another behaves to us. The woman who is too indifferent and too forgiving is also inconsiderate. Remember 'the unmoored boat floats about.' Is it not so?"

Tô-no-Chiûjiô quickly nodded assent, as he said, "Quite true! A woman who has no strength of emotion, no passion of sorrow or of joy, can never be holders of us. Nay even jealousy, if not carried to the extent of undue suspicion, is not undesirable. If we ourselves are not in fault, and leave the matter alone, such jealousy may easily be kept within due bounds. But stop"—added he suddenly—"Some women have to bear, and do bear, every grief that they may encounter with unmurmuring and suffering patience."

CHAPTER 13

Europe in the Middle Ages

13.1

A Letter to Pope Leo III and The Capitulary on the Missi, Charlemagne

Charlemagne ruled most of continental Europe for close to half a century (768-814). Charles' efforts to expand Christendom and impose order based on Christian principles won him a reputation that extended all the way to the court of Caliph Harun al-Rashid in Baghdad. His *Carolingian* (the family of Charles) successors, however, were less fortunate and probably less able. In 843, Charles' three grandsons divided the empire into three kingdoms, signaling continental Europe's return to political pluralism.

Before the collapse of the Carolingian Empire, Charlemagne established a sense of order and unity—if not its total reality, that served as an inspiration for many of Europe's later emperors and kings. These included the king of Germany, Otto I, who laid the basis for the Germanic *Holy Roman Empire* with his imperial coronation in 962, and Napoleon, who in the early nineteenth century attempted to create a pan-European empire centered on France.

Charlemagne's counselors and secretaries composed the following two sources in his name. They illustrate the ideals of Charles' court and the realities that faced it. The first document is a letter to Pope Leo III written in 796, shortly after the pope's accession to the papal throne—some four years before Charles' imperial coronation. The second is a *capitulary,* so called because it consists of many regulatory chapters (*capitula* in Latin), which Emperor Charles issued in 802. Known as the *Capitulary on the Missi,* it established regulations regarding the *missi dominici* (the sovereign's envoys) whom Charles sent throughout his empire. These *missi* were not career officials. They were high-ranking churchmen and lay lords who exercised special commissions. Working in pairs of one layman and one churchman, they traveled to assigned regions far from their homes and examined the state of affairs, correcting irregularities and reporting to the emperor.

Sources:

1. Oliver J. Thatcher and Edgar H. McNeal, trans., *A Source Book for Medieval History* (New York: Charles Scribner's Sons, 1905), p. 107.
2. D. C. Munro, trans., *University of Pennsylvania Translations and Reprints* (Philadelphia: University of Pennsylvania, 1900), vol. 6, no. 5, pp. 16-27, passim.

A Letter to Pope Leo III

Charles, by the grace of God king of the Franks and Lombards, and patrician of the Romans, to his holiness, Pope Leo, greeting. . . . Just as I entered into an agreement with the most holy father, your predecessor, so also I desire to make with you an inviolable treaty of mutual fidelity and love; that, on the one hand, you shall pray for me and give me the apostolic benediction, and that, on the other, with the aid of God I will ever defend the most holy seat of the holy Roman Church. For it is our part to defend the holy Church of Christ from the attacks of pagans and infidels from without, and within to enforce the acceptance of the Catholic faith. It is your part, most holy father, to aid us in the good fight by raising your hands to God as Moses did so that by your intercession the Christian people under the leadership of God may always and everywhere have the victory over the enemies of His holy name, and the name of our Lord Jesus Christ may be glorified throughout the world. Abide by the canonical law in all things and obey the precepts of the Holy Fathers always, that your life may be an example of sanctity to all, and your holy admonitions be observed by the whole world, and that your light may so shine before men that they may see your good works and glorify your father who is in Heaven. May omnipotent God preserve your holiness unharmed through many years for the exalting of His holy Church.

The Capitulary on the *Missi*

1. Concerning the embassy sent out by the lord emperor.

Therefore, the most serene and most Christian lord emperor Charles has chosen from his nobles the wisest and most prudent men, both archbishops and some of the other bishops also, and venerable abbots and pious laymen, and has sent them throughout his whole kingdom, and through them he would have all the various classes of persons mentioned in the following chapters live in accordance with the correct law. Moreover, where anything which is not right and just has been enacted in the law, he has ordered them to inquire into this most diligently and to inform him of it. He desires, God granting, to reform it. And let no one, through his cleverness or craft, dare to oppose or thwart the written law, as many are wont to do, or the judicial sentence passed upon him, or to do injury to the churches of God, or the poor, or the widows, or the wards, or any Christian. But all shall live entirely in accordance with God's precept, honestly and under a just rule, and each one shall be admonished to live in harmony with his fellows in his business or profession; the canonical clergy ought to observe in every respect a canonical life without heeding base gain; nuns ought to keep diligent watch over their lives; laymen and the secular clergy ought rightly to observe their laws without malicious fraud; and all ought to live in mutual charity and perfect peace.

And let the *missi* themselves make a diligent investigation whenever any man claims that an injustice has been done him by any one, just as they desire to deserve the grace of omnipotent God and to keep their fidelity promised to Him, so that in all cases, in accordance with the will and fear of God, they shall administer the law fully and justly in the case of the holy churches of God and of the poor, of wards and widows, and of the whole people. And if there be anything of such a nature that they, together with the provincial counts, are not able of themselves to correct it and to do justice concerning it, they shall, without any reservation, refer it, together with their reports, to the judgment of the emperor; and the straight path of justice shall not be impeded by any one on account of flattery or gifts, or on account of any relationship, or from fear of the powerful.

2. Concerning the fidelity to be promised to the lord emperor.

He has commanded that every man in his whole kingdom, whether ecclesiastic or layman, and each one according to his vow and occupation, should now promise to him as emperor the fidelity which he had previously promised to him as king; and all of those who had not yet made that promise should do likewise, down to those who were twelve years old. And that it shall be announced to all in public, so that each one might know, how great and how many things are comprehended in that oath; not merely, as many have thought hitherto, fidelity to the lord emperor as regards his life, and not introducing any enemy into his kingdom out of enmity, and not consenting to or concealing another's faithlessness to him; but that all may know that this oath contains in itself the following meaning:

3. First, that each one voluntarily shall strive, in accordance with his knowledge and ability, to live completely in the holy service of God, in accordance with the precept of God and in accordance with his own promise, because the lord emperor is unable to give to all individually the necessary care and discipline. . . .

5. That no one shall presume to rob or do any injury fraudulently to the churches of God, or widows, or orphans, or pilgrims, for the lord emperor himself, under God and His saints, has constituted himself their protector and defender.

6. That no one shall dare to lay waste a benefice of the lord emperor, or to make it his own property.

7. That no one shall presume to neglect a summons to war from the lord emperor; and that no one of the counts shall be so presumptuous as to dare to excuse any one of those who owe military service, either on account of relationship, or flattery, or gifts from any one.

8. That no one shall presume to impede at all in any way a ban or command of the lord emperor, or to tamper with his work, or to impede, or to lessen, or in any way to act contrary to his will or commands. And that no one shall dare to neglect to pay his dues or tax.

9. That no one, for any reason, shall make a practice in court of defending another unjustly, either from any desire of gain when the cause is weak, or by impeding a just judgment by his skill in reasoning, or by a desire of oppressing when the cause is weak. But each one shall answer for his own cause or tax or debt, unless someone is infirm or ignorant of pleading. . . . But in every case it shall be done in accordance with justice and the law; and no one shall have the power to impede justice by a gift, reward, or any kind of evil flattery, or from any hindrance of relationship. And no one shall unjustly consent to another in anything, but with all zeal and good-will all shall be prepared to carry out justice.

For all the above mentioned ought to be observed by the imperial oath.

10. [We ordain] that bishops and priests shall live according to the canons and shall teach others to do the same.

11. That bishops, abbots, and abbesses who are in charge of others, with the greatest veneration shall strive to surpass their subjects in this diligence and shall not oppress their sub-

jects with a harsh rule or tyranny, but with a sincere love shall carefully guard the flock committed to them with mercy and charity, or by the examples of good works. . . .

14. That bishops, abbots and abbesses, and counts shall be mutually in accord, following the law in order to render a just judgment with all charity and unity of peace, and that they shall live faithfully in accordance with the will of God, so that always everywhere through them and among them a just judgment shall be rendered. The poor, widows, orphans, and pilgrims shall have consolation and defense from them; so that we, through the good-will of these, may deserve the reward of eternal life rather than punishment. . . .

19. That no bishops, abbots, priests, deacons, or other members of the clergy shall presume to have dogs for hunting, or hawks, falcons, and sparrow-hawks, but each shall observe fully the canons or rule of his order. If any one shall presume to do so, let him know that he shall lose his office. And in addition he shall suffer such punishment for his misconduct that the others will be afraid to possess such things for themselves. . . .

27. And we command that no one in our whole kingdom shall dare to deny hospitality to rich, or poor, or pilgrims; that is, let no one deny shelter and fire and water to pilgrims traversing our country in God's name, or to any one traveling for the love of God, or for the safety of his own soul.

28. Concerning embassies coming from the lord emperor. That the counts and *centenarii* shall provide most carefully, as they desire the good-will of the lord emperor, for the *missi* who are sent out, so that they may go through their territories without any delay; and the emperor commands all everywhere that they see to it that no delay is encountered anywhere, but they shall cause the *missi* to go on their way in all haste and shall provide for them in such a manner as they may direct. . . .

32. Murders, by which a multitude of the Christian people perish, we command in every way to be shunned and to be forbidden. . . . Nevertheless, lest sin should also increase, in order that the greatest enmities may not arise among Christians, when by the persuasions of the Devil murders happen, the criminal shall immediately hasten to make amends and with all speed shall pay to the relatives of the murdered man the fitting composition for the evil done. And we forbid firmly that the relatives of the murdered man shall dare in any way to continue their enmities on account of the evil done, or shall refuse to grant peace to him who asks it, but, having given their pledges, they shall receive the fitting composition and shall make a perpetual peace; moreover, the guilty one shall not delay to pay the composition. . . . But if any one shall have scorned to make the fitting composition, he shall be deprived of his property until we shall render our decision. . . .

40. Lastly, therefore, we desire all our decrees to be known in the whole kingdom through our *missi* now sent out, either among the men of the Church, bishops, abbots, priests, deacons, canons, all monks or nuns, so that each one in his ministry or profession may keep our ban or decree, or where it may be fitting to thank the people for their good-will, or to furnish aid, or where there may be need still of correcting anything. . . . Where we believe there is anything unpunished, we shall so strive to correct it with all our zeal and will that with God's aid we may bring it to correction, both for our own eternal glory and that of all our faithful.

13.2

Call for a Crusade, Pope Urban II

The series of crusades initiated in the eleventh century brought the West into greater contact with Byzantium and Islam. These crusades displayed the expansiveness of the West during the High Middle Ages and the increasing power and activism of the papacy. In 1095 Pope Urban II called the first of these crusades in response to a request for help from the Byzantine Emperor Alexius Comnenus. At the Council of Clermont, Urban made the following plan, recorded by Robert the Monk.

Source: James Harvey Robinson, ed., *Readings in European History,* Vol. I (Boston: Ginn, 1904), pp. 314-317.

"From the confines of Jerusalem and from the city of Constantinople a grievous report has gone forth and has repeatedly been brought to our ears; namely, that a race from the kingdom of the Persians, an accursed race, a race wholly alienated from God, 'a generation that set not their heart aright, and whose spirit was not steadfast with God', has violently invaded the lands of those Christians and has depopulated them by pillage and fire. They have led away a part of the captives into their own country, and a part they have killed by cruel tortures. They have either destroyed the churches of God or appropriated them for the rites of their own religion. They destroy the altars, after having defiled them with their uncleanness. . . . The kingdom of the Greeks is now dismembered by them and has been deprived of territory so vast in extent that it could not be traversed in two months' time.

"On whom, therefore, is the labor of avenging these wrongs and of recovering this territory incumbent, if not upon you,—you, upon whom, above all other nations, God has conferred remarkable glory in arms, great courage, bodily activity, and strength to humble the heads of those who resist you? Let the deeds of your ancestors encourage you and incite your minds to manly achievements:—the glory and greatness of King Charlemagne, and of his son Louis, and of your other monarchs, who have destroyed the kingdoms of the Turks and have extended the sway of the holy Church over lands previously pagan. Let the holy sepulcher of our Lord and Saviour, which is possessed by the unclean nations, especially arouse you, and the holy places which are now treated with ignominy and irreverently polluted with the filth of the unclean. Oh, most valiant soldiers and descendants of invincible ancestors, do not degenerate, but recall the valor of your progenitors.

"But if you are hindered by love of children, parents, or wife, remember what the Lord says in the Gospel, 'He that loveth father or mother more than me is not worthy of me.' 'Every one that hath forsaken houses, or brethren, or sisters, or father, or mother, or wife, or children, or lands, for my name's sake, shall receive an hundredfold, and shall inherit everlasting life.' Let none of your possessions retain you, nor solicitude for your family affairs. For this land which you inhabit, shut in on all sides by the seas and surrounded by the mountain peaks, is too narrow for your large population; nor does it abound in wealth; and it furnishes scarcely food enough for its cultivators. Hence it is that you murder and devour one another, that you wage war, and that very many among you perish in intestine strife.

"Let hatred therefore depart from among you, let your quarrels end, let wars cease, and let all dissensions and controversies slumber. Enter upon the road to the Holy Sepulcher; wrest that land from the wicked race, and subject it to yourselves. That land which, as the Scripture says, 'floweth with milk and honey' was given by God into the power of the children of Israel. Jerusalem is the center of the earth; the land is fruitful above all others, like another paradise of delights. This spot the Redeemer of mankind has made illustrious by his advent, has beautified by his sojourn, has consecrated by his passion, has redeemed by his death, has glorified by his burial.

"This royal city, however, situated at the center of the earth, is now held captive by the enemies of Christ and is subjected, by those who do not know God, to the worship of the heathen. She seeks, therefore, and desires to be liberated and ceases not to implore you to come to her aid. From you especially she asks succor, because, as we have already said, God has conferred upon you above all other nations great glory in arms. Accordingly, undertake this journey eagerly for the remission of your sins, with the assurance of the reward of imperishable glory in the kingdom of heaven."

CHAPTER 14

Civilization in the Americas, ca. 400-1500

14.1

Memoirs: The Aztecs, Bernal Diaz del Castillo

The Aztecs arrived in Mesoamerica around 1218. They slowly developed, until the mid-1400s when they came to dominate the region. Although they based their empire on the plunder of war and human sacrifice, the Aztecs were also great lovers of beauty. There are indications that when Cortés conquered Mexico in 1519, Aztec culture was about to decline. Bernal Díaz (1492?-1581), one of Cortés' companions, wrote this selection a half-century later. It gives a sense of the highly-developed civilization and the splendor of the Aztec capital.

SOURCE: I. I. Lockhart, trans., *The Memoirs of the Conquistador Bernal de Castillo* (London: J. Hatchard and Son, 1844), pp. 220-221, 235-238.

When we gazed upon all this splendour . . . we scarcely knew what to think, and we doubted whether all that we beheld was real. A series of large towns stretched themselves along the banks of the lake, out of which still larger ones rose magnificently above the waters. Innumerable crowds of canoes were plying everywhere around us; at regular distances we continually passed over new bridges, and before us lay the great city of Mexico in all its splendour. . . .

Motecusuma himself, according to his custom, was sumptuously attired, had on a species of half boot, richly set with jewels, and whose soles were made of solid gold. The four grandees who supported him were also richly attired, which they must have put on somewhere on the road, in order to wait upon Motecusuma; they were not so sumptuously dressed when they first came out to meet us. Besides these distinguished caziques, there were many other grandees around the monarch, some of whom held the canopy over his head, while others again occupied the road before him, and spread cotton cloths on the ground that his feet might not touch the bare earth. No one of his suite ever looked at him full in the face; every one in his presence stood with eyes downcast, and it was only his four nephews and cousins who supported him that durst look up. . . .

Our commander, attended by the greater part of our cavalry and foot, all well armed, as, indeed, we were at all times, had proceeded to the Tlatelulco. . . . The moment we arrived in this immense market, we were perfectly astonished at the vast numbers of people, the profusion of merchandise which was there exposed for sale, and at the good police and order that reigned throughout. The grandees who accompanied us drew our attention to the smallest circumstance, and gave us full explanation of all we saw. Every species of merchandise had a separate spot for its sale. We first of all visited those divisions of the market appropriated for the sale of gold and silver wares, of jewels, of cloths interwoven with feathers, and of other manufactured goods; besides slaves of both sexes. . . . Next to these came the dealers in coarser wares—cotton, twisted thread, and cacao. . . . In one place were sold the stuffs manufactured of nequen; ropes, and sandals; in another place, the sweet maguey root, ready cooked, and various other things made from this plant. In another division of the market were exposed the skins of tigers, lions, jackals, otters, red deer, wild cats, and of other beasts of prey, some of which were tanned. In another place were sold beans and sage, with other herbs and vegetables. A particular market was assigned for the merchants in fowls, turkeys, ducks, rabbits, hares, deer, and dogs; also for fruit-sellers, pastry-cooks, and tripe-sellers. Not far from these were exposed all manner of earthenware, from the large earthen cauldron to the smaller pitchers. Then came the dealers in honey and honey-cakes, and other sweetmeats. Next to these, the timber-merchants, furniture-dealers, with their stores of tables, benches, cradles, and all sorts of wooden implements, all separately arranged. . . .

In this market-place there were also courts of justice, to which three judges and several constables were appointed, who inspected the goods exposed for sale. . . . I wish I had completed the enumeration of all this profusion of merchandise. The variety was so great that it would occupy more space than I can well spare to note them down in; besides which, the market was so crowded with people, and the thronging so excessive in the porticoes, that it was quite impossible to see all in one day. . . .

Indeed, this infernal temple, from its great height, commanded a view of the whole surrounding neighbourhood. From this place we could likewise see the three causeways which led into Mexico. . . . We also observed the aqueduct which ran from Chapultepec, and provided the whole town with sweet water. We could also distinctly see the bridges across the openings, by which these causeways were intersected, and through which the waters of the lake ebbed and flowed. The lake itself was crowded with canoes, which were bringing provisions, manufactures, and other merchandize to the city. From here we also discovered that the only communication of the houses in this city, and of all the other towns built in the lake, was by means of drawbridges or canoes. In all these towns the beautiful white plastered temples rose above the smaller ones, . . . and this, it may be imagined, was a splendid sight.

After we had sufficiently gazed upon this magnificent picture, we again turned our eyes toward the great market, and beheld the vast numbers of buyers and sellers who thronged them. The bustle and noise occasioned by this multitude of human beings was so great that it could be heard at a distance of more than four miles.

14.2

The Chronicle of Peru: The Incas

The Incas of South America established one of the most complex and sophisticated empires in world history. Centered in the highlands of Peru, by the time of the European discovery, they had developed a political and economic system that extended along the edge of South America's western coast for about 2500 miles. Much of our written information about the Incas comes from accounts of Western conquerors, explorers, and missionaries who streamed into South America during the sixteenth century. The following selection is a description of Inca culture by an early member of Spain's conquering armies. He sought to document the complexity of the Inca civilization just as the Spaniards were about to destroy it. Pedro Cieza de Leon (1518-1560) was involved in several campaigns in Ecuador and Colombia between 1535 and 1547. He wrote what is now considered the authoritative account between 1547 and 1550 and based much of his writing on first-hand accounts he transcribed from the Incas themselves.

Source: Piedro Cieza de Leon, *The Second Part of the Chronicle of Peru,* Clements R. Markham, trans. and ed. (London: The Hakluyt Society, 1883), pp. 36-38, 42.

It should be well understood that great prudence was needed to enable these kings to govern such large provinces, extending over so vast a region, parts of it rugged and covered with forests, parts mountainous, with snowy peaks and ridges, parts consisting of deserts of sand, dry and without trees or water. These regions were inhabited by many different nations, with varying languages, laws, and religions, and the kings had to maintain tranquillity and to rule so that all should live in peace and in friendship towards their lord. Although the city of Cuzco was the head of the empire, as we have remarked in many places, yet at certain points, as well shall also explain, the king stationed his delegates and governors, who were the most learned, the ablest, and the bravest men that could be found, and none was so youthful that he was not already in the last third part of his age. As they were faithful and none betrayed their trusts, and as they had the *mitimaes* on their side, none of the natives, though they might be more powerful, attempted to rise in rebellion; or if such a thing ever did take place, the town where the revolt broke out was punished, and the ringleaders were sent prisoners to Cuzco. . . .

. . . All men so feared the king, that they did not dare to speak evil even of his shadow. And this was not all. If any of the king's captains or servants went forth to visit a distant part of the empire on some business, the people came out on the road with presents to receive them, not daring, even if one came alone, to omit to comply with all his commands.

So great was the veneration that the people felt for their princes, throughout this vast region, that every district was as well regulated and governed as if the lord was actually present to chastise those who acted contrary to his rules. This fear arose from the known valour of the lords and their strict justice. It was felt to be certain that those who did evil would receive punishment without fail, and that neither prayers nor bribes would avert it. At the same time, the Incas always did good to those who were under their sway, and would not allow them to be ill-treated, nor that too much tribute should be exacted from them. Many who dwelt in a sterile country where they and their ancestors had lived with difficulty, found that through the orders of the Inca their lands were made fertile and abundant, the things being supplied which before were wanting. In other districts, where there was scarcity of clothing, owing to the people having no flocks, orders were given that cloth should be abundantly provided. In short, it will be understood that as these lords knew how to enforce service and the payment of tribute, so they provided for the maintenance of the people, and took care that they should want for nothing. Through these good works, and because the lord always gave women and rich gifts to his principal vassals, he gained so much on their affections that he was most fondly loved.

One of the things which I admired most, in contemplating and noting down the affairs of this kingdom, was to think how and in what manner they can have made such grand and admirable roads as we now see, and what a number of men would suffice for their construction, and with what tools and instruments they can have levelled the mountains and broken through the rocks to make them so broad and good as they are. For it seems to me that if the Emperor should desire to give orders for another royal road to be made, like that which goes from Quito to Cuzco, or the other from Cuzco to go to Chile, with all his power I believe that he could not get it done; nor could any force of men achieve such results unless there was also the perfect order by means of which the commands of the Incas were carried into execution. For if the road to be made was fifty leagues long, or one hundred or two hundred, and though the ground was of the most rugged character, it would be done with diligent care. But their roads were much longer, some of them extending for over one thousand one hundred leagues along such dizzy and frightful abysses that, looking down, the sight failed one. In some places, to secure the regular width, it was necessary to hew a path out of the living rock; all which was done with fire and their picks. In other places the ascents were so steep and high that steps had to be cut from below to enable the ascent to be made, with wider spaces at intervals for resting-places. In other parts there were great heaps of snow, which were more to be feared, and not at one spot only, but often recurring. Where these snows obstructed the way, and where there were forests of trees and loose clods of earth, the road was leveled and paved with stones when necessary.

CHAPTER 15

Europe in the Renaissance and Reformation

15.1

The Spark for the Reformation: Indulgences, Johann Tetzel

The medieval struggle for power between the popes and the Holy Roman emperors created longstanding tension between Italy and Germany. The bitter struggle between the Hohenstaufens and the popes, followed by the Babylonian Captivity, bred, in the Germans, a lasting suspicion of the Roman Catholic Church that bore fruit in the nationalism of the Reformation.

In the fifteenth century, various church councils attempted moderate reform, but repeated postponement of reform made the radical Reformation of the sixteenth century inevitable.

Although there were many causes of the Reformation, the immediate cause that sparked Luther into the position of a reformer was the sale of indulgences. Indulgences were remissions or exemptions of an individual's time in purgatory for the sins he had committed in life. The papacy could grant them because it could draw on the treasury of merit or pool of spiritual wealth left by Christ and extraordinarily good Christians over time. As with other Church practices, what was once used for spiritual purposes, such as rewarding acts of penitence or the Crusaders, was by the sixteenth century being "abused" for secular purposes, such as providing money for Church officers. This was apparently the case with the sale of indulgences. In 1517 Archbishop Albert of Mainz appointed Johann Tetzel (1465?-1519), a persuasive, popular Dominican friar to sell indulgences in Germany. Proceeds of the sale were to be split between Albert and the papacy. The following is an excerpt from a sermon on indulgences by Tetzel.

The idea of "buying one's way into heaven" was one corruption within the church that sparked Martin Luther to begin the Reformation.

SOURCE: James Harvey Robinson and Merrick Whitcomb, eds., "Period of the Early Reformation in Germany," in *Translations and Reprints from the Original Sources of European History,* vol. II, no. 6, ed. Department of History of the University of Pennsylvania (Philadelphia: University of Pennsylvania Press, 1898), pp. 4-5.

You may obtain letters of safe conduct from the vicar of our Lord Jesus Christ, by means of which you are able to liberate your soul from the hands of the enemy, and convey it by means of contrition and confession, safe and secure from all pains of Purgatory, into the happy kingdom. For know, that in these letters are stamped and engraven all the merits of Christ's passion there laid bare. Consider, that for each and every mortal sin it is necessary to undergo seven years of penitence after confession and contrition, either in this life or in Purgatory.

How many mortal sins are committed in a day, how many in a week, how many in a month, how many in a year, how many in the whole extent of life! They are well-nigh numberless, and those that commit them must needs suffer endless punishment in the burning pains of Purgatory.

But with these confessional letters you will be able at any time in life to obtain full indulgence for all penalties imposed upon you, in all cases except the four reserved to the Apostolic See. Thence throughout your whole life, whenever you wish to make confession, you may receive the same remission, except in cases reserved to the Pope, and afterwards, at the hour of death, a full indulgence as to all penalties and sins, and your share of all spiritual blessings that exist in the church militant and all its members.

Do you not know that when it is necessary for anyone to go to Rome, or undertake any other dangerous journey, he takes his money to a broker and gives a certain per cent—five or six or ten—in order that at Rome or elsewhere he may receive again his funds intact, by means of the letters of this same broker? Are you not willing, then, for the fourth part of a florin, to obtain these letters, by virtue of which you may bring, not your money, but your divine and immortal soul, safe and sound into the land of Paradise?

15.2

Ninety-five Theses, Martin Luther

Martin Luther, the leader of the Protestant Reformation, was born at Eisleben, Prussian Saxony, November 10, 1483. He studied jurisprudence at the University of Erfurt, where he later lectured on physics and ethics. In 1505 he entered the Augustinian monastery at Erfurt, two years later was ordained a priest, and in 1508 became a professor of philosophy at the University of Wittenberg.

The starting point of Luther's career as a reformer was his posting on the church door of Wittenberg the *Ninety-five Theses* on October 31, 1517. These formed a passionate statement of the true nature of penitence, and a protest against the sale of indulgences. In issuing the *Theses*, Luther expected the support of his ecclesiastical superiors. It was only after three years of controversy, during which he refused a summons to Rome, that he proceeded to publish those works that brought about his expulsion from the Church.

The year 1520 saw the publication of the three great documents which laid down the fundamental principles of the Reformation. In the "Address to the Christian Nobility of the German Nation," Luther attacked the corruptions of the Church and the abuses of its authority, and asserted the right of the layman to spiritual independence. In "Concerning Christian Liberty," he expounded the doctrine of justification by faith, and gave a complete presentation of his theological position. In the "Babylonish Captivity of the Church," he criticized the sacramental system, and set up the Scriptures as the supreme authority in religion.

In the midst of this activity came his formal excommunication and his renunciation of allegiance to the Pope. He was proscribed by the Emperor Charles V and taken into the protection of prison in Wartburg by the friendly Elector of Saxony, where he translated the New Testament into the German vernacular. The complete translation of the Bible, issued in 1534, marks the establishment of the modern literary language of Germany.

The rest of Luther's life was occupied with a vast amount of literary and controversial activity. He died at Eisleben, February 18, 1546.

Source: Martin Luther, *Ninety-five Theses* (New York: P. F. Collier, 1910), pp. 251-258.

Disputation of Dr. Martin Luther Concerning Penitence and Indulgences

In the desire and with the purpose of elucidating the truth, a disputation will be held on the underwritten propositions at Wittenberg, under the presidency of the Reverend Father Martin Luther, Monk of the Order of St. Augustine, Master of Arts and of Sacred Theology, and ordinary Reader of the same in that place. He therefore asks those who cannot be present and discuss the subject with us orally, to do so by letter in their absence. In the name of our Lord Jesus Christ. Amen.

1. Our Lord and Master Jesus Christ, in saying "Repent ye," etc., intended that the whole life of believers should be penitence.

2. This word cannot be understood of sacramental penance, that is, of the confession and satisfaction which are performed under the ministry of priests.

3. It does not, however, refer solely to inward penitence; nay such inward penitence is naught, unless it outwardly produces various mortifications of the flesh.

4. The penalty thus continues as long as the hatred of self—that is, true inward penitence—continues: namely, till our entrance into the kingdom of heaven.

5. The Pope has neither the will nor the power to remit any penalties, except those which he has imposed by his own authority, or by that of the canons.

6. The Pope has no power to remit any guilt, except by declaring and warranting it to have been remitted by God; or at most by remitting cases reserved for himself; in which cases, if his power were despised, guilt, would certainly remain.

7. God never remits any man's guilt, without at the same time subjecting him, humbled in all things, to the authority of his representative the priest.

8. The penitential canons are imposed only on the living, and no burden ought to be imposed on the dying, according to them.

9. Hence the Holy Spirit acting in the Pope does well for us, in that, in his decrees, he always makes exception of the article of death and of necessity.

10. Those priests act wrongly and unlearnedly, who, in the case of the dying, reserve the canonical penances for purgatory.

11. Those tares about changing of the canonical penalty into the penalty of purgatory seem surely to have been sown while the bishops were asleep.

12. Formerly the canonical penalties were imposed not after, but before absolution, as tests of true contrition.

13. The dying pay all penalties by death, and are already dead to the canon laws, and are by right relieved from them.

14. The imperfect soundness or charity of a dying person necessarily brings with it great fear; and the less it is, the greater the fear it brings.

15. This fear and horror is sufficient by itself, to say nothing of other things, to constitute the pains of purgatory, since it is very near to the horror of despair.

16. Hell, purgatory, and heaven appear to differ as despair, almost despair, and peace of mind differ.

17. With souls in purgatory it seems that it must needs be that, as horror diminishes, so charity increases.

18. Nor does it seem to be proved by any reasoning or any scriptures, that they are outside of the state of merit or of the increase of charity.

19. Nor does this appear to be proved, that they are sure and confident of their own blessedness, at least all of them, though we may be very sure of it.

20. Therefore the Pope, when he speaks of the plenary remission of all penalties, does not mean simply of all, but only of those imposed by himself.

21. Thus those preachers of indulgences are in error who say that, by the indulgences of the Pope, a man is loosed and saved from all punishment.

22. For in fact he remits to souls in purgatory no penalty which they would have had to pay in this life according to the canons.

23. If any entire remission of all penalties can be granted to any one, it is certain that it is granted to none but the most perfect—that is, to very few.

24. Hence the greater part of the people must needs be deceived by this indiscriminate and high-sounding promise of release from penalties.

25. Such power as the Pope has over purgatory in general, such has every bishop in his own diocese, and every curate in his own parish, in particular.

26. The Pope acts most rightly in granting remission to souls, not by the power of the keys (which is of no avail in this case), but by the way of suffrage.

27. They preach mad, who say that the soul flies out of purgatory as soon as the money thrown into the chest rattles.

28. It is certain that, when the money rattles in the chest, avarice and gain may be increased, but the suffrage of the Church depends on the will of God alone.

29. Who knows whether all the souls in purgatory desire to be redeemed from it, according to the story told of Saints Severinus and Paschal?

30. No man is sure of the reality of his own contrition, much less of the attainment of plenary remission.

31. Rare as is a true penitent, so rare is one who truly buys indulgences—that is to say, most rare.

32. Those who believe that, through letters of pardon, they are made sure of their own salvation, will be eternally damned along with their teachers.

33. We must especially beware of those who say that these pardons from the Pope are that inestimable gift of God by which man is reconciled to God.

34. For the grace conveyed by these pardons has respect only to the penalties of sacramental satisfaction, which are of human appointment.

35. They preach no Christian doctrine, who teach that contrition is not necessary for those who buy souls out of purgatory or buy confessional licences.

36. Every Christian who feels true compunction has of right plenary remission of pain and guilt, even without letters of pardon.

37. Every true Christian, whether living or dead, has a share in all the benefits of Christ and of the Church given him by God, even without letters of pardon.

38. The remission, however, imparted by the Pope is by no means to be despised, since it is, as I have said, a declaration of the Divine remission.

39. It is a most difficult thing, even for the most learned theologians, to exalt at the same time in the eyes of the people the ample effect of pardons and the necessity of true contrition.

40. True contrition seeks and loves punishment; while the ampleness of pardons relaxes it, and causes men to hate it, or at least gives occasion for them to do so.

41. Apostolical pardons ought to be proclaimed with caution, lest the people should falsely suppose that they are placed before other good works of charity.

42. Christians should be taught that it is not the mind of the Pope that the buying of pardons is to be in any way compared to works of mercy.

43. Christians should be taught that he who gives to a poor man, or lends to a needy man, does better than if he bought pardons.

44. Because, by a work of charity, charity increases and the man becomes better; while, by means of pardons, he does not become better, but only freer from punishment.

45. Christians should be taught that he who sees any one in need, and passing him by, gives money for pardons, is not purchasing for himself the indulgences of the Pope, but the anger of God.

46. Christians should be taught that, unless they have superfluous wealth, they are bound to keep what is necessary for the use of their own households, and by no means to lavish it on pardons.

47. Christians should be taught that, while they are free to buy pardons, they are not commanded to do so.

48. Christians should be taught that the Pope, in granting pardons, has both more need and more desire that devout prayer should be made for him, than that money should be readily paid.

49. Christians should be taught that the Pope's pardons are useful, if they do not put their trust in them; but most hurtful, if through them they lose the fear of God.

50. Christians should be taught that, if the Pope were acquainted with the exactions of the preachers of pardons, he would prefer that the Basilica of St. Peter should be burnt to ashes, than that it should be built up with the skin, flesh and bones of his sheep.

51. Christians should be taught that, as it would be the duty, so it would be the wish of the Pope, even to sell, if necessary, the Basilica of St. Peter, and to give of his own money to very many of those from whom the preachers of pardons extract money.

52. Vain is the hope of salvation through letters of pardon, even if a commissary—nay, the Pope himself—were to pledge his own soul for them.

53. They are enemies of Christ and of the Pope who, in order that pardons may be preached, condemn the word of God to utter silence in other churches.

54. Wrong is done to the word of God when, in the same sermon, an equal or longer time is spent on pardons than on it.

55. The mind of the Pope necessarily is, that if pardons, which are a very small matter, are celebrated with single bells, single processions, and single ceremonies, the Gospel, which is a very great matter, should be preached with a hundred bells, a hundred processions, and a hundred ceremonies.

56. The treasures of the Church, whence the Pope grants indulgences, are neither sufficiently named nor known among the people of Christ.

57. It is clear that they are at least not temporal treasures, for these are not so readily lavished, but only accumulated, by many of the preachers.

58. Nor are they the merits of Christ and of the saints, for these, independently of the Pope, are always working grace to the inner man, and the cross, death, and hell to the outer man.

59. St. Lawrence said that the treasures of the Church are the poor of the Church, but he spoke according to the use of the word in his time.

60. We are not speaking rashly when we say that the keys of the Church, bestowed through the merits of Christ, are that treasure.

61. For it is clear that the power of the Pope is alone sufficient for the remission of penalties and of reserved cases.

62. The true treasure of the Church is the Holy Gospel of the glory and grace of God.

63. This treasure, however, is deservedly most hateful, because it makes the first to be last.

64. While the treasure of indulgences is deservedly most acceptable, because it makes the last to be first.

65. Hence the treasures of the gospel are nets, wherewith of old they fished for the men of riches.

66. The treasures of indulgences are nets, wherewith they now fish for the riches of men.

67. Those indulgences, which the preachers loudly proclaim to be the greatest graces, are seen to be truly such as regards the promotion of gain.

68. Yet they are in reality in no degree to be compared to the grace of God and the piety of the cross.

69. Bishops and curates are bound to receive the commissaries of apostolical pardons with all reverence.

70. But they are still more bound to see to it with all their eyes, and take heed with all their ears, that these men do not preach their own dreams in place of the Pope's commission.

71. He who speaks against the truth of apostolical pardons, let him be anathema and accursed.

72. But he, on the other hand, who exerts himself against the wantonness and licence of speech of the preachers of pardons, let him be blessed.

73. As the Pope justly thunders against those who use any kind of contrivance to the injury of the traffic in pardons.

74. Much more is it his intention to thunder against those who, under the pretext of pardons, use contrivances to the injury of holy charity and of truth.

75. To think that Papal pardons have such power that they could absolve a man even if—by an impossibility—he had violated the Mother of God, is madness.

76. We affirm, on the contrary, that Papal pardons cannot take away even the least of venal sins, as regards its guilt.

77. The saying that, even if St. Peter were now Pope, he could grant no greater graces, is blasphemy against St. Peter and the Pope.

78. We affirm, on the contrary, that both he and any other Pope have greater graces to grant—namely, the Gospel, powers, gifts of healing, etc. (I Cor. xii. 9.)

79. To say that the cross set up among the insignia of the Papal arms is of equal power with the cross of Christ, is blasphemy.

80. Those bishops, curates, and theologians who allow such discourses to have currency among the people, will have to render an account.

81. This licence in the preaching of pardons makes it no easy thing, even for learned men, to protect the reverence due to the Pope against the calumnies, or, at all events, the keen questionings of the laity.

82. As for instance:—Why does not the Pope empty purgatory for the sake of most holy charity and of the supreme necessity of souls—this being the most just of all reasons—if he redeems an infinite number of souls for the sake of that most fatal thing, money, to be spent on building a basilica—this being a very slight reason?

83. Again: why do funeral masses and anniversary masses for the deceased continue, and why does not the Pope return, or permit the withdrawal of the funds bequeathed for this purpose, since it is a wrong to pray for those who are already redeemed?

84. Again: what is this new kindness of God and the Pope, in that, for money's sake, they permit an impious man and an enemy of God to redeem a pious soul which loves God, and yet do not redeem that same pious and beloved soul, out of free charity, on account of its own need?

85. Again: why is it that the penitential canons, long since abrogated and dead in themselves in very fact and not only by usage, are yet still redeemed with money, through the granting of indulgences, as if they were full of life?

86. Again: why does not the Pope, whose riches are at this day more ample than those of the wealthiest of the wealthy, build the one Basilica of St. Peter with his own money, rather than with that of poor believers?

87. Again: what does the Pope remit or impart to those who, through perfect contrition, have a right to plenary remission and participation?

88. Again: what greater good would the Church receive if the Pope, instead of once, as he does now, were to bestow these remissions and participations a hundred times a day on any one of the faithful?

89. Since it is the salvation of souls, rather than money, that the Pope seeks by his pardons, why does he suspend the letters and pardons granted long ago, since they are equally efficacious?

90. To repress these scruples and arguments of the laity by force alone, and not to solve them by giving reasons, is to expose the Church and the Pope to the ridicule of their enemies, and to make Christian men unhappy.

91. If, then, pardons were preached according to the spirit and mind of the Pope, all these questions would be resolved with ease—nay, would not exist.

92. Away, then, with all those prophets who say to the people of Christ, "Peace, peace," and there is no peace!

93. Blessed be all those prophets who say to the people of Christ, "The cross, the cross," and there is no cross!

94. Christians should be exhorted to strive to follow Christ their Head through pains, deaths, and hells,

95. And thus trust to enter heaven through many tribulations, rather than in the security of peace.

15.3

Condemnation of Peasant Revolt, Martin Luther

In 1524 a major peasant revolt broke out in Germany. Long-standing economic and social conflicts came to a head as peasants rose against their lords, the German princes. The peasants expected Luther to support them because he had so recently turned on the Church in the name of Christian liberty. Luther's concerns, however, were primarily spiritual; he did not intend to extend his challenge to papal authority to social and political authority. Hesitant at first, Luther clearly sided with the princes as the peasant revolt spread and became more serious. Luther lost much popular support, particularly among peasants, who turned instead to more radical groups like the Anabaptists. But Luther gained important political allies among the princes, who savagely put down the revolt. Lutheranism became cast as a movement that supported strong secular authority. The following is an excerpt from Luther's condemnation of the peasant revolt.

SOURCE: James Harvey Robinson, ed., *Readings in European History*, Vol. II (Boston: Ginn, 1904), pp. 106-108.

In my preceding pamphlet [on the "Twelve Articles"] I had no occasion to condemn the peasants, because they promised to yield to law and better instruction, as Christ also demands (Matt. Vii. I). But before I can turn around, they go out and appeal to force, in spite of their promises, and rob and pillage and act like mad dogs. From this it is quite apparent what they had in their false minds, and that what they put forth under the name of the gospel in the "Twelve Articles" was all vain pretense. In short, they practice mere devil's work, and it is the arch-devil himself who reigns at Mühlhausen, indulging in nothing but robbery, murder, and bloodshed; as Christ says of the devil in John viii. 44, "he was a murderer from the beginning." Since, therefore, those peasants and miserable wretches allow themselves to be led astray and act differently from what they declared, I likewise must write differently concerning them; and first bring their sins before their eyes, as God commands (Isa. lviii. I; Ezek. ii. 7), whether perchance some of them may come to their senses; and, further, I would instruct those in authority how to conduct themselves in this matter.

With threefold horrible sins against God and men have these peasants loaded themselves, for which they have deserved a manifold death of body and soul.

First, they have sworn to their true and gracious rulers to be submissive and obedient, in accord with God's command (Matt. xxii. 21), "Render therefore unto Caesar the things which are Caesar's," and (Rom. xiii. I), "Let every soul be subject unto the higher powers." But since they have deliberately and sacrilegiously abandoned their obedience, and in addition have dared to oppose their lords, they have thereby forfeited body and soul, as perfidious, perjured, lying, disobedient wretches and scoundrels are wont to do. Wherefore St. Paul judges them, saying (Rom. xiii. 2), "And they that resist shall receive to themselves damnation." The peasants will incur this sentence, sooner or later; for God wills that fidelity and allegiance shall be sacredly kept.

Second, they cause uproar and sacrilegiously rob and pillage monasteries and castles that do not belong to them, for which, like public highwaymen and murderers, they deserve the twofold death of body and soul. It is right and lawful to slay at the first opportunity a rebellious person, who is known as such, for he is already under God's and the emperor's ban. Every man is at once judge and executioner of a public rebel; just as, when a fire starts, he who can extinguish it first is the best fellow. Rebellion is not simply vile murder, but is like a great fire that kindles and devastates a country; it fills the land with murder and bloodshed, makes widows and orphans, and destroys everything, like the greatest calamity. Therefore, whosoever can, should smite, strangle, and stab, secretly or publicly, and should remember that there is nothing more poisonous, pernicious, and devilish than a rebellious man. Just as one must slay a mad dog, so, if you do not fight the rebels, they will fight you, and the whole country with you.

Third, they cloak their frightful and revolting sins with the gospel, call themselves Christian brethren, swear allegiance, and compel people to join them in such abominations. Thereby they become the greatest blasphemers and violators of God's holy name, and serve and honor the devil under the semblance of the gospel, so that they have ten times deserved death of body and soul, for never have I heard of uglier sins. And I believe also that the devil foresees the judgment day, that he undertakes such an unheard-of measure; as if he said, "It is the last and therefore it shall be the worst; I'll stir up the dregs and knock the very bottom out." May the Lord restrain him! Lo, how mighty a prince is the devil, how he holds the world in his hands and can put it to confusion: who else could so soon capture so many thousands of peasants, lead them astray, blind and deceive them, stir them to revolt, and make them the willing executioners of his malice. . . .

And should the peasants prevail (which God forbid!),—for all things are possible to God, and we know not but that he is preparing for the judgment day, which cannot be far distant, and may purpose to destroy, by means of the devil, all order and authority and throw the world into wild chaos,—yet surely they who are found, sword in hand, shall perish in the wreck with clear consciences, leaving to the devil the kingdom of this world and receiving instead the eternal kingdom. For we are come upon such strange times that a prince may more easily win heaven by the shedding of blood than others by prayers.

CHAPTER 16

Global Interaction

16.1

Journal (1492), Christopher Columbus

Christopher Columbus (1451-1506) initiated Spain's emergence as a dominant power in the Americas in the sixteenth century. Born in Genoa, Italy, he had seafaring experience before sailing west into the Atlantic for King Ferdinand II and Queen Isabella I.

Columbus envisioned a sea route to "the Indies" (Asia) by westward passage, although learned men and mathematicians had rejected that idea as impractical. Note that they thought it was impractical, not that the earth was flat. Despite the persistence of the popular myth, virtually every educated person in Europe in 1492 understood that the earth was round. He embarked from Europe on August 3, 1492 on the most important voyage in world history. On October 12, the lookout on the *Pinta* spotted the sandy Bahaman island that Columbus named San Salvador (now Watlings) and claimed for Spain. He believed he was off the China mainland.

He explored the coast of Cuba, crossed the Windward Passage to Hispaniola (Haiti), and kept notes on the Native Americans and the unknown flora and fauna. On his return, Spain gave him a hero's welcome and saluted him as a grandee of Spain.

During the 1992 quincentennial of Columbus' first voyage, a heated debate occurred over the place of Columbus in world history. Was he a hero for his exploits, or was he responsible for the "holocaust" which resulted in the deaths of millions of Native Americans?

The selection here is an excerpt from the journal Columbus kept during his voyage. Oddly, it is written in the third person. Most likely, the journal was copied from Columbus' original and the scribe referred to Columbus in the third person, e.g. "the Admiral."

Source: From The Journal of Christopher Columbus, translated by Clements R. Markham. Reprint of 1893 edition published by the Hakluyt Society.

Wednesday, 10th of October.

The people could endure no longer. They complained of the length of the voyage. But the Admiral cheered them up in the best way he could, giving them good hopes of the advantages they might gain from it. He added that, however much they might complain, he had to go to the Indies, and that he would go on until he found them, with the help of our Lord.

THURSDAY, 11TH OF OCTOBER.

They saw sandpipers, and a green reed near the ship. Those of the caravel *Pinta* saw a cane and a pole, and they took up another small pole which appeared to have been worked with iron; also another bit of cane, a land-plant, and a small board. The crew of the caravel *Niña* also saw signs of land, and a small branch covered with berries. Everyone breathed afresh and rejoiced at these signs.

After sunset the Admiral returned to his original west course. . . . As the caravel *Pinta* was a better sailer, and went ahead of the Admiral, she found the land, and made the signals ordered by the Admiral. The land was first seen by a sailor named Rodrigo de Triana. But the Admiral, at ten in the previous night, being on the castle of the poop, saw a light, though it was so uncertain that he could not affirm it was land. He called Pero Gutierrez, a gentleman of the King's bedchamber, and said that there seemed to be a light, and that he should look at it. He did so, and saw it. The Admiral said the same to Rodrigo Sanchez of Segovia, whom the King and Queen had sent with the fleet as inspector, but he could see nothing, because he was not in a place whence anything could be seen. After the Admiral had spoken he saw the light once or twice, and it was like a wax candle rising and falling. It seemed to few to be an indication of land; but the Admiral made certain that land was close. When they said the *Salve,* which all the sailors were accustomed to sing in their way, the Admiral asked and admonished the men to keep a good look-out on the forecastle, and to watch well for land; and to him who should first cry out that he saw land, he would give a silk doublet, besides the other rewards promised by the Sovereigns, which were 10,000 maravedis to him who should first see it. At two hours after midnight the land was sighted at a distance of two leagues. The vessels were hove to, waiting for daylight; and on Friday they arrived at a small island of the Lucayos, called in the language of the Indians, *Guanahani.* Presently they saw naked people. The Admiral went on shore in the armed boat, and Martin Alonso Pinzon, and Vicente Yañez, his brother, who was captain of the *Niña.* The Admiral took the royal standard, and the captains went with two banners of the green cross, which the Admiral took in all the ships as a sign, with an F and a Y and a crown over each letter, one on one side of the cross and the other on the other. Having landed, they saw trees very green, and much water, and fruits of diverse kinds. The Admiral called to the two captains, and to the others who leaped on shore, and to Rodrigo Escovedo, secretary of the whole fleet, and to Rodrigo Sanchez of Segovia, and said that they should bear faithful testimony that he, in presence of all, had taken, as he now took, possession of the said island for the King and for the Queen, his Lords making the declarations that are required, as is more largely set forth in the testimonies which were then made in writing.

Presently many inhabitants of the island assembled. What follows is in the actual words of the Admiral in his book of the first navigation and discovery of the Indies. "I," he says, "that we might form great friendship, for I knew that they were a people who could be more easily freed and converted to our holy faith by love than by force, gave to some of them red caps, and glass beads to put round their necks, and many other things of little value, which gave them great pleasure, and made them so much our friends that it was a marvel to see. They afterwards came to the ship's boats where we were, swimming and bringing us parrots, cotton threads in skeins, darts, and many other things; and we exchanged them for other things that we gave them, such as glass beads and small bells. In fine, they took all, and gave what they had with good will. It appeared to me to be a race of people very poor in everything. They go as naked as when their mothers bore them, and so do the women, although I did not see more than one young girl. All I saw were youths, none more than thirty years of age. They are very well made, with very handsome bodies, and very good countenances. Their hair is short and coarse, almost like the hairs of a horse's tail. They wear the hairs brought down to the eyebrows, except a few locks behind, which they wear long and never cut. They paint themselves black, and they are the colour of the Canarians, neither black nor white. Some paint themselves white, others red, and others of what colour they find. Some paint their faces, others the whole body, some only round the eyes, others only on the nose. They neither carry nor know anything of arms, for I showed them swords, and they took them by the blade and cut themselves through ignorance. They have no iron, their darts being wands without iron, some of them having a fish's tooth at the end, and others being pointed in various ways. They are all of fair stature and size, with good faces, and well made. I saw some with marks of wounds on their bodies, and I made signs to ask what it was, and they gave me to understand that people from other adjacent islands came with the intention of seizing them, and that they defended themselves. I believed, and still believe, that they come here from the mainland to take them prisoners. They should be good servants and intelligent, for I observed that they quickly took in what was said to them, and I believe that they would easily be made Christians, as it appeared to me that they had no religion. I, our Lord being pleased, will take hence, at the time of my departure, six natives for your Highnesses, that they may learn to speak. I saw no beast of any kind except parrots, on this island."

SATURDAY, 13TH OF OCTOBER.

"As soon as dawn broke many of these people came to the beach, all youths, as I have said, and all of good stature, a very handsome people. Their hair is not curly, but loose and coarse, like horse hair. In all the forehead is broad, more so than in any other people I have hitherto seen. Their eyes are very beautiful and not small, and themselves far from black, but the colour of the Canarians. Nor should anything else be expected, as this island is in a line east and west from the island of Hierro in the Canaries. Their legs are very straight, all in one line, and no belly, but very well formed. They came to the ship in small canoes, made out of the trunk of a tree like a long boat, and all of one piece, and wonderfully worked, considering the country. They are large, some of them holding 40 to 45 men, others smaller, and some only large enough to old one man. They are propelled with a paddle like a baker's shovel, and go at a marvelous rate. If the canoe capsizes they all promptly begin to swim, and to bale it out with calabashes that they take with them. They brought skeins of cotton thread, parrots, darts, and other small things which it would be tedious to recount, and they give all in exchange for anything that may be given to them. I was attentive, and took trouble to ascertain if there was gold. I saw that some of them had a small piece fastened in a hole they have in the nose, and by signs I was able to make out that to the south, or going from the island to the south, there was a king who had great cups full, and who possessed a great quantity. I tried to get them to go there, but afterwards I saw that they had no inclination. I resolved to wait until to-morrow in the afternoon and then to depart, shaping a course to the S.W., for, according to what many of them told me, there was land to the S., to the S.W., and N.W., and that the natives from the N.W. often came to attack them, and went on to the S.W. in search of gold and precious stones.

"This island is rather large and very flat, with bright green trees, much water, and a very large lake in the centre, without any mountain, and the whole land so green that it is a pleasure to look on it. The people are very docile, and for the longing to possess our things, and not having anything to give in return, they take what they can get, and presently swim away. Still, they give away all they have got, for whatever may be given to them, down to broken bits of crockery and glass. I saw one give 16 skeins of cotton for three *ceotis* of Portugal, equal to one *blanca* of Spain, the skeins being as much as an *arroba* of cotton thread. I shall keep it, and shall allow no one to take it, preserving it all for your Highnesses, for it may be obtained in abundance. It is grown in this island, though the short time did not admit of my ascertaining this for a certainty. Here also is found the gold they wear fastened in their noses. But, in order not lose time, I intend to go and see if I can find the island of Cipango. Now, as it is night, all the natives have gone on shore with their canoes."

"It is a very green island, level and very fertile, and I have no doubt that they sow and gather corn all the year round, as well as other things. I saw many trees very unlike those of our country. Many of them have their branches growing in different ways and all from one trunk, and one twig is one form, and another in a different shape, and so unlike that it is the greatest wonder in the world to see the great diversity; thus one branch has leaves like those of a cane, and others like those of a mastick tree: and on a single tree there are five or six different kinds. Nor are these grafted, for it may be said that grafting is unknown, the trees being wild, and untended by these people. They do not know any religion, and I believe they could easily be converted to Christianity, for they are very intelligent. Here the fish are so unlike ours that it is wonderful. Some are the shape of dories, and of the finest colours in the world, blue, yellow, red, and other tints, all painted in various ways, and the colours are so bright that there is not a man who would not be astonished, and would not take great delight in seeing them. There are also whales. I saw no beasts on the land of any kind, except parrots and lizards. A boy told me that he saw a large serpent. I saw neither sheep, nor goats, nor any other quadruped. It is true I have been here a short time, since noon, yet I could not have failed to see some if there had been any.

Sunday, 21st of October.

After breakfast I went on shore, and found only one house, in which there was no one, and I supposed they had fled from fear, because all their property was left in the house. I would not allow anything to be touched, but set out with the captains and people to explore this island. If the others already seen are very beautiful, green, and fertile, this is much more so, with large trees and very green. Here there are large lagoons with wonderful vegetation on their banks. Throughout the island all is green, and the herbage like April in Andalusia. The songs of the birds were so pleasant that it seemed as if a man could never wish to leave the place.

The flocks of parrots concealed the sun; and the birds were so numerous, and of so many different kinds, that it was wonderful. There are trees of a thousand sorts, and all have their several fruits; and I feel the most unhappy man in the world not to know them, for I am well assured that they are all valuable. I bring home specimens of them, and also of the land. Thus walking along round one of the lakes I saw a serpent, which we killed, and I bring home the skin for your Highnesses. As soon as it saw us it went into the lagoon, and we followed, as the water was not very deep, until we killed it with lances. It is 7 *palmos* long, and I believe that there are many like it in these lagoons. Here I came upon some aloes, and I have determined to take ten quintals on board to-morrow, for they tell me that they are worth a good deal. Also, while in search of good water, we came to a village about half a league from our anchorage. The people, as soon as they heard us, all fled and left their houses, hiding their property in the wood. I would not allow a thing to be touched, even the value of a pin. Presently some men among them came to us, and one came quite close. I gave him some bells and glass beads, which made him very content and happy. That our friendship might be further increased, I resolved to ask him for something; I requested him to get some water. After I had gone on board, the natives came to the beach with calabashes full of water, and they delighted much in giving it to us. I ordered another string of glass beads to be presented to them, and they said they would come again to-morrow. I wished to fill up all the ships with water at this place, and, if there should be time, I intended to search the island until I had had speech with the king, and seen whether he had the gold of which I had heard. I shall then shape a course for another much larger island, which I believe to be Cipango, judging from the signs made by the Indians I bring with me. They call it *Cuba,* and they say that there are ships and many skilful sailors there. Beyond this island there is another called *Bosio,* which they also say is very large, and others we shall see as we pass, lying between. According as I obtain tidings of gold or spices I shall settle what should be done. I am still resolved to go to the mainland and the city of Guisay, and to deliver the letters of your Highnesses to the Gran Can, requesting a reply and returning with it."

The Admiral says that, on the previous Sunday, the 11th of November, it seemed good to take some persons from amongst those at *Rio de Mares,* to bring to the Sovereigns, that they might learn our language, so as to be able to tell us what there is in their lands. Returning, they would be the mouthpieces of the Christians, and would adopt our customs and the things of the faith. "I saw and knew" (says the Admiral) "that these people are without any religion, not idolaters, but very gentle, not knowing what is evil, nor the sins of murder and theft, being without arms, and so timid that a hundred would fly before one Spaniard, although they joke with them. They, however, believe and know that there is a God in heaven, and say that we have come from heaven. At any prayer that we say, they repeat, and make the sign of the cross. Thus your Highnesses should resolve to make them Christians, for I believe that, if the work was begun, in a little time a multitude of nations would be converted to our faith, with the acquisition of great lordships, peoples, and riches for Spain. Without doubt, there is in these lands a vast quantity of gold, and the Indians I have on board do not speak without reason when they say that in these islands there are places where they dig out gold, and wear it on their necks, ears, arms, and legs, the rings being very large. There are also precious stones, pearls, and an infinity of spices. In this river of Mares, whence we departed to-night, there is undoubtedly a great quantity of mastick, and much more could be raised, because the trees may be planted, and will yield abundantly. The leaf and fruit are like the mastick, but the tree and leaf are larger. I ordered many of these trees to be tapped, to see if any of them would yield resin; but, as it rained all the time I was in that river, I could not get any, except a very little, which I am bringing to your Highnesses. It may not be the right season for tapping, which is, I believe, when the trees come forth after winter and begin to flower. But when I was there the fruit was nearly ripe. Here also there is a great quantity of cotton, and I believe it would have a good sale here without sending it to Spain, but to the great cities of the Gran Can, which will be discovered without doubt and many others ruled over by other lords, who will be pleased to serve your Highnesses, and whither will be brought other commodities of Spain and of the Eastern lands; but these are to the west as regards us. There is also here a great yield of aloes, though this is not a commodity that will yield great profit. The mastick, however, is important, for it is only obtained from the said island of Chios, and I believe the harvest is worth 50,000 ducats, if I remember right. There is here, in the mouth of the river, the best port I have seen up to this time, wide, deep, and clear of rocks. It is an excellent site for a town and fort, for any ship could come close up to the walls; the land is high, with a temperate climate, and very good water.

"Yesterday a canoe came alongside the ship, with six youths in it. Five came on board, and I ordered them to be detained. They are now here. I afterwards sent to a house on the western side of the river, and seized seven women, old and young, and three children. I did this because the men would behave better in Spain if they had women of their own land, than without them. For on many occasions the men of Guinea have been brought to learn the language in Portugal, and afterwards, when they returned, and it was expected that they would be useful in their land, owing to the good company they had enjoyed and the gifts they had received, they never appeared after arriving. Others may not act thus. But, having women, they have the wish to perform what they are required to do; besides, the women would teach our people their language, which is the same in all these islands, so that those who make voyages in their canoes are understood everywhere. On the other hand, there are a thousand different languages in Guinea, and one native does not understand another.

"The same night the husband of one of the women came alongside in a canoe, who was father of three children—one boy and two girls. He asked me to let him come with them, and besought me much. They are now all consoled at being with one who is a relation of them all. He is a man of about 45 years of age."

He met a canoe in the middle of the gulf, with a single Indian in it. The Admiral was surprised how he could have kept afloat with such a gale blowing. Both the Indian and his canoe were taken on board, and he was given glass beads, bells, and brass trinkets, and taken in the ship, until she was off a village 17 miles from the former anchorage, where the Admiral came to again. The village appeared to have been lately built, for all the houses were new. The Indian then went on shore in his canoe, bringing the news that the Admiral and his companions were good people; although the intelligence had already been conveyed to the village from the place where the natives had their interview with the six Spaniards. Presently more than five hundred natives with their king came to the shore opposite the ships, which were anchored very close to the land. Presently one by one, then many by many, came to the ship without bringing anything with them, except that some had a few grains of very fine gold in their ears and noses, which they readily gave away. The Admiral ordered them all to be well treated; and he says: "for they are the best people in the world, and the gentlest; and above all I entertain the hope in our Lord that your Highnesses will make them all Christians, and that they will be all your subjects, for as yours I hold them." He also saw that they all treated the king with respect, who was on the seashore. The Admiral sent him a present, which he received in great state. He was a youth of about 21 years of age, and he had with him an aged tutor, and other councillors who advised and answered him, but he uttered very few words. One of the Indians who had come in the Admiral's ship spoke to him, telling him how the Christians had come from heaven, and how they came in search of gold, and wished to find the island of *Baneque*. He said that it was well, and that there was much gold in the said island. He explained to the alguazil of the Admiral that the way they were going was the right way, and that in two days they would be there; adding, that if they wanted anything from the shore he would give it them with great pleasure. This king, and all the others, go naked as their mothers bore them, as do the women without any covering, and these were the most beautiful men and women that had yet been met with. They are fairly white, and if they were clothed and protected from the sun and air, they would be almost as fair as people in Spain. This land is cool, and the best that words can describe. It is very high, yet the top of the highest mountain could be ploughed with bullocks; and all is diversified with plains and valleys. In all Castille there is no land that can be compared with this for beauty and fertility. All this island, as well as the island of Tortuga, is cultivated like the plain of Cordova. They raise on these lands crops of yams, which are small branches, at the foot of which grow roots like carrots, which serve as bread. They powder and knead them, and make them into bread; then they plant the same branch in another part, which again sends out four or five of the same roots, which are very nutritious, with the taste of chesnuts. Here they have the largest the Admiral had seen in any part of the world, for he says that they have the same plant in Guinea. At this place they were as thick as a man's leg. All the people were stout and lusty, not thin, like the natives that had been seen before, and of a very pleasant manner, without religious belief. The trees were so luxuriant that the leaves left off being green. It was a wonderful thing to see those valleys, and rivers of sweet water, and the cultivated fields, and land fit for cattle, though they have none, for orchards, and for anything in the world that a man could seek for.

In the afternoon the king came on board the ship, where the Admiral received him in due form, and caused him to be told that the ships belonged to the Sovereigns of Castille, who were the greatest Princes in the world. But neither the Indians who were on board, who acted as interpreters, nor the king, believed a word of it. They maintained that the Spaniards came from heaven, and that the Sovereigns of Castille must be in heaven, and not in this world. They placed Spanish food before the king to eat, and he ate a mouthful, and gave the rest to his councillors and tutor, and to the rest who came with him.

"Your Highnesses may believe that these lands are so good and fertile, especially these of the island of Española, that there is no one who would know how to describe them, and no one who could believe if he had not seen them. And your Highnesses may believe that this island, and all the others, are as much yours as Castille. Here there is only wanting a settlement and the order to the people to do what is required. For I, with the force I have under me, which is not large, could march over all these islands without opposition. I have seen only three sailors land, without wishing to do harm, and a multitude of Indians fled before them. They have no arms, and are without warlike instincts; they all go naked, and are so timid that a thousand would not stand before three of our men. So that they are good to be ordered about, to work and sow, and do all that may be necessary, and to build towns, and they should be taught to go about clothed and to adopt our customs."

That Cacique showed that he was well disposed to the Admiral. Presently the canoe departed, and afterwards they said to the Admiral that there was more gold in Tortuga than in Española, because it is nearer to Baneque. The Admiral did not think that there were gold mines either in Española or Tortuga, but that the gold was brought from *Baneque* in small quantities, there being nothing to give in return. That land is so rich that there is no necessity to work much to sustain life, nor to clothe themselves, as they go naked. He believed that they were very near the source, and that our Lord would point out where the gold has its origin. He had information that from here to *Baneque* was four days' journey, about 34 leagues, which might be traversed with a fair wind in a single day.

Tuesday, 18th of December.

The Admiral remained at the same anchorage, because . . . the Cacique had said that he had sent for gold. The Admiral did not expect much from what might be brought, but he wanted to understand better whence it came. Presently he ordered the ship and caravel to be adorned with arms and dressed with flags, in honour of the feast of Santa Maria de la commemoration of the Annunciation, which was on that day, and many rounds were fired from the lombards. The king of that island of Española had got up very early and left his house, which is about five leagues away, reaching the village at three in the morning. There were several men from the ship in the village, who had been sent by the Admiral to see if any gold had arrived. They said that the king came with two hundred men; that he was carried in a litter by four men; and that he was a youth, as has already been said. To-day, when the Admiral was dining under the poop, the king came on board with all his people.

The Admiral says to the Sovereigns: "Without doubt, his state, and the reverence with which he is treated by all his people, would appear good to your Highnesses, though they all go naked. When he came on board, he found that I was dining at a table under the poop, and, at a quick walk, he came to sit down by me, and did not wish that I should give place by coming to receive him or rising from the table, but that I should go on with my dinner. I thought that he would like to eat of our viands, and ordered them to be brought for him to eat. When he came under the poop, he made signs with his hand that all the rest should remain outside, and so they did, with the greatest possible promptitude and reverence. They all sat on the deck, except the men of mature age, whom I believe to be his councillors and tutor, who came and sat at his feet. Of the viands which I put before him, he took of each as much as would serve to taste it, sending the rest to his people, who all partook of the dishes. The same thing in drinking: he just touched with his lips, giving the rest to his followers. They were all of fine presence and very few words. What they did say, so far as I could make out, was very clear and intelligent. The two at his feet watched his mouth, speaking to him and for him, and with much reverence. After dinner, an attendant brought a girdle, made like those of Castille, but of different material, which he took and gave to me, with pieces of worked gold, very thin. I believe they get very little here, but they say that they are very near the place where it is found, and where there is plenty. I saw that he was pleased with some drapery I had over my bed so I gave it him, with some very good amber beads I wore on my neck, some coloured shoes, and a bottle of orange-flower water. He was marvellously well content, and both he and his tutor and councillors were very sorry that they could not understand me, nor I them. However, I knew that they said that, if I wanted anything, the whole island was at my disposal. I sent for some beads of mine, with which, as a charm, I had a gold *excelente,* on which your Highnesses were stamped. I showed it to him, and said, as I had done yesterday, that your Highnesses ruled the best part of the world, and that there were no Princes so great. I also showed him the royal standards, and the others with a cross, of which he thought much. He said to his councillors what great lords your Highnesses must be to have sent me from so far, even from heaven to this country, without fear. Many other things passed between them which I did not understand, except that it was easy to see that they held everything to be very wonderful."

When . . . the king wanted to go, the Admiral sent him on shore in his boat very honourably, and saluted him with many guns. Having landed, he got into his litter, and departed with his 200 men, his son being carried behind on the shoulders of an Indian, a man highly respected. All the sailors and people from the ships were given to eat, and treated with much honour wherever they like to stop. One sailor said that he had stopped in the road and seen all the things given by the Admiral. A man carried each one before the king, and these men appeared to be among those who were most respected. His son came a good distance behind the king, with a similar number of attendants, and the same with a brother of the king, except that the brother went on foot, supported under the arms by two honoured attendants. This brother came to the ship after the king, and the Admiral presented him with some of the things used for barter. It was then that Admiral learnt that a king was called *Cacique* in their language. This day little gold was got by barter, but the Admiral heard from an old man that there were many neighbouring islands, at a distance of a hundred leagues or more, as he understood, in which much gold is found; and there is even one island that was all gold. In the others there was so much that it was said they gather it with sieves, and they fuse it and make bars, and work it in a thousand ways. They explained the work by signs. This old man pointed out to the Admiral the direction and position, and he determined to go there, saying that if the old man had not been a principal councillor of the king he would detain him, and make him go, too; or if he knew the language he would ask him, and he believed, as the old man was friendly with him and the other Christians, that he would go of his own accord. But as these people were now subjects of the King of Castille, and it would not be right to injure them, he decided upon leaving him. The Admiral set up a very large cross in the centre of the square of that village, the Indians giving much help; they made prayers and worshipped it, and, from the feeling they show, the Admiral trusted in our Lord that all the people of those islands would become Christians.

All the people went with them to the village, which they said was the largest, and the best laid out with streets, of any they had seen. The canoes go very fast with paddles; so they went ahead to apprise the *Cacique,* as they call the chief. They also have another greater name—

Nitayno; but it was not clear whether they used it for lord, or governor, or judge. At last the Cacique came to them, and joined them in the square, which was clean-swept, as was all the village. The population numbered over 2,000 men. This king did great honour to the people from the ship, and every inhabitant brought them something to eat and drink. Afterwards the king gave each of them cotton cloths such as women wear, with parrots for the Admiral, and some pieces of gold. The people also gave cloths and other things from their houses to the sailors; and as for the trifles they got in return, they seemed to look upon them as relics. When they wanted to return in the afternoon, he asked them to stay until the next day, and all the people did the same. When they saw that the Spaniards were determined to go, they accompanied them most the way, carrying the gifts of the Cacique on their backs as far as the boats, which had been left at the mouth of the river.

Monday, 24th of December.

Among the numerous Indians who had come to the ship yesterday, and had made signs that there was gold in the island, naming the places whence it was collected, the Admiral noticed one who seemed more fully informed, or who spoke with more willingness, so he asked him to come with the Christians and show them the position of the gold mines. This Indian has a companion or relation with him, and among other places they mentioned where gold was found, they named *Cipango,* which they called *Civao.* Here they said that there was a great quantity of gold, and that the Cacique carried banners of beaten gold. But they added that it was very far off to the eastward.

Here the Admiral addresses the following words to the Sovereigns: "Your Highnesses may believe that there is no better nor gentler people in the world. Your Highnesses ought to rejoice that they will soon become Christians, and that they will be taught the good customs of your kingdom. A better race there cannot be, and both the people and the lands are such quantity that I know the people and the lands are in such quantity that I know not how to write it. I have spoken in the superlative degree of the country and people of Juana, which they call Cuba, but there is as much difference between them and this island and people as between day and night. I believe that no one who should see them could say less than I have said, and I repeat that the things and the great villages of this island of Española, which they call *Bohio,* are wonderful. All here have a loving manner and gentle speech, unlike the others, who seem to be menacing when they speak. Both men and women are of good stature, and not black. It is true that they all paint, some with black, others with other colours, but most with red. I know that they are tanned by the sun, but this does not affect them much. Their houses and villages are pretty, each with a chief, who acts as their judge, and who is obeyed by them. All these lords use few words, and have excellent manners. Most of their orders are given by a sign with the hand, which is understood with surprising quickness."

Tuesday, 25th of December. Christmas.

"The king and all his people wept. They are a loving people, without covetousness, and fit for anything; and I assure your Highnesses that there is no better land nor people. They love their neighbours as themselves, and their speech is the sweetest and gentlest in the world, and always with a smile. Men and women go as naked as when their mothers bore them. Your Highnesses should believe that they have very good customs among themselves. The king is a man of remarkable presence, and with a certain self-contained manner that is a pleasure to see. They have good memories, wish to see everything, and ask the use of what they see.

WEDNESDAY, 26TH OF DECEMBER.

To-day, at sunrise, the king of that land came to the caravel *Niña,* where the Admiral was, and said to him, almost weeping, that he need not be sorry, for that he would give him all he had; that he had placed two large houses at the disposal of the Christians who were on shore, and that he would give more if they were required, and as many canoes as could load from the ship and discharge on shore, with as many people as were wanted. This had all been done yesterday, without so much as a needle being missed. "So honest are they," says the Admiral, "without any covetousness for the goods of others, and so above all was that virtuous king." While the Admiral was talking to him, another canoe arrived from a different place, bringing some pieces of gold, which the people in the canoe wanted to exchange for a hawk's bell; for there was nothing they desired more than these bells. They had scarely come alongside when they called and held up the gold, saying *Chuq chuq* for the bells, for they are quite mad about them. After the king had seen this, and when the canoes which came from other places had departed, he called the Admiral and asked him to give orders that one of the bells was to be kept for another day, when he would bring four pieces of gold the size of a man's hand. The Admiral rejoiced to hear this, and afterwards a sailor, who came from the shore, told him that it was wonderful what pieces of gold the men on shore were getting in exchange for next to nothing. For a needle they got a piece of gold worth two *castellanos,* and that this was nothing to what it would be within a month. The king rejoiced much when he saw that the Admiral was pleased. He understood that his friend wanted much gold, and he said, by signs, that he knew where there was, in the vicinity, a very large quantity; so that he must be in good heart, for he should have as much as he wanted. He gave some account of it, especially saying that in *Cipango,* which they call *Cibao,* it is so abundant that it is of no value, and that they will bring it, although there is also much more in the island of *Española,* which they call *Bohio,* and in the province of *Caritaba.* The king dined on board the caravel with the Admiral and afterwards went on shore, where he received the Admiral with much honour. He gave him a collation consisting of three or four kinds of yams, with shellfish and game, and other viands they have, besides the bread they call *cazavi.* He then took the Admiral to see some groves of trees near the houses, and they were accompanied by at least a thousand people, all naked. The Lord had on a shirt and a pair of gloves, given to him by the Admiral, and he was more delighted with the gloves than with anything else. In his manner of eating, both as regards the high-bred air and the peculiar cleanliness he clearly showed his nobility. After he had eaten, he remained some time at table, and they brought him certain herbs, with which he rubbed his hands. The Admiral thought that this was done to make them soft, and they also gave him water for his hands. After the meal he took the Admiral to the beach. The Admiral then sent for a Turkish bow and a quiver of arrows, and took a shot at a man of his company, who had been warned. The chief, who knew nothing about arms, as they neither have them nor use them, thought this a wonderful thing. He, however, began to talk of those of *Caniba,* whom they call *Caribes*. They come to capture the natives, and have bows and arrows without iron, of which there is no memory in any of these lands, nor of steel, nor any other metal except gold and copper. Of copper the Admiral had only seen very little. The Admiral said, by signs, that the Sovereigns of Castille would order the Caribs to be destroyed, and that all should be taken with their heads tied together. He ordered a lombard and a hand-gun to be fired off, and seeing the effect caused by its force and what the shots penetrated, the king was astonished. When his people heard the explosion they all fell on the ground. They brought the Admiral a large mask, which had pieces of gold for the eyes and ears and in other parts, and this they gave, with other trinkets of gold that the same king had put on the head and round the neck of the Admiral, and of other Christians, to whom they also gave many pieces. The Admiral received much pleasure and consolation from these things, which tempered the anxiety and sorrow he felt at the loss of the ship. He knew our Lord had caused the ship to stop here, that a settlement might be formed. "From this", he says, "originated so many things that, in truth, the disaster was really a piece of good fortune. For it is certain that, if I had not lost the ship, I should have gone on without anchoring in this place, which is within a great bay, having two or three reefs of rock. I should not have left people in the country during this voyage, nor even, if I had desired to leave them, should I have been able to obtain so much information, nor such supplies and provisions for a fortress. And true it is that many people had asked me to give them leave to remain. Now I have given orders for a tower and a fort, both well built, and a large cellar, not because I believe that such defences will be necessary. I believe that with the force I have with me I could subjugate the whole island, which I believe to be larger than Portugal, and the population double. But they are naked and without arms, and hopelessly timid. Still, it is advisable to build this tower, being so far from your Highnesses. The people may thus know the skill of the subjects of your Highnesses, and what they can do; and will obey them with love and fear. So they make preparations to build the fortress, with provision of bread and wine for more than a year, with seeds for sowing, the ship's boat, a caulker and carpenter, a gunner and cooper. Many among these men have a great desire to serve your Highnesses and to please me, by finding out where the mine is whence the gold is brought. Thus everything is got in readiness to begin the work. Above all, it was so calm that there was scarcely wind nor wave when the ship ran aground." This is what the Admiral says; and he adds more to show that it was great good luck, and the settled design of God, that the ship should be lost in order that people might be left behind. If it had not been for the treachery of the master and his boat's crew, who were all or mostly his countrymen, in neglecting to lay out the anchor so as to haul the ship off in obedience to the Admiral's orders, she would have been saved. In that case, the same knowledge of the land as has been gained in these days would not have been secured, for the Admiral always proceeded with the object of discovering, and never intended to stop more than a day at any one place, unless he was detained by the wind. Still, the ship was very heavy and unsuited for discovery. It was the people of Palos who obliged him to take such a ship, by not complying "with what they had promised to the King and Queen, namely, to supply suitable vessels for this expedition. This they did not do. Of all that there was on board the ship, not a needle, nor a board, nor a nail was lost, for she remained as whole as when she sailed, except that it was necessary to cut away and level down in order to get out the jars and merchandise, which were landed and carefully guarded." He trusted in God that, when he returned from Spain, according to his intention, he would find a ton of gold collected by barter by those he was to leave behind, and that they would found the mine, and spices in such quantities that the sovereigns would, in three years, be able to undertake and fit out an expedition to go and conquer the Holy Sepulchre. "Thus", he says, "I protest to your Highnesses that all the profits of this my enterprise may be spent in the conquest of Jerusalem. Your Highnesses may laugh, and say that it is pleasing to you, and that, without this, you entertain that desire."

THURSDAY, 27TH OF DECEMBER.

The king of that land came alongside the caravel at sunrise, and said that he had sent for gold, and that he would collect all he could before the Admiral departed; but he begged him not to go.

SUNDAY, 13TH OF JANUARY.

The Admiral . . . sent the boat on shore to a beautiful beach to obtain yams for food. They found some men with bows and arrows, with whom they stopped to speak, buying two bows and many arrows from them. They asked one of them to come on board the caravel and see the Admiral; who says that he was very wanting in reverence, more so than any native he had yet seen. His face was all stained with charcoal, but in all parts there is the custom of painting the body different colours. He wore his hair very long, brought together and fastened behind, and put into a small net of parrots' feathers. He was naked, like all the others. The Admiral supposed that he belong to the Caribs, who eat men, and that the gulf he had seen yesterday formed this part of the land into an island by itself. The Admiral asked about the Caribs, and he pointed to the east, near at hand, which means that he saw the Admiral yesterday before he entered the bay. The Indian said there was much gold to the east, pointing to the poop of the caravel, which was a good size, meaning that there were pieces as large. He called gold *tuob,* and did not understand *caona,* as they call it in the first part of the island that was visited, nor *nozay,* the name in San Salvador and the other islands. Copper is called *tuob* in Española. He also spoke of the island of *Goanin,* where there was much *tuob.* The Admiral says that he had received notices of these islands from many persons; that in the other islands the natives were in great fear of the *Caribs,* called by some of them *Caniba,* but in Española *Carib.* He thought they must be an audacious race, for they go to all these islands and eat the people they can capture. He understood a few words, and the Indians who were on board comprehended more, there being a difference in the languages owing to the great distance between the various islands. The Admiral ordered that the Indian should be fed, and given pieces of green and red cloth, and glass beads, which they like very much, and then sent on shore. He was told to bring gold if he had any, and it was believed that he had, from some small things he brought with him. When the boat reached the shore there were fifty-five men behind the trees, naked, and with very long hair, as the women wear it in Castille. Behind the head they wore plumes of feathers of parrots and other birds, and each man carried a bow. The Indian landed, and signed to the others to put down their bows and arrows, and a piece of a staff, which is like . . . ., very heavy, carried instead of a sword. As soon as they came to the boat the crew landed, and began to buy the bows and arrows and other arms, in accordance with an order of the Admiral. Having sold two bows, they did not want to give more, but began to attack the Spaniards, and to take hold of them. They were running back to pick up their bows and arrows where they had laid them aside, and took cords in their hands to bind the boat's crew. Seeing them rushing down, and being prepared—for the Admiral always warned them to be on their guard—the Spaniards attacked the Indians, and gave one a stab with a knife in the buttocks, wounding another in the breast with an arrow. Seeing that they could gain little, although the Christians were only seven and they numbered over fifty, they fled, so that none were left, throwing bows and arrows away. The Christians would have killed many, if the pilot, who was in command, had not prevented them. The Spaniards presently returned to the caravel with the boat. The Admiral regretted the affair for one reason, and was pleased for another. They would have fear of the Christians, and they were no doubt an ill-conditioned people, probably Caribs, who eat men. But the Admiral felt alarm lest they should do some harm to the 39 men left in the fortress and town of *Navidad,* in the event of their coming here in their boat. Even if they are not Caribs, they are a neighbouring people, with similar habits, and fearless, unlike the other inhabitants of the island, who are timid, and without arms. The Admiral says all this, and adds that he would have liked to have captured some of them. He says that they lighted many smoke signals, as is the custom in this island of Española.

MONDAY, 14TH OF JANUARY.

This evening the Admiral wished to find the houses of the Indians and to capture some of them, believing them to be Caribs. . . . Many Indians were seen on shore. The Admiral, therefore, ordered the boat to be sent on shore, with the crew well armed. Presently the Indians came to the stern of the boat, including the man who had been on board the day before, and had received presents from the Admiral. With him there came a king, who had given to the said Indian some beads in token of safety and peace for the boat's crew. This king, with three of his followers, went on board the boat and came to the caravel. The Admiral ordered them to be given biscuit and treacle to eat, and gave a chief a red cap, some beads, and a piece of red cloth. The others were also given pieces of cloth. The chief said that next day he would bring a mask made of gold, affirming that there was much here, and in *Carib* and *Matinino.* They afterwards went on shore well satisfied.

The Admiral here says that the caravels were making much water. . . . But, notwithstanding that the caravels were making much water, he trusted in the favour and mercy of our Lord, for his high Majesty well knew how much controversy there was before the expedition could be dispatched from Castille, that no one was in the Admiral's favour save Him alone who knew his heart, and after God came our Highnesses, while all others were against him without any reason. He further says: "And this has been the cause that the royal crown of your Highnesses has not a hundred *cuentos* of revenue more than after I entered your service, which is seven years ago in this very month, the 20th of January. The increase will take place from now onwards. For the almighty God will remedy all things."

TUESDAY, 15TH OF JANUARY.

The Admiral now wished to depart, for there was nothing to be gained by further delay, after these occurrences and the tumult with the Indians. To-day he had heard that all the gold was in the district of the town of *Navidad,* belonging to their Highnesses; and that in the island of *Carib* there was much copper, as well as in *Matinino.* The intercourse at *Carib* would, however, be difficult, because the natives are said to eat human flesh. Their island would be in sight from thence, and the Admiral determined to go there, as it was on the route, and thence to *Matinino,* which was said to be entirely peopled by women, without men. He would thus see both islands, and might take some of the natives. The Admiral sent the boat on shore, but the king of that district had not come, for his village was distant. He, however, sent his crown of gold, as he had promised; and many other natives came with cotton, and bread made from yams, all with their bows and arrows. After the bartering was finished, four youths came to the caravel. They appeared to the Admiral to give such a clear account of the islands to the eastward, on the same route as the Admiral would have to take, that he determined to take them to Castille with him. He says that they had no iron nor other metals; at least none was seen, but it was impossible to know much of the land in so short a time, owing to the difficulty with the language, which the Admiral could not understand except by guessing, nor could they know what was said to them, in such a few days. The bows of these people are as large as those of France or England. The arrows are similar to the darts of the natives who have been met with previously, which are made of young canes, which grow very straight, and a *vara* and a half of two *varas* in length. They point them with a piece of sharp wood, a *palmo* and a half long, and at the end some of them fix a fish's tooth, but most of them anoint it with an herb. They do not shoot as in other parts, but in a certain way which cannot do much harm. Here they have a great deal of fine and long cotton, and plenty of mastick. The bows appeared to be of yew, and there is gold and copper. There is also plenty of *aji,* which is their pepper, which is more valuable than pepper, and all the people eat nothing else, it being very wholesome. Fifty caravels might be annually loaded with it from Española. The Admiral says that he found a great deal of weed in this bay, the same as was met with at sea when he came on this discovery. He therefore supposed that there were islands to the eastward, in the direction of the position where he began to meet with it; for he considers it certain that this weed has its origin in shallow water near the land, and, if this is the case, these Indies must be very near the Canary Islands. For this reason he thought the distance must be less than 400 leagues.

WEDNESDAY, 16TH OF JANUARY.

There was a west wind, which was fair to go to the island of *Carib* on an E.N.E. course. This was where the people live of whom all the natives of the other islands are so frightened, because they roam over the sea in canoes without number, and eat the men.

THURSDAY, 14TH OF FEBRUARY.

This night the wind increased, and the waves were terrible, rising against each other, and so shaking and straining the vessel that she could make no headway, and was in danger of being stove in. . . . The Admiral ordered that a pilgrimage should be made to Our Lady of Guadaloupe, carrying a candle of 6 lbs. of weight in wax, and that all the crew should take an oath that the pilgrimage should be made by the man on whom the lot fell. As many beans were got as there were persons on board, and on one a cross was cut with a knife. They were then put into a cap and shaken up. The first who put in his hand was the Admiral, and he drew out the bean with a cross, so the lot fell on him; and he was bound to go on the pilgrimage and fulfil the vow. Another lot was drawn, to go on pilgrimage to Our Lady of Loreto, which is in the march of Ancona, in the Papal territory, a house where Our lady works many and great miracles. The lot fell on a sailor of the port of Santa Maria, named Pedro de Villa, and the Admiral promised to pay his travelling expenses. Another pilgrimage was agreed upon, to watch for one night in Santa Clara at Moguer, and have a Mass said, for which they again used the beans, including the one with a cross. The lot again fell on the Admiral. After this the Admiral and all the crew made a vow that, on arriving at the first land, they would all go in procession, in their shirts, to say their prayers in a church dedicated to Our Lady.

Besides these general vows made in common, each sailor made a special vow; for no one expected to escape, holding themselves for lost, owing to the fearful weather from which they were suffering. . . . On account of the favourable weather enjoyed among the islands, the Admiral had omitted to make provision for this need, thinking that ballast might be taken on board at the island inhabited by women, which he had intended to visit. The only thing to do was to fill the barrels that had contained wine or fresh water with water from the sea, and this supplied a remedy.

Admiral writes of the causes which made him fear that he would perish, and of others that gave him hope that God would work his salvation, in order that such news as he was bringing to the Sovereigns might not be lost. It seemed to him that the strong desire he felt to bring such great news, and to show that all he had said and offered to discover had turned out true, suggested the fear that he would not be able to do so, and that each stinging insect would be able to thwart and impede the work. He attributes this fear to his little faith, and to his want of confidence in Divine Providence. He was comforted, on the other hand, by the mercies of God in having vouchsafed him such a victory, in the discoveries he had made, and in that God had complied with all his desires in Castille, after much adversity and many misfortunes. As he had before put all his trust in God, who had heard him and granted all he sought, he ought now to believe that God would permit the completion of what had been begun, and ordain that he should be saved. Especially as he had freed him on the voyage out, when he had still greater reason to fear, from the trouble caused by the sailors and people of his company, who all with one voice declared their intention to return, and protested that they would rise against him. But the eternal God gave him force and valour to withstand them all, and in many other marvellous ways had God shown his will in this voyage besides those known to their Highnesses. Thus he ought not to fear the present tempest, though his weakness and anxiety prevent him from giving tranquillity to his mind. He says further that it gave him great sorrow to think of the two sons he had left at their studies in Cordova, who would be left orphans, without father or mother, in a strange land; while the Sovereigns would not know of the services he had performed in this voyage, nor would they receive the prosperous news which would move them to help the orphans. To remedy this, and that their Highnesses might know how our Lord had granted a victory in all that could be desired respecting the Indies, and that they might understand that there were no storms in those parts, which may be known by the herbs and trees which grow even within the sea; also that the Sovereigns might still have information, even if he perished in the storm, he took a parchment and wrote on it as good an account as he could of all he had discovered, entreating anyone who might pick it up to deliver it to the Sovereigns. He rolled this parchment up in waxed cloth, fastened it very securely, ordered a large wooden barrel to be brought, and put it inside, so that no one else knew what it was. They thought that it was some act of devotion, and so he ordered the barrel to be thrown into the sea. Afterwards, in the showers and squalls, the wind veered to the west, and they went before it, only with the foresail, in a very confused sea, for five hours. They made 2 1/2 leagues N.E. They had taken in the reefed mainsail, for fear some wave of the sea should carry all away.

Friday, 15th of February.

After sunrise they sighted land. . . . Some said it was the island of Madeira, others that it was the rock of Cintra, in Portugal, near Lisbon. . . . The Admiral found by his reckoning that he was close to the Azores.

At sunrise he steered S.S.W., and reached the island at night, but could not make out what island it was, owing to the thick weather.

Monday, 18th of February.

Yesterday, after sunset, the Admiral was sailing round the island, to see where he could anchor and open communications. He let go one anchor, which he presently lost, and then stood off and on all night. After sunrise he again reached the north side of the island, where he anchored, and sent the boat on shore. They had speech with the people, and found that it was the island of Santa Maria, one of the Azores. They pointed out the port to which the caravel should go. They said that they had never seen such stormy weather as there had been for the last fifteen days, and they wondered how the caravel could have escaped. They gave many thanks to God, and showed great joy at the news that the Admiral had discovered the Indies. The Admiral says that his navigation had been very certain, and that he had laid the discoveries down on the chart. Many thanks were due to our Lord, although there had been some delay. But he was sure that he was in the region of the Azores, and that this was one of them. He pretended to have gone over more ground, to mislead the pilots and mariners who pricked off the charts, in order that he might remain master of that route to the Indies, as, in fact, he did. For none of the others kept an accurate reckoning, so that no one but himself could be sure of the route to the Indies.

Tuesday, 19th of February.

After sunset three natives of the island came to the beach and hailed. The Admiral sent the boat, which returned with fowls and fresh bread. It was carnival time, and they brought other things which were sent by the captain of the island, named Juan de Castañeda, saying that he knew the Admiral very well, and that he did not come to see him because it was night, but that at dawn he would come with more refreshments, bringing with him three men of the boat's crew, whom he did not send back owing to the great pleasure he derived from hearing their account of the voyage. The Admiral ordered much respect to be shown to the messengers, and that they should be given beds to sleep in that night, because it was late, and the town was far off. As on the previous Thursday, when they were in the midst of the storm, they had made a vow to go in procession to a church of Our Lady as soon as they came to land, the Admiral arranged that half the crew should go to comply with their obligation to a small chapel, like a hermitage, near the shore; and that he would himself go afterwards with the rest. Believing that it was a peaceful land, and confiding in the offers of the captain of the island, and in the peace that existed between Spain and Portugal, he asked the three men to go to the town and arrange for a priest to come and say Mass. The half of the crew then went in their shirts, in compliance with their vow. While they were at their prayers, all the people of the town, horse and foot, with the captain at their head, came and took them all prisoners. The Admiral, suspecting nothing, was waiting for the boat to take him and the rest to accomplish the vow. At 11 o'clock, seeing that they did not come back, he feared that they had been detained, or that the boat had been swamped, all the island being surrounded by high rocks. He could not see what had taken place, because the hermitage was round a point. He got up the anchor, and made sail until he was in full view of the hermitage, and he saw many of the horsemen dismount and get into the boat with arms. They came to the caravel to seize the Admiral. The captain stood up in the boat, and asked for an assurance of safety from the Admiral, who replied that he granted it; but, what outrage was this, that he saw none of his people in the boat? The Admiral added that they might come on board, and that he would do all that might be proper. The Admiral tried, with fair words, to get hold of this captain, that he might recover his own people, not considering that he broke faith by giving him security, because he had offered peace and security, and had then broken his word. The captain, as he came with an evil intention, would not come on board. Seeing that he did not come alongside, the Admiral asked that he might be told the reason for the detention of his men, an act which would displease the King of Portugal, because the Portuguese received much honour in the territories of the King of Castille, and were as safe as if they were in Lisbon. He further said that the Sovereigns had given him letters of recommendation to all the Lords and Princes of the world, which he would show the captain if he would come on board; that he was the Admiral of the Ocean Sea, and Viceroy of the Indies, which belonged to their Highnesses, and that he would show the commissions signed with their signatures, and attested by their seals, which he held up from a distance. He added that his Sovereigns were in friendship and amity with the King of Portugal, and had ordered that all honour should be shown to ships that came from Portugal. Further, that if the captain did not surrender his people, he would still go on to Castille, as he had quite sufficient to navigate as far as Seville, in which case the captain and his followers would be severely punished for their offence. Then the captain and those with him replied that they did not know the King and Queen of Castille there, nor their letters, nor were they afraid of them, and they would give the Admiral to understand that this was Portugal, almost menacing him. On hearing this the Admiral was much moved, thinking that some cause of disagreement might have arisen between the two kingdoms during his absence, yet he could not endure that they should not be answered reasonably. Afterwards he turned to the captain, and said that he should go to the port with the caravel, and that all that had been done would be reported to the King his Lord. The Admiral made those who were in the caravel bear witness to what he said, calling to the captain and all the others, and promising that he would not leave the caravel until a hundred Portuguese had been taken to Castille, and all that island had been laid waste.

Thursday, 21st of February.

Yesterday the Admiral left that island of Santa Maria for that of San Miguel, to see if a port could be found to shelter his vessel from the bad weather. The Admiral knew the land, which was the rock of Cintra, near the river of Lisbon, and he resolved to run in because there was nothing else to be done. So terrible was the storm, that in the village of Cascaes, at the mouth of the river, the people were praying for the little vessel all that morning. After they were inside, the people came off, looking upon their escape as a miracle. At the third hour they passed Rastelo, within the river of Lisbon, where they were told that such a winter, with so many storms, had never before been known, and that 25 ships had been lost in Flanders, while others had been wind-bound in the river for four months. Presently the Admiral wrote to the King of Portugal, who was then at a distance of nine leagues, to state that the Sovereigns of Castille had ordered him to enter the ports of his Highness, and ask for what he required for payment, and requesting that the King would give permission for the caravel to come to Lisbon, because some ruffians, hearing that he had much gold on board, might attempt a robbery in an unfrequented port, knowing that they did not come from Guinea, but from the Indies.

Tuesday, 5th of March.

To-day the great ship of the King of Portugal was also at anchor off Rastelo, with the best provision of artillery and arms that the Admiral had ever seen. The master of her, named Bartolomé Diaz, of Lisbon, came in an armed boat to the caravel, and ordered the Admiral to get into the boat, to go and give an account of himself to the agents of the king and to the captain of that ship. The Admiral replied that he was the Admiral of the Sovereigns of Castille, and that he would not give an account to any such persons, nor would he leave the ship except by force, as he had not the power to resist. The master replied that he must then send the master of the caravel. The Admiral answered that neither the master nor any other person should go except by force, for if he allowed anyone to go, it would be as if he went himself; and that such was the custom of the Admirals of the Sovereigns of Castille, rather to die than to submit, or to let any of their people submit. The master then moderated his tone, and told the Admiral that if that was his determination he might do as he pleased. He, however, requested that he might be shown the letters of the Kings of Castille, if they were on board. The Admiral readily showed them, and the master returned to the ship and reported what had happened to the captain, named Alvaro Dama. That officer, making great festival with trumpets and drums, came to the caravel to visit the Admiral, and offered to do all that he might require.

Wednesday, 6th of March.

As soon as it was known that the Admiral came from the Indies, it was wonderful how many people came from Lisbon to see him and the Indians, giving thanks to our Lord, and saying that the heavenly Majesty had given all this to the Sovereigns of Castille as a reward for their faith and their great desire to serve God.

Thursday, 7th of March.

To-day an immense number of people came to the caravel, including many knights, and amongst them the agents of the king, and all gave infinite thanks to our Lord for so wide an increase of Christianity granted by our Lord to the Sovereigns of Castille; and they said that they received it because their Highnesses had worked and laboured for the increase of the religion of Christ.

Wednesday, 14th of March

[illegible]

Thursday, 15th of March

[illegible]

CHAPTER 17

Constitutionalism in Europe

17.1

The Divine Right of Kings, James I

James Stuart (James VI of Scotland, 1567-1625; James I of England, 1603-1625) was an intellectual who was rarely able to carry out his ideas. He had hoped to unify England, Scotland, and Ireland, but both political realities and his personal failings thwarted him. He sought to ease international tensions, but his efforts to prevent the conflict that would become the Thirty Years' War were unsuccessful. The outbreak of the Thirty Years' War also destroyed his hope of negotiating a European religious compromise. Besides his duties as monarch, James I wrote on a variety of topics. His most famous work, the *True Law of a Free Monarchy,* is a classic argument for divine-right monarchy. Interestingly, although James penned this work in 1598 before he assumed the throne of England, he never tried to set up divine-right rule in England. He believed that his power derived from God but acknowledged that as king of England, he had sworn oaths to govern according to the "laws and customs of England."

Source: The Political Works of James I (1616), intro. Charles Howard McIlwain (Cambridge, Mass.: Harvard University Press, 1918), 53-70.

The Trew Law of Free Monarchies: or the Reciprock and Mutuall Duetie Betwixt a Free King and His Naturall Subjects

As there is not a thing so necessarie to be knowne by the people of any land, next the knowledge of their God, as the right knowledge of their alleageance, according to the forme of governement established among them, especially in a Monarchie (which forme of government, as resembling the Divinitie, approacheth nearest to perfection, as all the learned and wise men from the beginning have agreed upon; Unitie being the perfection of all things,) So hath the ignorance, and (which is worse) the seduced opinion of the multitude blinded by them, who thinke themselves able to teach and instruct the ignorants, procured the wracke and overthrow of sundry flourishing Commonwealths; and heaped heavy calamities, threatening utter destruction upon others. And the smiling successe, that unlaw rebellions have oftentimes had against Princes in ages past (such hath bene the misery, and the iniquitie of the time) hath by way of practise strengthened many of their errour: albeit there cannot be a more deceivable argument; then to judge by the justnesse of the cause by the event thereof; as hereafter shall be proved more at length. And among others, no Common-wealth, that ever hath bene since the beginning, hath had greater need of the trew knowledge of this ground, then this our so long disordered, and distracted Common-wealth hath: the misknowledge hereof being the onely spring, from whence have flowed so many endlesse calamities, miseries, and confusions, as is better felt by many, then the cause thereof well knowne, and deepely considered. The naturall zeale therefore, that I beare to this my native countrie, with the great pittie I have to see the so-long disturbance thereof for lack of the trew knowledge of this ground (as I have said before) hath compelled me at last to breake silence, to discharge my conscience to you my deare country men herein, that knowing the ground from whence these your many endlesse troubles have proceeded, as well as ye have already too-long tasted the bitter fruites thereof, ye may by knowledge, and eschewing of the cause escape, and divert the lamentable effects that ever necessarily follow thereupon. I have chosen the onely to set downe in this short Treatise, the trew grounds of the mutuall deutie, and alleageance betwixt a free and absolute Monarche, and his people.

First then, I will set downe the trew grounds, whereupon I am to build, out of the Scriptures, since Monarchie is the trew paterne of Divinitie, as I have already said: next, from the fundamental Lawes of our own Kingdome, which nearest must concerne us: thirdly, from the law of Nature, by divers similitudes drawne out of the same.

By the Law of Nature the King becomes a naturall Father to all his Lieges at his Coronation: And as the Father of his fatherly duty is bound to care for the nourishing, education, and vertuous government of his children; even so is the king bound to care for all his subjects. As all the toile and paine that the father can take for his children, will be thought light and well bestowed by him, so that the effect thereof redound to their profite and weale; so ought the Prince to doe towards his people. As the kindly father ought to foresee all inconvenients and dangers that may arise towards his children, and though with the hazard of his owne person presse to prevent the same; so ought the King towards his people. As the fathers wrath and correction upon any of his children that offendeth, ought to be by a fatherly chastisement seasoned with pitie, as long as there is any hope of amendment in them; so ought the King towards any of his Lieges that offend in that measure. And shortly, as the Fathers chiefe joy ought to be in procuring his childrens welfare, rejoicing at their weale, sorrowing and pitying at their evil, to hazard for their safetie, travell for their rest, wake for their sleepe; and in a word, to thinke that his earthly felicitie and life standeth and liveth more in them, nor in himself; so ought a good Prince thinke of his people.

As to the other branch of this mutuall and reciprock band, is the duety and alleageance that the Lieges owe to their King: the ground whereof, I take out of the words of Samuel, dited by Gods Spirit, when God had given him commandement to heare the peoples voice in choosing and anointing them a King. And because that place of Scripture being well understood, is so pertinent for our purpose, I have insert herein the very words of the Text.

10. So Samuel tolde all the wordes of the Lord unto the people that asked a King of him.

11. And he said, this shall be the maner of the King that shall raigne over you: hee will take your sonnes, and appoint them to his Charets, and to be his horsemen, and some shall runne before his Charet.

12. Also, hee will make them his captaines over thousands, and captaines over fifties, and to eare his ground, and to reape his harvest, and to make instruments of warre and the things that serve for his charets.

13. Hee will also take your daughters, and make them Apothicaries, and Cookes, and Bakers.

14. And hee will take your fields, and your vineyards, and your best Olive trees, and give them to his servants.

15. And hee will take the tenth of your seed, and of your Vineyards, and give it to his Eunuches, and to his servants.

16. And hee will take your men servants, and your maid-servants, and the chief of your young men, and your asses, and put them to his worke.

17. Hee will take the tenth of your sheepe: and ye shall be his servants.

18. And ye shall cry out at that day, because of your King, whom ye have chosen you: and the Lord God will not heare you at that day.

19. But the people would not heare the voice of Samuel, but did say: Nay, but there shall be a King over us.

20. And we also will be all like other Nations, and our King shall judge us, and goe out before us, and fight out battles.

As likewise, although I have said, a good king will frame all his actions to be according to the Law; yet is hee not bound thereto but of his good will, and for good example—giving to his subjects: For as in the law of abstaining from eating of flesh in Lenton, the king will, for examples sake, make his owne house to observe the Law; yet no man will thinke he needs to take a licence to eate flesh. And although by our Lawes, the bearing and wearing of hag-buts, and pistolets be forbidden, yet no man can find any fault in the King, for causing his traine use them in any raide upon the Borderers, or other malefactours or rebellious subjects. So as I have already said, a good King, although hee be above the Law, will subject and frame his actions thereto, for examples sake to his subjects, and of his owne free-will, but not as subject or bound thereto.

And the agreement of the Law of nature in this our ground with the Lawes and constitutions of God, and man, already alleged, will by two similitudes easily appeare. The King towards his people is rightly compared to a father of children, and to a head of a body composed of divers members: For as fathers, the good Princes, and Magistrates of the people of God acknowledged themselves to their subjects. And for all other well ruled Common-wealths, the stile of Pater patriae was ever, and is commonly used to Kings. And the proper office of a King towards his Subjects, agrees very wel with the office of the head towards the body, and all members thereof: For from the head, being the seate of Judgement, proceedeth the care and foresight of guiding, and preventing all evill that may come to the body, so doeth the King for his people. As the discourse and direction flowes from the head, and the execution according thereunto belongs to the rest of the members, every one according to their office: so it is betwixt a wise Prince, and his people. As the judgement coming from the head may not onely imploy the members, every one in their owne office, as long as they are able for it; but likewise in case any of them be affected with any infirmitie must care and provide for their remedy, incase it be curable, and if otherwise, gar cut them off for feare of infecting of the rest: even so is it betwixt the Prince, and his people. And as there is ever hope of curing any diseased member of the direction of the head, as long as it is whole; but by contrary, if it be troubled, all the members are partakers of that paine, so is it betwixt the Prince and his people.

And now first for the fathers part (whose naturally love to his children I described in the first part of this my discourse, speaking of the dutie that Kings owe to their Subjects) consider, I pray you what duetie his children owe to him, & whether upon any pretext whatsoever, it wil not be thought monstrous and unnaturall to his sons, to rise up against him, to control him at their appetite, and when they thinke good to sley him, or to cut him off, and adopt to themselves any other they please in his roome: Or can any pretence of wickedness or rigor on his part be a just excuse for his children to put hand into him? And although wee see by the course of nature, that love useth to descend more than to ascend, in case it were trew, that the father hated and wronged the children never so much, will any man, endued with the least sponke of reason, thinke it lawful for them to meet him with the line? Yea, suppose the father were furiously following his sonnes with a drawen sword, is it lawful for them to turne and strike againe, or make any resistance but by flight? I thinke surely, if there were no more but the example of bruit beasts & unreasonable creatures, it may serve well enough to qualifie and prove this my argument. We reade often the pietie that the Storkes have to their olde and decayed parents: And generally wee know, that there are many sorts of beasts and fowles, that with violence and many bloody strokes will beat and banish their yong ones from them, how soone they perceive them to be able to fend themselves; but wee never read or heard of any resistance on their part, except among the vipers; which prooves such persons, as ought to be reasonable creatures, and yet unnaturally follow this example, to be endued with their viperous nature.

And it is here likewise to be noted, that the duty and alleageance, which the people sweareth to their prince, is not bound to themselves, but likewise to their lawfull heires and posterity, the lineall to their lawfull heires and posterity, the lineall succession of crowns being begun among the people of God, and happily continued in divers Christian commonwealths: So as no objection either of heresie, or whatsoever private statute or law may free the people from their oathgiving to their king, and his succession, established by the old fundamentall lawes of the kingdom: For, as hee is their heritable over-lord, and so by birth, not by any right in the coronation, commeth to his crowne; it is a like unlawful (the crowne ever standing full) to displace him that succeedeth thereto, as to eject the former: For at the very moment of the expiring of the king reigning, the nearest and lawful heire entreth in his place: And so to refuse him, or intrude another, is not to holde out uncomming in, but to expell and put out their righteous King. And I trust at this time whole France acknowledgeth the superstitious rebellion of the liguers, who upon pretence of heresie, by force of armes held so long out, to the great desolation of their whole country, their native and righteous king from possessing of his owne crowne and naturall kingdome.

Not that by all this former discourse of mine, and Apologie for kings, I meane that whatsoever errors and intollerable abominations a sovereigne prince commit, hee ought to escape all punishment, as if thereby the world were only ordained for kings, & they without controlment to turne it upside down at their pleasure: but by the contrary, by remitting them to God (who is their onely ordinary Judge) I remit them to the sorest and sharpest school-master that can be devised for them: for the further a king is preferred by God above all other ranks & degrees of men, and the higher that his seat is above theirs, the greater is his obligation to his maker. And therefore in case he forget himselfe (his unthankfulness being in the same measure of height) the sadder and sharper will be correction be; and according to the greatnes of the height he is in, the weight of his fall wil recompense the same: for the further that any person is obliged to God, his offence becomes and growes so much the greater, then it would be in any other. Joves thunderclaps light oftner and sorer upon the high & stately oaks, then on the low and supple willow trees: and the highest bench is sliddriest to sit upon. Neither is it ever heard that any king forgets himself towards God, or in his vocation; but God with the greatness of the plague revengeth the greatnes of his ingratitude: Neither thinke I by the force of argument of this my discourse so to perswade the people, that none will hereafter be raised up, and rebell against wicked Princes. But remitting to the justice and providence of God to stirre up such scourges as pleaseth him, for punishment of wicked kings (who made the very vermine and filthy dust of the earth to bridle the insolencie of proud Pharaoh) my onely purpose and intention in this treatise is to perswade, as farre as lieth in me, by these sure and infallible grounds, all such good Christian readers, as beare not onely the naked name of a Christian, but kith the fruites thereof in their daily forme of life, to keep their hearts and hands free from such monstrous and unnaturall rebellions, whensoever the wickednesse of a Prince shall procure the same at Gods hands: that, when it shall please God to cast such scourges of princes, and instruments of his fury in the fire, ye may stand up with cleane handes, and unspotted consciences, having prooved your selves in all your actions trew Christians toward God, and dutifull subjects towards your King, having remitted the judgement and punishment of all his wrongs to him, whom to onely of right it appertaineth.

But craving at God, and hoping that God shall continue his blessing with us, in not sending such fearefull desolation, I heartily wish our kings behaviour so to be, and continue among us, as our God in earth, and loving Father, endued with such properties as I described a King in the first part of this Treatise. And that ye (my deare countreymen, and charitable readers) may presse by all means to procure the prosperitie and welfare of your King; that as hee must on the one part thinke all his earthly felicitie and happiness grounded upon your weale, caring more for himselfe for your sake then for his owne, thinking himselfe onely ordained for your weale; such holy and happy emulation may arise betwixt him and you, as his care for your quietnes, and your care for his honor and preservation, may in all your actions daily strive together, that the Land may thinke themselves blessed with such a King, and the king may thinke himself most happy in ruling over so loving and obedient subjects.

17.2

English Bill of Rights (1689)

Because of the Glorious Revolution (1688), England's reigning Catholic monarch James II, who had angered his subjects by his infringements upon due process and constitutional liberties, and by favoring Catholics, was forced to flee to France, by his daughter Mary and her husband Prince William (III) of Orange. Parliament took advantage of this usurpation of the throne by agreeing to support and legitimize William and Mary's claims to the royal succession in return for their signature on the English Bill of Rights of 1689.

The English Bill of Rights asserted that James had abdicated and established William and Mary as monarchs. It forbade Roman Catholics from succeeding to the throne. Finally, it declared that the exercise of royal power, such as the maintenance of an army in peacetime, without the consent of Parliament was illegal. From that moment, Parliament became the dominant branch of government.

Four hundred seventy-four years after the Magna Charta, the English reasserted the idea that the King is under the law and, by now, subject to the will of Parliament. It also reflected the English commitment to the English Reformation of Henry VIII that established Protestantism as the official religion.

Source: From Readings in English History Drawn from the Original Sources by Edward P. Cheyney, Ginn & Company, 1908.

Whereas the said late King James II having abdicated the government, and the throne being thereby vacant, his Highness the prince of Orange (whom it hath pleased Almighty God to make the glorious instrument of delivering this kingdom from popery and arbitrary power) did (by the advice of the lords spiritual and temporal, and diverse principal persons of the Commons) cause letters to be written to the lords spiritual and temporal, being Protestants, and other letters to the several counties, cities, universities, boroughs, and Cinque Ports, for the choosing of such persons to represent them, as were of right to be sent to parliament, to meet and sit at Westminster upon the two-and-twentieth day of January, in this year 1689, in order to such an establishment as that their religion, laws, and liberties might not again be in danger of being subverted; upon which letters elections have been accordingly made.

And thereupon the said lords spiritual and temporal and Commons, pursuant to their respective letters and elections, being now assembled in a full and free representation of this nation, taking into their most serious consideration the best means for attaining the ends aforesaid, do in the first place (as their ancestors in like case have usually done), for the vindicating and asserting their ancient rights and liberties, declare:

1. That the pretended power of suspending laws, or the execution of laws, by regal authority, without consent of parliament, is illegal.
2. That the pretended power of dispensing with laws, or the execution of laws, by regal authority, as it hath been assumed and exercised of late, is illegal.
3. That the commission for erecting the late court of commissioners for ecclesiastical causes, and all other commissions and courts of like nature, are illegal and pernicious.
4. That levying money for or to the use of the crown by pretense of prerogative, without grant of parliament, for longer time or in other manner than the same is or shall be granted, is illegal.
5. That it is the right of the subjects to petition the king, and all commitments and prosecutions for such petitioning are illegal.
6. That the raising or keeping a standing army within the kingdom in time of peace, unless it be with consent of parliament, is against law.
7. That the subjects which are Protestants may have arms for their defense suitable to their conditions, and as allowed by law.
8. That election of members of parliament ought to be free.
9. That the freedom of speech, and debates or proceedings in parliament, ought not to be impeached or questioned in any court or place out of parliament.
10. That excessive bail ought not to be required, nor excessive fines imposed, nor cruel and unusual punishments inflicted.
11. That jurors ought to be duly impaneled and returned, and jurors which pass upon men in trials for high treason ought to be freeholders.
12. That all grants and promises of fines and forfeitures of particular persons before conviction are illegal and void.

And that for redress of all grievances, and for the amending, strengthening, and preserving of the laws, parliament ought to be held frequently. . . .

CHAPTER 18

New Western World-View

18.1

On Patriotism and Toleration, Voltaire

François Marie Arouet, known to the world by his pen name, Voltaire, was a *philosophe*, a leader of the French Enlightenment during his long life (1694-1778). He was critical of the *ancien régime* and an advocate of rational criteria. As a philosopher, wit, playwright, and cultural critic, he dedicated himself to confronting power and prejudice with skepticism and reason. Partly because of his biting wit, he was imprisoned in the Bastille and exiled from his native France to England and Prussia. After his return to France, however, Voltaire's country house near Switzerland attracted so many intellectuals from all over Europe that it became a kind of cultural capital of the continent.

Basic to the Enlightenment was the idea that people could use reason to overcome the bias and self-interest of their own region, nation, religion, group, or tribe and empathize with a larger group.

Source: From A Philosophical Dictionary by Voltaire, J.P. Mendum, 1852.

Patrie (Country)

A young journeyman pastry cook who had been to school, and who still knew a few of Cicero's phrases, boasted one day of loving his country. "What do you mean by your 'country'?" a neighbor asked him. "Is it your oven? Is it the village where you were born and which you have never seen since? Is it the street where dwelled your father and mother who have been ruined and have reduced you to baking little pies for a living? Is it the town hall where you will never be a police superintendent's clerk? Is it the Church of Our Lady where you have not been able to become a choirboy, while an absurd man is archbishop and duke with an income of twenty thousand golden louis?"

The journeyman pastry cook did not know what to answer. A thinker who was listening to this conversation, concluded that in a large country there were often many thousand men who had no country at all.

You, pleasure-loving Parisian, who have never made any great journey save that to Dieppe to eat fresh fish; who know nothing but your varnished town house, your pretty country house, and your box at that Opera where the rest of Europe persists in feeling bored; who speak your own language agreeably enough because you know no other, you love all that, and you love further the girls you keep, the champagne which comes to you from Rheims, the dividends which the Hôtel de Ville pays you every six months, and you say you love your country!

In all conscience, does a financier cordially love his country? The officer and the soldier who will pillage their winter quarters, if one lets them, have they a very warm love for the peasants they ruin? . . . Where was the country of Attila and of a hundred heroes of this type? I would like someone to tell me which was Abraham's country. The first man to write that the country is wherever one feels comfortable was, I believe, Euripides in his *Phaeton.* But the first man who left his birthplace to seek his comfort elsewhere had said it before him.

Where then is the country? Is it not a good field, whose owner, lodged in a well-kept house, can say: "This field that I till, this house that I have built, are mine; I live there protected by laws which no tyrant can infringe. When those who, like me, possess fields and houses, meet in their common interest, I have my voice in the assembly; I am a part of everything, a part of the community, a part of the dominion; there is my country"?

Well, now, is it better for your country to be a monarchy or a republic? For four thousand years has this question been debated. Ask the rich for an answer, they all prefer aristocracy; question the people, they want democracy; only kings prefer royalty. How then is it that nearly the whole world is governed by monarchs? . . . It is sad that often in order to be a good patriot one is the enemy of the rest of mankind. To be a good patriot is to wish that one's city may be enriched by trade, and be powerful by arms. It is clear that one country cannot gain without another losing, and that it cannot conquer without making misery. Such then is the human state that to wish for one's country's greatness is to wish harm to one's neighbors. He who should wish his country might never be greater, smaller, richer, poorer, would be the citizen of the world.

On Universal Tolerance

It does not require great art, or magnificently trained eloquence, to prove that Christians should tolerate each other. I, however, am going further: I say that we should regard all men as our brothers. What? The Turk my brother? The Chinaman my brother? The Jew? The Siam? Yes, without doubt; are we not all children of the same father and creatures of the same God?

But these people despise us; they treat us as idolaters! Very well! I will tell them that they are grievously wrong. It seems to me that I would at least astonish the proud, dogmatic Islam imam or Buddhist priest, if I spoke to them as follows:

"This little globe, which is but a point, rolls through space, as do many other globes; we are lost in the immensity of the universe. Man, only five feet high, is assuredly only a small thing in creation." One of these imperceptible beings says to another one of his neighbors, in Arabia or South Africa: "Listen to me, because God of all these worlds has enlightened me: there are nine hundred million little ants like us on the earth, but my ant-hole is the only one dear to God; all the others are cast off by Him for eternity; mine alone will be happy, and all the others will be eternally damned."

They would then interrupt me, and ask which fool blabbed all this nonsense. I would be obliged to answer, "You, yourselves."

TOLERATION

What is toleration? It is the endowment of humanity. We are all steeped in weaknesses and errors; let us forgive each other our follies; that is the first law of nature.

In the stock exchanges of Amsterdam, London, Surat, or Basra, the Gheber, the Banian, the Jew, the Mahometan, the Chinese Deist, the Brahmin, the Greek Christian, the Roman Christian, the Protestant Christian, the Quaker Christian, trade with one another: they don't raise their dagger against each other to gain souls for their religion. Why then have we butchered one another almost without interruption since the first Council of Nicaea?

Constantine began by issuing an edict which tolerated all religions; but he ended up by persecuting. Before him, people denounced the Christians only because they had started to build a party in the state. The Romans permitted all cults, even that of the Jews, even that of the Egyptians, although they had so much contempt for both. Why did Rome tolerate these cults? Because neither the Egyptians nor even the Jews tried to exterminate the ancient religion of the empire; they didn't cross land and sea to make proselytes, but thought only of making money. It is undeniable, however, that the Christians wanted their religion to be the dominant one. The Jews didn't want the statue of Jupiter in Jerusalem; but the Christians didn't want it in the capitol. St. Thomas was candid enough to confess that if the Christians hadn't dethroned the emperors, it was because they couldn't. It was their view that the whole world should be Christian. They were therefore necessarily the enemies of the whole world, until it was converted.

Among themselves, they battled each other over every controversial point. First of all, was it necessary to regard Jesus Christ as God? Those who denied it were anathematized under the name of Ebionites, who in turn anathematized the worshipers of Jesus.

When some of them wanted all goods to be held in common, as they supposedly were in the age of the apostles, their adversaries called them Nicolaites and accused them of the most infamous crimes. When others laid claim to mystical devotion, they were called Gnostics, and people attacked them furiously. When Marcion disputed over the Trinity, he was called an idolator.

Tertullian, Praxeas, Origen, Novatus, Novatian, Sabellius, Donatus, were all persecuted by their brethren before Constantine; and hardly had Constantine made the Christian religion prevail than the Athanasians and the Eusebians tore each other to pieces; and from that time on down to our day the Christian Church has been inundated in blood.

I admit the Jewish people was a pretty barbarous people. It butchered without pity all the inhabitants of an unfortunate little country to which it had no more right than it had to Paris and London. Still, when Naaman was cured of his leprosy by plunging seven times into the Jordan; when, to show his gratitude to Elisha, who had taught him this secret, he told him that he would worship the God of the Jews out of gratitude, he reserved to himself the liberty to worship the God of his king at the same time; he asked Elisha's permission to do so, and the prophet didn't hesitate to give it to him. The Jews worshiped their God; but they were never astonished that each nation should have its own. They thought it right that Chemosh gave a certain disrict to the Moabites, provided their God gave them one too. Jacob didn't hesitate to marry the daughters of an idolator. Laban had his God as Jacob had his. These are examples of toleration among the most intolerant and cruel nation of all antiquity: we have imitated it in its irrational frenzies and not in its leniency.

It is clear that every individual who persecutes a man, his brother, because he is not of his opinion, is a monster. There is no problem about that. But the government, the magistrates, the princes, how shall they deal with those who have a religion different from theirs? If they are powerful foreigners, it is certain that a prince will make an alliance with them. Francis I, Most Christian, allies himself with the Muslims against Charles the Fifth, Most Catholic. Francis I gives money to the Lutherans of Germany to support their rebellion against the emperor; but he begins by having the Lutherans in his own country burned, as is the practice. He pays them in Saxony for political reasons; he burns them in Paris for political reasons. But what will happen? The persecutions make proselytes; soon France is full of new Protestants. At first they allow themselves to be hanged, and afterward they do some hanging in their own turn. There are civil wars, then comes Saint Bartholomew, and this corner of the world is worse than anything the ancients and the moderns ever said about hell.

Maniacs, who have never been able to offer pure worship to the God who made you! Wretches, who could never learn from the example of the Noachides, the Chinese literati, the Parsis, and all the sages! Monsters, who need superstitions as the gizzard of a raven needs carrion! We have already told you, and there is nothing more to say: if there are two religions in your country, they will cut one another's throats; if there are thirty of them, they will live in peace. Look at the Grand Turk: He governs Ghebers, Banians, and Greek, Nestorian, Roman Christians. The first man who stirs up a tumult is impaled, and all is peaceful.

TOLÉRANCE • TOLERATION

Second Section

Of all religions, the Christian should of course inspire the most toleration, but till now the Christians have been the most intolerant of all men.

Because Jesus stooped to be born in poverty and humble estate, like his brothers, he never deigned to practice the art of writing. The Jews had a law written in the greatest detail, but we don't have a single line from the hand of Jesus. The apostles disagreed on a number of points. St. Peter and St. Barnabas ate forbidden meat with foreigners recently turned Christians. St. Paul reproached them for this conduct, and this very St. Paul—Pharisee, disciple of the Pharisee Gamaliel, the very St. Paul who had persecuted the Christians with fury, and who turned Christian himself after he broke with Gamaliel—nevertheless went afterward to sacrifice in the temple Jerusalem, in the temple of his apostolate. For a week he publicly observed all the ceremonies of the Judaic law, which he had renounced; he even performed supererogatory devotions and purifications; he Judaized completely. For a week the greatest apostle of the Christians did the very things for which men are condemned to the stake in most Christian nations.

Theodas and Judas had called themselves Messiahs before Jesus. Dositheus, Simon, Menander, called themselves Messiahs after Jesus. From the first century of the Church onward, and even before the name of Christian was known, there was a score of sects in Judaea.

The contemplative Gnostics, the Dositheans, the Corinthians, existed before the disciples of Jesus took the name of Christians. Soon there were thirty gospels, each of which belonged to a different society; and from the end of the first century we can count thirty sects of Christians in Asia Minor, Syria, Alexandria, and even Rome.

All these sects, despised by the Roman government and concealed in their obscurity, nevertheless persecuted each other in the tunnels in which they crept; that is, they insulted each other, for that was all they were able to do in their abjectness: they were almost wholly made up of the scum of the people.

When at last some Christians adopted the doctrines of Plato and mixed a little philosophy with their religion, they separated from the Jewish cult and gradually won some eminence. But they remained divided into sects; there was never a time when the Christian Church was united. It was born amid the divisions of the Jews—Samaritans, Pharisees, Sadducees, Essenes, Judaites, disciples of John, Therapeutes. It was divided in its cradle; it was even divided during the occasional persecutions it endured under the first emperors. Often the martyr was regarded as an apostate by his brethren, and the Carpocratian Christian expired under the sword of the Roman executioner, excommunicated by the Ebionite Christian, which Ebionite had been anathematized by the Sabellian.

The terrible dissension which has endured for so many centuries is a striking lesson teaching us mutually to forgive our errors; dissension is the great evil of mankind, and toleration is its only remedy.

There is nobody who doesn't agree with this truth, whether he meditates calmly in his study or amicably examines the truth with his friends. Why then do the very men who embrace, kindness, beneficence, and justice in private denounce these virtues in public with so much fury? Why? Because their self-interest is their god, because they sacrifice everything to the monster they worship.

I possess a dignity and power founded on ignorance and credulity; I tread on the heads of men prostrate at my feet: if they stand up and look me in the face, I am lost; therefore I must keep them bound to the ground with chains of iron.

Thus argue the men whom centuries of fanaticism have made powerful. They have other powerful men below them, and these have still others, who all enrich themselves at the expense of the poor, fatten on their blood, and laugh at their foolishness. They all detest toleration as political backers who have enriched themselves at the public's expense are afraid to give an accounting and as tyrants dread the word freedom. Then, to top it all off, they hire fanatics to shout in a great voice: "Respect the absurdities of my master, tremble, pay, and shut up."

This is how people have acted for a long time in a large part of the world; but today, when so many sects balance each other in power, how shall we choose among them? Every sect, as we know, is a certificate of error; there are no sects of geometers, algebraists, and arithmeticians because all the propositions of geometry, algebra, and arithmetic are true. In all other sciences men may make mistakes. What Thomist or Scotist theologian would dare to say seriously that he is sure of his facts?

If there is one sect that recalls the times of the first Christians, it is surely the Quakers. None resembles the apostles more closely. The apostles received the spirit, and the Quakers receive the spirit. The apostles and disciples spoke three or four at a time in the assembly on the third floor; the Quakers do the same on the ground floor. According to St. Paul women were allowed to preach, and according to the same St. Paul they were forbidden to; female Quakers preach by virtue of the first permission.

The apostles and disciples swore by Yes and No, the Quakers swear no differently.

No rank, no difference in attire among the disciples and the apostles; the Quakers have sleeves without buttons, and all dress in the same manner.

Jesus Christ did not baptize any of his apostles; the Quakers are not baptized.

It would be easy to push the parallel further; it would be even easier to see how the Christian religion of today differs from the religion Jesus practiced. Jesus was a Jew, and we are not Jews. Jesus abstained from pork because it was impure, and from rabbit because it ruminated and did not have a cloven foot; we boldly eat pork because for us it is not impure, and rabbit which has a cloven foot and doesn't ruminate.

Jesus was circumcised, and we retain our foreskin. Jesus ate the paschal lamb with lettuce, he celebrated the feast of the tabernacles, and we do neither. He observed the Sabbath, and we have changed it; he sacrificed, and we do not sacrifice.

Jesus always concealed the mystery of his incarnation and his rank; he did not say that he was equal to God; St. Paul says expressly in his Epistle to the Hebrews that God created Jesus lower than the angels; and despite all the words of St. Paul, Jesus was acknowledged to be God at the Council of Nicaea.

Jesus gave the pope neither the borderland of Ancona, nor the duchy of Spoleto; and yet the pope had them by divine right.

Jesus did not make a sacrament of marriage or of holy orders; and with us, holy orders and marriage are sacraments.

If we wish to study the matter closely: the Catholic, apostolic, and Roman religion is in all its ceremonies and dogmas the opposite of the religion of Jesus.

But really! Must we all Judaize because Jesus Judaized all his life?

If we were allowed to argue consistently in religious matters, it is clear that we should all turn Jews, because Jesus Christ our Saviour was born a Jew, lived as a Jew, and died as a Jew, and because he said expressly that he came to realize, to fulfill, the Jewish religion. But it is even clearer that we should all mutually tolerate each other, because we are all weak, inconsistent, a prey to change and error. Should a reed bowed into the mud by the wind say to the neighboring reed, bowed in the opposite direction: "Creep in my fashion, wretch, or I'll send in a request to have you uprooted and burned"?

18.2

The Social Contract (1762), Jean-Jacques Rousseau

Jean-Jacques Rousseau (1712-1778) was born in Geneva and raised by his unstable father. He became an important French political philosopher, educationist, and essayist. Alternately neglected and overprotected, Rousseau received little formal education and was largely self-taught. Eventually apprenticed to an engraver, he carried on a variety of menial occupations. He escaped from service and traveled throughout Europe before settling in Paris in 1741. He was taken up by the leaders of the salons, the fashionable meetings of the French intellectuals, where he came to know Diderot and the Encyclopedists. In 1754 he wrote *Discourse on the Origin of Inequality* (1755), emphasizing the natural goodness of human beings, and the corrupting influences of institutionalized life. Rousseau gained wide popularity for his writings on educational and social issues. Living in constant motion, fearing both his friends and his enemies, he finally settled down and married his longtime mistress. He moved to Luxembourg (1757), where he wrote his masterpiece, *The Social Contract* (1762). The same year he published his major work on education, *Emile*, in novel form. Its views on monarchy and governmental institutions forced him to flee to Switzerland, and then England, at the invitation of David Hume. There he wrote most of his *Confessions* (published posthumously in 1782). He returned to Paris in 1767, where he continued to write, but gradually became insane.

The *Social Contract* is Rousseau's most significant political work. Despite his own experiences, he had an optimistic view of human nature. He believed that people were essentially good, and that they formed governments to provide the greatest possible amount of personal freedom. His ideas were a great influence on the thought and reforms of the French Revolution, and he introduced the slogan "Liberty, Equality, Fraternity."

Source: From Contrat Social ou Principes Du Droit Politique by JJ Rousseau, translated by Theodore Kallman.

I suppose man arrived at a point where obstacles, which prejudice his preservation in the state of nature, outweigh, by their resistance, the force which each individual can employ to maintain himself in this condition. Then the primitive state can no longer exist; and mankind would perish did it not change its way of life.

Now, as men cannot engender new forces, but can only unite and direct those which exist, they have no other means of preservation than to form by aggregation a sum of forces which could prevail against resistance, and to put them in play by a single motive and make them act in concert.

This sum of forces can be established only by the concurrence of many; but the strength and liberty of each man being the primary instruments of his preservation, how can he pledge them without injury to himself and without neglecting the care which he owes to himself? This difficulty as related to my subject may be stated as follows: "To find a form of association which shall defend and protect with the public force the person and property of each associate, and by means of which each, uniting with all, shall obey however only himself, and remain as free as before." Such is the fundamental problem which the *Social Contract* gives the solution.

The clauses of this contract are so determined by the nature of the act, that the least modification would render them vain and of no effect; so that, although they may, perhaps never have been formally enunciated, they are everywhere the same, everywhere tacitly admitted and recognized until, the social compact being violated, each enters again into his first rights and resumes his natural liberty, thereby losing the conventional liberty which he renounced it.

These clauses, clearly understood, may be reduced to one; that is the total alienation of each associate with all his rights to the entire community, for, first, each giving himself entirely, the condition is the same for all, no one has an interest in making onerous for the others.

Further, the alienation being without reserve, the union is as complete as it can be, and no associate has anything to claim: for, if some rights remained to individuals, as there would be no common superior who could decide between them and the public, each, being in some points his own judge, would soon profess to be so in everything; the state of nature would exist, and the association would necessarily become tyrannical and useless.

Finally, each giving himself to all, gives himself to none; and as there is not an associate over whom he does not acquire the same right as is ceded, an equivalent is gained for all that is lost, and more force to keep what he has.

If, then, we remove from the social contract all that is not of its essence, it will be reduced to the following terms: "Each of us gives in common his person and all his force under the supreme direction of the general will; and we receive each member as an indivisible part of the whole."

Immediately, instead of the individual person of each contracting party, this act of association produces a moral and collective body, composed of as many members as the assembly has votes, which receives from this same act its unity—its common being, its life and its will. This public personage, thus formed by the union of all the others, formerly took the name of the city, and now takes that of republic or body politic. This is called the *state* by its members when it is passive; the *Sovereign* when it is active; and a *power* when comparing it to its equals. With regard to the associated, they take collectively the name *people,* and call themselves individually *citizens,* as participating in the sovereign authority, and *subjects,* as submitted to the laws of the state. But these terms are often confounded and are taken one for the other. It is enough to know how to distinguish them when they are employed with all precision.

Signs of a Good Government

When it is asked positively which is the best government, a question is asked which is unanswerable as it is indeterminate; or, if you will, it has as many good answers as there are continuations possible in the absolute and relative positions of peoples.

But if it be asked by what sign it may be known whether a given people is well or ill governed, it would be another thing, and the question of fact could be answered.

However, it is not answered because each wishes to answer it in his own way. Subjects vaunt public tranquility; citizens, individual liberty; one prefers the safety of property, and the other that of the person; one thinks that the best government is the most severe, the other maintains that it is the most gentle; this one wishes that crimes be punished, and that one that they be prevented; one finds it delightful to be feared by his neighbors, another prefers to be unknown to them: one is content when money circulates, another requires that the people have bread. Even were an agreement reached on these and similar points, would an advance be made? Moral qualities lacking exact measurements—if an agreement were reached as to the sign, how could it be reached as to the estimate to be put upon them?

As for me, I am always astonished that so simple a sign fails to be recognized, or that such bad faith prevails that it is not acknowledged. What is the *object* of political association? The preservation and prosperity of its members. And what is the surest sign that they are preserved and prospered? It is their number and population. Do not look elsewhere for this much disputed sign. Other things being equal, the government under which—without outside means, without naturalization, without colonies—the citizens increase and multiply most, is invariably the best. That under which a people diminishes and perishes is the worst. Statisticians, it is now your affair; count, measure, compare.

The General Will Is Indestructible

As long as men united together look upon themselves as a single body, they have but one will relating to the common preservation and general welfare. Then all the energies of the state are vigorous and simple; its maxims are clear and luminous; there are no mixed contradictory interests; the common prosperity shows itself everywhere, and requires only good sense to be appreciated. Peace, union, and equality are enemies of political subtleties. Upright, honest men are difficult to deceive, because of their simplicity; decoys and pretexts do not impose upon them, they are not cunning enough to be dupes. When we see among the happiest peoples of the world groups of peasants regulating the affairs of state under an oak, and conducting themselves wisely, can we help despising the refinements of other nations, who make themselves illustrious and miserable with so much art and mystery?

A state thus governed has need of few laws; and, in proportion as it becomes necessary to promulgate new ones this necessity will be universally recognized. The first to propose them will say only what they have already felt, and it requires neither intrigues nor eloquence to cause to become laws what each has already resolved upon, as soon as he can be sure that others will do likewise.

But when the social knot begins to relax, and the state to weaken, when individual interests commence to be felt, and small societies to influence the great, the common interest changes and finds opponents: unanimity no longer rules in the suffrages; the general will is no longer the will of all; contradictions and debates arise, and the best counsel does not prevail without dispute.

Finally, when the state, near its fall, exists only by a vain and illusory form; when the social tie is broken in all hearts; when the vilest interests flaunt boldly in the sacred name of the public welfare, then the general will becomes silent; all being guided by secret motives think no more like citizens than if the state had never existed. Iniquitous decrees are passed falsely under the name of the law, which have for object individual interests only.

Does it follow that the general will is annihilated or corrupted? No; it is always constant, inalterable, and pure; but it is subordinated to others which overbalance it. Each, in detaching his interest from the common interest, sees that he cannot separate it entirely; but his part of the public misfortune seems nothing to him compared to the exclusive good which he thinks he has appropriated to himself. This particular good excepted, he desires the general well-being for his own interest as strongly as any other. Even in selling his vote for money he has not extinguished in himself the general will—he eludes it.

The fault which he commits is in evading the question and answering something which has not been asked him; instead of saying by his vote, "It is advantageous to the state," he says, "It is advantageous to such a man or party that such or such counsel prevail." The law of public order in assemblies is not so much to maintain the general will there, as to see that it is always interrogated and always answers.

I should have here many reflections to make upon the simple right to vote upon each act of sovereignty, a right which nothing can take from citizens, and upon the right to think, to propose, to divide, to discuss, which the government has always taken great care to allow only to its members; but this important matter will require a separate treatise, and I cannot consider it fully here.

CHAPTER 19

Africa, 1400-1800

19.1

The Life of Olaudah Equiano, Olaudah Equiano

Surely, the most poignant account of the slave trade by a native African is that of Olaudah Equiano, as told by himself. Equiano was born in an Ibo village in 1745, where, at the age of eleven, African slave traders captured him. He spent ten years in Virginia and served in the British navy before he earned his freedom in 1766. Then, as a free man, he confronted challenges that would change the course of his life. While living in the Americas, Europe, and Africa he campaigned vigorously for the abolition of slavery until his death in 1797.

The following selection is from his well-written autobiography. The conditions of the slave trade in Africa varied, and enslaved individuals were forced to adjust to many changes. Equiano was one of about 50,000 Africans brought to the New World in 1756. In the Americas, the slave captain took him to Barbados to sell to sugar plantation owners. To Equiano's good fortune, he was not purchased there, probably because he was so young, for most slaves sold into Barbados during the eighteenth century died from the work. Consequently, he was sent to Virginia, where a tobacco planter bought him, and in 1757 an officer of the British navy purchased him. Serving on British warships until he was seventeen, he began to understand who he was and the world in which he found himself. He also learned to read and write English. This skill gave him the opportunity to succeed when a Quaker merchant purchased him and allowed him to buy his freedom in 1766.

Source: From The Life of Olaudah Equiano by Olaudah Equiano, Knapp, 1837.

That part of Africa, known by the name of Guinea, to which the trade for slaves is carried on, extends along the coast about 3400 miles, from Senegal to Angola, and includes a variety of kingdoms. Of these the most considerable is the kingdom of Benin, both as to extent and wealth, the richness and cultivation of the soil, the power of its king, and the number and warlike disposition of the inhabitants. It extends along the coast about 170 miles, but runs back into the interior part of Africa to a distance hitherto, I believe, unexplored by any traveler, and seems only terminated at length by the empire of Abyssinia, near 1500 miles from its beginning. This kingdom is divided into many provinces or districts, in one of the most remote and fertile of which, I was born, in the year 1745, situated in a charming fruitful vale, named Essaka. The distance of this province from the capital of Benin and the sea coast must be very considerable, for I had never heard of white men or Europeans, nor of the sea; and our subjection to the king of Benin was little more than nominal, for every transaction of the government, as far as my slender observation extended, was conducted by the chief or elders of the place. The manners and government of a people who have little commerce with other countries are generally very simple, and the history of what passes in one family or village may serve as a specimen of the whole nation. My father was one of those elders or chiefs I have spoken of, and was styled Embrenche, a term, as I remember, importing the highest distinction, and signifying in our language a *mark* of grandeur. This mark is conferred on the person entitled to it, by cutting the skin across at the top of the forehead, and drawing it down to the eyebrows; and while it is in this situation applying a warm hand, and rubbing it until it shrinks up into a thick *weal* across the lower part of the forehead. Most of the judges and senators were thus marked; my father had long borne it; I had seen it conferred on one of my brothers, and I also was *destined* to receive it by my parents. Those Embrenche, or chief men, decided disputes and punished crimes, for which purpose they always assembled together. The proceedings were generally short, and in most cases the law of retaliation prevailed.

We are almost a nation of dancers, musicians, and poets. Thus every great event, such as a triumphant return from battle or other cause of public rejoicing, is celebrated in public dances, which are accompanied with songs and music suited to the occasion. The assembly is separated into four divisions, which dance either apart or in succession, and each with a character peculiar to itself. The first division contains the married men, who in their dances frequently exhibit feats of arms and the representation of a battle. To these succeed the married women, who dance in the second division. The young men occupy the third, and the maidens the fourth. Each represents some interesting scene of real life, such as a great achievement, domestic employment, a pathetic story, or some rural sport; and as the subject is generally founded on some recent event, it is therefore ever new. This gives our dances a spirit and variety, which I have scarcely seen elsewhere. We have many musical instruments, particularly drums of different kinds, a piece of music which resembles a guitar, and another much like a stickado. These last are chiefly used by betrothed virgins, who play on them on all grand festivals.

As our manners are simple, our luxuries are few. The dress of both sexes is nearly the same. It generally consists of a long piece of calico, or muslin, wrapped loosely round the body, somewhat in the form of a highland plaid. This is usually dyed blue, which is our favorite color. It is extracted from a berry, and is brighter and richer than any I have seen in Europe. Besides this, our women of distinction wear golden ornaments, which they dispose with some profusion on their arms and legs. When our women are not employed with the men in tillage, their usual occupation is spinning and weaving cotton, which they afterwards dye, and make into garments. They also manufacture earthen vessels, of which we have many kinds. Among the rest, tobacco pipes, made after the same fashion, and used in the same manner, as those in Turkey.

Our manner of living is entirely plain; for as yet the natives are unacquainted with those refinements in cookery which debauch the taste; bullocks, goats, and poultry supply the greatest part of their food. (These constitute likewise the principal wealth of the country, and the chief articles of its commerce.) The flesh is usually stewed in a pan; to make it savory we sometimes use pepper, and other spices, and we have salt made of wood ashes. Our vegetables are mostly plantains, eadas, yams, beans, and Indian corn. The head of the family usually eats alone; his wives and slaves have also their separate tables. Before we taste food we always wash our hands; indeed, our cleanliness on all occasions is extreme, but on this it is an indispensable ceremony. After washing, libation is made, by pouring out a small portion of the drink on the floor, and tossing a small quantity of the food in a certain place, for the spirits of departed relations, which the natives suppose to preside over their conduct and guard them from evil. They are totally unacquainted with strong or spirituous liquors; and their principal beverage is palm wine. This is got from a tree of that name, by tapping it at the top and fastening a large gourd to it; and sometimes one tree will yield three or four gallons in a night. When just drawn it is of a most delicious sweetness; but in a few days it acquires a tartish and more spirituous flavor, though I never saw anyone intoxicated by it. The same tree also produces nuts and oil. Our principal luxury is in perfumes: one sort of these is an odoriferous wood of delicious fragrance, the other a kind of earth, a small portion of which thrown into the fire diffuses a most powerful odor. We beat this wood into powder, and mix it with palm oil, with which both men and women perfume themselves.

In our buildings we study convenience rather than ornament. Each master of a family has a large square piece of ground, surrounded with a moat or fence, or enclosed with a wall made of red earth tempered, which, when dry, is as hard as brick. Within this, are his houses to accommodate his family and slaves, which, if numerous, frequently present the appearance of a village. The last we esteemed a great rarity, as our waters were only brooks and springs. They barter with us for odoriferous woods and earth, and our salt of wood ashes. They always carry slaves through our land; but the strictest account is exacted of their manner of procuring them before they are suffered to pass. Sometimes, indeed, we sold slaves to them, but they were only prisoners of war, or such among us as had been convicted of kidnapping, or adultery, and some other crimes, which we esteemed heinous. This practice of kidnapping induces me to think, that, notwithstanding all our strictness, their principal business among us was to capture our people. I remember too, they carried great sacks along with them, which not long after, I had an opportunity of fatally seeing applied to that infamous purpose.

Our land is uncommonly rich and fruitful, and produces all kinds of vegetables in great abundance. We have plenty of Indian corn, and vast quantities of cotton and tobacco. Our pineapples grow without culture; they are about the size of the largest sugar-loaf, and finely flavored. We have also spices of different kinds, particularly pepper, and a variety of delicious fruits which I have never seen in Europe, together with gums of various kinds, and honey in abundance. All our industry is exerted to improve these blessings of nature. Agriculture is our chief employment; and everyone, even the children and women, are engaged in it. Thus we are all habituated to labor from our earliest years. Everyone contributes something to the common stock; and, as we are unacquainted with idleness, we have no beggars. The benefits of such a mode of living are obvious. The West India planters prefer the slaves of Benin or Eboe to those of any other part of Guinea, for their hardiness, intelligence, integrity, and zeal. Those benefits are felt by us in the general healthiness of the people, and in their vigor and activity; I might have added, too, in their comeliness. Deformity is indeed unknown amongst us, I mean that of shape. Numbers of the natives of Eboe now in London might be brought in support of this assertion: for, in regard to complexion, ideas of beauty are wholly relative. I remember while in Africa to have seen three Negro children who were tawny, and another quite white, who were universally regarded by myself, and the natives in general, as far as related to their complexions, as deformed. Our women, too, were, in my eye at least, uncommonly graceful, alert, and modest to a degree of bashfulness; nor do I remember to have heard of an instance of incontinence amongst them before marriage. They are also remarkably cheerful. Indeed, cheerfulness and affability are two of the leading characteristics of our nation.

Our tillage is exercised in a large plain or common, some hour's walk from our dwellings, and all the neighbors resort thither in a body. They use no beasts of husbandry; and their only instruments are hoes, axes, shovels, and beaks, or pointed iron, to dig with. Sometimes we are visited by locusts, which come in large clouds, so as to darken the air, and destroy our harvest. This, however, happens rarely, but when it does, a famine is produced by it. I remember an instance or two wherein this happened. This common is often the theatre of war; and therefore when our people go out to till their land, they not only go in a body, but generally take their arms with them for fear of a surprise; and when they apprehend an invasion, they guard the avenues to their dwellings, by driving sticks into the ground, which are so sharp at one end as to pierce the foot, and are generally dipt in poison. From what I can recollect of these battles, they appear to have been eruptions of one little state or district on the other, to obtain prisoners or booty. Perhaps they were incited to this by those traders who brought the European goods I mentioned, amongst us. Such a mode of obtaining slaves in Africa is common; and I believe more are procured this way, and by kidnapping, than any other. When a trader wants slaves, he applies to a chief for them, and tempts him with his wares. It is not extraordinary, if on this occasion he yields to the temptation with as little firmness, and accepts the price of his fellow creature's liberty, with as little reluctance as the enlightened merchant. Accordingly he falls on his neighbors, and a desperate battle ensues. If he prevails and takes prisoners, he gratifies his avarice by selling them; but, if his party be vanquished, and he falls into the hands of the enemy, he is put to death; for, as he has been known to foment their quarrels, it is thought dangerous to let him survive, and no ransom can save him, though all other prisoners may be redeemed. We have fire-arms, bows and arrows, broad two-edged swords and javelins; we have shields also which cover a man from head to foot. All are taught the use of these weapons; even our women are warriors, and march boldly out to fight along with the men. Our whole district is a kind of militia: on a certain signal given, such as the firing of a gun at night, they all rise in arms and rush upon their enemy. It is perhaps something remarkable, that when our people march to the field a red flag or banner is borne before them. I was once a witness to a battle in our common. We had been all at work in it one day as usual, when our people were suddenly attacked. I climbed a tree at some distance, from which I beheld the fight. There were many women as well as men on both sides; among others my mother was there, and armed with a broad sword. After fighting for a considerable time with great fury, and many had been killed, our people obtained the victory, and took their enemy's Chief a prisoner. He was carried off in great triumph, and, though he offered a large ransom for his life, he was put to death. A virgin of note among our enemies had been slain in the battle, and her arm was exposed in our marketplace, where our trophies were always exhibited. The spoils were divided according to the merit of the warriors. Those prisoners which were not sold or redeemed, we kept as slaves; but how different was their condition from that of the slaves in the West Indies! With us, they do no more work than other members of the community, even their master; their food, clothing, and lodging were nearly the same as theirs (except that they were not permitted to eat with those who were free-born); and there was scarce any other difference between them, than a superior degree of importance which the head of a family possesses in our state, and that authority which, as such, he exercises over every part of his household. Some of these slaves have even slaves under them as their own property, and for their own use.

As to religion, the natives believe that there is one Creator of all things, and that he lives in the sun, and is girted round with a belt; that he may never eat or drink, but, according to some, he smokes a pipe, which is our own favorite luxury. They believe he governs events, especially our deaths or captivity; but, as for the doctrine of eternity, I do not remember to have ever heard of it; some, however, believe in the transmigration of souls in a certain degree. Those spirits which were not transmigrated, such as their dear friends or relations, they believe always attend them, and guard them from the bad spirits or their foes. For this reason they always, before eating, as I have observed, put some small portion of the meat, and pour some of their drink, on the ground for them; and they often make oblations of the blood of beasts or fowls at their graves. I was very fond of my mother, and almost constantly with her. When she went to make these oblations at her mother's tomb, which was a kind of small solitary thatched house, I sometimes attended her. There she made her libations, and spent most of the night in cries and lamentations. I have been often extremely terrified on these occasions. The loneliness of the place, the darkness of the night, and the ceremony of libation, naturally awful and gloomy, were heightened by my mother's lamentations; and these concurring with the doleful cries of birds, by which these places were frequented, gave an inexpressible terror to the scene.

We compute the year, from the day on which the sun crosses the line, and on its setting that evening, there is a general shout throughout the land; at least, I can speak from my own knowledge, throughout our vicinity. The people at the same time make a great noise with rattles, not unlike the basket rattles used by children here, though much larger, and hold up their hands to heaven for a blessing. It is then the greatest offerings are made; and those children whom our wise men foretell will be fortunate are then presented to different people. I remember many used to come to see me, and I was carried about to others for that purpose. They have many offerings, particularly at full moons; generally two, at harvest, before the fruits are taken out of the ground; and when any young animals are killed, sometimes they offer up part of them as a sacrifice. These offerings, when made by one of the heads of a family, serve for the whole. I remember we often had them at my father's and my uncle's, and their families have been present. Some of our offerings are eaten with bitter herbs. We had a saying among us to anyone of a cross temper, "That if they were to be eaten, they should be eaten with bitter herbs."

We practiced circumcision like the Jews, and made offerings and feasts on that occasion, in the same manner as they did.

CHAPTER 20

Islamic World, 1450-1800

20.1

Turkish Letters (1589), Ogier Ghiselin de Busbecq

Suleiman I, known to Europeans as Suleiman the Magnificent, is remembered largely for his military conquests, but his accomplishments go beyond battlefield exploits. He was a patron of history and literature, oversaw the codification of Ottoman law (hence his honorific title *the Lawgiver*), and contributed to the architectural grandeur of Istanbul, the seat of Ottoman government. He was one of the outstanding rulers of the age.

The following observations of Suleiman and Ottoman society were recorded by Ogier Ghiselin de Busbecq (1522-1590), a Flemish nobleman who spent most of his life in the service of the Hapsburgs, in particular Ferdinand I, who was the archduke of Austria, king of Hungary and Bohemia, and, from 1558 to 1564, Holy Roman Emperor. In 1555 Ferdinand sent Busbecq to Suleiman's court in Istanbul to represent his interests in a dispute over the status of Transylvania, a region that had been part of Hungary, and is today part of Romania. After six years of discussions, the two sides agreed on a compromise by which Transylvania became an autonomous state in theory but paid an annual tribute to the sultan.

During his six years in Ottoman lands Busbecq recorded his observations and impressions and sent them in the form of four long letters to his friend Nicholas Michault. A Hapsburg diplomat himself, Michault was in a position to communicate some of Busbecq's views to high-ranking Hapsburg officials. All four letters were published in Paris in 1589. Subsequently appearing in numerous Latin versions and translated into the major European languages, Busbecq's letters provide a wealth of information about Ottoman society.

Source: From Ogier Ghiselin de Busbecq, London: Kegan Paul, 1881.

First Impressions

On our arrival . . . we were taken to call on Achmet Pasha (the chief Vizier) and the other pashas—for the Sultan himself was not then in the town—and commenced our negotiations with them touching the business entrusted to us by King Ferdinand. The pashas . . . told us that the whole matter depended on the Sultan's pleasure. On his arrival we were admitted to an audience; but the manner and spirit in which he . . . listened to our address, our arguments, and our message was by no means favorable. . . .

On entering we were separately conducted into the royal presence by the chamberlains, who grasped our arms. . . . After having gone through a pretense of kissing his [Suleiman's] hand, we were conducted backwards to the wall opposite his seat, care being taken that we should never turn our backs on him. The sultan then listened to what I had to say; but the language that I used was not at all to his taste, for the demands of Archduke Ferdinand breathed a spirit of independence and dignity, which was by no means acceptable to one who deemed that his wish was law; and so he made no answer beyond saying in an impatient way, "Giusel, giusel," i.e. well, well. After this we were dismissed to our quarters.

The Sultan's hall was crowded with people, among whom were several officers of high rank. Besides these were all the troopers of the Imperial guard, and a large force of Janissaries (slave soldiers), but there was not in all that great assembly a single man who owed his position to anything save his valor and his merit. No distinction is attached to birth among the Turks; the respect to be paid to a man is measured by the position he holds in the public service. There is no fighting for precedence; a man's place is marked out by the duties he discharges. . . . It is by merit that men rise in the service, a system which ensures that posts should only be assigned to the competent. . . . Those who receive the highest offices from the Sultan are for the most part the sons of shepherds or herdsmen, and so far from being ashamed of their parentage, they actually glory in it, and consider it a matter of boasting that they owe nothing to the accident of birth; for they do not believe that high qualities are either natural or hereditary, nor do they think that they can be handed down from father to son, but that they are partly the gift of God, and partly the result of good training, great industry, and unwearied zeal. . . . Among the Turks, therefore, honors, high posts, and judgeships are the rewards of great ability and good service.

Ottoman Military Strength

Against us stands Suleiman, that foe whom his own and his ancestors' exploits have made so terrible; he tramples the soil of Hungary with 200,000 horses, he is at the very gates of Austria, threatens the rest of Germany, and brings in his train all the nations that extend from our borders to those of Persia. The army he leads is equipped with the wealth of many kingdoms. Of the three regions, into which the world is divided (Asia, Europe, Africa), there is not one that does not contribute its share towards our destruction. . . .

The Turkish monarch going to war takes with him over 40,000 camels and nearly as many baggage mules, of which a great part, when he is invading Persia, are loaded with rice and other kinds of grain. These mules and camels also serve to carry tents and armor, and likewise tools and munitions for the campaign. The territories, which bear the name of Persia, . . . are less fertile than our country, and even such crops as they bear are laid waste by the inhabitants in time of invasion in hopes of starving out the enemy, so that it is very dangerous for an army to invade Persia if it is not furnished with abundant supplies. . . .

After dinner I practice the Turkish bow, in the use of which weapon people here are marvelously expert. From the eighth, or even the seventh, year of their age they begin to shoot at a mark, and practice archery ten or twelve years. This constant exercise strengthens the muscles of their arms, and gives them such skill that they can hit the smallest marks with their arrows. . . . So sure is their aim that in battle they can hit a man in the eye or in any other exposed part they choose.

No nation in the world has shown greater readiness than the Turks to avail themselves of the useful inventions of foreigners, as is proved by their employment of cannons and mortars, and many other things invented by Christians. . . . The Turks are much afraid of carbines and pistols, such as are used on horseback. The same, I hear, is the case with the Persians, on which account someone advised Rustem, when he was setting out with the Sultan on a campaign against them, to raise from his household servants a troop of 200 horsemen and arm them with firearms, as they would cause much alarm . . . in the ranks of the enemy. Rustem, in accordance with this advice, raised a troop of dragoons, furnished them with firearms, and had them drilled. But they had not completed half the journey when their guns began to get out of order. Every day some essential part of their weapons was lost or broken, and it was not often that armorers could be found capable of repairing them. So, a large part of their firearms having been rendered unserviceable, the men took a dislike to the weapon; and this prejudice was increased by the dirt which its use entailed, the Turks being a very cleanly people, for the dragoons had their hands and clothes begrimed with gunpowder, and moreover presented such a sorry appearance, with their ugly boxes and pouches hanging about them, that their comrades laughed at them and called them apothecaries. So, . . . they gathered around Rustem and showing him their broken and useless firearms, asked what advantage he hoped to gain from them when they met the enemy, and demanded that he should relieve them, and give them their old arms again. Rustem, after considering their request carefully, thought there was no reason for refusing to comply with it, and so they got permission to resume their bows and arrows.

Problems of the Succession

Suleiman had a son by a concubine who came from the Crimea. . . . His name was Mustafa, and at the time of which I am speaking he was young, vigorous, and of high repute as a soldier. But Suleiman had also several other children, by a Russian woman. . . . To the latter he was so much attached that he placed her in the position of wife. . . .

Mustafa's high qualities and matured years marked him out to the soldiers who loved him, and the people who supported him, as the successor of his father, who was now in the decline of life. On the other hand, his step-mother [Roxelana], by throwing the claim of a lawful wife onto the balance, was doing the utmost to counterbalance his personal merits and his rights as eldest son, with a view to obtaining the throne for her own children. In this intrigue, she received the advice and assistance of Rustem, whose fortunes were inseparably linked with hers by his marriage with a daughter she had by Suleiman. . . .

Inasmuch as Rustem was chief Vizier, . . . he had no difficulty . . . in influencing his master's mind. The Turks, accordingly, are convinced that it was by the calumnies of Rustem and the spells of Roxelana, who was in ill repute as a practitioner of sorcery, that the Sultan was so estranged from his son as to entertain the design of getting rid of him. A few believe that Mustafa, being aware of the plans, . . . decided to anticipate them, and thus engaged in designs against his father's throne and person. The sons of Turkish Sultans are in the most wretched position in the world, for, as soon as one of them succeeds his father, the rest are doomed to certain death. The Turk can endure no rival to the throne, and, indeed, the conduct of the Janissaries renders it impossible for the new Sultan to spare his brothers; for if one of them survives, the Janissaries are forever asking generous favors, If these are refused, the cry is heard, "Long live the brother!" "God preserve the brother!"—a tolerably broad hint that they intend to place him on the throne. So that the Turkish Sultans are compelled to celebrate their succession by staining their hands with the blood of their nearest relatives. . . .

Being at war with Shah Tahmasp, Shah of the Persians, he {Suleiman} had sent Rustem against him as commander-in-chief of his armies. Just as he was about to enter Persian territory, Rustem suddenly halted, and hurried off dispatches to Suleiman, informing them that affairs were in a very critical state; that treason was rife; . . . that the soldiers had been tampered with, and cared for no one but Mustafa; . . . and he must come at once if he wished to preserve his throne. Suleiman was seriously alarmed by these dispatches. He immediately hurried to the army, sent a letter to summon Mustafa to his presence, inviting him to clear himself of those crimes of which he was suspected. . . .

There was great uneasiness among the soldiers, when Mustafa arrived. . . . He was brought to his father's tent, and there everything betokened peace. . . . But there were in the tent certain mutes— . . . strong and sturdy fellows, who had been appointed as his executioners. As soon as he entered the inner tent, they threw themselves upon him, and endeavored to put the fatal noose around his neck. Mustafa, being a man of considerable strength, made a stout defense and fought—there being no doubt that if he escaped . . . and threw himself among the Janissaries, the news of this outrage on their beloved prince would cause such pity and indignation that they would not only protect him, but also proclaim him Sultan. Suleiman felt how critical the matter was, being only separated by the linen hangings of his tent from the stage on which this tragedy was being enacted. When he found that there was an unexpected delay in the execution of his scheme, he thrust out his head from the chamber of his tent, and glared on the mutes with fierce and threatening eyes; at the same time, with signs full of hideous meaning, he sternly rebuked their slackness. Hereon, the mutes, gaining fresh strength from the terror he inspired, threw Mustafa down, got the bowstring around his neck, and strangled him. Shortly afterwards they laid his body on a rug in front of the tent, that the Janissaries might see the man they had desired as their Sultan. . . .

Meanwhile, Roxelana, not content with removing Mustafa from her path, . . . did not consider that she and her children were free from danger, so long as his offspring survived. Some pretext, however, she thought necessary, in order to furnish a reason for the murder, but this was not hard to find. Information was brought to Suleiman that, whenever his grandson appeared in public, the boys of Ghemlik—where he was being educated—shouted out, "God save the Prince, and may he long survive his father:" and the meaning of these cries was to point him out as his grandsire's future successor, and his father's avenger. Moreover, he was bidden to remember that the Janissaries would be sure to support the son of Mustafa, so that the father's death had in no way secured the peace of the throne and realm. . . .

Suleiman was easily convinced by these arguments to sign the death-warrant of his grandson. He commissioned Ibrahim Pasha to go to the Ghemlik with all speed, and put the innocent child to death.

20.2

Akbarnama (1602), Abul Fazl

Only Ashoka, who ruled in the third century B.C.E. is as highly regarded as Akbar among India's rulers. Humayan, Akbar's father, was driven from India in 1540, and did not regain his kingdom until 1555. Shortly after returning, he died (1556). His thirteen-year-old son was now emperor. Akbar's mother and an advisor to his father assumed control for Akbar. They issued orders in his name, and trained him to become emperor.

Akbar had great charisma and became strong enough to forge an infrastructure and administrative system that supported the empire for a century. Religious and ethnic tolerance characterized his reign, but he exercised a firm hand over the bureaucracy. He may be the only Muslim ruler of India whose Hindu subjects not only respected but even loved him. A key to his success was his diplomacy. He married a Rajput princess, a Hindu, strengthening his standing with Hindus and bringing former foes, the Rajputs, into the political structure. He also suspended the jitza, a tax on non-Muslims. Akbar was "the real builder of the Mughal empire." Many Europeans visited his court and discussed philosophical and religious ideas with Akbar.

Abul Fazl, Akbar's close companion, kept conscientious accounts of Akbar's activities, including his philosophical and religious explorations. He meticulously recorded the details of his sovereign's practices and interests. When, in 1602, a supporter of Jahangir, Akbar's estranged son and successor, assassinated Abul Fazl, the emperor became despondent.

Abul Fazl recorded both personal and institutional features of Akbar's reign. His account is a laudatory history of the emperor's personality and exploits.

The *Akbarnama* also contains many descriptions of Indian society such as the following passage on Hinduism. Abul Fazl shared Akbar's tolerant religious views and tried to present Hinduism favorably to Muslims, many of whom opposed the religious freedom Akbar offered his Hindu subjects. More disturbing to Muslims was Akbar's interest not just in Hinduism but also Christianity, Jainism, and Zoroastrianism, all of which he drew upon to found a new religious cult, *Din Illahi,* or Divine Faith. Abul Fazl sought to lessen the concerns of Muslims that Hindus were guilty of two great sins against the majesty and oneness of God—idolatry (worship of idols) and polytheism (belief in many gods). He also explained the religious basis of the Hindu caste system, the rigid hierarchies of which were far removed from the Muslim belief in the equality of all believers before Allah.

Akbar's imperial harem was spectacular. At Fatehpur Sikri, a gigantic chess board was constructed. The ladies of the harem served as the chess pieces. Akbar and his royal guests would stand in a tower overlooking the court and direct the ladies where to move. Fatehpur Sikri still exists as a tourist attraction, as does the chess board.

SOURCE: In Abul Fazl, "The Ain-i-Akari," ed. and trans. by H. S. Jarrett. Calcutta, India: Baptist Mission Press, 1868-1894.

[Hindus] one and all believe in the unity of God, and as to the reverence they pay to images of stone and wood and the like, which simpletons regard as idolatry, it is not so. The writer of these has exhaustively discussed the object with many enlightened and upright men, and it became evident that these images . . . are fashioned as aids to fix the mind and keep the thoughts from wandering, while the worship of God alone is required as indispensable. In all their ceremonial observances and usage they ever implore the favor of the world-illumining sun and regard the pure essence of the Supreme Being as transcending the idea of power in operation.

Brahma . . . they hold to be the Creator; Vishnu, the Nourisher and Preserver: and Shiva, called also Mahadeva, the Destroyer. Some maintain that God who is without equal, manifested himself under these three divine forms, without thereby sullying the garment of His inviolate sanctity, as the Nazarenes hold of the Messiah. Others assert that these were human creatures exalted to these dignities through perfectness of worship, probity of thought and righteousness of deed. The godliness and self-discipline of this people is such as is rarely to be found in other lands.

They hold that the world had a beginning, and some are of the opinion that it will have an end. . . . They allow of no existence external to God. The world is a delusive appearance, and as a man in sleep sees fanciful shapes, and is affected by a thousand joys and sorrows, so are its seeming realities. . . .

Brahma is the Supreme Being; and is essential existence and wisdom and also bliss. . . .

Since according to their belief, the Supreme Deity can assume an elemental form without defiling the skirt of the robe of omnipotence, they first make the various idols of gold and other substances to represent the ideal and gradually withdrawing the mind from this material worship, they become meditatively absorbed in the ocean of His mysterious being. . . .

They believe that the Supreme Being in the wisdom of His counsel, assumes an elementary form of a special character for the good of the creation, and many of the wisest of the Hindus accept this doctrine. . . .

Caste

The Hindu philosophers reckon four states of auspiciousness which they term *varna.* 1. *Brahmin.* 2. *Kshatriya.* 3. *Vaisya.* 4. *Sudra.* Other than these are termed *Mlechchha* ("untouchables" or outcastes). At the creation of the world the first of these classes was produced from the mouth of Brahma . . . ; the second, from his arms; the third, from his thigh and the fourth from his feet; the fifth from the cow *Kamadhenu,* the name of Mlechchha being employed to designate them.

The *Brahmins* have six recognized duties: 1. The study of the Vedas and other sciences. 2. The instruction of others (in the sacred texts). 3. The performance of the *Jag,* that is oblation (a religious offering) of money and kind to the Devatas (deities). 4. Inciting others to the same. 5. Giving presents. 6. Receiving presents.

Of these six the *Kshatriya* must perform three. 1. Perusing the holy texts. 2. The performance of the Jag. 3. Giving presents. Further they must, 1. Minister to Brahmins. 2. Control the administration of worldly government and receive the reward thereof. 3. Protect religion. 4. Exact fines for delinquency and observe adequate measure therein. 5. Punish in proportion to the offense. 6. Amass wealth and duly expend it. 7. Supervise the management of elephants, horses, and cattle and the functions of ministerial subordination. 8. Levy war on due occasion. 9. Never ask for alms. 10. Favor the meritorious and the like.

The *Vaisya* also must perform the same three duties of the Brahmin, and, in addition, must occupy himself in: 1. Service. 2. Agriculture. 3. Trade. 4. The care of cattle. 5. The carrying of loads. . . .

The Sudra is incapable of any other privilege than to serve these three castes, wear their cast-off garments and eat their leavings. He may be a painter, goldsmith, blacksmith, carpenter, and trade in salt, honey, milk, butter-milk, clarified butter and grain.

Those of the fifth class, are reckoned as beyond the pale of religion, like infidels, Jews, and the like. By the intermarriages of these, sixteen other classes are formed. The son of Brahmin parents is acknowledged as a Brahmin. If the mother be a Kshatriya (the father being a Brahmin), the progeny is called *Murdhavasikta.* If the mother be a Vaisya, the son is named *Ambastha,* and if a Sudra girl, *Nishada.* If the father and mother are both Kshatriya, the progeny if Kshatriya. If the mother be a Brahmin (which is illicit), the progeny is *Vaideha* but if she be a Kshatriya, which also is regarded as improper, he is *Magadha.* From the Vaisya by a Sudra mother is produced a *Karana.* When both parents are Sudra, the progeny is Sudra. If the mother be a Brahmin, the progeny is *Chandala.* If she be a Kshatriya, it is called *Chatta.* From a Sudra by a Vaisya girl is produced the *Ayogava.*

In the same way still further ramifications are formed, each with different customs and modes of worship and each with infinite distinctions of habitation, profession, and rank of ancestry that defy computation. . . .

KARMA

. . . This is a system of knowledge of amazing and extraordinary character, in which the learned of Hindustan concur without dissenting opinion. It reveals the particular class of actions performed in a former birth which have occasioned the events that befall men in this present life, and prescribes the special expiation of each sin, one by one. It is of four kinds.

The first kind discloses the particular action which has brought a man into existence in one of the five classes into which mankind is divided, and the action which occasions the assumption of male or female form. A *Kshatriya* who lives continently will, in his next birth, be born a *Brahmin.* A *Vaisya* who hazards his transient life to protect a Brahmin, will become a *Kshatriya.* A *Sudra* who lends money without interest and does not defile his tongue by demanding repayment, will be born a *Vaisya.* A *Mlechchha* who serves a *Brahmin* and eats food from his house till his death, will become a *Sudra.* A *Brahmin* who undertakes the profession of a *Kshatriya* will become a *Kshatriya,* and thus a *Kshatriya* will become a *Vaisya,* and a *Vaisya* a *Sudra,* and a *Sudra* a *Mlechchha.* Whosoever accepts in alms . . . the bed on which a man has died (an unclean object) . . . will, in the next birth, from a man become a woman. Any woman or *Mlechchha,* who in the temple . . . sees the form of *Narayana,* and worships him with certain incantations, will in the next birth, if a woman, become a man, and if a *Mlechchha,* a *Brahmin.* . . .

The second kind shows the strange effects of actions on health of body and in the production of manifold diseases.

Madness is the punishment of disobedience to father and mother.

Pain in the eyes arises from having looked upon another's wife. . . .

Dumbness is the consequence of killing a sister. . . .

Colic results from having eaten with an imperious person or a liar. . . .

Consumption is the punishment of killing a *Brahmin*. . . .

The third kind indicates the class for actions which have caused sterility and names suitable remedies. . . .

A woman who does not menstruate, in a former existence . . . roughly drove away the children of her neighbors who had come as usual to play at her house. . . .

A woman who gives birth to only daughters is thus punished for having contemptuously regarded her husband from pride. . . .

A woman who has given birth to a son that dies and a daughter that lives, has, in her former existence, taken animal life. Some say that she had killed goats. . . .

The fourth kind treats of riches and poverty, and the like. Whoever distributes alms at auspicious times, as during eclipses of the moon and sun, will become rich and bountiful (in his next existence). Whoso at the times, visits any place of pilgrimage . . . and there dies, will possess great wealth, but will be avaricious and of a surly disposition. Whosoever when hungry and with food before him, hears the supplication of a poor man and bestows it all upon him, will be rich and {generous}.

The Imperial Harem

His majesty is a great friend of good order and propriety in business. Through order, the world becomes a meadow of truth and reality; and that which is but external, receives through it a spiritual meaning. For this reason, the large number of women—a vexatious question even for a great statesman—furnished his Majesty with an opportunity to display his wisdom, and to rise from the low level of worldly dependence to the eminence of perfect freedom. The imperial palace and household are therefore in the best order.

His Majesty forms matrimonial alliances with princes of Hindustan, and of other countries; and secures by these ties of harmony the peace of the world.

As the sovereign, by the light of his wisdom, has raised fit persons from the dust of obscurity, and appointed them to various offices, so does he also elevate faithful persons to the several ranks in the service of the seraglio. Short-sighted men think of impure gold, which will gradually turn into pure gold; but the far-sighted know that his Majesty understands how to use elixirs and chemical processes. Any kind of growth will alter the constitution of a body; copper and iron will turn to gold, and tin and lead to silver; hence it is no matter of astonishment if an excellent being changes the worthless into men. "The saying of the wise is true that the eye of the exalted is the elixir for producing goodness." Such also are the results flowing from the love of order of his Majesty, from his wisdom, insight, regard to rank, his respect for others, his activity, his patience. Even when he is angry, he does not deviate from the right path; he looks at everything with kindly feelings, weighs rumors well, and is free from all prejudice; he considers it a great blessing to have good wishes of the people, and does not allow the intoxicating pleasures of this world to overpower his calm judgement.

His Majesty has made a large enclosure with fine buildings inside where he reposes. Though there are more than five thousand women, he has given to each a separate apartment. He has also divided them into sections, and keeps them attentive to their duties. Several chaste women have been appointed as *daroghas,* and superintendents over each section, and one has been selected for the duties of writer. Thus, as in the imperial offices, everything is here also in proper order. The salaries are sufficiently liberal. Not counting the presents, which his Majesty most generously bestows, the women of the highest rank receive from 1610 to 1028 Rs. *per mensem.* Some of the servants have from 51 to 20, others from 40 to 2 Rs. Attached to a private audience hall of the palace is a clever and zealous writer, who superintends the expenditure of the Harem, and keeps an account of the cash and the stores. If a woman wants anything, within the limit of her salary, she applies one of the *Tahwildars* (cash-keepers) of the seraglio. The *Tahwildars* then sends a memorandum to the writer, who checks it, when the General Treasurer makes the payment in cash, as for claims of this nature no checks are given.

The writer also makes out an estimate of the annual expenditure, writes out summarily a receipt, which is countersigned by the ministers of the state. It is then stamped with a peculiar imperial seal, which is only used in grants connected with the Harem, when the receipt becomes payable. The money itself is paid by the cash-keeper of the General Treasury to the General *Tahwildar,* who on the order of the writer of the Harem, hands it over to the several Sub-*Tahwildars* for distribution among the servants of the seraglio. All moneys are reckoned in their salaries at the current rate.

The inside of the Harem is guarded by sober and active women; the most trustworthy of them are placed about the apartments of his Majesty. Outside the enclosure the eunuchs are placed; and at a proper distance, there is a guard of faithful *Rajputs,* beyond whom are the porters of the gates. Besides, on all four sides, there are guards of Nobles, *Ahadis,* and other troops, according to their ranks.

Whenever *Begams,* or the wives of nobles, or other women of chaste character, desire to be presented, they first notify their wish to the servants of the seraglio, and wait for a reply. From thence they send their request to the officers of the palace, after which those who are eligible are permitted to enter the Harem. Some women of rank obtain permission to remain there for a whole month.

Notwithstanding the great number of faithful guards, his Majesty does not dispense with his own vigilance, but keeps the whole in proper order.

CHAPTER 21

East Asia, 1400-1800

21.1

Letter from China (1683), Ferdinand Verbiest

Ferdinand Verbiest (1632-1688) was a Flemish missionary and astronomer who served at the court of the Manchu emperor Kangxi (1661-1722). Although Kangxi's father had put Jesuit missionaries to death, Father Verbiest particularly impressed the young emperor when he made a crucial readjustment to the Chinese calendar. Verbiest instructed the emperor in astronomy and mathematics, learning the Tartar language to do so, and was allowed considerable access to the court. Verbiest accompanied Kangxi on two military expeditions into the south, where pockets of resistance remained against the Manchu dynasty, which had recently usurped power. Owing to his mathematical skill, Verbiest was ultimately able to figure out the exact location of the Chinese-Russian border.

The excerpt printed here is Verbiest's account of his second voyage into the Crimea with Emperor Kangxi. It is a letter written from China to Jesuit officials in Europe. Verbiest's description of the emperor and his entourage is the best portrait of the early Manchus. His wonder at the Great Wall of China is still shared today.

Source: From HISTORY OF THE TWO TARTAR CONQUERORS OF CHINA, translated and edited by The Earl of Ellesmere, New York: Burt Franklin Publisher, 1854.

Letter of Father Ferdinand Verbiest, sent from Pekin, the capital of China, to Europe; concerning a Second Journey which he made with the Emperor of China, beyond the great Chinese Wall into Tartary.

The emperor of China, on the 6th day of July, A.D. 1683, being the thirtieth year of his life, with the queen, his grandmother, and a great attendance, to the amount of 60,000 persons and 100,000 horses, commenced a journey to West Tartary, having expressed a special desire that I should accompany him. The causes of this journey were several. The first was, to keep the military during peace in constant movement and practice, to fit it for the exigencies of war. For this motive the emperor, in this same year (having made a levy from all his provinces of his best troops), returning to Pekin, after having established a solid peace throughout the vast empire of China, resolved to his council to make annually three such expeditions, each at a certain season, during which he might, on the pretext of the chase and of practicing his soldiers in the pursuit of stags, wild boars, and tigers, procure an image and representation of war with human enemies and rebels, and a rehearsal of conflicts which might thereafter ensue. He had in view at the least to prevent for his soldiers and especially his Tartar troops, that infection of Chinese luxury and corruption which might otherwise naturally ensue from the idleness of peace. And, in fact, this fashion in which the emperor went forth to the chase, had all the form and appearance of a royal progress to war; for he went attended by 100,000 horses and more than 60,000 men, all armed with bow and arrows and saber, and divided into troops and companies, and with all the military accompaniments of banners and music. In the chase these surrounded mountains and forests in a wide circuit like those who invest a town to be besieged; in which they observed the process pursued by the Western Tartars in their great hunts. The army, again, is divided into an advanced, a centre, and a rear-guard, and into wings right and left. The command of each of these bodies is committed to officers of eminence, and to members of the imperial house.

Inasmuch, however, as this expedition was planned for a march of more than seventy days (the emperor being on each day from morning till evening devoted to the chase), and all the provisions, and baggage and other heavy impediments had to be conveyed over continual ascents and descents, partly on wagons, partly on camels, mules, and horses, the labours and difficulties of each day's march are not to be described. For in the whole of this West Tartary nothing is met with but mountain and valley. It has no towns, and no villages, no, not even a house. All its inhabitants live as herdsmen under tents or hovels, which they convey from valley to valley when they move in search of fresh and better pasture for their herds, which consist solely of oxen, sheep, and horses; for of pigs, dogs, and other animals, which abound among an agricultural peasantry, they have none. I say that they possess nothing but these cattle, which graze the uncultivated soil.

These Tartars are a slothful people, and little disposed to any toil, even to that of the chase. They neither sow nor reap, nor plough nor harrow. They live for the most part on milk, cheese, and flesh. They make certain wine which resembles our brandy, and which they delight to swallow to repletion, till they fling themselves down and are reduced, soul and body, to the condition of the very cattle.

They hold, meanwhile, their priests, called lamas, in great veneration, and in this respect are distinguished from some neighbouring Tartar tribes, who practice no religious observances, or next to none, and live as Atheists.

Both being equally slaves, and bound to the service of their lords, are on this account difficult of conversion to our faith; following the nod of the latter, in matters of religion, like the cattle which follow where they are led, not where they choose to go.

In this manner did the emperor lead his troops a march of many days, through such desert districts, over ridges of mountains almost linked with each other, over many acclivities, beyond measure steep and far removed from the ordinary track. He followed the chase every day, riding in advance of the troops, often under a blazing sun, sometimes in heavy rain. Many who had taken part in the campaigns of preceding years, openly confessed to me that they had never, in actual war, endured such hardships as in this factitious campaign. Thus the emperor fully compassed his primary object, that of inuring his troops.

It appears, however, that another motive for the expedition was, the political object of keeping these Western Tartars in obedience, and checking the plots and intrigues of their councils. This was one reason for the magnitude of the force, and the imperial pomp with which the emperor penetrated their country. For this he conveyed also thither some pieces of cannon . . . These he occasionally caused to be discharged in the winding valleys, in which the reverberation from the cliffs added to the effect of those thundering salutes with which the emperor's movements from his palace in Pekin are usually attended; and which, as also the accompanying music of trumpets, drums, and copper cymbals, were now employed on the occasions of the emperor's marching, or at meal times, to dazzle and fill the eyes and ears of the barbarous tribes. For the Chinese empire has, from remote times, feared no enemy so much as these Tartars, who starting from this Eastern district, encompass Northern and Western China with a countless multitude of tribes, to repel the invasion, or, so to speak, the inundation of which, former emperors constructed the great Wall. I had four times passed over and personally inspected that work. In truth, the seven wonders of the world condensed into one, could not be compared with it. That which I have seen with my own eyes of it, far exceeds all report of it which has yet reached Europe.

There are two circumstances which exalt this work to the skies. The first is, that it is carried not alone over level places, but in many places over the highest summits of the mountains from east to west, and follows all the acclivities; towers of a lasting construction rising high into the air, at intervals of two bow-shots apart. On our return we ascertained by our instruments the height of a portion of the Wall above the horizon at 1037 geometrical feet.

We might well wonder how the builders could draw to such a height, up the steepest places, from the lowest valleys, which are destitute themselves of water, such a quantity of stones, lime, water, etc.

The other circumstance is, that the Wall should be carried, not with one, but with a variety of curves, following all the prominences of the mountain; so that it may be considered not a single, but a triple Wall, which protects the whole Tartarian frontier of China.

The emperor has divided the immeasurable districts of West Tartary into forty-eight provinces, and has made them all subject and tributary; and thus may this sovereign of the Chinese and of both Tartaries, be justly named as the greatest and mightiest monarch and sole ruler in the world; as one who has incorporated into one body so many districts and nations under one authority, without the interposition of any other prince. He may, I say, be named, as the monarch most essentially and most singularly worthy of the name, for this reason, that he of all rulers the most by himself governs so vast a multitude of men; for what is most remarkable in him and distinctive from all others, is that from the beginning of his reign to this present day since he took the helm of government, he has never permitted any one to govern for him or in his place, nor allowed any one, whether of the princes of the realm, or of the kolaos, or other authorities who may be familiar with him, or who enjoy his favour and are near his heart, more than others to dispose of or settle any public matter by their own separate deliberation. Nay, not within the innermost recesses of the palace has he ever so condescended to any of the eunuchs or the youth of the court, his contemporaries with whom he had been brought up from infancy, as to allow any one of them to act on his own behalf in public matters; facts which are altogether singular, and may be regarded as miracles in this kind of government, when the practice of his predecessors is taken into consideration.

This emperor chastises offenders of the highest as well as lowest class with marvelous impartiality, according to the misdeeds, deriving them of rank and dignity. He himself, after considering the proceedings and sentences of the Imperial council or the Courts of Law, determines and directs the issue. On this account men of all ranks and dignities whatsoever, even the nearest to him in blood, stand in his presence with the deepest awe, and recognize him as sole ruler.

As a point which concerns ourselves and our objects, I must refer to my former observations on the Tartar priests or lamas, and that these, by reason of the policy pursued in the government of the Tartaries, have easy access to the princes and dignitaries, a circumstance which makes the introduction of our faith among these people the more difficult. These priests have much influence with the queen-mother, who sprung from West Tartary, and has attained the age of fifty, and they have for many years past enjoyed her warm affection.

Inasmuch as this queen is held in great consideration by the emperor, and knows well from these priests that we are strong opponents of the superstition to which she clings, it is a wonder, nay a miracle, at the least a singular proof of God's power and providence, that the emperor should have hitherto treated us with such benignity and with familiarity and honour, even beyond these lamas themselves.

The third and last cause of this expedition was that the emperor wished to consult the condition of his health; for experience had taught him, that while he remained at Pekin his health from various annoyances often failed him, which he hoped by his present movement and change of life to provide against, and even to gain strength . . .

It may be added that by this movement he with the queen-mother avoided the summer heat, which in the dog-days at Pekin is tremendous. For in this part of Tartary not only is the air very cooling, but wintry, especially at night, so that the inhabitants not only wear woolens but betake themselves to furs and peltry for clothing. The cause of this is the mountainous character of the country and its elevation, such that for five days' journey we were constantly traversing high ridges, and climbing higher and higher.

The emperor desired to know how much this mountain was elevated above the level of Pekin, from which capital it is about three hundred miles distant, and commenced us to devise some means of measuring the difference. We therefore on our return, after measuring the heights and distances of more than one hundred summits, found that the horizon, or rather the circular level of Pekin was three thousand geometrical paces lower than the highest ridge or top of this mountain.

Several petty kings of West Tartary came in to see the emperor from distances of three and even five hundred Italian miles, with their sons and kinsmen. They all saluted us with great demonstration of good will, which they evinced openly by looks and gestures of hand and body. For any of them could speak no language but their own, which is different from that of the East Tartars. Some also had formerly been presented to us at Pekin, and some had visited our church there.

One day as we were arriving at the town which was the end and object of our journey, we met towards dusk a very old prince, who was returning from the emperor's tents, and on our appearance halted with all his attendants, which was very numerous, and asked, through an interpreter, which of us was Nau Hoay Gi? One of our followers pointing me out with voice and gesture, he approached us with much appearance of pleasure and benignity, and said, "I have long since heard of your name; are you well?" He approached father Grimaldi with the like demeanour, and asked how he was. From this conduct, we derived some hope that at some time or other our worship might find access to these secular princes, especially should some of our scientific brethren find means to open the door of such access by pleasing exhibitions of knowledge, and if the people could be cajoled by presents.

The emperor throughout our whole journey exhibited to us a benevolence and attention, such as, in truth, he displayed to no one else, not even of the princes or his own kinsmen, and this both in word and deed in presence of the whole army.

One day as the emperor fell in with us in an extensive valley, while we were employed in a scientific operation for ascertaining the height and distance of certain mountains, he halted with all his court and escort, and while still at some distance, shouted out in the Chinese tongue, "Hao mo?" That is, are you well? He then asked some questions in the Tartar language as to the heights of the mountains, which I answered in the same. He then turned to his attendants and spoke much in our praise, all which his uncle, who was present, reported to me that evening.

The same goodwill he showed us on many other occasions, to wit, in frequently sending us dishes from his own table to our tent, in the sight of all his grandees. He even ordered us sometimes to be entertained in his own tent. Sometimes when he knew we were abstaining from flesh, he would send us dishes suited to our wants. For he well knew our habits of keeping fast days, and would often ask whether the days were a fast day or not.

His eldest son, following the example of his father, showed us similar goodwill. Once having hurt his shoulder by a fall from his horse, he was obliged to remain still for ten days, which we also did with the greater part of the army. On this occasion, his father being far absent with the chase, he almost every day, and often twice a-day, at midday and evening, sent to our huts dishes from his own table.

This constant benevolence of the emperor is so much the more to be ascribed to the special favour and providence of God, because to others, and even to the princes of his blood, he is very mutable and unstable in his disposition.

21.2

A Secret Plan for Managing the Country (1798), Honda Toshiaki

Honda Toshiaki (1744-1821) was a Japanese political economist and navigator. He learned Dutch to get knowledge of the West. After surveying Japan's northern island of Hokkaido, he advocated a program to increase Japan's wealth and power by focusing on the manufacture of gunpowder and metals, the encouragement of shipping, and colonization. Honda's program envisioned an end to the traditional policy of isolation *(sakoku)* and the promotion of state-sponsored foreign trade, thus anticipating developments after the Meiji Restoration (1868).

Source: From Keene, Donald, The Japanese Discovery of Europe, 1720-1830. Copyright © 1952, 1969 by Donald Keene. All rights reserved. Used with the permission of Stanford University Press, www.sup.org

A Secret Plan of Government

Not until Tokugawa Ieyasu used his power to control the strong and give succor to the weak did the warfare that had lasted for three hundred years without a halt suddenly abate. Arrows were left in their quivers and spears in their racks. If now, in such a time of peace, the country were ruled in accordance with the four imperative needs, the prices of all commodities would be stabilized, and the discontent of the people would thus be cut off at the root. This is the true method of establishing a permanent foundation for the nation, so that the people will become honest in their hearts and cultivate orderly ways even if they are not governed. It must have been because he realized how difficult it would be to preserve the empire for all ages to come if the people were not honest in their hearts that Ieyasu, exhorted shoguns who would succeed him to abstain from any irregularities in government, and to rule on a basis of benevolence and honesty. It was his counsel that the shoguns should serve as models to the people, and by their honesty train the people in the ways of humanity and justice. He taught that the shogun should not compel obedience merely by the use of force, but by his acts of benevolence should keep the nation at peace.

Ieyasu had the great lords of the empire leave their families behind in Edo, where they themselves had to be in attendance every other year. In that way he could learn of the government of the domains. This is an example of the profound insight of Ieyasu. He taught the daimyo that the duties of a governor consisted in the careful attempt to guide the people of their domains in such a way as both to bring about the prosperity of the land and to encourage the literary and military arts.

However, in recent days there has been the spectacle of lords confiscating the allocated property of their retainers on the pretext of paying back debts to the merchants. The debts do not then decrease, but usually seem rather to grow larger. One daimyo with an income of 60,000 *koku* so increased his borrowings that he could not make good his debts, and there was a public suit. The court judgment in the case was said to have been over 1,180,800 *ryō*. Even if repayment had been attempted on the basis of his income of 60,000 koku, the debt would not have been completely settled for fifty or sixty years, so long a time that it is difficult to imagine the day would actually come.

All the daimyo are not in this position, but there is not one who has not borrowed from the merchants. Is this not a sad state of affairs? The merchant, watching this spectacle, must feel like a fisherman who sees a fish swim into his net. Officials of the daimyo harass the farmers for money, which they claim they need to repay the daimyo's debts, but the debts do not diminish. Instead, the daimyo go on contracting new ones year after year. The officials are blamed for this situation, and are dismissed as incompetent. New officials then harass and afflict the farmers in much the same way as the old ones, and so it goes on. However talented the officials may be, they become disgusted and abandon the effort. Some pretend sickness and remain in their homes; others are indiscreet and die young.

No matter how hard the daimyo and his officials rack their brains, they do not seem to be able to reduce the debts. The lords are "sunk in a pool of debts," as it is popularly said, a pool from which their children and grandchildren will be unable to escape. Everything will be as the merchants wish it. The daimyo turn over their domains to the merchants, receiving in return an allowance with which to pay their public and private expenses. Such daimyo give no thought at all to Heaven, to fulfilling their duties as samurai, or to the proper way of looking after the farmers.

Many fields have turned into wasteland since the famine of 1783, when thousands of farmers starved to death. Wherever one goes from the Kantō to Ōu, one hears people say, "There used to be a village here. . . . The land over there was once part of such-and-such a county, but now there is no village and no revenue comes from the land." This condition prevails especially in Ōu, in which province alone five counties have reverted to wasteland. During the three years of bad crops and famine that followed 1783, over two million people in the province of Ōu alone starved to death. When so many farmers starved, reducing still further their already insufficient numbers, the amount of uncultivated land greatly increased. If the wicked practice of infanticide, now so prevalent, is not stopped, the farming population will dwindle until it tends to die out altogether. Generous protective and relief measures must be put into effect immediately if this evil practice is to be stamped out.

A wise ruler could end this practice in short order and create an atmosphere favorable to the prosperity of the nation by establishing a system based on generosity and compassion. When a woman of one of the lower classes becomes pregnant, a government agent should be sent to investigate the situation. The mother of the child should then be given two sacks of rice each year from the month the child is born until he is ten years old. The practice of infanticide would soon stop. Thus by spending a mere twenty sacks of rice over a period of ten years, the country would at the same time gain a good farmer and atone for the misery caused in the past.

Though I say "misery," there are no words capable of expressing the feeling that everyone must have when he thinks of people killing with their own hands the children they have brought into the world. Dumb animals and birds all experience love and compassion for their young. How can it be that man kills his children? The Confucian scholars of ancient and modern times have talked a great deal about benevolence and compassion, but they possess neither in their hearts. Officials and authorities talk about benevolent government, but they have no understanding of what that means. Whose fault is it that the farmers are dying of starvation and that good fields are turning into wasteland? The fault lies entirely with the ruler. I am at a loss to describe the disloyalty and faithlessness of such actions. The rage that overpowers me when I consider how slow in coming is the punishment sent by Heaven is a sincere expression of my thoughts on the matter.

I have traveled three times through the provinces of the country examining conditions. Since I am a poor person, I have at times been forced to sleep in fields or in the mountains. I have experienced all kinds of physical hardships and want. I have noted the conditions of farm roads in the provinces, roads so poor that produce was left to rot on the ground for want of a way to transport it. I have described such things as the location of mines, the activities of robbers in different places, and the secret disposal at some remote port of goods that were being shipped from one harbor to another and that had been stolen from the owner under the pretense of a shipwreck. These records I leave to future men of goodwill. I have sought to give to the nation what I have come to understand about the significance of the four imperative needs in the humble hope that my plan will relieve the suffering of the farmers and help to bring about the disappearance of infanticide. I am hesitant about leaving behind these crude writings when there are so many learned and brilliant persons in the world today, but if it is true, as the proverb says, that a three-year-old child can show the way over a dangerous crossing, persons who condescend to read these lines carefully may derive profit from them.

Of all the countries of Europe, Africa, Asia, and America, the one with the longest history is Egypt, which lies on the eastern shores of Africa. Over six thousand years ago Egypt was civilized. The Egyptians knew the art of writing, had a calendar at that remote date, and had a system of time notation that was in use throughout the country.

There later appeared a man named Christ in a country called Judea at the northwest end of Asia; he established the Catholic religion, which spread northward of Europe. In India, to the east, Sakyamuni appeared, and in China there were the sage-rulers Yao, Shun, Yu, T'ang, Wen, and Wu. All these men were teachers. Although what they taught differed, their doctrines amounted in each instance to an explanation of the way countries should be ruled and kept at peace. The particulars differed from country to country, but in all cases their meaning could be reduced to the principle of encouraging virtue and punishing vice.

Every country has a system of writing with which it transmits the teachings of its sages. Our country adopted Chinese writing and philosophy. Thus there are persons who enjoy a reputation for wide scholarship when all they know is the origin and history of one country, China. China became civilized three thousand years ago, and was thus over three thousand years slower than Egypt. Because of this difference in antiquity there are many faults in Chinese state policies that time has not as yet corrected.

The great number and inconvenience of Chinese character make them useless in dealings with foreign countries. There are now barely three countries besides China where they may be understood: Korea, the Ryukyus, and Japan. And even in these countries it is considered a difficult task to gain a thorough knowledge of them. The European alphabet has twenty-five letters, each of which may be written in eight different forms. With these letters one can describe anything in the world. Nothing could be simpler. If one tried to memorize all the hundreds of thousands of Chinese characters and devoted one's life's energies to the task, how many could one actually learn? One would be sure to forget a great many. Even supposing that some man could learn them all, the best he could do would be to copy in Japan all the old Chinese stories. Rather than attempt to help the nation in this way, it would be simpler to turn to profit those resources with which Japan is naturally endowed.

There is a country called Italy at the southern end of Europe, lying between 35° and 36° N. Lat. The good laws of Judea, which is separated from the southern tip of Italy by the Mediterranean Sea, appear to have been transmitted there. Thus it was that an enlightened ruler established a benevolent rule in Italy that was cheerfully obeyed by the people. He was considered so wise a man that he was given the title of Emperor of Europe, and for many generations afterward all Europe was under one sovereign. However, there came a foolish emperor whose regime was disordered. The subject countries then rebelled, and now all the countries formerly under one emperor are independent.

The capitals of France, Spain, England, and Holland have become thriving places. There are reasons for their prosperity that I shall attempt to explain by using the example of one of them. France long ago became the first country to manufacture cannon, and she also invented the method of making gunpowder for military use. This gave her supremacy over the neighboring countries. She afterward used her inventions against those countries that were at war, thus compelling them to cease fighting. This was the great achievement of France. No matter how well equipped a nation was, even if it possessed mighty fortresses of steel, when French cannons were brought to bear or French privateers attacked, not only would its fortresses fall, but very few of its people would be left to tell the tale. For fear of loss of human life France has not yet transmitted her inventions to other countries.

Europe was first with all other important inventions as well. Because astronomy, calendar making, and mathematics are considered the ruler's business, the European kings are well versed in celestial and terrestrial principles, and instruct the common people in them. Thus even among the lower classes one finds men who show great ability in their particular fields. The Europeans as a result have been able to establish industries with which the rest of the world is unfamiliar. It is for this reason that all the treasures of the world are said to be attracted to Europe. There is nowhere the Europeans' ships do not go in order to obtain the different products and treasures of the world. They trade their own rare products, superior implements, and unusual inventions for the precious metals and valuable goods of others, which they bring back to enrich their own countries. Their prosperity makes them strong, and it is because of their strength that they are never invaded or pillaged, whereas for their part they have invaded countless non-European countries. Spain has conquered many of the best parts of North and South America, and has moved her capital there. Portugal, England, and France also have possessions in the Americas. The islands of the eastern oceans, such as Java, Sumatra, Borneo, and Luzon, are all European possessions. In those countries that have not as yet submitted to the Europeans, they have set up trading stations where they trade with the local rulers, seeking only to obtain the greatest possible profits. Even countries that have not yielded to European might are devoting all their energies to producing things for Europe. The real objectives of the European nations are thus achieved anyway.

There is no place in the world to compare with Europe. It may be wondered in what way this supremacy was achieved. In the first place, the European nations have behind them a history of five to six thousand years. In this period they have delved deep into the beauties of the arts, have divined the foundations of government, and have established a system based on a thorough examination of the factors that naturally make a nation prosperous. Because of their proficiency in mathematics, they have excelled also in astronomy, calendar making, and surveying. They have elaborated laws of navigation such that there is nothing simpler for them than to sail the oceans of the world.

There is no positive evidence on when European ships first reached the nations of the Far East, but it would appear from the descriptions in the "Foreign Events" section of the *Ming History* that they first came to China during the Wan-li era. It cannot have been so very long, in any case, since they first came. As far as our country's history is concerned, it was not until the opening years of the seventeenth century that Dutch ships came regularly every year for trade. It is by such trade that the European nations have become so wealthy.

Nothing can compare in size with the great bell of Moscow or the copper lantern of France. Nor is there elsewhere in the world anything to compare with their practice of building houses of stone. These are a product of their achievements in sailing over the world. To complete any great undertaking—for example, a major public works project or a powerful fortress—with the resources of one country alone is very difficult, and results in the exhaustion of the people; but when the resources of foreign countries are added, there is no undertaking, however great, that cannot be accomplished. This is true in particular of those nations of Europe celebrated for their strength and prosperity. Because they are cold northern countries, they could not afford any large-scale expenditures if they had only the resources of their own country to depend on. In spite of this example, however, the Japanese do not look elsewhere than to China for good or beautiful things, so tainted are the customs and temperament of Japan by Chinese teachings. Japanese are therefore unaware of such things as the four imperative needs, since they do not figure in the teachings of the Chinese sages.

China is a mountainous country that extends as far as Europe and Africa. It is bounded by the ocean to the south, but water communication within the country is not feasible. Since it is impossible to feed the huge population of cities when transport can be effected only by human or animal strength, there are no big cities in China away from the coast. China is therefore a much less favored country than Japan, which is surrounded by water, and this factor shows in the deficiencies and faults of Chinese state policies. China does not merit being used as a model. Since Japan is a maritime nation, shipping and trade should be the chief concerns of the ruler. Ships should be sent to all countries to obtain products needed for national consumption and to bring precious metals to Japan. A maritime nation is equipped with the means to increase her national strength.

By contrast, a nation that attempts to get along on its own resources will grow steadily weaker. The nation's weakness will affect the farmers, and there will be a tendency for the number of farmers to decrease over the years. It becomes a grave national problem when this crisis is reached. To put the matter more bluntly, the policies followed by the various ruling families until now have determined that the lower classes must lead a hand-to-mouth existence. The best part of the harvests of the farmers who live on the domains of the empire is wrenched away from them. The lords spend all they take within the same year, and if they then do not have enough, they oppress the farmers all the more cruelly in an effort to obtain additional funds. This goes on year after year. It is no wonder that when, on top of the grave afflictions that have exhausted the farmers in recent times, there have come bad harvests and famines in the years since 1783, farmers from the Kantō to Ōu have starved to death, and good fields that could produce millions of koku of rice have been turned into wasteland. Is it not true that the people living on a daimyo's domains are imperial subjects left in his care? Is there any reason why even a single one of their precious lives should be left to the caprices of a lord? Is not caring for them the function of a governor and the concern of the ruler?

During the first twenty years of a man's life he is supported by the efforts of his parents, consuming huge quantities of food without producing any himself. If then he reaches manhood and is at long last able to be of service to his country, it is the worst possible loss for him to be left to die by his lord. Man, unlike other creatures, becomes of service to his country only after twenty years of life have gone by, and thus every single subject is precious.

Is it not true that if the ruler fails to cherish his people, he is remiss in his duties, and that the fate of the nation is determined by his actions? The ruler who is lax in looking after the people's needs will fall naturally into profligacy and idleness, and his extravagances will mount without limit. In extreme cases he may go so far as to destroy his house and ruin his province, but even if this does not occur, the gods will surely punish him for his wickedness. He will sink into a pool of debts from which his children and grandchildren will not be able to escape, and in this manner his domains will pass into the hands of the merchants. He will be trapped and forced by this means to pay his debts. There is no point in my expanding further on the fact that samurai, who enjoy hereditary stipends, are falling into the traps of the stipend-less merchants. The samurai pretend that this is actually not so bad, but it represents a terrible state of affairs. The tribute paid by the farmers of the domains, the product of their tears of blood and their hardships of a year, is seized before it reaches their lords and delivered directly into the hands of the merchants. The ruling class does not even dream that these offerings are made only after great exertions and tears of blood.

It is great shame that such conditions prevail, but it is said that "even the thoughts of an ant may reach up to Heaven." Though their conditions differ, the highest and the lowest alike are human beings, and the rulers ought to think about those who are less fortunate than themselves. Soon all the gold and silver currency will pass into the hands of the merchants, and only merchants will be deserving of the epithets "rich" and "mighty." Their power will thus grow until they stand first among the four classes. When I investigated the incomes of present-day merchants, I discovered that fifteen-sixteenths of the total income of Japan goes to the merchants, with only one-sixteenth left for the samurai. As proof of this statement, I cite the following case. When there are good rice harvests at Yonezawa in Dewa or in Semboku-gun in Akita the price is five to six *mon* for one *shō*. The rice is sold to merchants who ship it to Edo, where the price is about 100 mon, regardless of the original cost. At this rate, if one bought 10,000 ryō's worth of rice in Dewa, sent it to Edo and sold it there, one's capital would be increased to 160,000 ryō. If the 160,000 ryō in turn were used as capital, the return in Edo would be 2,560,000 ryō. With only two exchanges of trade it is possible to make enormous profits.

It may be claimed that of this sum part must go for shipping expenses and pack-horse charges, but the fact remains that one gets back sixteen times what one has paid for the rice. It is thus apparent that fifteen-sixteenths of the nation's income goes to the merchants. In terms of the production of an individual farmer, out of thirty days a month he works twenty-eight for the merchants and two for the samurai; or, out of 360 days in a year, he works 337 1/2 for the merchants and 22 1/2 for the samurai. Clearly, then, unless the samurai store grain it is impossible for them to offer any relief to the farmers in years of famine. This may be why they can do no more than look on when the farmers are dying of starvation. And all this because the right system has not been established. It is a most lamentable state of affairs that the farmers have to shoulder the weight of this error and die of starvation as inevitably as "water collecting in a hollow."

The price of rice determines that of other cereals and also affects foodstuff prices as a whole; as it fluctuates so will the others. One can thus judge its importance. Since the market price of rice concerns the ruler, it should not be left for merchants to determine, but should be controlled by the government authorities. The present attitude is that since trade involves buying and selling, and since buying and selling is the merchants' profession, involving a contest with the people for profits, the samurai are absolutely resolved not to engage in trade. This is an unintelligent and ill-informed attitude.

Japan is a long, narrow country that stretches over ten degrees of latitude from its northeastern extreme to its southwest corner, a distance of about 550 ri. Even in bad years, when the crops failed to ripen in one place, there has never been a case when the drought extended to every part of the nation. It is therefore the parental duty of the ruler toward the people to relieve their hunger by shipping grain from provinces with rich harvests to those with poor ones, thus ministering to their wants. This is imperative. There is a difference between this duty of the ruler and what the merchants do to make a living. The merchants buy up produce at a low price at the place where it is harvested and then store it. They wait for a drought or for other natural disasters to harm the crops and cause the price of rice to go up. They then sell the grain at the place where it was originally purchased at a price several times what they paid. In this way they struggle with the people in their greed for high profits. Gentlemen would never do this.

In the summer of 1787 the price of one hundred 35-shō sacks of rice climbed from 250 ryō to 300 ryō in the capital. There was a plot to make the prices go even higher. It was announced that the stocks of rice in the city had been exhausted. This was really not true; there was a perfectly adequate supply, but the merchants planned the announcement in order to get even bigger profits In view of the disgraceful motives that inspire merchants, it is impossible to live in security unless some plan is devised to deal with them once and for all. Trading stations should therefore be established at important inland ports and seaports throughout Japan. Rice and other grain offered for sale should be bought during the year at the natural market price, as determined by the quality of the harvest, and stored at the station. A survey should be made of crop conditions in all parts of the nation, and the information obtained should be quickly circulated by couriers in boats. Every year each country should estimate the amount of food it will need, and leave that amount in the appropriate station. The remainder should be transported on station ships to provinces that have had bad crops distributed there to relieve hunger. In all provinces, including the capital, the normal price paid to the farmers during the previous year should be used as the price standard. If the price does not go up or down more than ten to twenty percent from this level, the station should not buy or sell; if it rises above the limit, the station should sell. Buying and selling would thus maintain prices within ten to twenty percent of the average price paid to farmers during the previous year. The stations could then keep the highest price of rice fixed according to the price in the capital. It is inevitable that there should be some discrepancies, since shipping costs to places nearer or farther away will differ, but the prices would be roughly the same, and the people would be greatly helped. This plan would give the farmers a new lease on life.

Then, even if no formal regulations are made on the subject, the evil practice of infanticide would stop. Within twenty years not only would there be a better race increasing in numbers, but the abandoned fields would gradually be cultivated again and return to their original fertile state. This plan will permit millions of koku of additional income to be raised without persecuting the farmers. When a policy truly designed to bring peace and prosperity to the country is adopted, the people will show honest obedience, and they will share in the fifteen-sixteenths of the national income the merchants now take. Then in two or three years provinces now so impoverished that infanticide is the general rule will be put on their feet, and the farmers will be rehabilitated.

Even during the short period that Hideyoshi was in power, he managed to distribute 465,000 ryō (767,250 ryō in current exchange) among the lords of the empire in the fourth moon of 1588. If he had lived to old age, he would probably have made even China a tributary nation of Japan, but unhappily he died in his sixty-third year on September 18, 1598. Because the country was at war at the time, he gave the money to the lords; if peace had prevailed, he would have given it to the farmers for their relief.

Unless the ruler is possessed of great genius, the country will be poorly governed. Examples of this adage may be found throughout the ancient and modern histories of both Japan and China. The present times are the first since Minamoto Yoritomo founded the military order that the samurai have been in such a sorry state. This situation must be changed at once, and the old order of samurai, farmers, artisans, merchants, and idlers restored. Trading stations should be established steadily throughout the country, as I have suggested, and extensive trading carried out. The wants of one section should be supplied with what another possesses by transporting the produce in government-owned ships. This would both help the people and bring money into the government treasuries. If the ruler should become very wealthy without courting wealth and without seeking profit, proving himself thus worthy of the name "richest in the land," he would preserve his authority and his fortune. This would be a most felicitous and extraordinary thing, and would lay the cornerstone for ten thousand years of prosperity.

By means of the plans outlined in the account of the four imperative needs and the three great sources of worry, the present corrupt and jejune society could be restored to its former prosperity and strength. The ancient glories of the warrior-nation of Japan would be revived. Colonization projects would gradually be commenced and would meet with great success. A capital city would be built in eastern Ezo for northern Japan. The central capital would be at Edo, and the southern one at Osaka. The capital of the entire nation would alternate among these three locations. Then, under enlightened government, Japan could certainly be made the richest and strongest country in the world. This is because Japan, unlike other nations, has ample deposits of gold, silver, lead, and iron.

CHAPTER 22

Western Political Revolutions

22.1

Declaration of the Rights of Man and of the Citizen (1789)

Seldom have events moved more swiftly or dramatically than those that occurred in France from July 14 to August 27, 1789. The fall of the Bastille was followed by the Great Fear, which led to the abolition of feudal privilege and the drafting of the "Declaration of the Rights of Man and Citizen" by the French National Assembly.

The Declaration proclaimed liberty of conscience, property, and the press, and freedom from arbitrary imprisonment. It finally ended the privileged system of the *ancien regime*. To many it signified the ushering-in of a new basis for society in Europe and ultimately, the world. In the words of the English poet, William Wordsworth, "Bliss was it in that dawn to be alive; but to be young was very Heaven."

SOURCE: From The Evolution of Modern Liberty by George L. Scherger, Longmans, Green & Company, 1904.

Approved by the National Assembly of France, August 26, 1789

The representatives of the French people, organized as a National Assembly, believing that the ignorance, neglect, or contempt of the rights of man are the sole cause of public calamities and of the corruption of governments, have determined to set forth in a solemn declaration the natural, unalienable, and sacred rights of man, in order that this declaration, being constantly before all the members of the Social body, shall remind them continually of their rights and duties; in order that the acts of the legislative power, as well as those of the executive power, may be compared at any moment with the objects and purposes of all political institutions and may thus be more respected, and, lastly, in order that the grievances of the citizens, based hereafter upon simple and incontestable principles, shall tend to the maintenance of the constitution and redound to the happiness of all.

Therefore the National Assembly recognizes and proclaims, in the presence and under the auspices of the Supreme Being, the following rights of man and of the citizen:

Articles:

1. Men are born and remain free and equal in rights. Social distinctions may be founded only upon the general good.

2. The aim of all political association is the preservation of the natural and imprescriptible rights of man. These rights are liberty, property, security, and resistance to oppression.

3. The principle of all sovereignty resides essentially in the nation. No body nor individual may exercise any authority which does not proceed directly from the nation.

4. Liberty consists in the freedom to do everything which injures no one else; hence the exercise of the natural rights of each man has no limits except those which assure to the other members of the society the enjoyment of the same rights. These limits can only be determined by law.

5. Law can only prohibit such actions as are hurtful to society. Nothing may be prevented which is not forbidden by law, and no one may be forced to do anything not provided for by law.

6. Law is the expression of the general will. Every citizen has a right to participate personally, or through his representative, in its foundation. It must be the same for all, whether it protects or punishes. All citizens, being equal in the eyes of the law, are equally eligible to all indignities and to all public positions and occupations, according to their abilities, and without distinction except that of their virtues and talents.

7. No person shall be accused, arrested, or imprisoned except in the cases and according to the forms prescribed by law. Any one soliciting, transmitting, executing, or causing to be executed, any arbitrary order, shall be punished. But any citizen summoned or arrested in virtue of the law shall submit without delay, as resistance constitutes an offense.

8. The law shall provide for such punishments only as are strictly and obviously necessary, and no one shall suffer punishment except it be legally inflicted in virtue of a law passed and promulgated before the commission of the offense.

9. As all persons are held innocent until they shall have been declared guilty, if arrest shall be deemed indispensable, all harshness not essential to the securing of the prisoner's person shall be severely repressed by law.

10. No one shall be disquieted on account of his opinions, including his religious views, provided their manifestation does not disturb the public order established by law.

11. The free communication of ideas and opinions is one of the most precious of the rights of man. Every citizen may, accordingly, speak, write, and print with freedom, but shall be responsible for such abuses of his freedom as shall be defined by law.

12. The security of the rights of man and of the citizen requires public military forces. These forces are, therefore, established for the good of all and not for the personal advantage of those to whom they shall be entrusted.

13. A common contribution is essential for the maintenance of the public forces and for the cost of administration. This should be equitably distributed among all the citizens in proportion to their means.

14. All the citizens have a right to decide, either personally or by their representatives, as to the necessity of the public contribution; to grant this freely; to know to what uses it is put; and to fix the proportion, the mode of assessment and of collection and the duration of the taxes.

15. Society has the right to require of every public agent an account of his administration.

16. A society in which the observance of the law is not assured, nor the separation of powers defined, has no constitution at all.

17. Since property is an inviolable and sacred right, no one shall be deprived thereof except where public necessity, legally determined, shall clearly demand it, and then only on condition that the owner shall have been previously and equitably indemnified.

22.2

Declaration of the Rights of Woman and Citizen (1791), Olympe de Gouges

In this document Olympe de Gouges exposes the hypocrisy inherent in the previous one. Women, especially educated, wealthy bourgeois women in France, often were supporters of the revolutionary ideals embodied in the *Declaration of Independence* and the *Declaration of the Rights of Man and Citizen.* Many were outraged that the *Declaration of the Rights of Man* applied only to males. De Gouges published her *Declaration of the Rights of Woman* in 1791 to remedy the fatal flaw in the masculine assumptions of the *Declaration of the Rights of Man.* The leaders of the French Revolution ignored it. Later, the Napoleonic Code of 1804 declared women legally incompetent. In 1793 Olympe de Gouges was guillotined for her opposition to the execution of the French royal family.

Source: From European Women: A Documentary History, 1789-1945 by Eleanor S. Reimer and John C. Fout, copyright © 1980 by Schocken Books, a division of Random House, Inc. Used by permission of Schocken Books, a division of Random House, Inc.

The mothers, daughters, sisters, representatives of the nation, ask to constitute a National Assembly. Considering that ignorance, forgetfulness or contempt of the rights of women are the sole causes of public miseries, and of corruption of governments, they have resolved to set forth in a solemn declaration, the natural, unalterable and sacred rights of woman, so that this declaration, being ever present to all members of the social body, may unceasingly remind them of their rights and their duties; in order that the acts of women's power, as well as those of men, may be judged constantly against the aim of all political institutions, and thereby be more respected for it, in order that the complaints of women citizens, based henceforth on simple and indisputable principles, may always take the direction of maintaining the Constitution, good morals and the welfare of all.

In consequence, the sex superior in beauty and in courage in maternal suffering recognizes and declares, in the presence of and under the auspices of the Supreme Being, the following rights of woman and of the woman citizen.

Article I

Woman is born free and remains equal to man in rights. Social distinctions can be based only on common utility.

Article II

The aim of every political association is the preservation of the natural and imprescriptible rights of man and woman. These rights are liberty, prosperity, security, and above all, resistance to oppression.

Article III

The source of all sovereignty resides essentially in the Nation, which is nothing but the joining together of Man and Woman; no body, no individual, can exercise authority that does not emanate expressly from it.

Article IV

Liberty and justice consist in giving back to others all that belongs to them; thus the only limits on the exercise of women's natural rights are the perpetual tyranny by which man opposes her; these limits must be reformed by the laws of nature and of reason.

Article V

The laws of nature and reason forbid all actions that are harmful to society; all that is not forbidden by these wise and divine laws cannot be prevented, and no one can be constrained to do what they do not prescribe.

Article VI

Law must be the expression of the general will: all citizens, men and women alike, must personally or through their representatives concur in its formation; it must be the same for all; all citizens, men and women alike, being equal before it, must be equally eligible for all high offices, positions and public employments, according to their abilities, and without distinctions other than their virtues and talents.

Article VII

No woman can be an exception: she will be accused, apprehended and detained in cases determined by law; women, like men, will obey this rigorous rule.

Article VIII

The law must establish only those penalties which are strictly and clearly necessary, and no woman can be punished by virtue of a law established and promulgated prior to the offense, and legally applied to women.

Article IX

When a woman is declared guilty, full severity is exercised by the law.

Article X

No one ought to be disturbed for one's opinions, however fundamental they are; since a woman has the right to mount the scaffold, she must also have the right to address the House, provided her interventions do not disturb the public order as it has been established by law.

Article XI

The free communication of ideas and opinions is one of the most precious rights of woman, since this freedom ensures the legitimacy of fathers toward their children. Every woman citizen can therefore say freely: I am the mother of a child that belongs to you, without being forced to conceal the truth because of a barbaric prejudice; except to be answerable for abuses of this liberty as determined by law.

Article XII

The guarantee of the rights of woman and of the woman citizen is a necessary benefit; this guarantee must be instituted for the advantage of all, and not for the personal benefit of those to whom it is entrusted.

Article XIII

For the upkeep of public forces and for administrative expenses, the contributions of woman and man are equal; a woman shares in all the labors required by law, in the painful tasks; she must therefore have an equal share in the distribution of offices, employments, trusts, dignities, and work.

Article XIV

Women and men citizens have the right to ascertain by themselves or through their representatives the necessity of public taxes. Women citizens will not only assume an equal part in providing the wealth but also in the public administration and in determining the quota, the assessment, the collection and the duration of the impost.

Article XV

The mass of women, joined together to contribute their taxes with those of men, have the right to demand from every public official an accounting of his administration.

Article XVI

Any society in which the guarantee of rights is not assured, nor the separation of powers determined, has no Constitution; the Constitution is null if the majority of the individuals of whom the nation is comprised have not participated in its drafting.

Article XVII

Ownership of property is for both sexes, mutually and separately; it is for each a sacred and inviolable right; no one can be deprived of it as a true patrimony from nature, unless a public necessity, legally established, evidently demands it, and with the condition of a just and prior indemnity.

Afterword

Woman, wake up! The alarm bell of reason is making itself heard throughout the universe; recognize your rights. The powerful empire of nature is no longer beset by prejudices, fanaticism, superstition and lies. The torch of truth has dispelled all clouds of stupidity and usurpation. The enslaved man multiplied his forces but has had to resort to yours to break his chains. Once free he became unjust to his female companion. O women! women, when will you stop being blind? What advantages have you received from the Revolution? A more pronounced scorn, a more marked contempt? During the centuries of corruption, your only power was over the weaknesses of men. Your empire is destroyed, what then is left to you? The conviction that men are unjust. The claiming of your patrimony based on the wise laws of nature. The good word of the Lawgiver of the Marriage at Cana? Are you afraid that our French lawmakers, correctors of this morality, so long tied up with the politics which is no longer in style will say to you: "Women, what is there in common between you and us?—Everything, you would have to reply. If they persisted in their weakness, in putting forth this inconsistency which is a contradiction of their principles, you should courageously oppose these hale pretensions of superiority with the force of reason; unite under the banner of philosophy, unfold all the energy of your character and you will soon see these proud men, your servile adorers, crawling at your feet, but proud to share with you the treasures of the Supreme Being. Whatever the obstacles that oppose us may be, it is in your power to free us, you have only to will it. . . .

Since it is now a question of national education, let us see if our wise lawmakers will think wisely about the education of women.

CHAPTER 23

European Industrial Revolution

23.1

Condition of the Working Class in England in 1844, Friedrich Engels

Friedrich Engels (1820-1895) was a German socialist philosopher, a collaborator with Karl Marx, and a founder of "scientific socialism." From 1842 he lived mostly in England. He first met Marx in Brussels in 1844 and collaborated with him on the Communist Manifesto (1848). He died in London after spending his later years editing and translating Marx's writings.

Source: From The Condition of the Working-Class in England in 1844, translated by Florence Kelley Wischnewetzky, first published 1892.

I have now to prove that society in England daily and hourly commits what the workingmen's organs, with perfect correctness, characterize as social murder, that it has placed the workers under conditions in which they can neither retain health nor live long; that it undermines the vital force of these workers gradually, little by little, and so hurries them to the grave before their time. I have further to prove that society knows how injurious such conditions are to the health and the life of the workers, and yet does nothing to improve these conditions. That it *knows* the consequences of its deeds; that its act is, therefore, not mere manslaughter, but murder, I shall have proved, when I cite official documents, reports of Parliament and of the Government, in substantiation of my charge.

That a class which lives under the conditions already sketched and is so ill-provided with the most necessary means of subsistence, cannot be healthy and can reach no advanced age, is self-evident. Let us review the circumstances once more with especial reference to the health of the workers. The centralization of population in great cities exercises of itself an unfavourable influence; the atmosphere of London can never be so pure, so rich in oxygen, as the air of the country; two and a half million pairs of lungs, two hundred and fifty thousand fires, crowded upon an area three to four miles square, consume an enormous amount of oxygen, which is replaced with difficulty, because the method of building cities in itself impedes ventilation. The carbonic acid gas, engendered by respiration and fire, remains in the streets by reason of its specific gravity, and the chief air current passes over the roofs of the city. The lungs of the inhabitants fail to receive the due supply of oxygen, and the consequence is mental and physical lassitude and low vitality. For this reason, the dwellers in cities are far less exposed to acute, and especially to inflammatory, affections than rural populations, who live in a free, normal atmosphere; but they suffer the more from chronic affections. And if life in large cities is, in itself, injurious to health, how great must be the harmful influence of an abnormal atmosphere in the working-people's quarters, where, as we have seen, everything combines to poison the air. In the country, it may, perhaps, be comparatively innoxious to keep a dung-heap adjoining one's dwelling, because the air has free ingress from all sides; but in the midst of a large town, among closely built lanes and courts that shut out all movement of the atmosphere, the case is different. All putrefying vegetable and animal substances give off gases decidedly injurious to health, and if these gases have no free way to escape, they inevitably poison the atmosphere. The filth and stagnant pools of the working-people's quarters in the great cities have, therefore, the worst effect upon the public health, because they produce precisely those gases which engender disease; so, too, the exhalations from contaminated streams. But this is by no means all. The manner in which the great multitude of the poor is treated by society to-day is revolting. They are drawn into the large cities where they breathe a poorer atmosphere than in the country; they are relegated to districts which, by reason of the method of construction, are worse ventilated than any others; they are deprived of all means of cleanliness, of water itself, since pipes are laid only when paid for, and the rivers so polluted that they are useless for such purposes; they are obliged to throw all offal and garbage, all dirty water, often all disgusting drainage and excrement into the streets, being without other means of disposing of them; they are thus compelled to infect the region of their own dwellings. Nor is this enough. All conceivable evils are heaped upon the heads of the poor. If the population of great cities is too dense in general, it is they in particular who are packed into the least space. As though the vitiated atmosphere of the streets were not enough, they are penned in dozens into single rooms, so that the air which they breathe at night is enough in itself to stifle them. They are given damp dwellings, cellar dens that are not waterproof from below, or garrets that leak from above. Their houses are so built that the clammy air cannot escape. They are supplied bad, tattered, or rotten clothing, adulterated and indigestible food. They are exposed to the most exciting changes of mental condition, the most violent vibrations between hope and fear; they are hunted like game, and not permitted to attain peace of mind and quiet enjoyment of life. They are deprived of all enjoyments except that of sexual indulgence and drunkenness, are worked every day to the point of complete exhaustion of their mental and physical energies, and are thus constantly spurred on to the maddest excess in the only two enjoyments at their command. And if they surmount all this, they fall victims to want of work in a crisis when all the little is taken from them that had hitherto been vouchsafed them.

How is it possible, under such conditions, for the lower class to be healthy and long lived? What else can be expected than an excessive mortality, an unbroken series of epidemics, a progressive deterioration in the physique of the working population? Let us see how the facts stand.

That the dwellings of the workers in the worst portions of the cities, together with the other conditions of life of this class, engender numerous diseases, is attested on all sides. The article already quoted from the *Artisan* asserts with perfect truth, that lung diseases must be the inevitable consequence of such conditions, and that, indeed, cases of this kind are disproportionately frequent in this class. That the bad air of London, and especially of the working-people's districts, is in the highest degree favourable to the development of consumption, the hectic appearance of great numbers of persons sufficiently indicates. If one roams the streets a little in the early morning, when the multitudes are on their way to their work, one is amazed at the number of persons who look wholly or half-consumptive. Even in Manchester the people have not the same appearance; these pale, lank, narrow-chested, hollow-eyed ghosts, whom one passes at every step, these languid, flabby faces, incapable of the slightest energetic expression, I have seen in such startling numbers only in London, though consumption carries off a horde of victims annually in the factory towns of the North. In competition with consumption stands typhus, to say nothing of scarlet fever, a disease which brings most frightful devastation into the ranks of the working-class. Typhus, that universally diffused affliction, is attributed by the official report on the sanitary condition of the working-class, directly to the bad state of the dwellings in the matters of ventilation, drainage, and cleanliness. This report, compiled, it must not be forgotten, by the leading physicians of England from the testimony of other physicians, asserts that a single ill-ventilated court, a single blind alley without drainage, is enough to engender fever, and usually does engender it, especially if the inhabitants are greatly crowded. This fever has the same character almost everywhere, and develops in nearly every case into specific typhus. It is to be found in the working-people's quarters of all great towns and cities, and in single ill-built, ill-kept streets of smaller places, though it naturally seeks out single victims in better districts also. In London it has now prevailed for a considerable time; its extraordinary violence in the year 1837 gave rise to the report already referred to. According to the annual report of Dr. Southwood Smith on the London Fever Hospital, the number of patients in 1843 was 1,462, or 418 more than in any previous year. In the damp, dirty regions of the north, south, and east districts of London, this disease ranged with extraordinary violence. Many of the patients were working-people from the country, who had endured the severest privation while migrating, and, after their arrival, had slept hungry and half-naked in the streets, and so fallen victims to the fever. These people were brought into the hospital in such a state of weakness, that unusual quantities of wine, cognac, and preparations of ammonia and other stimulants were required for their treatment; 16 1/2 percent of all patients died. This malignant fever is to be found in Manchester; in the worst quarters of the Old Town, Ancoats, Little Ireland, etc., it is rarely extinct; though here, ads in the *English* towns generally, it prevails to a less extent than might be expected. In Scotland and Ireland, on the other hand, it rages with a violence that surpasses all conception. In Edinburgh and Glasgow it broke out in 1817, after the famine, and in 1826 and 1837 with especial violence, after the commercial crisis, subsiding somewhat each time after having ranged about three years. In Edinburgh about 6,000 persons were attacked by the fever during the epidemic of 1817, and about 10,000 in that of 1837, and not only the number of persons attacked but the violence of the disease increased with each repetition.

But the fury of the epidemic in all former periods seems to have been child's play in comparison with its ravages after the crisis of 1842. One-sixth of the whole indigent population of Scotland was seized by the fever, and the infection was carried by wandering beggars with fearful rapidity from one locality to another. It did not reach the middle and upper classes of the populations, yet in two months there were more fever cases than in twelve years before. In Glasgow, twelve per cent. of the population were seized in the year 1843; 32,000 persons, of whom thirty-two per cent. perished, while this mortality in Manchester and Liverpool does not ordinarily exceed eight per cent. The illness reached a crisis on the seventh and fifteenth days; on the latter, the patient usually became yellow, which our authority regards as an indication that the cause of the malady was to be sought in mental excitement and anxiety. In Ireland, too, these fever epidemics have become domesticated. During twenty-one months of the years 1817-1818, 39,000 fever patients passed through the Dublin hospital; and in a more recent year, according to Sheriff Alison, 60,000. In Cork the fever hospital received one-seventh of the population in 1817-1818, in Limerick in the same time one-fourth, and in the bad quarter of Waterford, nineteen-twentieths of the whole population were ill of the fever at one time.

When one remembers under what conditions the working-people live, when one thinks how crowded their dwellings are, how every nook and corner swarms with human beings, how sick and well sleep in the same room, in the same bed, the only wonder is that a contagious disease like this fever does not spread yet farther. And when one reflects how little medical assistance the sick have at command, how many are without any medical advice whatsoever, and ignorant of the most ordinary precautionary measures, the mortality seems actually small. Dr. Alison, who has made a careful study of this disease, attributes it directly to the want and the wretched condition of the poor. He asserts that privations and the insufficient satisfaction of vital needs are what prepare the fame for contagion and make the epidemic widespread and terrible. He proves that a period of privation, a commercial crisis or a bad harvest, has each time produced the typhus epidemic in Ireland as in Scotland, and that the fury of the plague has fallen almost exclusively on the working-class. It is a noteworthy fact, that according to his testimony, the majority of persons who perish by typhus are fathers of families, precisely the persons who can least be spared by those dependent upon them; and several Irish physicians whom he quotes bear the same testimony.

Another category of diseases arises directly from the food rather than the dwellings of the workers. The food of the labourer, indigestible enough in itself, is utterly unfit for young children, and he has neither means nor time to get his children more suitable food. Moreover, the custom of giving children spirits, and even opium, is very general; and these two influences, with the rest of the conditions of life prejudical to bodily development, give rise to the most diverse affections of the digestive organs, leaving life-long traces behind them. Nearly all workers have stomachs more or less weak, and are yet forced to adhere to the diet which is the root of the evil. How should they know what is to blame for it? And if they knew, how could they obtain a more suitable regimen so long as they cannot adopt a different way of living and are not better educated? But new disease arises during childhood from impaired digestion. Scrofula is almost universal among the working-class, and scrofulous parents have scrofulous children, especially when the original influences continue in full force to operate upon the inherited tendency of the children. The employment of the wife dissolves the family utterly and of necessity, and this dissolution, in our present society, which is based upon the family, brings the most demoralizing consequences for parents as well as children. A mother who has no time to trouble herself about her child, to perform the most ordinary loving services for it during its first year, who scarcely indeed sees it, can be no real mother to the child, must inevitably grow indifferent to it, treat it unlovingly like a stranger. The children who grow up under such conditions are utterly ruined for later family life, can never feel at home in the family which they themselves found, because they have always been accustomed to isolation, and they contribute therefore to the already general undermining of the family in the working-class. A similar dissolution of the family is brought about by the employment of the children. When they get on far enough to earn more than they cost their parents from week to week, they begin to pay the parents a fixed sum for board and lodging, and keep the rest for themselves. This often happens from the fourteenth or fifteenth year. In a word, the children emancipated themselves, and regard the paternal dwelling as a lodging-house, which they often exchange for another, as suits them.

In many cases the family is not wholly dissolved by the employment of the wife, but turned upside down. The wife supports the family, the husband sits at home, tends the children, sweeps the room and cooks. This case happens very frequently; in Manchester alone, many hundred such men could be cited, condemned to domestic occupations. It is easy to imagine the wrath aroused among the working-men by this reversal of all relations within the family, while the other social conditions remain unchanged. There lies before me a letter from an English working-man, Robert Pounder, Baron's Buildings, Wood-house, Moorside, in Leeds (the bourgeoisie may hunt him up there; I give the exact address for the purpose), written by him to Oastler:

He relates how another working-man, being on tramp, came to St. Helens, in Lancashire, and there looked up an old friend. He found him in a miserable, damp cellar, scarcely furnished; and when my poor friend went in, there sat poor Jack near the fire, and what did he, think you? why he sat and mended his wife's stockings with the bodkin; and as soon as he saw his old friend at the door-post, he tried to hide them. But Joe, that is my friend's name, had seen it, and said: "Jack, what the devil art thou going? Where is the missus? Why, is that thy work?" and poor Jack was ashamed, and said: "No, I know this is not my work, but my poor missus is i' th' factory; she has to leave at half-past five and works till eight at night, and then she is so knocked up that she cannot do aught when she gets home, so I have to do everything for her what I can, for I have no work, nor had any for more nor three years, and I shall never have any more work while I live;" and then he wept a big tear. Jack again said: "There is work enough for women folks and childer hearabouts, but none for men; thou mayest sooner find a hundred pound on the road than work for men—but I should never had believed that either thou or any one else would have seen me mending my wife's stockings, for it is bad work. But she can hardly stand on her feet; I am afraid she will be laid up, and then I don't know what is to become of us, for it's a good bit that she has been the man in the house and I the woman; it is bad work, Joe;" and he cried bitterly, and said, "It has not been always so." "No," said Joe; "but when thou hadn't no work, how has thou not shifted?" "I'll tell thee, Joe, as well as I can, but it was bad enough; thou knowest when I got married I had work plenty, and thou knows I was not lazy." "No, that thou wert not." "And we had a good furnished house, and Mary need not go to work. I could work for the two of us; but now the world is upside down. Mary has to work and I have to stop at home, mind the childer sweep and wash, bake and mend; and, when the poor woman comes home at night, she is knocked up. Thou knows, Joe, it's hard for one that was used different." "Yes, boy, it is hard." And then Jack began to cry again, and he wished he had never married, and that he had never been born; but he had never thought, when he wed Mary, that it would come to this. "I have often cried over it," said Jack. Now when Joe heard this, he told me that he had cursed and damned the factories, and the masters, and the Government, with all the curses that he had learned while he was in the factory from a child."

Can any one imagine a more insane state of things than that described in this letter? And yet this condition, which unsexes the man and takes from the woman all womanliness without being able to bestow upon the man true womanliness, or the woman true manliness—this condition which degrades, in the most shameful way, both sexes, and, through them, Humanity, is the last result of our much-praised civilisation, the final achievement of all the efforts and struggles of hundreds of generations to improve their own situation and that of their posterity. We must either despair of mankind, and its aims and efforts, when we see all our labour and toil result in such a mockery, or we must admit that human society has hitherto sought salvation in a false direction; we must admit that so total a reversal of the position of the sexes can have come to pass only because the sexes have been placed in a false position from the beginning. If the reign of the wife over the husband, as inevitably brought about by the factory system, is inhuman, the pristine rule of the husband over the wife must have been inhuman too. If the wife can now base her supremacy upon the fact that she supplies the greater part, nay, the whole of the common possession, the necessary inference is that this community of possession is no true and rational one, since one member of the family boasts offensively of contributing the greater share. If the family of our present society is being thus dissolved, this dissolution merely shows that, at bottom, the binding tie of this family was not family affection, but private interest lurking under the cloak of a pretended community of possessions.

CHAPTER 24

Isms and Upheaval

24.1

An Inquiry into the Nature and Causes of the Wealth of Nations (1776), Adam Smith

Adam Smith (1723-1790) was the most important representative of the eighteenth-century Scottish enlightenment. Though his father was a customs official, the younger Smith trained for a university career from an early age. He entered Glasgow University in 1737 at a period when it was a leading European center of learning. He studied moral philosophy and was so proficient in his subject that fifteen years later he was appointed to the chair of moral philosophy there. His interests turned to law and economics, and he began to formulate the principles that were to underlie his greatest work, *The Wealth of Nations.* Smith subsequently resigned his academic post to travel and lead a quiet life. He died in Edinburgh in 1790.

The Wealth of Nations is a classic of Western economic theory. In it, Smith postulates self-interest as the principal motivation of economic activity and explains how a free marketplace enhances economic exchange among self-interested traders. Smith's views remain central to modern capitalist organization and doctrine.

Source: From In Inquiry Into the Nature and Causes of the Wealth of Nations by Adam Smith, Oxford at Clarendon Press, 1880.

Chapter VII

Of the Natural and Market Price of Commodities

There is in every society or neighbourhood an ordinary or average rate both of wages and profit in every different employment of labour and stock. This rate is naturally regulated, as I shall show hereafter, partly by the general circumstances of the society, their riches or poverty, their advancing, stationary, or declining condition; and partly by the particular nature of each employment.

There is likewise in every society or neighbourhood an ordinary or average rate of rent, which is regulated too, as I shall show hereafter, partly by the general circumstances of the society or neighbourhood in which the land is situated, and partly by the natural or improved fertility of the land.

These ordinary or average rates may be called the natural rates of wages, profit, and rent, at the time and place in which they commonly prevail.

When the price of any commodity is neither more nor less than what is sufficient to pay the rent of the land, the wages of the labour, and the profits of the stock employed in raising, preparing, and bringing it to market, according to their natural rates, the commodity is then sold for what may be called its natural price.

The commodity is then sold precisely for what it is worth, or for what it really costs the person who brings it to market; for though in common language what is called the prime cost of any commodity does not comprehend the profit of the person who is to sell it again, yet if he sells it at a price which does not allow him the ordinary rate of profit in his neighbourhood, he is evidently a loser by the trade; since by employing his stock in some other way he might have made that profit. His profit, besides, is his revenue, the proper fund of his subsistence. As, while he is preparing and bringing the goods to market, he advances to his workmen their wages, or their subsistence; so he advances to himself, in the same manner, his own subsistence, which is generally suitable to the profit which he may reasonably expect from the sale of his goods. Unless they yield him this profit, therefore, they do not repay him what they may very properly be said to have really cost him.

Though the price, therefore, which leaves him this profit, is not always the lowest at which a dealer may sometimes sell his goods, it is the lowest at which he is likely to sell them for any considerable time; at least where there is perfect liberty, or where he may change his trade as often as he pleases.

The actual price at which any commodity is commonly sold is called its market price. It may either be above, or below, or exactly the same with its natural price.

The market price of every particular commodity is regulated by the proportion between the quantity which is actually brought to market, and the demand of those who are willing to pay the natural price of the commodity, or the whole value to the rent, labour, and profit, which must be paid in order to bring it thither. Such people may be called the effectual demanders, and their demand the effectual demand; since it may be sufficient to effectuate the bringing of the commodity to market. It is different from the absolute demand. A very poor man may be said in some sense to have a demand for a coach and six; he might like to have it; but his demand is not an effectual demand, as the commodity can never be brought to market in order to satisfy it.

When the quantity of any commodity which is brought to market falls short of the effectual demand, all those who are willing to pay the whole value of the rent, wages, and profit, which must be paid in order to bring it thither, cannot be supplied with the quantity which they want. Rather than want it altogether, some of them will be willing to give more. A competition will immediately begin among them, and the market price will rise more or less above the natural price, according as either the greatness of the deficiency, or the wealth and wanton luxury of the competitors, happen to animate more or less the eagerness of the competition. Among competitors of equal wealth and luxury the same deficiency will generally occasion a more or less eager competition, according as the acquisition of the commodity happens to be of more or less importance to them. Hence the exorbitant price of the necessaries of life during the blockade of a town or in a famine.

When the quantity brought to market exceeds the effectual demand, it cannot be all sold to those who are willing to pay the whole value of the rent, wages and profit, which must be paid in order to bring it thither. Some part must be sold to those who are willing to pay less, and the low price which they give for it must reduce the price of the whole. The market price will sink more or less below the natural price, according as the greatness of the excess increases more or less the competition of the sellers, or according as it happens to be more or less important to them to get immediately rid of the commodity. The same excess in the importation of perishable, will occasion a much greater competition than in that of durable commodities; in the importation of oranges, for example, than in that of old iron.

When the quantity brought to market is just sufficient to supply the effectual demand and no more, the market price naturally comes to be either exactly, or as nearly as can be judged of, the same with natural price. The whole quantity upon hand can be disposed of for this price, and cannot be disposed of for more. The competition of the different dealers obliges them all to accept of this price, but does not oblige them to accept of less.

The quantity of every commodity brought to market naturally suits itself to the effectual demand. It is the interest of all those who employ their land, labour, or stock, in bringing any commodity to market, that the quantity never should exceed the effectual demand; and it is the interest of all other people that it never should fall short of that demand.

If at any time it exceeds the effectual demand, some of the component parts of its price must be paid below their natural rate. If it is rent, the interest of the landlords will immediately prompt them to withdraw a part of their land; and if it is wages or profit, the interest of the labourers in the one case, and of their employers in the other, will prompt them to withdraw a part of their labour or stock from this employment. The quantity brought to market will soon be no more than sufficient to supply the effectual demand. All the different parts of its price will rise to their natural rate, and the whole price to its natural price.

If, on the contrary, the quantity brought to market should at any time fall short of the effectual demand, some of the component parts of its price must rise above their natural rate. If it is rent, the interest of all other landlords will naturally prompt them to prepare more land for the raising of this commodity; if it is wages or profit, the interest of all other labourers and dealers will soon prompt them to employ more labour and stock in preparing and bringing it to market. The quantity brought thither will soon be sufficient to supply the effectual demand. All the different parts of its price will soon sink to their natural rate, and the whole price to its natural price.

The natural price, therefore, is, as it were, the central price, to which the prices of all commodities are continually gravitating. Different accidents may sometimes keep them suspended a good deal above it, and sometimes force them down even somewhat below it. But whatever may be the obstacles which hinder them from settling in this center of repose and continuance, they are constantly tending towards it.

The whole quantity of industry annually employed in order to bring any commodity to market, naturally suits itself in this manner to the effectual demand. It naturally aims at bringing always that precise quantity thither which may be sufficient to supply, and no more than supply, that demand.

But in some employments the same quantity of industry will in different years produce very different quantities of commodities; while in others it will produce always the same, or very nearly the same. The same number of labourers in husbandry will, in different years, produce very different quantities of corn, wine, oil, hops, &c. But the same number of spinners and weavers will every year produce the same or very nearly the same quantity of linen and woolen cloth. It is only the average produce of the one species of industry which can be suited in any respect to the effectual demand; and as its actual produce is frequently much greater and frequently much less than its average produce, the quantity of the commodities brought to market will sometimes exceed a good deal, and sometimes fall short a good deal, of the effectual demand. Even though that demand therefore should continue always the same, their market price will be liable to great fluctuations, will sometimes fall a good deal below, and sometimes rise a good deal above, their natural price. In the other species of industry, the produce of equal quantities of labour being always the same, or very nearly the same, it can be more exactly suited to the effectual demand. While that demand continues the same, therefore, the market price of the commodities is likely to do so too, and to be either altogether, or as nearly as can be judged of, the same with the natural price. That the price of linen and woolen cloth is liable neither to such frequent nor to such great variations as the price of corn, every man's experience will inform him. The price of the one species of commodities varies only with the variations in the demand: That of the other varies not only with the variations in the demand, but with the much greater and more frequent variations in the quantity of what is brought to market in order to supply that demand.

The occasional and temporary fluctuations in the market price of any commodity fall chiefly upon those parts of its price which resolve themselves into wages and profit. That part which resolves itself into rent is less affected by them. A rent certain in money is not in the least affected by them either in its rate or in its value. A rent which consists either in a certain proportion or in a certain quantity of the rude produce, is no doubt affected in its yearly value by all the occasional and temporary fluctuations in the market price of that rude produce; but it is seldom affected by them in its yearly rate. In settling the terms of the lease, the landlord and farmer endeavour, according to their best judgment, to adjust that rate, not to the temporary and occasional, but to the average and ordinary price of the produce.

Such fluctuations affect both the value and the rate either of wages or of profit, according as the market happens to be either over-stocked or under-stocked with commodities or with labour; with work done, or with work to be done. A public mourning raises the price of black cloth (with which the market is almost always under-stocked upon such occasions), and augments the profits of the merchants who possess any considerable quantity of it. It has no effect upon the wages of the weavers. The market is under-stocked with commodities, not with labour; with work done, not with work to be done. It raises the wages of journeymen taylors. The market is here under-stocked with labour. There is an effectual demand for more labour, for more work to be done than can be had. It sinks the price of coloured silks and cloths, and thereby reduces the profits of the merchants who have any considerable quantity of them upon hand. It sinks too the wages of the workmen employed in preparing such commodities, for which all demand is stopped for six months, perhaps for a twelvemonth. The market is here over-stocked both with commodities and with labour.

But though the market price of every particular commodity is in this manner continually gravitating, if one may say so, towards the natural price, yet sometimes particular accidents, sometimes natural causes, and sometimes particular regulations of police, may, in many commodities, keep up the market price, for a long time together, a good deal above the natural price.

When by an increase in the effectual demand, the market price of some particular commodity happens to rise a good deal above the natural price, those who employ their stocks in supplying that market are generally careful to conceal this change. If it was commonly known, their great profit would tempt so many new rivals to employ their stocks in the same way, that, the effectual demand being fully supplied, the market price would soon be reduced to the natural price, and perhaps for some time even below it. If the market is at a great distance from the residence of those who supply it, they may sometimes be able to keep the secret for several years together, and may so long enjoy their extraordinary profits without any new rivals. Secrets of this kind, however, it must be acknowledged, can seldom be long kept; and the extraordinary profit can last very little longer than they are kept.

Secrets in manufactures are capable of being longer kept than secrets in trade. A dyer who has found the means of producing a particular colour with materials which cost only half the price of those commonly made use of, may, with good management, enjoy the advantage of his discovery as long as he lives, and even leave it as a legacy to his posterity. His extraordinary gains arise from the high price which is paid for his private labour. They properly consist in the high wages of that labour. But as they are repeated upon every part of his stock, and as their whole amount bears, upon that account, a regular proportion to it, they are commonly considered as extraordinary profits of stock.

Such enhancements of the market price are evidently the effects of particular accidents, of which, however, the operation may sometimes last for many years together.

Some natural productions require such a singularity of soil and situation, that all the land in a great country, which is fit for producing them, may not be sufficient to supply the effectual demand. The whole quantity brought to market, therefore, may be disposed of to those who are willing to give more than what is sufficient to pay the rent of the land which produced them, together with the wages of the labour, and the profits of the stock which were employed in preparing and bringing them to market, according to their natural rates. Such commodities may continue for whole centuries together to be sold at this high price; and that part of it which resolves itself into the rent of land is in this case the part which is generally paid above its natural rate. The rent of the land which affords such singular and esteemed productions, like the rent of some vineyards in France of a peculiarly happy soil and situation, bears no regular proportion to the rent of other equally fertile and equally well-cultivated land in its neighbourhood. The wages of the labour and the profits of the stock employed in bringing such commodities to market, on the contrary, are seldom out of their natural proportion to those of the other employments of labour and stock in their neighbourhood.

Such enhancements of the market price are evidently the effect of natural causes which may hinder the effectual demand from ever being fully supplied, and which may continue, therefore, to operate for ever.

A monopoly granted either to an individual or to a trading company has the same effect as a secret in trade or manufactures. The monopolists, by keeping the market constantly understocked, by never fully supplying the effectual demand, sell their commodities much above the natural price, and raise their emoluments, whether they consist in wages or profit, greatly above their natural rate.

The price of monopoly is upon every occasion the highest which can be got. The natural price, or the price of free competition, on the contrary, is the lowest which can be taken, not upon every occasion indeed, but for any considerable time together. The one is upon every occasion the highest which can be squeezed out of the buyers, or which, it is supposed, they will consent to give: The other is the lowest which the sellers can commonly afford to take, and at the same time continue their business.

The exclusive privileges of corporations, statutes of apprenticeship, and all those laws which restrain, in particular employments, the competition to a smaller number than might otherwise go into them, have the same tendency, though in a less degree. They are a sort of enlarged monopolies, and may frequently, for ages together, and in whole classes of employments, keep up the market price of particular commodities above the natural price, and maintain both the wages of the labour and the profits of the stock employed about them somewhat above their natural rate.

Such enhancements of the market price may last as long as the regulations of police which give occasion to them.

The market price of any particular commodity, though it may continue long above, can seldom continue long below, its natural price. Whatever part of it was paid below the natural rate, the persons whose interest it affected would immediately feel the loss, and would immediately withdraw either so much land, or so much labour, or so much stock, from being employed about it, that the quantity brought to market would soon be no more than sufficient to supply the effectual demand. Its market price, therefore, would soon rise to the natural price. This at least would be the case where there was perfect liberty.

The same statutes of apprenticeship and other corporation laws indeed, which, when a manufacture is in prosperity, enable the workman to raise his wages a good deal above their natural rate, sometimes oblige him, when it decays, to let them down a good deal below it.

24.2

The Communist Manifesto (1848), Karl Marx and Friedrich Engels

Karl Marx (1815-1883) was the German son of a Jewish lawyer and the founder of modern international communism. He studied law at Bonn and Berlin but took up history, Hegelian philosophy, and Feuerbach's materialism. He edited a radical newspaper in the Rhineland, and, after it was suppressed, moved to Paris (1843) and Brussels (1845). There, with Friedrich Engels as his closest collaborator and disciple, he reorganized the Communist League, which met in London in 1847. In 1848 they completed the *Communist Manifesto,* which attacked the state as the instrument of oppression, and religion and culture as the ideologies of the capitalist class. He was expelled from Brussels, and in 1849 settled in London, where he studied economics and wrote the first volume of his major work, *Das Kapital* (1867). Marx died with this work unfinished.

Source: From Manifesto of the Communist Party by Karl Marx and Friedrich Engels, C. H. Kerr, 1913.

I

Bourgeois and Proletarians

The history of all hitherto existing society is the history of class struggles.

Freeman and slave, patrician and plebeian, lord and serf, guild-master and journeyman, in a word, oppressor and oppressed, stood in constant opposition to one another, carried on uninterrupted, now hidden, now open fight, a fight that each time ended, either in a revolutionary re-constitution of society at large, or in the common ruin of the contending classes.

In the earlier epochs of history we find almost everywhere a complicated arrangement of society into various orders, a manifold gradation of social rank. In ancient Rome we have patricians, knights, plebeians, slaves; in the middle ages, feudal lords, vassals, guild-masters, journeymen, apprentices, serfs; in almost all of these classes, again, subordinate gradations.

The modern bourgeois society that has sprouted from the ruins of feudal society, has not done away with class antagonisms. It has but established new classes, new conditions of oppression, new forms of struggle in place of the old ones.

Our epoch, the epoch of the bourgeoisie, possesses, however, this distinctive feature; it has simplified the class antagonisms. Society as a whole is more and more splitting up into two great hostile camps, into two great classes directly facing each other: Bourgeoisie and Proletariat.

From the serfs of the middle ages sprang the chartered burghers of the earliest towns. From these burgesses the first elements of the bourgeoisie were developed.

The discovery of America, the rounding of the Cape, opened up fresh ground for the rising bourgeoisie. The East Indian and Chinese markets, the colonization of America, trade with the colonies, the increase in the means of exchange and in commodities generally, gave to commerce, to navigation, to industry, an impulse never before known, and thereby, to the revolutionary element in the tottering feudal society, a rapid development.

The feudal system of industry, under which industrial production was monopolized by closed guilds, now no longer sufficed for the growing wants of the new market. The manufacturing system took its place. The guild-masters were pushed on one side by the manufacturing middle-class: division of labor between the different corporate guilds vanished in the face of division of labor in each single workshop.

Meantime the markets kept ever growing, the demand ever rising. Even manufacture no longer sufficed. Thereupon, steam and machinery revolutionized industrial production. The place of manufacture was taken by the giant, Modern Industry, the place of the industrial middle-class, by industrial millionaires, the leaders of whole industrial armies, the modern bourgeois.

Modern industry has established the world market, for which the discovery of America paved the way. This market has given an immense development to commerce, to navigation, to communication by land.

The immediate aim of the Communists is the same as that of all the other proletarian parties: formation of the proletariat into a class, overthrow of the bourgeois of supremacy, conquest of political power by the proletariat.

The theoretical conclusions of the Communists are in no way based on ideas or principles that have been invented or discovered by this or that would-be universal reformer.

They merely express, in general terms, actual relations springing from an existing class struggle, from a historical movement going on under our very eyes. The abolition of existing property relations is not at all a distinctive feature of Communism.

All property relations in the past have continually been subject to historical change consequent upon the change in historical conditions.

The French Revolution, for example, abolished feudal property in favor of bourgeois property.

The distinguishing feature of Communism is not the abolition of property generally, but the abolition of bourgeois property. But modern bourgeois private property is the final and most complete expression of the system of producing and appropriating products, that is based on class antagonism, on the exploitation of the many by the few.

In this sense, the theory of the Communists may be summed up in the single sentence: Abolition of private property.

We Communists have been reproached with the desire of abolishing the right of personally acquiring property as the fruit of a man's own labor, which property is alleged to be the groundwork of all personal freedom, activity and independence.

Hard won, self-acquired, self-earned property! Do you mean the property of the petty artisan and of the small peasant, a form of property that preceded the bourgeois form? There is no need to abolish that; the development of industry has to a great extent already destroyed it, and is still destroying it daily.

Or do you mean modern bourgeois private property?

But does wage labor create any property for the laborer? Not a bit. It creates capital, *i.e.*, that kind of property which exploits wage labor, and which cannot increase except upon condition of getting a new supply of wage labor for fresh exploitation. Property, in its present form, is based on the antagonism of capital and wage labor. Let us examine both sides of this antagonism.

To be a capitalist is to have not only a purely personal, but a social status in production. Capital is a collective product, and only by the united action of many members, nay, in the last resort, only by the united action of all members of society, can it be set in motion.

Capital is therefore not a personal, it is a social power.

When, therefore, capital is converted into common property, into the property of all members of society, personal property is not thereby transformed into social property. It is only the social character of the property that is changed. It loses its class character.

Let us now take wage labor.

The average price of wage labor is the minimum wage, *i.e.*, that quantum of the means of subsistence which is absolutely requisite to keep the laborer in bare existence as a laborer. What, therefore, the wage laborer appropriates by means of his labor, merely suffices to prolong and reproduce a bare existence. We by no means intend to abolish this personal appropriation of the products of labor, an appropriation that is made for the maintenance and reproduction of human life, and that leaves no surplus where-with to command the labor of others. All that we want to do away with is the miserable character of this appropriation, under which the laborer lives merely to increase capital and is allowed to live only in so far as the interests of the ruling class require it.

In bourgeois society, living labor is but a means to increase accumulated labor. In Communist society accumulated labor is but a means to widen, to enrich, to promote the existence of the laborer.

In bourgeois society, therefore, the past dominates the present; in communist society the present dominates the past. In bourgeois society, capital is independent and has individuality, while the living person is dependent and has no individuality.

And the abolition of this state of things is called by the bourgeois abolition of individuality and freedom! And rightly so. The abolition of bourgeois individuality, bourgeois independence and bourgeois freedom is undoubtedly aimed at.

By freedom is meant, under the present bourgeois conditions of production, free trade, free selling and buying.

But if selling and buying disappears, free selling and buying disappears also. This talk about free selling and buying, and all the other "brave words" of our bourgeoisie about freedom in general have a meaning, if any, only in contrast with restricted selling and buying, with the fettered traders of the Middle Ages, but have no meaning when opposed to the Communistic abolition of buying and selling, of the bourgeois conditions of production, and of the bourgeoisie itself.

You are horrified at our intending to do away with private property. But in your existing society private property is already done away with for nine-tenths of the population; its existence for the few is solely due to its non-existence in the hands of those nine-tenths. You reproach us, therefore, with intending to do away with a form of property, the necessary condition for whose existence is the non-existence of any property for the immense majority of society.

In one word, you reproach us with intending to do away with your property. Precisely so: that is just what we intend.

From the moment when labor can no longer be converted into capital, money, or rent, into a social power capable of being monopolized, *i.e.*, from the moment when individual property can no longer be transformed into bourgeois property, into capital, from that moment, you say, individuality vanishes.

You must, therefore, confess that by "individual" you mean no other person than the bourgeois, than the middleclass owner of property. This person must, indeed, be swept out of the way and made impossible.

Communism deprives no man of the power to appropriate the products of society: all that it does is to deprive him of the power to subjugate the labor of others by means of such appropriation.

On what foundation is the present family, the bourgeois family, based? On capital, on private gain. In its completely developed form this family exists only among the bourgeoisie. But this state of things finds its complement in the practical absence of the family among the proletarians, and in public prostitution.

The bourgeois family will vanish as a matter of course when its complement vanishes, and both will vanish with the vanishing of capital.

Do you charge us with wanting to stop the exploitation of children by their parents? To this crime we plead guilty.

But, you will say, we destroy the most hallowed of relations when we replace home education by social.

And your education! Is not that also social, and determined by the social conditions under which you educate; by the intervention, direct or indirect, of society by means of schools, etc.? The Communists have not invented the intervention of society in education; they do but seek to alter the character of that intervention, and to rescue education from the influence of the ruling class.

The bourgeois clap-trap about the family and education, about the hallowed correlation of parent and child, become all the more disgusting, the more, by the action of Modern Industry, all family ties among the proletarians are torn asunder and their children transformed into simple articles of commerce and instruments of labor.

But you communists would introduce community of women, screams the whole bourgeoisie chorus.

The bourgeois sees in his wife a mere instrument of production. He hears that the instruments of production are to be exploited in common, and, naturally, can come to no other conclusion, than that the lot of being common to all will likewise fall to the women.

He has not even a suspicion that the real point aimed at is to do away with the status of women as mere instruments of production.

For the rest, nothing is more ridiculous than the virtuous indignation of our bourgeois at the community of women which, they pretend, is to be openly and officially established by the Communists. The Communists have no need to introduce community of women; it has existed almost from time immemorial.

Our bourgeois, not content with having the wives and daughters of their proletarians at their disposal, not to speak of common prostitutes, take the greatest pleasure in seducing each others' wives.

Bourgeois marriage is in reality a system of wives in common, and thus, at the most, what the Communists might possibly be reproached with, is that they desire to introduce, in substitution for a hypocritically concealed, an openly legalized community of women. For the rest, it is self-evident that the abolition of the present system of production must bring with it the abolition of the community of women springing from that system, *i.e.*, of prostitution both public and private.

The Communists are further reproached with desiring to abolish countries and nationalities.

The working men have no country. We cannot take from them what they don't possess. Since the proletariat must first of all acquire political supremacy, must rise to be the leading class of the nation, must constitute itself the nation, it is, so far, itself national, though not in the bourgeois sense of the word.

National differences and antagonisms between peoples are daily more and more vanishing, owing to the development of the bourgeoisie, to freedom of commerce, to the world-market, to uniformity in the mode of production and in the conditions of life corresponding thereto.

The supremacy of the proletariat will cause them to vanish still faster. United action, of the leading civilized countries at least, is one of the first conditions for the emancipation of the proletariat.

In proportion as the exploitation of one individual by another is put an end to, the exploitation of one nation by another will also be put an end to. In proportion as the antagonism between classes within the nation vanishes, the hostility of one nation to another will come to an end.

The charges against Communism made from a religious, a philosophical, and generally, from an ideological standpoint, are not deserving of serious examination.

Does it require deep intuition to comprehend that man's ideas, views and conceptions, in one word, man's consciousness, changes with every change in the conditions of his material existence, in his social relations and in his social life?

What else does the history of ideas prove than that intellectual production changes in character in proportion as material production is changed? The ruling ideas of each age have ever been the ideas of its ruling class.

When people speak of ideas that revolutionize society they do but express the fact that within the old society the elements of a new one have been created, and that the dissolution of the old ideas keeps even pace with the dissolution of the old conditions of existence.

When the ancient world was in its last throes the ancient religions were overcome by Christianity. When Christian ideas succumbed in the 18th century to rationalist ideas, feudal society fought its death-battle with the then revolutionary bourgeoisie. The ideas of religious liberty and freedom of conscience merely gave expression to the sway of free competition within the domain of knowledge.

"Undoubtedly," it will be said, "religious, moral, philosophical and judicial ideas have been modified in the course of historical development. But religion, morality, philosophy, political science, and law, constantly survived this change.

"There are, besides, eternal truths, such as Freedom, Justice, etc., that are common to all states of society. But Communism abolishes eternal truths, it abolishes all religion and all morality, instead of constituting them on a new basis; it therefore acts in contradiction to all past historical experience."

What does this accusation reduce itself to? The history of all past society has consisted in the development of class antagonisms, antagonisms that assumed different forms at different epochs.

But whatever form they may have taken, one fact is common to all past ages, viz., the exploitation of one part of society by the other. No wonder, then, that the social consciousness of past ages, despite all the multiplicity and variety it displays, moves within certain common forms, or general ideas, which cannot completely vanish except with the total disappearance of class antagonisms.

The Communist revolution is the most radical rupture with traditional property relations; no wonder that its development involves the most radical rupture with traditional ideas.

But let us have done with the bourgeois objections to Communism.

We have seen above that the first step in the revolution by the working class is to raise the proletariat to the position of ruling class, to win the battle of democracy.

The proletariat will use its political supremacy to wrest, by degrees, all capital from the bourgeoisie, to centralize all instruments of production in the hands of the State, *i.e.,* of the proletariat organized as a ruling class; and to increase the total productive forces as rapidly as possible.

Of course, in the beginning, this cannot be effected except by means of despotic inroads on the rights of property, and on the conditions of bourgeois production; by means of measures, therefore, which appear economically insufficient and untenable, but which in the course of the movement outstrip themselves, necessitate further inroads upon the old social order, and are unavoidable as a means of entirely revolutionizing the mode of production.

These measures will of course be different in different countries.

Nevertheless in the most advanced countries the following will be pretty generally applicable:

1. Abolition of property in land and application of all rents of land to public purposes.
2. A heavy progressive or graduated income tax.
3. Abolition of all right of inheritance.
4. Confiscation of the property of all emigrants and rebels.
5. Centralization of credit in the hands of the State, by means of a national bank with State capital and an exclusive monopoly.
6. Centralization of the means of communication and transport in the hands of the State.

The Communists turn their attention chiefly to Germany, because that country is on the eve of a bourgeois revolution, that is bound to be carried out under more advanced conditions of European civilization, and with a more developed proletariat, than that of England was in the seventeenth and of France in the eighteenth century, and because the bourgeois revolution in Germany will be but the prelude to an immediately following proletarian revolution.

In short, the Communists everywhere support every revolutionary movement against the existing social and political order of things.

In all these movements they bring to the front, as the leading question in each, the property question, no matter what its degree of development at the time.

Finally, they labor everywhere for the union and agreement of the democratic parties of all countries.

The Communists disdain to conceal their views and aims. They openly declare that their ends can be attained only by the forcible overthrow of all existing social conditions. Let the ruling classes tremble at a Communistic revolution. The proletarians have nothing to lose but their chains. They have a world to win.

Working men of all countries, unite!

CHAPTER 25

European Life: Late Nineteenth Century

25.1

The Origin of Species by Means of Natural Selection (1859), Charles Darwin

The nineteenth century was a period of great scientific ideas and discoveries. Perhaps the most important, and the most controversial, was Darwin's theory of evolution.

Charles Darwin (1809-1882), a British naturalist, gathered data while on voyages in the southern Pacific. He used that data to develop his theory of evolution by natural selection. This theory of evolution, particularly as applied to human beings, challenged biblical accounts of creation. He argued that all life, including human life, evolved from lower forms. Evolution was slow and extended over a much longer period than everyone assumed. Natural selection, or survival of the fittest, determined how species evolved. Darwin first formulated his findings and theory in an 1844 essay. However, it was only after 1859, when he published *The Origin of Species by Means of Natural Selection,* that his ideas became well known and widely controversial. He went on to publish *The Descent of Man* in 1871.

SOURCE: From Origin of Species by Means of Natural Selection by Charles Darwin, P. F. Collier & Son, 1900.

Can we doubt (remembering that many more individuals are born than can possibly survive) that individuals having any advantage, however slight, over others, would have the best chance of surviving and of procreating their kind? On the other hand, we may feel sure that any variation in the least degree injurious would be rigidly destroyed. This preservation of favorable individual differences and variations, and the destruction of those which are injurious, I have called Natural Selection, or the Survival of the Fittest. Variations neither useful nor injurious would not be affected by natural selection, and would be left either a fluctuating element, as perhaps we see in certain polymorphic species, or would ultimately become fixed, owing to the nature of the organism and the nature of the conditions.

Several writers have misapprehended or objected to the term Natural Selection. Some have even imagined that natural selection induces variability, whereas it implies only the preservation of such variations as arise and are beneficial to the being under its conditions of life. No one objects to agriculturists speaking of the potent effects of man's selection; and in this case the individual differences given by nature, which man for some objects selects, must of necessity first occur. Others have objected that the term selection implies conscious choice in the animals which become modified; and it has even been urged that, as plants have no volition, natural selection is not applicable to them! In the literal sense of the word, no doubt, natural selection is a false term; but who ever objected to chemists speaking of the elective affinities of the various elements?—and yet an acid cannot strictly be said to elect the base with which it in preference combines. It has been said that I speak of natural selection as an active power or Deity; but who objects to an author speaking of the attraction of gravity as ruling the movements of the planets? Every one knows what is meant and is implied by such metaphorical expressions; and they are almost necessary for brevity. So again it is difficult to avoid personifying the word Nature; but I mean by Nature only the aggregate action and product of many natural laws, and by laws the sequence of events as ascertained by us. With a little familiarity such superficial objections will be forgotten.

We shall best understand the probable course of natural selection by taking the case of a country undergoing some slight physical change, for instance, of climate. The proportional numbers of its inhabitants will almost immediately undergo a change, and some species will probably become extinct. We may conclude, from what we have seen of the intimate and complex manner in which the inhabitants of each country are bound together, that any change in the numerical proportions of the inhabitants, independently of the change of climate itself, would seriously affect the others. If the country were open on its borders, new forms would certainly immigrate, and this would likewise seriously disturb the relations of some of the former inhabitants. Let it be remembered how powerful the influence of a single introduced tree or mammal has been shown to be. But in the case of an island, or of a country partly surrounded by barriers, into which new and better adapted forms could not freely enter, we should then have places in the economy of nature which would assuredly be better filled up, if some of the original inhabitants were in some manner modified; for, had the area been open to immigration, these same places would have been seized on by intruders. In such cases, slight modifications, which in any way favored the individuals of any species, by better adapting them to their altered conditions, would tend to be preserved; and natural selection would have free scope for the work of improvement.

We have good reason to believe, as shown in the first chapter, that changes in the conditions of life give a tendency to increased variability; and in the foregoing cases the conditions have changed, and this would manifestly be favorable to natural selection, by affording a better chance of the occurrence of profitable variations. Unless such occur, natural selection can do nothing. Under the term of "variations," it must never be forgotten that mere individual differences are included. As man can produce a great result with his domestic animals and plants by adding up in any given direction individual differences, so could natural selection, but far more easily from having incomparably longer time for action. Nor do I believe that any great physical change, as of climate, or any unusual degree of isolation to check immigration, is necessary in order that new and unoccupied places should be left for natural selection to fill up by improving some of the varying inhabitants. For as all the inhabitants of each country are struggling together with nicely balanced forces, extremely slight modifications in the structure or habits of one species would often give it an advantage over others; and still further modifications of the same kind would often still further increase the advantage, as long as the species continued under the same conditions of life and profited by similar means of subsistence and defence. No country can be named in which all the native inhabitants are now so perfectly adapted to each other and to the physical conditions under which they live, that none of them could be still better adapted or improved; for in all countries the natives have been so far conquered by naturalized productions that they have allowed some foreigners to take firm possession of the land. And as foreigners have thus in every country beaten some of the natives, we may safely conclude that the natives might have been modified with advantage, so as to have better resisted the intruders.

As man can produce, and certainly has produced, a great result by his methodical and unconscious means of selection, what may not natural selection effect? Man can act only on external and visible characters: Nature, if I may be allowed to personify the natural preservation or survival of the fittest, cares nothing for appearances, except in so far as they are useful to any being. She can act on every internal organ, on every shade of constitutional difference, on the whole machinery of life. Man selects only for his own good: Nature only for that of the being which she tends. Every selected character is fully exercised by her, as is implied by the fact of their selection. Man keeps the natives of many climates in the same country; he seldom exercises each selected character in some peculiar and fitting manner; he feeds a long and a short beaked pigeon on the same food; he does not exercise a long-backed or long-legged quadruped in any peculiar manner; he exposes sheep with long and short wool to the same climate. He does not allow the most vigorous males to struggle for the females. He does not rigidly destroy all inferior animals, but protects during each varying season, as far as lies in his power, all his productions. He often begins his selection by some half-monstrous form; or at least by some modification prominent enough to catch the eye or to be plainly useful to him. Under nature, the slightest differences of structure or constitution may well turn the nicely-balanced scale in the struggle for life, and so be preserved. How fleeting are the wishes and efforts of man! how short his time! and consequently how poor will be his results, compared with those accumulated by Nature during whole geological periods! Can we wonder, then, that Nature's productions should be far "truer" in character than man's productions; that they should be infinitely better adapted to the most complex conditions of life, and should plainly bear the stamp of far higher workmanship?

Illustrations of the Action of Natural Selection, or the Survival of the Fittest

In order to make it clear how, as I believe, natural selection acts, I must beg permission to give one or two imaginary illustrations. Let us take the case of a wolf, which preys on various animals, securing some by craft, some by strength, and some by fleetness; and let us suppose that the fleetest prey, a deer for instance, had from any change in the country increased in numbers, or that other prey had decreased in numbers, during that season of the year when the wolf was hardest pressed for food. Under such circumstances the swiftest and slimmest wolves would have the best chance of surviving and so be preserved or selected—provided always that they retained strength to master their prey at this or some other period of the year, when they were compelled to prey on other animals. I can see no more reason to doubt that this would be the result than that man should be able to improve the fleetness of his greyhounds by careful and methodical selection, or by that kind of unconscious selection which follows from each man trying to keep the best dogs without any thought of modifying the breed. I may add, that, according to Mr. Pierce, there are two varieties of the wolf inhabiting the Catskill Mountains, in the United States, one with a light greyhound-like form, which pursues deer, and the other more bulky, with shorter legs, which more frequently attacks the shepherd's flocks.

To the effects of intercrossing in eliminating variations of all kinds, I shall have to recur; but it may be here remarked that most animals and plants keep to their proper homes, and do not needlessly wander about; we see this even with migratory birds, which almost always return to the same spot. Consequently each newly-formed variety would generally be at first local, as seems to be the common rule with varieties in a state of nature; so that similarly modified individuals would soon exist in a small body together, and would often breed together. If the new variety were successful in its battle for life, it would slowly spread from a central district, competing with and conquering the unchanged individuals on the margins of an ever-increasing circle.

It may be worth while to give another and more complex illustration of the action of natural selection. Certain plants excrete sweet juice, apparently for the sake of eliminating something injurious from the sap: this is effected, for instance, by glands at the base of the stipules in some Leguminosæ, and at the backs of the leaves of the common laurel. This juice, though small in quantity, is greedily sought by insects; but their visits do not in any way benefit the plant. Now, let us suppose that the juice or nectar was excreted from the inside of the flowers of a certain number of plants of any species. Insects in seeking the nectar would get dusted with pollen, and would often transport it from one flower to another. The flowers of two distinct individuals of the same species would thus get crossed; and the act of crossing, as can be fully proved, gives rise to vigorous seedlings, which consequently would have the best chance of flourishing and surviving. The plants which produced flowers with the largest glands or nectaries, excreting most nectar, would oftenest be visited by insects, and would oftenest be crossed; and so in the long run would gain the upper hand and form a local variety. The flowers, also, which had their stamens and pistils placed, in relation to the size and habits of the particular insect which visited them, so as to favor in any degree the transportal of the pollen, would likewise be favored. We might have taken the case of insects visiting flowers for the sake of collecting pollen instead of nectar; and as pollen is formed for the sole purpose of fertilization, its destruction appears to be a simple loss to the plant; yet if a little pollen were carried, at first occasionally and then habitually, by the pollen-devouring insects from flower to flower, and a cross thus effected, although nine-tenths of the pollen were destroyed it might still be a great gain to the plant to be thus robbed; and the individuals which produced more and more pollen, and had larger anthers, would be selected.

25.2

Social Darwinism: Poor Laws and The Coming Slavery (1884), Herbert Spencer

In *Social Statics and Man Versus the State* (1884), Herbert Spencer gives Darwinian evolution a political-economic dimension and uses it to support a policy of strict *laissez-faire*. Spencer argued that the struggle between the fit and unfit, which dominates the world of nature, must not be thwarted in human society by social welfare measures. In the long run, Spencer said, the protection of the unfit will ruin the human race.

Source: Herbert Spencer, *Social Statics and Man Versus the State* (New York: D. Appleton, 1892), pp. 149-154, 302-303, 321-323, 327-333.

Poor Laws

Pervading all Nature we may see at work a stern discipline which is a little cruel that it may be very kind. That state of universal warfare maintained throughout the lower creation, to the great perplexity of many worthy people, is at bottom the most merciful provision which the circumstances admit of. It is much better that the ruminant animal, when deprived by age of the vigour which made its existence a pleasure, should be killed by some beast of prey, than that it should linger out a life made painful by infirmities, and eventually die of starvation. By the destruction of all such, not only is existence ended before it becomes burdensome, but room is made for a younger generation capable of the fullest enjoyment; and, moreover, out of the very act of substitution happiness is derived for a tribe of predatory creatures. Note, further, that their carnivorous enemies not only remove from herbivorous herds individuals past their prime, but also weed out the sickly, the malformed, and the least fleet or powerful. By the aid of which purifying process, as well as by the fighting so universal in the pairing season, all vitiation of the race through the multiplication of its inferior samples is prevented; and the maintenance of a constitution completely adapted to surrounding conditions, and therefore most productive of happiness, is ensured.

The development of the higher creation is a progress towards a form of being, capable of a happiness undiminished by these drawbacks. It is in the human race that the consummation is to be accomplished. Civilization is the last stage of its accomplishment. And the ideal man is the man in whom all the conditions to that accomplishment are fulfilled. Meanwhile, the well-being of existing humanity and the unfolding of it into this ultimate perfection, are both secured by that same beneficial though severe discipline, to which the animate creation at large is subject. It seems hard that an unskilfulness which with all his efforts he cannot overcome, should entail hunger upon the artisan. It seems hard that a labourer incapacitated by sickness from competing with his stronger fellows, should have to bear the resulting privations. It seems hard that widows and orphans should be left to struggle for life or death. Nevertheless, when regarded not separately but in connexion with the interests of universal humanity, these harsh fatalities are seen to be full of beneficence—the same beneficence which brings to early graves the children of diseased parents, and singles out the intemperate and the debilitated as the victims of an epidemic.

There are many very amiable people who have not the nerve to look this matter fairly in the face. Disabled as they are by their sympathies with present suffering, from duly regarding ultimate consequences, they pursue a course which is injudicious, and in the end even cruel. We do not consider it true kindness in a mother to gratify her child with sweetmeats that are likely to make it ill. We should think it a very foolish sort of benevolence which led a surgeon to let his patient's disease progress to a fatal issue, rather than inflict pain by an operation. Similarly, we must call those spurious philanthropists who, to prevent present misery, would entail greater misery on future generations. That rigorous necessity which, when allowed to operate, becomes so sharp a spur to the lazy and so strong a bridle to the random, these paupers' friends would repeal, because of the wailings it here and there produces. Blind to the fact that under the natural order of things society is constantly excreting its unhealthy, imbecile, slow, vacillating, faithless members, these unthinking, though well-meaning, men advocate an interference which not only stops the purifying process, but even increases the vitiation—absolutely encourages the multiplication of the reckless and incompetent by offering them an unfailing provision, and *dis*courages the multiplication of the competent and provident by heightening the difficulty of maintaining a family. And thus, in their eagerness to prevent the salutary sufferings that surround us, these sigh-wise and groan-foolish people bequeath to posterity a continually increasing curse.

Returning again to the highest point of view, we find that there is a second and still more injurious mode in which law-enforced charity checks the process of adaptation. To become fit for the social state, man has not only to lose his savageness but he has to acquire the capacities needful for civilized life. Power of application must be developed; such modification of the intellect as shall qualify it for its new tasks must take place; and, above all, there must be gained the ability to sacrifice a small immediate gratification for a future great one. The state of transition will of course be an unhappy state. Misery inevitably results from incongruity between constitution and conditions. Humanity is being pressed against the inexorable necessities of its new position—is being moulded into harmony with them, and has to bear the resulting happiness as best it can. The process *must* be undergone and the sufferings *must* be endured. No power on Earth, no cunningly-devised laws of statesmen, no world-rectifying schemes of the humane, no communist panaceas, no reforms that men ever did broach or ever will broach, can diminish them one jot. Intensified they may be, and are; and in preventing their intensification the philanthropic will find ample scope for exertion. But there is bound up with the change a *normal* amount of suffering, which cannot be lessened without altering the very laws of life. Every attempt at mitigation of this eventuates in exacerbation of it. All that a poor-law or any kindred institution can do, is to partially suspend the transition—to take off for a time, from certain members of society, the painful pressure which is effecting their transformation. At best this is merely to postpone what must ultimately be borne. But it is more than this: it is to undo what has already been done. For the circumstances to which adaptation is taking place cannot be superseded without causing a retrogression; and as the whole process must some time or other be passed through, the lost ground must be gone over again, and the attendant pain borne afresh.

At first sight these considerations seem conclusive against *all* relief to the poor—voluntary as well as compulsory; and it is no doubt true that they imply a condemnation of whatever private charity enables the recipients to elude the necessities of our social existence. With this condemnation, however, no rational man will quarrel. That careless squandering of pence which has fostered into perfection a system of organized begging—which has made skillful mendicancy more profitable than ordinary manual labour—which induces the simulation of diseases and deformities—which has called into existence warehouses for the sale and hire of impostor's dresses—which has given to pity-inspiring babes a market value of 9*d*. per day—the unthinking benevolence which has generated all this, cannot but be disapproved by every one. Now it is only against this injudicious charity that the foregoing argument tells. To that charity which may be described as helping men to help themselves, it make no objection—countenances it rather. And in helping men to help themselves, there remains abundant scope for the exercise of a people's sympathies. Accidents will still supply victims on whom generosity may be legitimately expended. Men thrown off the track by unforeseen events, men who have failed for want of knowledge inaccessible to them, men ruined by the dishonesty of others, and men in whom hope long delayed has made the heart sick, may, with advantage to all parties, be assisted. Even the prodigal, after severe hardships has branded his memory with the unbending conditions of social life to which he must submit, may properly have another trial afforded him. And, although by these ameliorations the process of adaptation must be remotely interfered with, yet, in the majority of cases, it will not be so much retarded in one direction as it will be advanced in another.

Objectionable as we find a poor-law to be, even under the supposition that it does what it is intended to do—diminish present suffering—how shall we regard it on finding that in reality it does no such thing—cannot do any such thing? Yet, paradoxical as the assertion looks, this is absolutely the fact. Let but the observer cease to contemplate so fixedly one side of the phenomenon—pauperism and its relief, and begin to examine the other side—rates and the *ultimate* contributors of them, and he will discover that to suppose the sum-total of distress diminishable by act-of-parliament bounty is a delusion.

Here, at any specified period, is a given quantity of food and things exchangeable for food, in the hands or at the command of the middle and upper classes. A certain portion of this food is needed by these classes themselves, and is consumed by them at the same rate, or very near it, be there scarcity or abundance. Whatever variation occurs in the sum-total of food and its equivalents, must therefore affect the remaining portion, not used by these classes for personal sustenance. This remaining portion is paid by them to the people in return for their labour, which is partly expended in the production of a further supply of necessaries, and partly in the production of luxuries. Hence, by how much this portion is deficient, by so much must the people come short. A re-distribution by legislative or other agency cannot make that sufficient for them which was previously insufficient. It can do nothing but change the parties by whom the insufficiency is felt. If it gives enough to some who else would not have enough, it must inevitably reduce certain others to the condition of not having enough.

The Coming Slavery

The kinship of pity to love is shown among other ways in this, that it idealizes its object. Sympathy with one in suffering suppresses, for the time being, remembrance of his transgressions. The feeling which vents itself in "poor fellow!" on seeing one in agony, excludes the thought of "bad fellow," which might at another time arise. Naturally, then, if the wretched are unknown or but vaguely known, all the demerits they may have are ignored; and thus it happens that when the miseries of the poor are dilated upon, they are thought of as the miseries of the deserving poor, instead of being thought of as the miseries of the undeserving poor, which in large measure they should be. Those whose hardships are set forth in pamphlets and proclaimed in sermons and speeches which echo throughout society, are assumed to be all worthy souls, grievously wronged; and none of them are thought of as bearing the penalties of their misdeeds.

On hailing a cab in a London street, it is surprising how frequently the door is officiously opened by one who expects to get something for his trouble. The surprise lessens after counting the many loungers about tavern-doors, or after observing the quickness with which a street-performance, or procession, draws from neighbouring slums and stable-yards a group of idlers. Seeing how numerous they are in every small area, it becomes manifest that tens of thousands of such swarm through London. "They have no work," you say. Say rather that they either refuse work or quickly turn themselves out of it. They are simply good-for-nothings, who in one way or other live on the good-for-somethings—vagrants and sots, criminals and those on the way to crime, youths who are burdens on hard-worked parents, men who appropriate the wages of their wives, fellows who share the gains of prostitutes; and then, less visible and less numerous, there is a corresponding class of women.

Is it natural that happiness should be the lot of such? or is it natural that they should bring unhappiness on themselves and those connected with them? Is it not manifest that there must exist in our midst an immense amount of misery which is a normal result of misconduct, and ought not to be dissociated from it? There is a notion, always more or less prevalent and just now vociferously expressed, that all social suffering is removable, and that it is the duty of somebody or other to remove it. Both these beliefs are false. To separate pain from ill-doing is to fight against the constitution of things, and will be followed by far more pain. Saving men from the natural penalties of dissolute living, eventually necessitates the infliction of artificial penalties in solitary cells, on tread-wheels, and by the lash. I suppose a dictum on which the current creed and the creed of science are at one, may be considered to have as high an authority as can be found. Well, the command "if any would not work neither should he eat," is simply a Christian enunciation of that universal law of Nature under which life has reached its present height—the law that a creature not energetic enough to maintain itself must die: the sole difference being that the law which in the one case is to be artificially enforced, is, in the other case, a natural necessity. And yet this particular tenet of their religion which science so manifestly justifies, is the one which Christians seem least inclined to accept. The current assumption is that there should be no suffering, and that society is to blame for that which exists. . . ..

. . . Influences of various kinds conspire to increase corporate action and decrease individual action. And the change is being on all sides aided by schemers, each of whom thinks only of his pet plan and not at all of the general reorganization which his plan, joined with others such, are working out. It is said that the French Revolution devoured its own children. Here, an analogous catastrophe seems not unlikely. The numerous socialistic changes made by Act of Parliament, joined with the numerous others presently to be made, will by-and-by be all merged in State-socialism—swallowed in the vast wave which they have little by little raised.

"But why is this change described as 'the coming slavery'?" is a question which many will still ask. The reply is simple. All socialism involves slavery.

What is essential to the idea of a slave? We primarily think of him as one who is owned by another. To be more than nominal, however, the ownership must be shown by control of the slave's actions—a control which is habitually for the benefit of the controller. That which fundamentally distinguishes the slave is that he labours under coercion to satisfy another's desires. The relation admits of sundry gradations. Remembering that originally the slave is a prisoner whose life is at the mercy of his captor, it suffices here to note that there is a harsh form of slavery in which, treated as an animal, he has to expend his entire effort for his owner's advantage. Under a system less harsh, though occupied chiefly in working for his owner, he is allowed a short time in which to work for himself, and some ground on which to grow extra food. A further amelioration gives him power to sell the produce of his plot and keep the proceeds. Then we come to the still more moderated form which commonly arises where, having been a free man working on his own land, conquest turns him into what we distinguish as a serf; and he has to give to his owner each year a fixed amount of labour or produce, or both: retaining the rest himself. Finally, in some cases, as in Russia before serfdom was abolished, he is allowed to leave his owner's estate and work or trade for himself elsewhere, under the condition that he shall pay an annual sum. What is it which, in these cases, leads us to qualify our conception of the slavery as more or less severe? Evidently the greater or smaller extent to which effort is compulsorily expended for the benefit of another instead of for self-benefit. If all the slave's labour is for his owner the slavery is heavy, and if but little it is light. Take now a further step. Suppose an owner dies, and his estate with its slaves comes into the hands of trustees; or suppose the estate and everything on it to be bought by a company; is the condition of the slave any the better if the amount of his compulsory labour remains the same? Suppose that for a company we substitute the community; does it make any difference to the slave if the time he has to work for others is as great, and the time left for himself is as small, as before? The essential question is—How much is he compelled to labour for other benefit than his own, and how much can he labour for his own benefit? The degree of his slavery varies according to the ratio between that which he is forced to yield up and that which he is allowed to retain; and it matters not whether his master is a single person or a society. If without option, he has to labour for the society, and receives from the general stock such portion as the society awards him, he becomes a slave to the society. . . .

Evidently then, the changes made, the changes in progress, and the changes urged, will carry us not only towards State-ownership of land and dwellings and means of communication, all to be administered and worked by State-agents, but towards State-usurpation of all industries: the private forms of which, disadvantaged more and more in competition with the State, which can arrange everything for its own convenience, will more and more die away; just as many voluntary schools have, in presence of Board-schools. And so will be brought about the desired ideal of the socialists.

And now when there has been compassed this desired ideal, which "practical" politicians are helping socialists to reach, and which is so tempting on that bright side which socialists contemplate, what must be the accompanying shady side which they do not contemplate? It is a matter of common remark, often made when a marriage is impending, that those possessed by strong hopes habitually dwell on the promised pleasures and think nothing of the accompanying pains. A further exemplification of this truth is supplied by these political enthusiasts and fanatical revolutionists. Impressed with the miseries existing under our present social arrangements, and not regarding these miseries as caused by the ill-working of a human nature but partially adapted to the social state, they imagine them to be forthwith curable by this or that rearrangement. Yet, even did their plans succeed it could only be by substituting one kind of evil for another. A little deliberate thought would show that under their proposed arrangements, their liberties must be surrendered in proportion as their material welfares were cared for.

For no form of co-operation, small or great, can be carried on without regulation, and an implied submission to the regulating agencies. Even one of their own organizations for effecting social changes yields them proof. It is compelled to have its councils, its local and general officers, its authoritative leaders, who must be obeyed under penalty of confusion and failure. And the experience of those who are loudest in their advocacy of a new social order under the paternal control of a Government, shows that even in private voluntarily-formed societies, the power of the regulative organization becomes great, if not irresistible: often, indeed, causing grumbling and restiveness among those controlled. Trades-unions which carry on a kind of industrial war in defence of workers' interests *versus* employers' interests, find that subordination almost military in its strictness is needful to secure efficient action; for divided councils prove fatal to success. And even in bodies of co-operators, formed for carrying on manufacturing or distributing businesses, and not needing that obedience to leaders which is required where the aims are offensive or defensive, it is still found that the administrative agency gains such supremacy that there arise complaints about "the tyranny of organization." Judge then what must happen when, instead of relatively small combinations, to which men may belong or not as they please, we have a national combination in which each citizen finds himself incorporated, and from which he cannot separate himself without leaving the country. Judge what must under such conditions become the despotism of a graduated and centralized officialism, holding in its hands the resources of the community, and having behind it whatever amount of force it finds requisite to carry out its decrees and maintain what it calls order. Well may Prince Bismarck display leanings towards State-socialism.

And then after recognizing, as they must if they think out their scheme, the power possessed by the regulative agency in the new social system so temptingly pictured, let its advocates ask themselves to what end this power must be used. Not dwelling exclusively, as they habitually do, on the material well-being and the mental gratifications to be provided for them by a beneficent administration, let them dwell a little on the price to be paid. The officials cannot create the needful supplies: they can but distribute among individuals that which the individuals have joined to produce. If the public agency is required to provide for them, it must reciprocally require them to furnish the means. There cannot be, as under our existing system, agreement between employer and employed—this the scheme excludes. There must in place of it be command by local authorities over workers, and acceptance by the workers of that which the authorities assign to them. And this, indeed, is the arrangement distinctly, but as it would seem inadvertently, pointed to by the members of the Democratic Federation. For they propose that production should be carried on by "agricultural and industrial *armies* under State-control": apparently not remembering that armies pre-suppose grades of officers, by whom obedience would have to be insisted upon; since otherwise neither order nor efficient work could be ensured. So that each would stand toward the governing agency in the relation of slave to master.

"But the governing agency would be a master which he and others made and kept constantly in check; and one which therefore would not control him or others more than was needful for the benefit of each and all."

To which reply the first rejoinder is that, even if so, each member of the community as an individual would be a slave to the community as a whole. Such a relation has habitually existed in militant communities, even under quasi-popular forms of government. In ancient Greece the accepted principle was that the citizen belonged neither to himself nor to his family, but belonged to his city—the city being with the Greek equivalent to the community. And this doctrine, proper to a state of constant warfare, is a doctrine which socialism unawares reintroduces into a state intended to be purely industrial. The services of each will belong to the aggregate of all; and for these services, such returns will be given as the authorities think proper. So that even if the administration is of the beneficent kind intended to be secured, slavery, however mild, must be the outcome of the arrangement.

A second rejoinder is that the administration will presently become not of the intended kind, and that the slavery will not be mild. The socialist speculation is vitiated by an assumption like that which vitiates the speculations of the "practical" politician. It is assumed that officialism will work as it is intended to work, which it never does. The machinery of Communism, like existing social machinery, has to be framed out of existing human nature; and the defects of existing human nature will generate in the one the same evils as in the other. The love of power, the selfishness, the injustice, the untruthfulness, which often in comparatively short times bring private organizations to disaster, will inevitably, where their effects accumulate from generation to generation, work evils far greater and less remediable; since, vast and complex and possessed of all the resources, the administrative organization once developed and consolidated, must become irresistible. And if there needs proof that the periodic exercise of electoral power would fail to prevent this, it suffices to instance the French Government, which, purely popular in origin, and subject at short intervals to popular judgment, nevertheless tramples on the freedom of citizens to an extent which the English delegates to the late Trades Unions Congress say "is a disgrace to, and an anomaly in, a Republican nation."

The final result would be a revival of despotism. A disciplined army of civil officials, like an army of military officials, gives supreme power to its head—a power which has often led to usurpation, as in mediæval Europe and still more in Japan—nay, has thus so led among our neighbours, within our own times. The recent confessions of M. de Maupas have shown how readily a constitutional head, elected and trusted by the whole people, may, with the aid of a few unscrupulous confederates, paralyze the representative body and make himself autocrat. That those who rose to power in a socialistic organization would not scruple to carry out their aims at all costs, we have good reason for concluding. When we find that shareholders who, sometimes gaining but often losing, have made that railway-system by which national prosperity has been so greatly increased, are spoken of by the council of the Democratic Federation as having "laid hands" on the means of communication, we may infer that those who directed a socialistic administration might interpret with extreme perversity the claims of individuals and classes under their control. And when, further, we find members of this same council urging that the State should take possession of the railways, "with or without compensation," we may suspect that the heads of the ideal society desired, would be but little deterred by consideration of equity from pursuing whatever policy they thought needful: a policy which would always be one identified with their own supremacy. It would need but a war with an adjacent society, or some internal discontent demanding forcible suppression, to at once transform a socialistic administration into a grinding tyranny like that of ancient Peru; under which the mass of the people, controlled by grades of officials, and leading lives that were inspected out-of-doors and in-doors, laboured for the support of the organization which regulated them, and were left with but a bare subsistence for themselves. And then would be completely revived, under a different form, that *régime* of status—that system of compulsory co-operation, the decaying tradition of which is represented by the old Toryism, and towards which the new Toryism is carrying us back.

"But we shall be on our guard against all that—we shall take precautions to ward off such disasters," will doubtless say the enthusiasts. Be they "practical" politicians with their new regulative measures, or communists with their schemes for re-organizing labour their reply is ever the same;—"It is true that plans of kindred nature have, from unforeseen causes or adverse accidents, or the misdeeds of those concerned, been brought to failure; but this time we shall profit by past experiences and succeed." There seems no getting people to accept the truth, which nevertheless is conspicuous enough, that the welfare of a society and the justice of its arrangements are at bottom dependent on the characters of its members; and that improvement in neither can take place without that improvement in character which results from carrying on peaceful industry under the restraints imposed by an orderly social life. The belief, not only of the socialists but also of those so-called Liberals who are diligently preparing the way for them, is that by due skill an ill-working humanity may be framed into well-working institutions. It is a delusion. The defective natures of citizens will show themselves in the bad acting of whatever social structure they are arranged into. There is no political alchemy by which you can get golden conduct out of leaden instincts.

CHAPTER 26

Western Imperialism, 1800-1914

26.1

The White Man's Burden (1899), Rudyard Kipling

Active imperialists and the public often glorified imperialism. Part of this glorification involved perceiving imperialism as a Christian and nationalistic venture. It portrayed imperialism as a heroic deed carried out by Western idealists trying to spread the "benefits" of "true civilization" to "less advanced" peoples of the world. One popular expression of this idea was the writing of Rudyard Kipling (1865-1936), an Englishman who wrote *The White Man's Burden* in 1899 to celebrate the American annexation of the Philippines.

Source: From Collected Verse, Doubleday & Company, Inc., 1907.

Take up the White Man's burden—
    Send forth the best ye breed—
Go bind your sons to exile
    To serve your captives' need;
To wait in heavy harness,
    On fluttered folk and wild—
Your new-caught, sullen peoples,
    Half-devil and half-child

Take up the White Man's burden—
    In patience to abide,
To veil the threat of terror
    And check the show of pride;
By open speech and simple,
    An hundred times made plain,
To seek another's profit,
    And work another's gain.

Take up the White Man's burden—
    The savage wars of peace—
Fill full the mouth of Famine
    And bid the sickness cease;

And when your goal is nearest
    The end for others sought,
Watch Sloth and heathen Folly
    Bring all your hope to nought.

Take up the White Man's burden—
    No tawdry rule of kings,
But toil of serf and sweeper—
    The tale of common things.
The ports ye shall not enter,
    The roads ye shall not tread,
Go make them with your living,
    And mark them with your dead.

Take up the White Man's burden—
    And reap his old reward:
The blame of those ye better,
    The hate of those ye guard—
The cry of hosts ye humour
    (Ah, slowly!) toward the light:—
"Why brought ye us from bondage,
    "Our loved Egyptian night?"
Take up the White Man's burden—
    Ye dare not stoop to less—
Nor call too loud on Freedom
    To cloak your weariness
By all ye cry or whisper,
    By all ye leave or do,
The silent, sullen peoples
    Shall weigh your Gods and you.

Take up the White Man's burden—
    Have done with childish days—
The lightly proffered laurel,
    The easy, ungrudged praise.
Comes now, to search your manhood
    Through all the thankless years,
Cold, edged with dear-bought wisdom,
    The judgment of your peers!

26.2

Standard Treaty (1886), Royal Niger Company

The Royal Niger Company was a company founded to secure the Niger regions for the British against French competition. The British amalgamated their traders on the River Niger into the National African Company. In 1886 it obtained a royal charter to rule a large part of what later became Nigeria. They secured the navigable portions of the Niger, frustrated the French, and destroyed the power of African middlemen. The charter expired in 1898, and the British consolidated the various parts of Nigeria into a British colony, which achieved independence in 1960.

Source: In Edward Hertslet, ed., THE MAP OF AFRICA BY TREATY, 2nd edition, Her Majesty's Stationery Office, 1896.

We, the undersigned chiefs of ______, with the view to the bettering of the condition of our country and people, do this day cede to the Royal Niger Company, for ever, the whole of our territory extending from ______.

We also give to the said Royal Niger Company full power to settle all native disputes arising from any cause whatever, and we pledge ourselves not to enter into any war with other tribes without the sanction of the said Royal Niger Company.

We understand that the said Royal Niger Company have full power to mine, farm, and build in any portion of our country.

We bind ourselves not to have any intercourse with any strangers or foreigners except through the said Royal Niger Company.

In consideration of the foregoing, the said Royal Niger Company (Chartered and Limited) bind themselves not to interfere with any of the native laws or customs of the country, consistently with the maintenance of order and good government.

The said Royal Niger Company agree to pay native owners of land a reasonable amount for any portion they may require.

The said Royal Niger Company bind themselves to protect the said Chiefs from the attacks of any neighboring aggressive tribes.

The said Royal Niger Company also agree to pay the said Chiefs ______ measures native value.

We, the undersigned witnesses, do hereby solemnly declare that the ______ Chiefs whose names are placed opposite their respective crosses have in our presence affixed their crosses of their own free will and consent, and that the said ______ has in our presence affixed his signature.

Done in triplicate at ______, this ______ day of ______, 188 ___.

Declaration by interpreter I, ______, of ______, do hereby solemnly declare that I am well acquainted with the language of the country, and that on the ______ day of ______, 188 ___, I truly and faithfully explained the above Agreement to all the Chiefs present, and that they understood its meaning.

CHAPTER 27

Imperialism in Asia

27.1

Letter of Advice to Queen Victoria, Lin Tse-Hsü

Lin Tse-Hsü (Lin Zexu) (1785-1850) was a Chinese politician. The Chinese regarded him as the first great patriot to resist the incursions of foreign powers into China. Lin was appointed Imperial Commissioner to deal with the problem of the increase in the illegal imports of opium. At Guangzhou (Canton) he held members of the British community hostage in their warehouses until they surrendered their stocks of opium. This resulted in a British punitive expedition, the Opium War. When China suffered defeat, Lin was exiled to Chinese Turkestan, but later recalled.

Source: Reprinted by permission of the publisher from China's Response to the West: A Documentary Survey, 1839-1923, by Ssu-yu Teng and John King Fairbank, pp. 24-27, Cambridge, Mass.: Harvard University Press, Copyright © 1954, 1979 by the President and Fellows of Harvard College. Copyright renewed 1982 by Ssu-yu Teng and John King Fairbank.

A communication: Magnificently our great emperor soothes and pacifies China and the foreign countries, regarding all with the same kindness. If there is profit, then he shares it with the peoples of the world; if there is harm, then he removes it on behalf of the world. This is because he takes the mind of Heaven-and-earth as his mind.

The kings of your honorable country by a tradition handed down from generation to generation have always been noted for their politeness and submissiveness. We have read your successive tributary memorials saying: "In general our countrymen who go to trade in China have always received His Majesty the Emperor's gracious treatment and equal justice," and so on. Privately we are delighted with the way in which the honorable rulers of your country deeply understand the grand principles and are grateful for the Celestial grace. For this reason the Celestial Court in soothing those from afar has redoubled its polite and kind treatment. The profit from trade has been enjoyed by them continuously for two hundred years. This is the source from which your country has become known for its wealth.

But after a long period of commercial intercourse, there appear among the crowd of barbarians both good persons and bad, unevenly. Consequently there are those who smuggle opium to seduce the Chinese people and so cause the spread of the poison to all provinces. Such persons who only care to profit themselves, and disregard their harm to others, are not tolerated by the laws of Heaven and are unanimously hated by human beings. His Majesty the Emperor, upon hearing of this, is in a towering rage. He has specially sent me, his commissioner, to come to Guangdong, and together with the governor-general and governor jointly to investigate and settle this matter. . . .

We find that your country is sixty or seventy thousand *li* [one *li* is roughly a third of a mile] from China. Yet there are barbarian ships that strive to come here for trade for the purpose of making a great profit. The wealth of China is used to profit the barbarians. That is to say, the great profit made by barbarians is all taken from the rightful share of China. By what right do they then in return use the poisonous drug to injure the Chinese people? Even though the barbarians may not necessarily intend to do us harm, yet in coveting profit to an extreme, they have no regard for injuring others. Let us ask, where is your conscience? I have heard that the smoking of opium is very strictly forbidden by your country; that is because the harm caused by opium is clearly understood. Since it is not permitted to do harm to your own country, even less should you let the harm be passed on to other countries—much less to China! Of all that China exports to foreign countries, there is not a single thing that is not beneficial to people; they are of benefit when eaten, or of benefit when used, or of benefit when resold; all are beneficial. Is there a single article from China that has done any harm to foreign countries? Take tea and rhubarb, for example; the foreign countries cannot get along for a single day without them. If China cuts off these benefits with no sympathy for those who are to suffer, then what can the barbarians rely upon to keep themselves alive? Moreover the woolens, camlets, and longells [i.e., textiles] of foreign countries cannot be woven unless they obtain Chinese silk. If China again cuts off this beneficial export, what profit can the barbarians expect to make? As for other foodstuffs, beginning with candy, ginger, cinnamon, and so forth, and articles for use, beginning with silk, satin, chinaware, and so on, all the things that must be had by foreign countries are innumerable. On the other hand, articles coming from the outside to China can only be used as toys. We can take them or get along without them. Since they are not needed by China, what difficulty would there be if we closed the frontier and stopped the trade? Nevertheless, our Celestial Court lets tea, silk, and other goods be shipped without limit and circulated everywhere without begrudging it in the slightest. This is for no other reason but to share the benefit with the people of the whole world.

The goods from China carried away by your country not only supply your own consumption and use but also can be divided up and sold to other countries, producing a triple profit. Even if you do not sell opium, you still have this threefold profit. How can you bear to go further, selling products injurious to others in order to fulfill your insatiable desire? . . .

We have further learned that in London, the capital of your honorable rule, and in Scotland, Ireland, and other places originally no opium has been produced. Only in several places of India under your control, such as Bengal, Madras, Bombay, Patna, Benares, and Malwa, has opium been planted from hill to hill and ponds have been opened for its manufacture. For months and years work is continued in order to accumulate the poison. The obnoxious order ascends, irritating Heaven and frightening the spirits. Indeed you, O King, can eradicate the opium plant in these places, hoe over the fields entirely, and sow in its stead the five grains [i.e., millet, barley, wheat, and so on]. Anyone who dares again attempt to plant and manufacture opium should be severely punished. This would really be a great, benevolent government policy that will increase the commonweal and get rid of evil. For this, Heaven must support you and the spirits must bring you good fortune, prolonging your old age and extending your descendants. All will depend on this act. . . .

Now we have set up regulations governing the Chinese people. He who sells opium shall receive the death penalty and he who smokes it also the death penalty. Now consider this: If the barbarians do not bring opium, then how can the Chinese people resell it, and how can they smoke it? The fact is that the wicked barbarians beguile the Chinese people into a death trap. How then can we grant life only to these barbarians? He who takes the life of even one person still has to atone for it with his own life; yet is the harm done by opium limited to the taking of one life only? Therefore in the new regulations, in regard to those barbarians who bring opium to China, the penalty is fixed at decapitation or strangulation. This is what is called getting rid of a harmful thing on behalf of mankind. . . .

Our Celestial Dynasty rules over and supervises the myriad states and surely possesses unfathomable spiritual dignity. Yet the emperor cannot bear to execute people without having first tried to reform them by instruction. . . . May you, O King, check your wicked and sift out your vicious people before they come to China, in order to guarantee the peace of your nation, to show further the sincerity of your politeness and submissiveness, and to let the two countries enjoy together the blessings of peace. How fortunate, how fortunate indeed! After receiving this dispatch will you immediately give us a prompt reply regarding the details and circumstances of your cutting off the opium traffic. Be sure not to put this off. The above is what has to be communicated. [Vermilion endorsement of the emperor:] This is appropriately worded and quite comprehensive.

Letter to Wu Zixu on the Need for Western Guns and Ships

This letter to his friend Wu Zixu, written two years after the debacle at Guangzhou, expresses Lin's realization of the need for adopting modern weapons and methods of warfare. As one in official disgrace, however, Lin dared not speak out, nor even communicate his thoughts privately except in guarded fashion. Under such circumstances it is understandable that the advocacy of reform should have been hampered and the taking of concrete steps so long delayed.

The rebels' ships on the open sea came and went as they pleased, now in the south and now suddenly in the north, changing successively between morning and evening. If we tried to put up a defense everywhere, not only would we toil and expend ourselves with limit, but also how could we recruit and transport so many troops, militia, artillery, and ammunition, and come to their support quickly? . . .

When I was in office in Guangdong and Guangxi, I had made plans regarding the problems of ships and cannon and a water force. Afraid that there was not enough time to build ships, I at first rented them. Afraid that there was not enough time to cast cannon and that it would not be done according to the regulations, I at first bought foreign ones. The most painful thing was that when the Humen [the Bogue or "Tiger's Mouth," the entrance to the Pearl River] was broken into, a large number of good cannon fell into the hands of the rebellious barbarians. I recall that after I had been punished two years ago, I still took the risk of calling the emperor's attention to two things: ships and guns. At that time, if these things could have been made and prepared, they still could have been used with effect to fight against the enemy in Zhejiang last fall [1841]. Now it is even more difficult to check the wildfire. After all, ships, guns, and a water force are absolutely indispensable. Even if the rebellious barbarians had fled and returned beyond the seas, these things would still have to be urgently planned for, in order to work out the permanent defense of our sea frontiers. . . .

But at this time I must strictly observe the advice to seal my lips as one corks the mouth of a bottle. Toward those with identical aims and interests, however, I suddenly spit out the truth and am unable to control myself. I extremely regret my foolishness and carelessness. Nevertheless, when I turn my thoughts to the depth of your attention to me, then I cannot conceal these things from myself.

27.2

Advice about the Policy of Isolation, Ii Naosuke

Ii Naosuke (1815-60) was a Japanese feudal lord. He was Chief Counsellor, or Elder *(tairo)*, of the Tokugawa Shogunate in 1858-60. Ii took the initiative in signing a commercial treaty with the United States (July 1858), despite strong pro-seclusionist feelings both at the imperial court and among many feudal lords and samurai. He began repressive measures against his critics, which led to his eventual assassination by the retainers of one domain (Mito) that had borne the brunt of his repression.

SOURCE: From Select Documents on Japanese Foreign Policy, translated by W. G. Beasley, 1955. Reprinted by permission of Oxford University Press, Ltd.

II NAOSUKE TO BAKUFU, 1 OCTOBER 1853.

Before the year 1635 there were nine government-licensed trading vessels belonging to Nagasaki, Sakai, Kyoto, etc., but with the prohibition of Christianity in the time of the *Shōgun* Iemitsu the *bakufu* put an end to the voyages of these nine ships and laid down laws closing the country. Commerce was entirely limited to the Dutch and Chinese, no others being allowed to participate in it. Careful consideration of conditions as they are today, however, leads me to believe that despite the constant differences and debates into which men of patriotism and foresight have been led in recent years by their perception of the danger of foreign aggression, it is impossible in the crisis we now face to ensure the safety and tranquillity of our country merely by an insistence on the seclusion laws as we did in former times. Moreover, time is essential if we are to complete our coast defenses. Since 1609, when warships of over 500 *koku* were forbidden, we have had no warships capable of opposing foreign attack on our coasts with heavy guns. Thus I am much afraid that were the foreigners now to seize as bases such outlying islands as Hachijō-jima and Ōshima, it would be impossible for us to remain inactive, though without warships we should have no effective means of driving them off. There is a saying that when one is besieged in a castle, to raise the drawbridge is to imprison oneself and make it impossible to hold out indefinitely; and again, that when opposing forces face each other across a river, victory is obtained by those who cross the river and attack. It seems clear throughout history that he who takes action is in a position to advance, while he who remains inactive must retreat. Even though the *shōgun's* ancestors set up seclusion laws, they left the Dutch and the Chinese to act as a bridge [to the outside world]. Might not this bridge now be of advantage to us in handling foreign affairs, providing us with the means whereby we may for a time avert the outbreak of hostilities and then, after some time has elapsed, gain a complete victory?

I understand that the coal for which the Americans have expressed a desire is to be found in quantity in Kyushu. We should first tell them, as a matter of expediency, that we also have need of coal, but that should their need of it arise urgently and unexpectedly during a voyage, they may ask for coal at Nagasaki and if we have any to spare we will provide it. Nor will we grudge them wood and water. As for foodstuffs, the supply varies from province to province, but we can agree to provide food for the shipwrecked and unfortunate. Again, we can tell them, of recent years we have treated kindly those wrecked on our coasts and have sent them all home. There is no need for further discussion of this subject, and all requests concerning it should be made through the Dutch. Then, too, there is the question of trade. Although there is a national prohibition of it, conditions are not the same as they were. The exchange of goods is a universal practice. This we should explain to the spirits of our ancestors. And we should then tell the foreigners that we mean in the future to send trading vessels to the Dutch Company's factory at Batavia to engage in trade; that we will allocate some of our trading goods to America, some to Russia, and so on, using the Dutch to trade for us as our agents; but that there will be a delay of one or two years because we must [first] construct new ships for these voyages. By replying in this way we will take the Americans by surprise in offering to treat them generally in the same way as the Dutch.

We must revive the licensed trading vessels that existed before the Kanei period (1624-1644), ordering the rich merchants of such places as Osaka, Hyōgo, and Sakai to take shares in the enterprise. We must construct new steamships, especially powerful warships, and these we will load with goods not needed in Japan. For a time we will have to employ Dutchmen as masters and mariners, but we will put on board with them Japanese of ability and integrity who must study the use of large guns, the handling of ships, and the rules of navigation. Openly these will be called merchant vessels, but they will in fact have the secret purpose of training a navy. As we increase the number of ships and our mastery of technique, Japanese will be able to sail the oceans freely and gain direct knowledge of conditions abroad without relying on the secret reports of the Dutch. Thus we will eventually complete the organization of a navy. Moreover, we must shake off the panic and apprehensions that have beset us and abandon our habits of luxury and wasteful spending. Our defenses thus strengthened, and all being arranged at home, we can act so as to make our courage and prestige resound beyond the seas. By so doing, we will not in the future be imprisoning ourselves; indeed, we will be able, I believe, so to accomplish matters at home and broad as to achieve national security. Forestalling the foreigners in this way, I believe, is the best method of ensuring that the *bakufu* will at some future time find opportunity to reimpose its ban and forbid foreigners to come to Japan, as was done in the Kansei period. Moreover, it would make possible the strictest prohibition of Christianity. And since I understand that the Americans and Russians themselves have only recently become skilled in navigation, I do not see how the people of our country, who are cleaver and quick-witted, should prove inferior to Westerners if we begin training at once.

The national situation being what it is, if the *bakufu* protects our coasts peacefully without bringing upon us permanent foreign difficulties, then even if that entails complete or partial change in the laws of our ancestors I do not believe such action could really be regarded as contrary to the wishes of those ancestors. However, I think it is essential to win the support of the country for *bakufu* policy on this occasion, so the *bakufu* should first notify the [Imperial] Court and then arrange to send Imperial messengers to the Ise, Iwashimizu, and Kashima shrines and a Tokugawa messenger to the Nikkō shrine, announcing there its resolve to secure tranquility at home and security for the country. Trust in the will of the gods, after all, is the ancient custom of our land; and I believe, moreover, that by so doing the *bakufu* may be able to unite national opinion.

It is now no easy matter, by means of orders concerning the defense of Edo and the nearby coast, to ensure that all will be fully prepared for any sudden emergency, so not a moment must be wasted. However many firm walls we construct, they will certainly not be as effective as unity of mind if the unforeseen happens. The urgent task of the moment, therefore, is for the *bakufu* to resolve on relieving the nation's anxieties and issue the appropriate orders.

I am conscious of my temerity in putting forward views that conflict with the existing [seclusion] laws, but I have so reported in accordance with your orders that I was to do so fully and without reserve.

27.3

A Japanese Plan for a Modern Army, Aritomo Yamagata

Aritomo Yamagata (1838-1922) was a Japanese soldier and politician. Made commanding officer of the Kiheitai in 1863, he went on to become Vice-Minister of War (1871) and then Army Minister. In 1878, in an attempt to counteract the trend of liberalization, he issued the "Admonition to the Military." It emphasized the traditional virtues of bravery and loyalty to the Meiji Emperor. As Chief of Staff, he was the driving force in the promulgation of the 1882 Imperial Rescript to Soldiers and Sailors, and the 1890 Imperial Rescript on Education. He was Home Minister (1883-89) and was Japan's first Prime Minister (1889-91 and 1898-1900). His modernization of the Japanese military led to victories in the Sino-Japanese War (1894-95) and Russo-Japanese War (1904-5), and Japan's emergence as a significant force in world politics. He was rewarded by being made Prince *(Koshaku)*. From 1903 he alternated with Ito Hirobumi as President of the Privy Council; after Ito's death (1909), Yamagata was the dominant senior leader, with the backing of the military and the bureaucracy. His downfall came in 1921 when he interfered in the marriage of the Crown Prince. He was publicly censured and died in disgrace the following year.

Source: From JAPAN: A DOCUMENTARY HISTORY, VOLUME II: THE LATE TOKUGAWA PERIOD TO THE PRESENT, ed. David J. Lu (Armonk, NY: M. E. Sharpe, 1997), pp. 315-318. English translation copyright © 1997 by David J. Lu. Reprinted with permission of M. E. Sharpe, Inc.

Opinion on Military Affairs and Conscription, 1872. A military force is required to defend the country and protect its people. Previous laws of this country inculcated in the minds of the samurai these basic functions, and there was no separation between the civilian and military affairs. Nowadays civilian officials and military officials have separate functions, and the practice of having the samurai serve both functions has been abandoned. It is now necessary to select and train those who can serve the military functions, and herein lies the change in our military system . . .

As your subjects carefully consider this matter, we discover that we are now maintaining the Ministry of Military Affairs *(hyōbu)* to serve domestic purposes, but in the future it will be required to serve foreign policy purposes. When we probe the matter further, we find that foreign and domestic considerations are essentially one and cannot be separated. This is so because, if our defense establishment is organized sufficiently to defend ourselves against threat from foreign countries, we shall have no fear of our inability to cope with domestic situations.

The status of our armed forces today is as follows: We have the so-called Imperial Guards whose functions are nothing more than to protect the sacred person of His Majesty and to guard the Imperial Palace. We have altogether more than twenty battalions manning the four military garrisons who are deployed to maintain domestic tranquility, and are not equipped to fight against any foreign threat. As to our navy, we have a few battleships yet to be completed. How can they be sufficient to counteract foreign threats?

Since the time of the Restoration, day after day and month after month, we have made significant progress. The governing of the districts *(gun)* and prefectures *(ken)* has been in the hands of the imperial government. Soldiers maintained by the *han* have been disbanded and all the armaments have been returned to the central government. In this way the domestic conditions have been completely altered. This is the time to establish a firm national policy, and to adopt as our purpose the defense of our country against foreign threats.

The first concern of the Ministry of Military Affairs is to set up a system to defend our homeland. For this purpose two categories of soldiers are required: a standing army and those on the reserve list. The number of troops differ from country to country. Of the major countries, Russia maintains the largest number of troops and the United States the smallest. The reason for this discrepancy comes from the fact that the governmental system differs from one country to another. Consequently the regulations governing each of the countries also differ. The Netherlands and Belgium are among the smallest countries, but they are located between large countries, and in order to avoid contempt and scorn from their neighbors, they diligently go about the business of defending their countries. Even though one of these countries has a total area not exceeding one-third of the area of our country, it maintains a standing army numbering not less than forty to fifty thousand. If we apply the existing standards prevailing in our country to judge these two countries, they may appear to be concerned only with military affairs to the neglect of other matters. However, they do attend to hundreds of other affairs of state and do not abandon them. This is possible because their national goals are already set, and they can act accordingly to implement them.

Therefore the creation of a standing army for our country is a task which cannot be delayed. It is recommended that a certain number of strong and courageous young men be selected from each of the prefectures in accordance with the size of the prefectures, and that such young men be trained in the Western-type military science and placed under rigorous drills, so that they may be deployed as occasion demands.

The so-called reservists do not normally remain within the military barracks. During peacetime they remain in their homes, and in an emergency they are called to service. All of the countries in Europe have reservists, and amongst them Prussia has most of them. There is not a single able-bodied man in Prussia who is not trained in military affairs. Recently Prussia and France fought each other and the former won handily. This is due in large measure to the strength of its reservists.

It is recommended that our country adopt a system under which any able-bodied man twenty years of age be drafted into military service, unless his absence from home will create undue hardship for his family. There shall be no distinction made between the common man and those who are of the samurai class. They shall all be formed into ranks, and after completion of a period of service, they shall be returned to their homes [to become reservists]. In this way every man will become a soldier, and not a single region in the country will be without defense. Thus our defense will become complete.

The second concern of the Ministry is coastal defense. This includes building of warships and constructing coastal batteries. Actually, battleships are movable batteries. Our country has thousands of miles of coastline, and any mobile corner of our country can become the advance post of our enemy. However, since it is not possible to construct batteries along the coastline everywhere, it is imperative to expand our navy and construct the largest warships. The latter can cover the areas that cannot be reached by the batteries and protect our homeland. The topography which is formed by nature cannot be changed by man. Every time there is war, the important strategic points will suffer the consequences of warfare. Therefore, a defense line must be predetermined during peacetime, and a line must be drawn clearly which must be strictly guarded, and people must be told to evacuate.

The third concern of the Military is to create resources for the navy and the army. There are three items under consideration, namely military academies, a bureau of military supplies, and a bureau of munitions depots. It is not difficult to have one million soldiers in a short time, but it is difficult to gain one good officer during that span of time. Military academies are intended to train officers for these two services. If we pay little attention to this need today, we shall not be able to have the services of capable officers for another day. Therefore, without delay military academies must be created and be allowed to prosper. Students shall be adequately trained by the faculty consisting of experts from several countries. There shall be established a set of regulations in the teaching of military drills and other subjects. The goal is to gain a supply of capable officers in a number larger than needed. The bureau of military supplies shall be in charge of procuring military provisions and manufacturing weapons of war for the two services. The bureau of munitions depots shall store such provisions and munitions. If we lack military provisions depots shall store such provisions and munitions. If we lack military provisions and weapons and our munitions depots are empty, what good will the million soldiers in the army or thousands of warships do? Therefore, well-qualified craftsmen from various countries must be hired to make necessary machines and build strong storage houses. We must make our own weapons and store them, and must become self-sufficient without relying on foreign countries. The goal is to create a sufficient amount and if there is any surplus it may be sold to other [countries].

Some people may argue that while they are aware of the urgency in the need for the Ministry of Military Affairs, they cannot permit the entire national resources to be committed to the need of one ministry alone. They further aver that from the larger perspective of the imperial government, there are so many other projects covering a wide range of things which require governmental attention. They reason that everything in the country changes continuously and everything occurs simultaneously. Therefore if military affairs advance one step, all others must advance one step. In this way everything in the country can become orderly. This argument fails to discern the fundamental issues. The recommendations herein presented by the Ministry of Military Affairs in no way asks for the stoppage of all governmental activities or for the monopolization of all governmental revenues. But in a national emergency, a new set of priorities must be established. Those of us who are given the task of governing must learn from the past, discern the present, and weigh all matters carefully.

In the past there was Emperor Peter who was determined to make his country a great nation. He went overseas and studied naval sciences. After his return he built many battleships and constructed St. Petersburg. He created a standing army numbering several million, and was able to engage in the art of international politics against five or six of the strongest nations. As to domestic politics, he was satisfied to leave them to a woman. There were one or two internal quarrels, but they were eradicated almost immediately. It is to him that the credit is due for making Russia a great nation.

Those of us who govern must first of all discern the conditions prevailing in the world, set up priorities and take appropriate measures. In our opinion Russia has been acting very arrogantly. Previously, contrary to the provisions of the Treaty of Sevastopol [sic], she placed her warships in the Black Sea. Southward, she has shown her aggressive intent toward Moslem countries and toward India. Westward, she has crossed the borders of Manchuria and has been navigating the Amur River. Her intents being thus, it is inevitable that she will move eastward sooner or later by sending troops to Hokkaido, and then, taking advantage of the seasonal wind, move to the warmer areas.

At a time like this it is very clear where the priority of this country must lie. We must now have a well-trained standing army supplemented by a large number of reservists. We must build warships and construct batteries. We must train officers and soldiers. We must manufacture and store weapons and ammunitions. The nation may consider that it cannot bear the expenses. However, even if we wish to ignore it, this important matter cannot disappear from us. Even if we prefer to enter into this type of defense undertaking, we cannot do without our defense for a single day. This situation is repeated everywhere in every country. At a time when a strong enemy from the north threatens us, can we afford not to make grand preparations? As to the actual system of installations, feeding of soldiers, building of ships, and all other matters and the expenses connected with them, we shall make a detailed report at a later date. Meanwhile, the above recommendations from the Ministry of Military Affairs represent its considered judgment and show the goals it wishes to attain. We respectfully submit these for your consideration.

Conscription System and Regulations, 1873 Conscription is applicable to those who have reached the age of twenty who are to be drafted to serve in the navy or army. The army is divided into three categories. First, the standing army; second, reserve troops; and third, national guards. Also in accordance with the qualifications of the soldiers, the army is divided into five branches, namely artillery, cavalry, infantry, engineer corps, and transport corps. Soldiers for these branches of service are to be called from the prefectures and districts under the jurisdiction of a specific military garrison to serve in that garrison for a given period of time. They are to be assigned to the defense of that locality.

1. The standing army is formed by those soldiers who are selected by lot from those who are eligible for that given year, and are to serve three years. . . .

2. The reserve troops are formed by those who have completed their three-year term of service with the standing army, and are allowed to return home to engage in their own occupations. They are further divided into two categories, the first reserve and the second reserve.

The first reservists are to serve two years, and in time of war will immediately be called upon to become part of the standing army. They must be prepared for such emergencies, and therefore must be called to the military barracks once a year to review the military skills they learned previously. . . .

3. In addition to the standing army and the reserve troops, all men between the ages of seventeen through forty are to be placed in the military registry, and when there is a nationwide, large-scale war, they are to be incorporated into the ranks, and be assigned the task of defending the territories covered by the garrison.

ARTICLE 3. Exception from service in the standing army.

1. Those whose height is less than five feet *(shaku)* one inch *(sum).*
2. Those who cannot serve on account of infirmity, chronic illness or deformity.
3. Those who are officials of the Council of State, Ministries, special cities, or prefectures.
4. Those who are students at the naval and military academies.
5. Those who have graduated with special skills from schools publicly maintained by the Ministries of Education, Industry, Development and other bureaus. Those who from their professors, and certificates showing their specialization are required.
6. Those who are head of the household.
7. Those who are the heir, or the appointed heir of a grandfather.
8. Those who are the only child or the only grandchild.
10. Those whose father and elder brother may still be living but are incapacitated, and thus are assuming the responsibility for the household.
11. Those who are adopted to become the legitimate heir. However, this provision is not applicable to those who are still at the homes of the natural parents.
12. Those who have a brother currently serving in the standing army.

ARTICLE 6. Regulations.

15. At the year when his turn for the conscription comes, the eligible young man may be exempt from service in the standing army and in the reserve troops by remitting a sum of two hundred and seventy yen as a substitutionary fee. Such substitutionary fees are to be submitted to the head of the lesser district *(ku),* transmitted to the offices of special cities or prefectures, and then remitted to the Ministry of Army headquarters during the month of May.

CHAPTER 28

Nation Building

28.1

Monroe Doctrine (1823), James Monroe

James Monroe (1758-1831) was an American politician and the fifth president of the United States. After serving in the War of Independence, he entered politics, becoming a member of the Senate (1790-94), Minister to France (1794-96), Governor of Virginia (1799-1802), Minister to England and Spain (1803-07), and Secretary of State (1811-17). During his "era of good feeling" he signed the Missouri Compromise, acquired Florida, and set forth the principles of the Monroe Doctrine. He won an easy reelection in 1820.

The Monroe Doctrine was a major statement of American foreign policy, proclaimed in 1823, attributed to President James Monroe, but written by Secretary of State John Quincy Adams. Monroe issued the doctrine after renewed interest in the Americas by European powers, especially Britain and Russia, following the Spanish-American revolutions for independence. It announced (1) the existence of a separate political system in the Western Hemisphere, (2) American hostility to further European colonization or attempts to extend European influence, and (3) non-interference with existing European colonies and dependencies or in European affairs.

Source: U.S. National Archives & Records Administration www.ourdocuments.gov

---

. . . At the proposal of the Russian Imperial Government, made through the minister of the Emperor residing here, a full power and instructions have been transmitted to the minister of the United States at St. Petersburg to arrange by amicable negotiation the respective rights and interests of the two nations on the northwest coast of this continent. A similar proposal has been made by His Imperial Majesty to the Government of Great Britain, which has likewise been acceded to. The Government of the United States has been desirous by this friendly proceeding of manifesting the great value which they have invariably attached to the friendship of the Emperor and their solicitude to cultivate the best understanding with his Government. In the discussions to which this interest has given rise and in the arrangements by which they may terminate the occasion has been judged proper for asserting, as a principle in which the rights and interests of the United States are involved, that the American continents, by the free and independent condition which they have assumed and maintain, are henceforth not to be considered as subjects for future colonization by any European powers . . .

It was stated at the commencement of the last session that a great effort was then making in Spain and Portugal to improve the condition of the people of those countries, and that it appeared to be conducted with extraordinary moderation. It need scarcely be remarked that the results have been so far very different from what was then anticipated. Of events in that quarter of the globe, with which we have so much intercourse and from which we derive our origin, we have always been anxious and interested spectators. The citizens of the United States cherish sentiments the most friendly in favor of the liberty and happiness of their fellow-men on that side of the Atlantic. In the wars of the European powers in matters relating to themselves we have never taken any part, nor does it comport with our policy to do so. It is only when our rights are invaded or seriously menaced that we resent injuries or make preparation for our defense. With the movements in this hemisphere we are of necessity more immediately connected, and by causes which must be obvious to all enlightened and impartial observers. The political system of the allied powers is essentially different in this respect from that of America. This difference proceeds from that which exists in their respective Governments; and to the defense of our own, which has been achieved by the loss of so much blood and treasure, and matured by the wisdom of their most enlightened citizens, and under which we have enjoyed unexampled felicity, this whole nation is devoted. We owe it, therefore, to candor and to the amicable relations existing between the United States and those powers to declare that we should consider any attempt on their part to extend their system to any portion of this hemisphere as dangerous to our peace and safety. With the existing colonies or dependencies of any European power we have not interfered and shall not interfere. But with the Governments who have declared their independence and maintain it, and whose independence we have, on great consideration and on just principles, acknowledged, we could not view any interposition for the purpose of oppressing them, or controlling in any other manner their destiny, by any European power in any other light than as the manifestation of an unfriendly disposition toward the United States. In the war between those new Governments and Spain we declared our neutrality at the time of their recognition, and to this we have adhered, and shall continue to adhere, provided no change shall occur which, in the judgment of the competent authorities of this Government, shall make a corresponding change on the part of the United States indispensable to their security.

The late events in Spain and Portugal show that Europe is still unsettled. Of this important fact no stronger proof can be adduced than that the allied powers should have thought it proper, on any principle satisfactory to themselves, to have interposed by force in the internal concerns of Spain. To what extent such interposition may be carried, on the same principle, is a question in which all independent powers whose governments differ from theirs are interested, even those most remote, and surely none of them more so than the United States. Our policy in regard to Europe, which was adopted at an early stage of the wars which have so long agitated that quarter of the globe, nevertheless remains the same, which is, not to interfere in the internal concerns of any of its powers; to consider the government de facto as the legitimate government for us; to cultivate friendly relations with it, and to preserve those relations by a frank, firm, and manly policy, meeting in all instances the just claims of every power, submitting to injuries from none. But in regard to those continents circumstances are eminently and conspicuously different.

It is impossible that the allied powers should extend their political system to any portion of either continent without endangering our peace and happiness; nor can anyone believe that our southern brethren, if left to themselves, would adopt it of their own accord. It is equally impossible, therefore, that we should behold such interposition in any form with indifference. If we look to the comparative strength and resources of Spain and those new Governments, and their distance from each other, it must be obvious that she can never subdue them. It is still the true policy of the United States to leave the parties to themselves, in hope that other powers will pursue the same course. . . .

28.2

Thirteenth Amendment (1865)

The Thirteenth Amendment (1865) to the United States Constitution abolished slavery and was the first of the Civil War amendments. Although slavery as an institution was virtually dead at war's end, its legal status had not been determined. President Andrew Johnson required ratification of the Amendment by former seceded states as part of his Reconstruction program. In December the necessary votes had been secured, and the Amendment was proclaimed "valid as part of the Constitution of the United States."

Source: U.S. National Archives & Record Administration www.ourdocuments.gov

Section 1.

Neither slavery nor involuntary servitude, except as a punishment for crime whereof the party shall have been duly convicted, shall exist within the United States, or any place subject to their jurisdiction.

Section 2.

Congress shall have power to enforce this article by appropriate legislation.

Passed by Congress January 31, 1865. Ratified December 6, 1865.

28.3

Slavery in the Yucatan (1909), Arnold Channing and Frederick J. Tabor Frost

In the nineteenth and early twentieth century, the Yucatan exhibited extreme economic dependence on the "industrial North." Henequen (a cactus plant) created this dependency. Its fibers supplied the raw material for rope cables. First exported to the United States in the 1840s, it was initially used in outfitting clipper ships. Demand for henequen expanded greatly after the invention of a knotting mechanism for grain binders in 1878. During the late nineteenth and early twentieth centuries, harvesting machine companies in the United States, particularly Cyrus McCormick's, imported hundreds of thousands of tons of henequen. From 1875 to 1910, export from the Yucatan increased from 40,000 bales to 600,000. In 1902, McCormick's company merged with other companies to form International Harvester, and McCormick negotiated secretly with the governor of Yucatan to lower prices of henequen in return for steady purchases from the governor's export companies. With that agreement, International Harvester established its "informal empire" in Yucatan. The company needed neither to own land in Yucatan nor to produce henequen directly. Production was left in the hands of a small group of local landowners and merchants, who became fabulously wealthy, and controlled the Yucatecan state government. Nevertheless, they were dependent. By controlling credit and the henequen market in the United States, Cyrus McCormick bound the Yucatecan oligarchy to the interests of International Harvester.

The expansion of henequen production also affected land tenure and labor relations in Yucatan. Before the great growth of exports, traditional haciendas producing hides, corn, and small amounts of henequen, required little participation from the Mayan rural laborers *(campesinos)* inhabiting the peninsula. The work regime on the traditional hacienda allowed Mayan workers enough time to cultivate their own plots of corn *(milpas)*. As well, in areas remote from the haciendas, Indian communities maintained a traditional agricultural lifestyle, free of hacienda obligations. When henequen became king, new plantations absorbed Indian communal land and imposed on their workers a much stricter regime of work. The new, efficient henequen plantations required constant attention, especially regarding harvesting the leaves of mature plants (after seven years) and weeding seedlings. No time was left for traditional agriculture. Because of labor shortages, plantation owners experimented with importation of captured Yaqui Indians from northern Mexico, and Puerto Rican and Korean workers. Most of all they relied on the local Mayan campesinos, whether they wanted to work on the plantation or not. The following selection, written by two visiting Englishmen in 1909, reveals the slavelike conditions on the henequen plantations.

SOURCE: From AMERICAN EGYPT: A RECORD OF TRAVEL IN YUCATAN, London: Hutchinson and Company, 1909.

The Yucatecans have a cruel proverb, *"Los Indios no oigan sino por las nalgas"* ("The Indians can hear only with their backs"). The Spanish half-breeds have taken a race once noble enough and broken them on the wheel of a tyranny so brutal that the heart of them is dead. The relations between the two peoples is ostensibly that of master and servant; but Yucatan is rotten with a foul slavery-the fouler and blacker because of its hypocrisy and pretence.

The peonage system of Spanish America, as specious and treacherous a plan as was ever devised for race-degradation, is that by which a farm labourer is legally bound to work for the land-owner, if in debt to him, until that debt is paid. Nothing could sound fairer; nothing could lend itself better to the blackest abuse. In Yucatan every Indian peon is in debt to his Yucatecan master. Why? Because every Indian is a spendthrift? Not at all; but because the master's interest is to get him and keep him in debt. This is done in two ways. The plantation-slave must buy the necessaries of his humble life at the plantation store, where care is taken to charge such prices as are beyond his humble earnings of sixpence a day. Thus he is always in debt to the farm; and if an Indian is discovered to be scraping together the few dollars he owes, the books of the hacienda are "cooked,"—yes, deliberately "cooked,"—and when he presents himself before the magistrate to pay his debt, say, of twenty dollars (£2) the haciendado can show scored against him a debt of fifty dollars. The Indian pleads that he does not owe it. The haciendado-court smiles. The word of an Indian cannot prevail against the Señor's books, it murmurs sweetly, and back to his slave-work the miserable peon must go, first to be cruelly flogged to teach him that freedom is not for such as he, and that struggle as he may he will never escape the cruel master who under law as at present administered in Yucatan has as complete a disposal of his body as of one of the pigs which root around in the hacienda yard.

Henequen (Spanish *jeniquen* or *geniquen*) is a fibre commercially known as Sisal hemp, from the fact that it is obtained from a species of cactus, the *Agave Sisalensis,* first cultivated around the tiny port of Sisal in Yucatan. The older Indian name for the plant is *Agave Ixtli.* From its fleshy leaves is crushed out a fine fibre which, from the fact that it resists damp better than ordinary hemp, is valuable for making ships' cables, but the real wealth-producing use of which is so bizarre that no one in a hundred guesses would hit on it. It is used in the myriad corn-binding machines of America and Canada. They cannot use wire, and cheap string is too easily broken. Henequen is at once strong enough and cheap enough. Hence the piles of money heaping up to the credit of Yucatecans in the banks of Merida . . .

[At the mill] three or four Indians set to work to arrange the leaves so that their black-pointed ends are all in one direction. Next these thorny points are severed by a machete and in small bundles of six or eight the leaves are handed to men who are feeding a sliding belt-like platform about a yard wide, and on this they are conveyed to the machine. Before they enter its great blunt-toothed, gaping jaws, they are finally arranged, as the sliding belt goes its unending round, so that they do not enter more than one at a time. Woe betide the Indian who has the misfortune to get his fingers in these revolving jaws of the gigantic crusher, and many indeed are there fingerless, handless, and armless from this cause . . .

For there is money for every one who touches the magic fibre except the miserable Indian, by whose never-ending labours the purse-proud monopolists of the Peninsula are enabled to be ever adding to their ill-gotten gold. There are in Yucatan to-day some 400 henequen plantations of from 25 to 20,000 acres, making the total acreage under cultivation some 140,000 acres. The cost of production including shipping expenses, export duties, etc., is now about 7 pesos (14*s.*) per 100 kilogrammes. The average market price of henequen is 28 pesos per kilogrammes, so the planter gets a return of 400 per cent. All this is obviously only possible as long as he can get slave-labour and the hideous truth about the exploitation of the Mayans is kept dark. The Indian gets a wage of 50 centavos for cutting a thousand leaves, and if he is to earn this in a day he must work ten hours. Near the big towns, 75 centavos are paid, but practically, on many haciendas, it is so managed that the labour is paid for by his bare keep.

CHAPTER 29

War and Revolution

29.1

What Is to Be Done?, V. I. Lenin

Vladimir Ilyich Lenin (1870-1924) was a Russian Marxist revolutionary and political leader. He studied at the Universities of Kazan and St. Petersburg, where he graduated in law. From 1895 to 1897 he was in prison, and from 1897 to 1900, he was in exile in Siberia for participating in underground revolutionary activities. There he used his time to study and write extensively about Marxism.

At the Second Congress of the Russian Social Democratic Labor Party (1903) Lenin caused a split between the Bolshevik and Menshevik factions and became the leader of the Bolshevik Party. Apart from the frustrating period of the Russian Revolution of 1905, he spent the entire period until 1917 abroad, developing and publicizing his political views.

After the tsarist regime collapsed in the February Revolution (1917), the provisional government fumbled in its attempts to continue Russian participation in the First World War against Germany. The war was causing enormous hardship, including food shortages, among the Russian people. Into this situation, Lenin returned to Petrograd from Zurich, and urged the early seizure of power by the proletariat under the slogan "All Power to the Soviets." His skills as a charismatic public speaker and seductive promises of a Communist paradise of plenty became the spark of the party's revolutionary takeover in October 1917. It established the Soviet Union, and Lenin became the head of the first Soviet government. He made peace with Germany at Brest-Litovsk to concentrate on defeating the Whites in the Russian Civil War (1918-21) that followed. Then he changed tactics by switching from a ruthless centralized policy of "war communism" to the New Economic Policy, which party critics saw as a "compromise with capitalism" and a retreat from socialist planning. On his death, his body was embalmed and placed in a mausoleum in front of the Moscow Kremlin. In 1924 Petrograd (formerly St. Petersburg) was renamed Leningrad in his honor. Much was subsequently done in his name by Stalin and others, some of which he would not have approved. However, the nature of the Soviet Union (USSR) and the reasons for its final collapse in 1991 owed much to him. It was not altogether surprising that the citizens of Leningrad voted for their city to resume the name of St. Petersburg.

Source: From V. I. Lenin, What is to be Done. Copyright International Publishers. Reprinted by permission.

The strikes of the nineties revealed far greater flashes of consciousness; definite demands were advanced, the strike was carefully timed, known cases and instances in other places were discussed, etc. The revolts were simply the resistance of the oppressed, whereas the systematic strikes represented the class struggle in embryo, but only in embryo. Taken by themselves, these strikes were simply trade union struggles, not yet Social-Democratic struggles. They marked the awakening antagonisms between workers and employers; but the workers were not, and could not be, conscious of the irreconcilable antagonism of their interests to the whole of the modern political and social system, i.e., theirs was not yet Social-Democratic consciousness. In this sense, the strikes of the nineties, despite the enormous progress they represented as compared with the "revolts," remained a purely spontaneous movement.

We have said that *there could not have been* Social-Democratic consciousness among the workers. It would have to be brought to them from without. The history of all countries shows the working class, exclusively by its own effort, is able to develop only trade-union consciousness, i.e., the conviction that it is necessary to combine in unions, fight the employers, and strive to compel the government to pass necessary labour legislation, etc. The theory of socialism, however, grew out of the philosophic, historical, and economic theories elaborated by educated representatives of the propertied classes, by intellectuals. By their social status, the founders of modern scientific socialism, Marx and Engels, themselves belonged to the bourgeois intelligentisia. In the very same way, in Russia, the theoretical doctrine of Social-Democracy arose altogether independently of the spontaneous growth of the working-class movement; it arose as a natural and inevitable outcome of the development of thought among the revolutionary socialist intelligentisa. In the period under discussion, the middle nineties, this doctrine not only represented the completely formulated programme of the Emancipation of Labour group, but had already won over to its side the majority of the revolutionary youth in Russia.

Trade-unionism does not exclude "politics" altogether, as some imagine. Trade unions have always conducted some political (but not Social-Democratic) agitation and struggle. We shall deal with the difference between trade-union politics and Social-Democratic politics in the next chapter.

Hence, we had both the spontaneous awakening of the working masses, their awakening to conscious life and conscious struggle, and a revolutionary youth, armed with Social-Democratic theory and straining towards the workers. In this connection it is particularly important to state the oft-forgotten (and comparatively little-known) fact that, although the *early* Social-Democrats of that period *zealously carried on economic agitation* (being guided in this activity by the truly useful indications contained in the pamphlet *On Agitation,* then still in manuscript), they did not regard this as their sole task. On the contrary, *from the very beginning* they set for Russian Social-Democracy the most far-reaching historical tasks, in general, and the task of overthrowing the autocracy, in particular.

Since there can be no talk of an independent ideology formulated by the working masses themselves in the process of their movement, the *only* choice is—either bourgeois or socialist ideology. There is no middle course (for mankind has not created a "third" ideology, and, moreover, in a society torn by class antagonisms there can never be a non-class or an above-class ideology). Hence, to belittle the socialist ideology *in any way, to turn aside from it in the slightest degree* means to strengthen bourgeois ideology. There is much talk of spontaneity.

But the *spontaneous* development of the working-class movement leads to its subordination to bourgeois ideology, *to its development along the lines of the Credo programme;* for the spontaneous working-class movement is trade-unionism, and trade-unionism means the ideological enslavement of the workers by the bourgeoisie. Hence, our task, the task of Social-Democracy, is to *combat spontaneity, to divert* the working-class movement from this spontaneous, trade-unionist striving to come under the wing of the bourgeoisie, and to bring it under the wing of revolutionary Social-Democracy. The sentence employed by the authors of the "Economist" letter published in *Iskra,* No. 12, that the efforts of the most inspired ideologists fail to divert the working-class movement from the path that is determined by the interaction of the material elements and the material environment *is* therefore *tantamount to renouncing socialism.* If these authors were capable of fearlessly, consistently, and thoroughly considering what they say, as everyone who enters the arena of literary and public activity should be, there would be nothing left for them but to "fold their useless arms over their empty breasts" and—surrender the field of action to the Struves and Prokopoviches, who are dragging the working-class movement "along the line of least resistance", i.e., along the line of bourgeois trade-unionism, or to the Zubatovs, who are dragging it along the line of clerical and gendarme "ideology".

This does not mean, of course, that the workers have no part in creating such an ideology. They take part, however, not as workers, but as a socialist theoreticians, as Proudhons and Weitlings; in order words, they take part only when they are able, and to the extent that they are able, more or less, to acquire the knowledge of their age and develop that knowledge. But in order that working men *may succeed in this more often,* every effort must be made to raise the level of the consciousness of the workers in general; it is necessary that the workers do not confine themselves to the artificially restricted limits of *"literature for workers"* but that they learn to an increasing degree to master *general literature.* It would be even truer to say "are not confined", instead of "do not confine themselves", because the workers themselves wish to read and do read all that is written for the intelligentsia, and only a few (bad) intellectuals believe that it is enough "for workers" to be told a few things about factory conditions and to have repeated to them over and over again what has long been known.

Let us recall the example of Germany. What was the historic service Lassalle rendered to the German working-class movement? It was that he *diverted* that movement from the path of progressionist trade-unionism and co-operativism towards which it had been spontaneously moving. To fulfill such a task it was necessary to do something quite different from talking of underrating the spontaneous element, of tactics-as-process, of the interaction between elements and environment, etc. *A fierce struggle against spontaneity* was necessary, and only after such a struggle, extending over many years, was it possible, for instance, to convert the working population of Berlin from a bulwark of the progressionist party into one of the finest strongholds of Social-Democracy. This struggle is by no means over even today (as might seem to those who learn the history of the German movement from Prokopovich, and its philosophy from Struve). Even now the German working class is, so to speak, split up among a number of ideologies.

Political Exposures and "Training in Revolutionary Activity"

In advancing against *Iskra* his theory of "raising the activity of the working masses", Marynov actually betrayed an urge *to belittle* that activity, for he declared the very economic struggle before which all economists grovel to be the preferable, particularly important, and "most widely applicable" means of rousing this activity and its broadest field. This error is characteristic, precisely in that it is by no means peculiar to Martynov. In reality, it is possible to "raise the activity of the working masses" *only* when this activity *is not restricted* to "political agitation on an economic basis". A basic condition for the necessary expansion of political agitation is the organization of *comprehensive* political exposure. *In no way* except by means of such exposures *can* the masses be trained in political consciousness and revolutionary activity. Hence, activity of this kind is one of the most important functions of international Social-Democracy as a whole, for even political freedom does not in anyway eliminate exposures; it merely shifts somewhat their sphere of direction. Thus, the German party is especially strengthening its positions and spreading its influence, thanks particularly to the untiring energy with which it is conducting its campaign of political exposure. Working-class consciousness cannot be genuine political consciousness unless the workers are trained to respond to *all* cases of tyranny, oppression, violence, and abuse, no matter *what class* is affected—unless they are trained, moreover, to respond from a Social-Democratic point of view and no other. The consciousness of the working masses cannot be genuine class-consciousness, unless the workers learn, from concrete, and above all from topical, political facts and events to observe *every* other social class in *all* the manifestations of its intellectual, ethical, and political life; unless they learn to apply in practice the materialist analysis and the materialist estimate of *all* aspects of the life and activity of *all* classes, strata, and groups of the population. Those who concentrate the attention, observation, and consciousness of the working class exclusively, or even mainly, upon itself alone are not Social-Democrats; for the self-knowledge of the working class is indissolubly bound up, not solely with a fully clear theoretical understanding—it would be even truer to say, not so much with the theoretical, as with the practical, understanding—of the relationships between *all* the various classes of modern society, acquired through the experience of political life. For this reason the conception of the economic struggle as the most widely applicable means of drawing the masses into the political movement, which our Economists preach, is so extremely harmful and reactionary in its practical significance. In order to become a Social-Democrat, the worker must have a clear picture in his mind of the economic nature and the social and political features of the landlord and the priest, the high state official and the peasant, the student and the vagabond; he must know their strong and weak points; he must grasp the meaning of all the catchwords and sophisms by which each class and each stratum *camouflages* its selfish strivings and its real "inner workings"; he must understand what interests are reflected by certain institutions and certain laws and how they are reflected by certain institutions and certain laws. But this "clear picture" cannot be obtained from any book. It can be obtained only from living examples and from exposures that follow close upon what is going on about us at a given moment; upon what is being discussed, in whispers perhaps, by each one in his own way; upon what finds expression in such and such events, in such and such statistics, in such and such court sentences, etc., etc. These comprehensive political exposures are an essential and *fundamental* condition for training the masses in revolutionary activity.

Why do the Russian workers still manifest little revolutionary activity in response to the brutal treatment of the people by the police, the persecution of religious sects, the flogging of peasants, the outrageous censorship, the torture of soldiers, the persecution of the most innocent cultural undertakings, etc.? Is it because the "economic struggle" does not "stimulate" them to this, because such activity does not "promise palpable results", because it produces little that is "positive"? To adopt such an opinion, we repeat, is merely to direct the charge where it does not belong, to blame the working masses for one's own philistinism (or Bernsteinism). The "activity" you want to stimulate among us workers, by advancing concrete demands that promise palpable results, we are already displaying and in our everyday, limited trade-union work we put forward these concrete demands, very often without any assistance whatever from the intellectuals. But *such* activity is not enough for us; we are not children to be fed on the thin gruel of "economic" politics alone; we want to know everything that others know, we want to learn the details of *all* aspects of political life and to take part *actively* in every single political event. In order that we may do this, the intellectuals must talk to us less of what we already know and tell us more about what we do not yet know and what we can never learn from our factory and "economic" experience, namely, political knowledge. You intellectuals can acquire this knowledge, and it is your *duty* to bring it to us in a hundred—and a thousand-fold greater measure than you have done up to now; and you must bring it to us, not only if the form of discussions, pamphlets, and articles (which very often—pardon our frankness—are rather dull), but precisely in the form of vivid *exposures* of what our government and our governing classes are doing at this very moment in all spheres of life. Devote more zeal to carrying out this duty and *talk less about "raising the activity of the working masses"*. We are far more active than you think, and we are quite able to support, by open street fighting, even demands that do not promise any "palpable results" whatever. It is not for you to "raise" our *activity,* because *activity is precisely the thing you yourselves lack.* Bow less in subservience to spontaneity, and think more about raising *your own* activity, gentlemen!

This, in fact, is what actually happens; so that when we speak of organisation, we literally speak in different tongues. I vividly recall, for example, a conversation I once had with a fairly consistent Economist, with whom I had not been previously acquainted. We were discussing the pamphlet, *Who Will Bring About The Political Revolution?* and were soon of a mind that its principal defect was its ignoring of the question of organisation. We had begun to assume full agreement between us; but, as the conversation proceeded, it became evident that we were talking of different things. My interlocutor accused the author of ignoring strike funds, mutual benefit societies, etc., whereas I had in mind an organisation of revolutionaries as an essential factor in "bringing about" the political revolution. As soon as the disagreement became clear, there was hardly, as I remember, a single question of principle upon which I was in agreement with the Economist!

What was the source of our disagreement? It was the fact that on questions both of organisation and of politics the Economists are forever lapsing from Social-Democracy into trade-unionism. The political struggle of Social-Democracy is far more extensive and complex than the economic struggle of the workers against the employers and the government. Similarly (indeed for that reason), the organisation of the revolutionary Social-Democratic Party must inevitably be of *a kind different* from the organisation of the workers designed for this struggle. The workers' organisation must in the first place be a trade-union organisation; secondly, it must be as broad as possible; and thirdly, it must be as public as conditions will allow (here, and further on, of course, I refer only to absolutist Russia). On the other hand, the organisation of the revolutionaries must consist first and foremost of people who make revolutionary activity their profession (for which reason I speak of the organisation of *revolutionaries,* meaning revolutionary Social-Democrats). In view of this common characteristic of the members of such an organisation, *all distinctions as between workers and intellectuals,* not to speak of distinctions of trade and profession, in both categories, *must be effaced.* Such an organisation must perforce not be very extensive and must be as secret as possible. Let us examine this threefold distinction.

In countries where political liberty exists the distinction between a trade-union and a political organisation is clear enough, as is the distinction between trade unions and Social-Democracy. The relations between the latter and the former will naturally vary in each country according to historical, legal, and other conditions; they may be more or less close, complex, etc. (in our opinion they should be as close and as little complicated as possible); but there can be no question in free countries of the organisation of trade unions coinciding with the organisation of the Social-Democratic Party. In Russia, however, the yoke of the autocracy appears at first glance to obliterate all distinctions between the Social-Democratic organisation and the workers' associations, since *all* workers' associations and *all* study circles are prohibited, and since the principal manifestation and weapon of the workers' economic struggle—the strike—is regarded as a criminal (and sometimes even as a political!) offence. Conditions in our country, therefore, on the one hand, strongly "impel" the workers engaged in economic struggle to concern themselves with political questions, and, on the other, they "impel" Social-Democrats to confound trade-unionism with Social-Democracy (and our Krichevskys, Martynovs, and Co., while diligently discussing the first kind of "impulsion", fail to notice the second). Indeed, picture to yourselves people who are immersed ninety-nine per cent in "the economic struggle against the employers and the government". Some of them will never, during the *entire* course of their activity (from four to six months), be impelled to think of the need for a more complex organisation of revolutionaries. Others, perhaps, will come across the fairly widely distributed Bernsteinian literature, from which they will become convinced of the profound importance of the forward movement of "the drab everyday struggle". Still others will be carried away, perhaps, by the seductive idea of showing the world a new example of "close and organic contact with the proletarian struggle"—contact between the trade-union and the Social-Democratic movements. But since you raise the question of *organisations* being unearthed and persist in your opinion, I assert that it is far more difficult to unearth a dozen wise men than a hundred fools. This position I will defend, no matter how much you instigate the masses against me for my "anti-democratic" views, etc. As I have stated repeatedly, by "wise men", in connection with organisation, I mean *professional revolutionaries,* irrespective of whether they have developed from among students or working men. I assert: (1) that no revolutionary movement can endure without a stable organisation of leaders maintaining continuity; (2) that the broader the popular mass drawn spontaneously into the struggle, which forms the basis of the movement and participates in it, the more urgent the need for such an organisation, and the more solid this organisation must be (for it is much easier for all sorts of demagogues to side-track the more backward sections of the masses); (3) that such an organisation must consist chiefly of people professionally engaged in revolutionary activity; (4) that in an autocratic state, the more we *confine* the membership of such an organisation to people who are professionally engaged in revolutionary activity and who have been professionally trained in the art of combating the political police, the more difficult will I be to unearth the organisation; and (5) the *greater* will be the number of people from the working class and from the other social classes who will be able to join the movement and perform active work in it.

I invite our Economists, terrorists, and "Economists-terrorists" to confute these propositions. At the moment, I shall deal only with the last two points. The question as to whether it is easier to wipe out "a dozen wise men" or "a hundred fools" reduces itself to the question, above considered, whether it is possible to have a mass *organisation* when the maintenance of strict secrecy is essential. We can never give a mass organisation that degree of secrecy without which there can be no question of persistent and continuous struggle against the government. To concentrate all secret functions in the hands of as small a number of professional revolutionaries as possible does not mean that the latter will "do the thinking for all" and that the rank and file will not take an active part in the *movement.* On the contrary, the membership will promote increasing numbers of the professional revolutionaries from its ranks; for it will know that it is not enough for a few students and for a few working men waging the economic struggle to gather in order to form a "committee", but that it takes years to train oneself to be a professional revolutionary; and the rank and file will "think", not only of amateurish methods, but of such training. Centralisation of the secret functions of the *organisation* by no means implies centralization of all the functions of the *movement.* Active participation of the widest masses in the illegal press will not diminish because a "dozen" professional revolutionaries centralise the secret functions connected with this work; on the contrary, it will *increase* tenfold. In this way, and in this way alone, shall we ensure that reading the illegal press, writing for it, and to some extent even distributing it, will *almost cease to be secret work,* for the police will soon come to realise the folly and impossibility of judicial and administrative red-tape procedure over every copy of a publication that is being distributed in the thousands. This holds not only for the press, but for every function of the movement, even for demonstration. The active and widespread participation of the masses will not suffer; on the contrary, it will benefit by the fact that a "dozen" experienced revolutionaries, trained professionally no less than the police, will centralise all the secret aspects of the work—the drawing up of leaflets, the working out of approximate plans; and the appointing of bodies of leaders for each urban district, for each factory district, and for each educational institution, etc. (I know that exception will be taken to my "undemocratic" views, but I shall reply below fully to this anything but intelligent objection.) Centralisation of the most secret functions in an organisation of revolutionaries will not diminish, but rather increase the extent and enhance the quality of the activity of a large number of other organisations, that are intended for a broad public and are therefore as loose and as non-secret as possible, such as workers' trade unions; workers' self-education circles and circles for reading illegal literature; and socialist, as well as democratic, circles among *all* other sections of the population; etc., etc. We must have such circles, trade unions, and organisations everywhere in *as large a number as possible* and with the widest variety of functions; but it would be absurd and harmful *to confound* them with the organisation of *revolutionaries,* to efface the border-line between them, to make still more hazy the all too faint recognition of the fact that in order to "serve" the mass movement we must have people who will devote themselves exclusively to Social-Democratic activities, and that such people must *train* themselves patiently and steadfastly to be professional revolutionaries.

Yes, this recognition is incredibly dim. Our worst sin with regard to organisation consists in the fact that *by our primitiveness we have lowered the prestige of revolutionaries in Russia.* A person who is flabby and shaky on questions of theory, who has a narrow outlook, who pleads the spontaneity of the masses as an excuse for his own sluggishness, who resembles a trade-union secretary more than a spokesman of the people, who is unable to conceive of a broad and bold plan that would command the respect even of opponents, and who is inexperienced and clumsy in his own professional art—the art of combating the political police—such a man is not a revolutionary, but a wretched amateur!

Let no active worker take offence at these frank remarks, for as far as insufficient training is concerned, I apply them first and foremost to myself.

29.2

Fourteen Points (1918), Woodrow Wilson

Woodrow Wilson (1856-1924) was a United States politician and the twenty-eighth president. He practiced law in Atlanta, later became a university professor, and, in 1902, president of Princeton University. He served as Democratic Governor of New Jersey (1911-13) and was elected president in 1912, running against Theodore Roosevelt and William Taft, and served two terms (1913-21). His "New Freedom" program proposed equality and opportunity for all men, and created the Federal Reserve Board and the Clayton Anti-Trust Act, which accorded many rights to labor unions. Wilson tried to keep the United States out of World War I, but events compelled him to enter the war in 1917 to "make the world safe for democracy." He laid out his proposed peace plan in the Fourteen Points, and actively championed the idea of a League of Nations, which was part of the Treaty of Versailles. The United States Senate shattered his idealistic vision of world peace by rejecting the treaty. In 1919 he received the Nobel Peace Prize, but after that his health declined severely, and he never recovered.

The Fourteen Points was Woodrow Wilson's peace program outlined in a message to Congress in 1918, at the end of World War I. The program offered the possibility of an acceptable peace to the Central Powers, and as a result Wilson became perceived as a moral leader. It was largely instrumental in causing Germany's surrender and the beginning of peace talks. In the final Treaty of Versailles, however, the other delegates compromised or defeated several of Wilson's points.

Source: U.S. National Archives & Records Administration www.ourdocuments.gov

---

We entered this war because violations of right had occurred which touched us to the quick and made the life of our own people impossible unless they were corrected and the world secure once for all against their recurrence. What we demand in this war, therefore, is nothing peculiar to ourselves. It is that the world be made fit and safe to live in; and particularly that it be made safe for every peace-loving nation which, like our own, wishes to live its own life, determine its own institutions, be assured of justice and fair dealing by the other peoples of the world as against force and selfish aggression. All the peoples of the world are in effect partners in this interest, and for our own part we see very clearly that unless justice be done to others it will not be done to us. The programme of the world's peace, therefore, is our programme; and that programme, the only possible programme, as we see it, is this:

I. Open covenants of peace, openly arrived at, after which there shall be no private international understandings of any kind but diplomacy shall proceed always frankly and in the public view.

II. Absolute freedom of navigation upon the seas, outside territorial waters, alike in peace and in war, except as the seas may be closed in whole or in part by international action for the enforcement of international covenants.

III. The removal, so far as possible, of all economic barriers and the establishment of an equality of trade conditions among all the nations consenting to the peace and associating themselves for its maintenance.

IV. Adequate guarantees given and taken that national armaments will be reduced to the lowest point consistent with domestic safety.

V. A free, open-minded, and absolutely impartial adjustment of all colonial claims, based upon a strict observance of the principle that in determining all such questions of sovereignty the interests of the populations concerned must have equal weight with the equitable claims of the government whose title is to be determined.

VI. The evacuation of all Russian territory and such a settlement of all questions affecting Russia as will secure the best and freest cooperation of the other nations of the world in obtaining for her an unhampered and unembarrassed opportunity for the independent determination of her own political development and national policy and assure her of a sincere welcome into the society of free nations under institutions of her own choosing; and, more than a welcome, assistance also of every kind that she may need and may herself desire. The treatment accorded Russia by her sister nations in the months to come will be the acid test of their good will, of their comprehension of her needs as distinguished from their own interests, and of their intelligent and unselfish sympathy.

VII. Belgium, the whole world will agree, must be evacuated and restored, without any attempt to limit the sovereignty which she enjoys in common with all other free nations. No other single act will serve as this will serve to restore confidence among the nations in the laws which they have themselves set and determined for the government of their relations with one another. Without this healing act the whole structure and validity of international law is forever impaired.

VIII. All French territory should be freed and the invaded portions restored, and the wrong done to France by Prussia in 1871 in the matter of Alsace-Lorraine, which has unsettled the peace of the world for nearly fifty years, should be righted, in order that peace may once more be made secure in the interest of all.

IX. A readjustment of the frontiers of Italy should be effected along clearly recognizable lines of nationality.

X. The peoples of Austria-Hungary, whose place among the nations we wish to see safeguarded and assured, should be accorded the freest opportunity to autonomous development.

XI. Rumania, Serbia, and Montenegro should be evacuated; occupied territories restored; Serbia accorded free and secure access to the sea; and the relations of the several Balkan states to one another determined by friendly counsel along historically established lines of allegiance and nationality; and international guarantees of the political and economic independence and territorial integrity of the several Balkan states should be entered into.

XII. The Turkish portion of the present Ottoman Empire should be assured a secure sovereignty, but the other nationalities which are now under Turkish rule should be assured an undoubted security of life and an absolutely unmolested opportunity of autonomous development, and the Dardanelles should be permanently opened as a free passage to the ships and commerce of all nations under international guarantees.

XIII. An independent Polish state should be erected which should include the territories inhabited by indisputably Polish populations, which should be assured a free and secure access to the sea, and whose political and economic independence and territorial integrity should be guaranteed by international covenant.

XIV. A general association of nations must be formed under specific covenants for the purpose of affording mutual guarantees of political independence and territorial integrity to great and small states alike.

In regard to these essential rectifications of wrong and assertions of right we feel ourselves to be intimate partners of all the governments and peoples associated together against the Imperialists. We cannot be separated in interest or divided in purpose. We stand together until the end.

For such arrangements and covenants we are willing to fight and to continue to fight until they are achieved; but only because we wish the right to prevail and desire a just and stable peace such as can be secured only by revolving the chief provocations to war, which this programme does remove. We have no jealousy of German greatness, and there is nothing in this programme that impairs it. We grudge her no achievement or distinction of learning or pacific enterprise such as have made her record very bright and very enviable. We do not wish to injure her or to block in any way her legitimate influence or power. We do not wish to fight her either with arms or with hostile arrangements of trade if she is willing to associate herself with us and the other peace-loving nations of the world in covenants of justice and law and fair dealing. We wish her only to accept a place of equality among the peoples of the world,—the new world in which we now live,—instead of a place of mastery.

CHAPTER 30

Asian Nationalism

30.1

Sykes-Picot Agreement (1916)

The Sykes-Picot Agreement (1916) was a secret agreement concluded by British diplomat Sir Mark Sykes and Georges Picot (for France) that partitioned the Ottoman Empire after World War I. France was to be dominant power in Syria and Lebanon, and Britain in Transjordan, Iraq, and Northern Palestine. The rest of Palestine was to be under international control, and an Arab state was to be established.

SOURCE: Historical Documents From www.mideastweb.org

It is accordingly understood between the French and British Governments:

That France and Great Britain are prepared to recognize and protect an independent Arab states or a confederation of Arab . . . under the suzerainty of an Arab chief. That in area (a) France, and in area (b) Great Britain, shall have priority of right of enterprise and local loans. That in area (a) France, and in area (b) Great Britain, shall alone supply advisers or foreign functionaries at the request of the Arab state or confederation of Arab states.

That in the blue area France, and in the red area Great Britain, shall be allowed to establish such direct or indirect administration or control as they desire and as they may think fit to arrange with the Arab state or confederation of Arab states.

That in the brown area there shall be established an international administration, the form of which is to be decided upon after consultation with Russia, and subsequently in consultation with the other allies, and the representatives of the sheriff of Mecca.

That Great Britain be accorded (1) the ports of Haifa and Acre, (2) guarantee of a given supply of water from the Tigres and Euphrates in area (a) for area (b). His majesty's government, on their part, undertake that they will at no time enter into negotiations for the cession of Cyprus to any third power without the previous consent of the French government.

That Alexandretta shall be a free port as regards the trade of the British empire, and that there shall be no discrimination in port charges or facilities as regards British shipping and British goods; that there shall be freedom of transit for British goods through Alexandretta and by railway through the blue area, or (b) area, or area (a); and there shall be no discrimination, direct or indirect, against British goods on any railway or against British goods or ships at any port serving the areas mentioned.

That Haifa shall be a free port as regards the trade of France, her dominions and protectorates, and there shall be no discrimination in port changes or facilities as regards French shipping and French goods. There shall be freedom of transit for French goods through Haifa and by the British railway through the brown area, whether those goods are intended for or originate in the blue area, area (a), or area (b), and there shall be no discrimination, direct or indirect, against French goods on any railway, or against French goods or ships at any port serving the areas mentioned.

That in area (a) the Baghdad railway shall not be extended southwards beyond Mosul, and in area (b) northwards beyond Samarra, until a railway connecting Baghdad and Aleppo via the Euphrates valley has been completed, and then only with the concurrence of the two governments.

That Great Britain has the right to build, administer, and be sole owner of a railway connecting Haifa with area (b), and shall have a perpetual right to transport troops along such a line at all times. It is to be understood by both governments that this railway is to facilitate the connection of Baghdad with Haifa by rail, and it is further understood that, if the engineering difficulties and expense entailed by keeping this connecting line in the brown area only make the project unfeasible, that the French government shall be prepared to consider that the line in question may also traverse the Polgon Banias Keis Marib Salkhad tell Otsda Mesmie before reaching area (b).

For a period of twenty years the existing Turkish customs tariff shall remain in force throughout the whole of the blue and red areas, as well as in areas (a) and (b), and no increase in the rates of duty or conversions from *ad valorem* to specific rates shall be made except by agreement between the two powers.

There shall be no interior customs barriers between any of the above mentioned areas. The customs duties leviable on goods destined for the interior shall be collected at the port of entry and handed over to the administration of the area of destination.

It shall be agreed that the French government will at no time enter into any negotiations for the cession of their rights and will not cede such rights in the blue area to any third power, except the Arab state or confederation of Arab states, without the previous agreement of His Majesty's government, who, on their part, will give a similar undertaking to the French government regarding the red area.

The British and French government, as the protectors of the Arab state, shall agree that they will not themselves acquire and will not consent to a third power acquiring territorial possessions in the Arabian peninsula, nor consent to third power installing a naval base either on the east coast, or on the islands, of the Red Sea. This, however, shall not prevent such adjustment of the Aden frontier as may be necessary in consequence of recent Turkish aggression.

The negotiations with the Arabs as to the boundaries of the Arab states shall be continued through the same channel as heretofore on behalf of the two powers.

It is agreed that measures to control the importation of arms into the Arab territories will be considered by the two governments.

30.2

Balfour Declaration (1917), Arthur Balfour

Arthur Balfour (1848-1930) was a British politician. He entered Parliament in 1874, becoming Secretary for Scotland (1886) and Chief Secretary for Ireland (1887-91), where his policy of suppression earned him the name of "Bloody Balfour." A conservative, he was Prime Minister (1902-5) and First Lord of the Admiralty (1915-16). As Foreign Secretary (1916-19) he was responsible for the "Balfour Declaration" (1917). Balfour resigned in 1922, but served again as Lord President (1925-29).

The Balfour Declaration (Nov. 2, 1917) was a short communication from Foreign Secretary Balfour to Lord Rothschild of the British Zionist Federation, expressing the British government's advocacy of a Jewish national home in Palestine, which was formerly part of the Ottoman Empire. In 1920 the Treaty of Versailles ceded Palestine to the British as a League of Nations Mandate. In 1922, when challenged over the Mandate in Parliament by Lord Islington, Balfour defended his decision.

In 1923 Britain clarified the vagueness of the Balfour Declaration: Jewish immigration was to be encouraged; an appropriate Jewish body formed to that end; the British would protect the rights of non-Jews, and they would give English, Hebrew, and Arabic peoples equal status. However, the next two decades showed Britain either unwilling or unable to deliver its promise to the Jews, especially in view of increasing Arab hostility to Jewish immigration.

Source: Historical Documents From www.mideastweb.org

November 2nd, 1917

Dear Lord Rothschild,

I have much pleasure in conveying to you, on behalf of His Majesty's Government, the following declaration of sympathy with Jewish Zionist aspirations which has been submitted to, and approved by, the Cabinet.

"His Majesty's Government view with favour the establishment in Palestine of a national home for the Jewish people, and will use their best endeavours to facilitate the achievement of this object, it being clearly understood that nothing shall be done which may prejudice the civil and religious rights of existing non-Jewish communities in Palestine, or the rights and political status enjoyed by Jews in any other country."

I should be grateful if you would bring this declaration to the knowledge of the Zionist Federation.

Yours sincerely,

Arthur Balfour

30.3

Indian Home Rule, Mohandas Gandhi

Mohandas K. (Mahatma) Gandhi (1869-1948) was not the only Indian Nationalist, but he will always be the best-remembered Indian leader of the twentieth century, and we will forever link his name to the destruction of Western colonialism.

Gandhi attended law school in London, England and began a law practice in India. He had difficulty being accepted into the profession, however, and was unable to find a position with an established firm. Fortunately, his brother helped him establish his own small law office in Bombay and steered many clients to Gandhi. One of these early clients gave Gandhi a commission to represent a firm that had a large claim in a South African court. In April 1893 he went to Pretoria, South Africa, where he spent twenty-one years opposing discriminatory legislation against Indians. He encountered racial insults that he faced for the rest of his life. He found the intolerable situation of racial persecution and ethnic harassment in Africa impossible to solve.

In 1914 Gandhi returned to India, the "jewel in the crown" of the British empire, and the world's wealthiest, most populous colony. He supported the Home Rule Movement and became the leader of the Indian National Congress and a founder of the Indian Congress Party. He assumed the moral high ground through his Satyagraha ("Soul Force") which advocated a policy of nonviolent non-cooperation to achieve independence. Following his first major non-cooperation and civil disobedience campaign (1919-22), the British jailed him for conspiracy (1922-24). He led a 200-mile march to the sea in 1930 to collect salt in a symbolic defiance of the government monopoly. This marked the beginning of the second major campaign of civil disobedience designed to attract the glare of international publicity. On his release from prison (1931), he attended the London Round Table Conference on Indian constitutional reform. In 1946 he negotiated with the Cabinet Mission that recommended the new constitutional structure. The Mahatma finally accomplished the liquidation of the British Raj in 1947. After independence, he tried to stop the Hindu/Muslim conflict in Bengal, a policy that led to his assassination in Delhi by a Hindu fanatic who opposed Gandhi's efforts to compromise with the Muslims.

Source: From Mohandas Gandhi, "Indian Home Rule", India: Ganesh & Co., 1922.

CHAPTER VI

Civilization

READER: Now you will have to explain what you mean by civilization . . .

EDITOR: Let us first consider what state of things is described by the word "civilization." Its true test lies in the fact that people living in it make bodily welfare the object of life. We will take some examples: the people of Europe today live in better-built-houses than they did a hundred years ago. This is considered an emblem of civilization, and this is also a matter to promote bodily happiness. Formerly, they wore skins, and used as their weapons spears. Now, they wear long trousers, and for embellishing their bodies they wear a variety of clothing, and, instead of spears, they carry with them revolvers containing five or more chambers. If people of a certain country, who have hitherto not been in the habit of wearing much clothing, boots, etc., adopt European clothing, they are suppose to have become civilized out of savagery. Formerly, in Europe, people plowed their lands mainly by manual labor. Now, one man can plow a vast tract by means of steam-engines, and can thus amass great wealth. This is called a sign of civilization. Formerly, the fewest men wrote books, that were most valuable. Now, anybody writes and prints anything he likes and poisons people's minds. Formerly, men traveled in wagons; now they fly through the air, in trains at the rate of four hundred and more miles per day. This is considered the height of civilization. It has been stated that, as men progress, they shall be able to travel in airships and reach any part of the world in a few hours. Men will not need the use of their hands and feet. They will press a button, and they will have their clothing by their side. They will press another button, and they will have their newspaper. A third, and a motor-car will be in waiting for them. They will have a variety of delicately dished up food. Everything will be done by machinery. Formerly, when people wanted to fight with one another, they measured between them their bodily strength; now it is possible to take away thousands of lives by one man working behind a gun from a hill. This is civilization. Formerly, men worked in the open air only so much as they liked. Now, thousands of workmen meet together and for the sake of maintenance work in factories or mines. Their condition is worse than that of beasts. They are obliged to work, at the risk of their lives, at most dangerous occupations, for the sake of millionaires. Formerly, men were made slaves under physical compulsion, now they are enslaved by temptation of money and of the luxuries that money can buy. There are now diseases of which people never dreamed before, and an army of doctors is engaged in finding out their cures, and so hospitals have increased. This is a test of civilization. Formerly, special messengers were required and much expense was incurred in order to send letters; today, anyone can abuse his fellow by means of a letter for one penny. True, at the same cost, one can send one's thanks also. Formerly, people had two or three meals consisting of homemade bread and vegetables; now, they require something to eat every two hours, so that they have hardly leisure for anything else. What more need I say? All this you can ascertain from several authoritative books. These are all true tests of civilization. And, if any one speaks to the contrary, know that he is ignorant. This civilization takes note neither of morality nor of religion . . .

This civilization is irreligion, and it has taken such a hold on the people in Europe that those who are in it appear to be half mad. They lack real physical strength or courage. They keep up their energy by intoxication. They can hardly be happy in solitude. Women, who should be the queens of households, wander in the streets, or they slave away in factories. For the sake of a pittance, half a million women in England alone are laboring under trying circumstances in factories or similar institutions. This awful fact is one of the causes of the daily growing suffragette movement.

This civilization is such that one has only to be patient and it will be self-destroyed.

CHAPTER X

The Condition of India (Continued)

The Hindus and the Muslims

READER: But I am impatient to hear your answer to my question. Has the introduction of Islam not unmade the nation?

EDITOR: India cannot cease to be one nation because people belonging to different religions live in it. The introduction of foreigners does not necessarily destroy the nation, they merge in it. A country is one nation only when such a condition obtains in it. That country must have a faculty for assimilation. India has ever been such a country. In reality, there are as many religions as there are individuals, but those who are conscious of the spirit of nationality do not interfere with one another's religion. If they do, they are not fit to be considered a nation. If the Hindus believe that India should be peopled only by Hindus, they are living in dreamland. The Hindus, the Muslims, the Parsees and the Christians who have made India their country are fellow-countrymen, and they will have to live in unity if only for their own interest. In no part of the world are one nationality and one religion synonymous terms; nor has it ever been so in India.

READER: But what about the inborn enmity between Hindus and Muslim?

EDITOR: That phrase has been invented by our mutual enemy. When the Hindus and Muslims fought against one another, they certainly spoke in that strain. They have long since ceased to fight. How, then, can there be any inborn enmity? Pray remember this too, that we did not cease to fight only after British occupation. The Hindus flourished under Muslim sovereigns and Muslims under the Hindu. Each party recognized that mutual fighting was suicidal, and that neither party would abandon its religion by force of arms. Both parties, therefore, decided to live in peace. With the English advent the quarrels recommenced . . .

Hindus and Muslims own the same ancestors, and the same blood runs through their veins. Do people become enemies because they change their religion? Is the God of the Muslim different from the God of the Hindu? Religions are different roads converging to the same point. What does it matter that we take different roads, so long as we reach the same goal? Wherein is the cause for quarreling?

CHAPTER XIII

What Is True Civilization?

READER: You have denounced railways, lawyers and doctors. I can see that you will discard all machinery. What, then, is civilization?

EDITOR: The answer to that question is not difficult. I believe that the civilization India has evolved is not to be beaten in the world. Nothing can equal the seeds sown by our ancestors. Rome went, Greece shared the same fate, the might of the Pharaohs was broken, Japan has become westernized, of China nothing can be said, but India is still, somehow or other, sound at the foundation. The people of Europe learn their lessons from the writings of the men of Greece or Rome, which exist no longer in their former glory. In trying to learn from them, the Europeans imagine that they will avoid the mistakes of Greece and Rome. Such is their pitiable condition. In the midst of all this, India remains immovable, and that is her glory. It is a charge against India that her people are so uncivilized, ignorant, and stolid, that it is not possible to induce them to adopt any changes. It is a charge really against our merit. What we have tested and found true on the anvil of experience, we dare not change. Many thrust their advice upon India, and she remains steady. This is her beauty; it is the sheet-anchor of our hope.

Civilization is that mode of conduct which points out to man the path of duty. Performance of duty and observance of morality are convertible terms. To observe morality is to attain mastery over our mind and our passions. So doing, we know ourselves. The Gujarati equivalent for civilization means "good conduct."

If this definition be correct, Then India, as so many writers have shown, has nothing to learn from any body else, and this is as it should be.

CHAPTER XVII

Passive Resistance

READER: Is there any historical evidence as to the success of what you have called soul-force or truth-force? No instance seems to have happened of any nation having risen through soul-force. I still think that the evil-doers will not cease doing evil without physical punishment.

EDITOR. . . . The force of love is the same as the force of the soul or truth. We have evidence of its working at every step. The universe would disappear without the existence of that force. But you ask for historical evidence. It is, therefore, necessary to know what history means . . .

The fact that there are so many men still alive in the world shows that it is based not on the force of arms but on the force of truth or love. Therefore the greatest and most unimpeachable evidence of the success of this force is to be found in the fact that, in spite of the wars of the world, it still lives on.

Thousands, indeed, tens of thousands, depend for their existence on a very active working of this force. Little quarrels of millions of families in their daily lives disappear before the exercise of this force. Hundreds of nations live in peace. History does not and cannot take note of this fact. History is really a record of every interruption of the even working of the force of love or of the soul. . . . Soul-force, being natural, is not noted in history.

READER: According to what you say, it is plain that instances of the kind of passive resistance are not to be found in history. It is necessary to understand this passive resistance more fully. It will be better, therefore, if you enlarge upon it.

EDITOR: Passive resistance is a method of securing rights by personal suffering; it is the reverse of resistance by arms. When I refuse to do a thing that is repugnant to my conscience, I use soul-force. For instance, the government of the day has passed a law which is applicable to me: I do not like it; if, by using violence, I force the government to repeal the law, I am employing what may be termed body-force. If I do not obey the law and accept the penalty for its breach, I use soul-force. It involves sacrifice of self.

Everybody admits that sacrifice of self is infinitely superior to sacrifice of others. Moreover, if this kind of force is used in a cause that is unjust, only the person using it suffers. He does not make others suffer for his mistakes. Men have before now done many things which were subsequently found to have been wrong. No man can claim to be absolutely in the right, or that a particular thing is wrong, because he thinks so, but it is wrong for him so long as that is his deliberate judgment. It is, therefore, meet [proper] that he should not do that which he knows to be wrong, and suffer the consequence whatever it may be. This is the key to the use of soul-force . . .

READER: From what you say, I deduce that passive resistance is a splendid weapon of the weak but that, when they are strong, they may take up arms.

EDITOR: This is gross ignorance. Passive resistance, that is, soul-force, is matchless. It is superior to the force of arms. How, then, can it be considered only a weapon of the weak? Physical-force men are strangers to the courage that is requisite in a passive resister. Do you believe that a coward can ever disobey a law that he dislikes? Extremists are considered to be advocates of brute-force. Why do they, then, talk about obeying the laws? I do not blame them. They can say nothing else. When they succeed in driving out the English, and they themselves become governors, they will want you and me to obey their laws. And that is a fitting thing for their constitution. But a passive resister will say he will not obey a law that is against his conscience, even though he may be blown to pieces at the mouth of a cannon.

What do you think? Wherein is courage required—in blowing others to pieces from behind a cannon or with a smiling face to approach a cannon and to be blown to pieces? Who is the true warrior—he who keeps death always as a bosom-friend or he who controls the death of others? Believe me that a man devoid of courage and manhood can never be a passive resister.

This, however, I will admit: that even a man, weak in body, is capable of offering this resistance. One man can offer it just as well as millions. Both men and women can indulge in it. It does not require the training of any army; it needs no Jiu-jitsu. Control over the mind is alone necessary, and, when that is attained, man is free like the king of the forest, and his very glance withers the enemy.

Passive resistance is an all-sided sword; it can be used anyhow; it blesses him who uses it and him against whom it is used. Without drawing a drop of blood, it produces far-reaching results.

30.4

Revolutionary Ideology, Mao Zedong

Mao Zedong (Mao Tse-tung) (1893-1976) was a Chinese political leader. He was the leading theorist of the Chinese communist revolution that won national power in China in 1949. The son of a farmer, at the age of twelve he sought an education in Changsha, where he encountered Western ideas. After graduating from a teacher's training college there, he went to Beijing, where he came under the influence of Li Dazhao. He took a leading part in the May Fourth Movement, then became a Marxist and a founding member of the Chinese Communist Party (CCP) (1921). During the first United Front with the Nationalist Party, Mao concentrated on political work among the peasants of his native province, where he advocated a rural revolution and created the Jiangxi Soviet. After the break with the nationalists in 1927, the communists were driven from the cities, after which Mao evolved the guerilla tactics of the "people's war."

In 1934 the nationalist government destroyed the Jiangxi Soviet, and in the subsequent Long March the communist forces retreated to Shaanxi to set up a new base. When, in 1936, under the increased threat of a Japanese invasion, the nationalists renewed their alliance with the communists, Mao restored and vastly increased the political and military power of his party. His claim to a share in the government led to civil war during which he ousted Chiang Kai-shek's regime from the mainland, and proclaimed the People's Republic of China (Oct. 1, 1949) with himself as Chairman of the CCP and President of the Republic. He followed the Soviet model of economic development and social change until 1958, then launched his Great Leap Forward, which encouraged rural industry and the use of surplus rural labor to create a new agricultural infrastructure. The failure of the Great Leap lost him most of his influence.

By 1965, with China's armed forces securely in the hands of his ally, Lin Biao, he launched a Cultural Revolution, and cautiously revived the Great Leap strategy when the left wing was victorious in the political struggles that followed (1965-71). He died in Beijing after a prolonged illness, which may have well weakened his judgment during his last years. A strong reaction set in against the excessive collectivism and egalitarianism that had emerged, but his successors retained and strengthened his anti-Stalinist emphasis on rural industry and local initiative.

Source: From Selected Works of Mao Tse-Tung, Lawrence and Wishart, London 1954 and International Publishers, New York 1954, 1956. Reprinted by permission of Lawrence & Wishart, UK.

The Importance of the Peasant Problem

During my recent visit to Hunan I conducted an investigation on the spot into the conditions in the five countries of Xiangtan, Xiangsiang, Hengshan, Liling, and Changsha. In the thirty-two days from January 4 to February 5, in villages and in county towns, I called together for fact-finding conferences experienced peasants and comrades working for the peasant movement, listened attentively to their reports, and collected a lot of material. Many of the hows and whys of the peasant movement were quite the reverse of what I had heard from the gentry in Hankou and Changsha. And many strange things there were that I had never seen or heard before. I think these conditions exist in many other places.

All kinds of arguments against the peasant movement must be speedily set right. The erroneous measures taken by the revolutionary authorities concerning the peasant movement must be speedily changed. Only thus can any good be done for the future of the revolution. For the rise of the present movement is a colossal event. In a very short time, in China's central, southern and northern provinces, several hundred million peasants will rise like a tornado or tempest, a force so extraordinarily swift and violent that no power, however great, will be able to suppress it. They will break all trammels that now bind them and rush forward along the road to liberation. They will send all imperialists, warlords, corrupt officials, local bullies, and bad gentry to their graves. All revolutionary parties and all revolutionary comrades will stand before them to be tested and to be accepted or rejected as they decide.

To march at their head and lead them? Or to follow at their rear, gesticulating at them and criticizing them? Or to face them as opponents?

Every Chinese is free to choose among the three alternatives, but circumstances demand that quick choice be made.

Down with the Local Bullies and Bad Gentry!

All Power to the Peasant Association!

The peasants attack as their main targets the local bullies and bad gentry and the lawless landlord, hitting in passing against patriarchal ideologies and institutions, corrupt officials in the cities, and evil customs in the rural areas. In force and momentum, the attack is like a tempest or hurricane; those who submit to it survive and those who resist it perish.

"An Awful Mess!" and "Very Good Indeed!"

The revolt of the peasants in the countryside disturbed the sweet dreams of the gentry. When news about the countryside reached the cities, the gentry there immediately burst into an uproar. When I first arrived in Changsha, I met people from various circles and picked up a good deal of street gossip. From the middle strata upward to the right-wingers of the Nationalists, there was not a single person who did not summarize the whole thing in one phrase: "An awful mess!" . . .

But the fact is . . . that the broad peasant masses have risen to fulfill their historic mission, that the democratic forces in the rural areas have risen to overthrow the rural feudal power.

The Question of "Going Too Far"

There is another section of people who say, "Although the peasant association ought to be formed, it has gone rather too far in its present actions." This is the opinion of the middle-of-the-roaders. But . . .

The opinion of this group, reasonable on the surface, is erroneous at bottom.

First, the things described above have all been the inevitable results of the doings of the local bullies and bad gentry and lawless landlords themselves.

Second, a revolution is not the same as inviting people to dinner, or writing an essay, or painting a picture, or doing fancy needlework; it cannot be anything so refined, so calm and gentle, or so mild, kind, courteous, restrained, and magnanimous. A revolution is an uprising, an act of violence whereby one class overthrows another. A rural revolution is a revolution by which the peasantry overthrow the authority of the feudal landlord class. If the peasants do not use the maximum of their strength, they can never overthrow the authority of the landlords, which has been deeply rooted for thousands of years. In the rural areas, there must be a great fervent revolutionary upsurge, which alone can arouse hundreds and thousands of the people to form a great force.

Vanguard of the Revolution

The main force in the countryside that has always put up the bitterest fight is the poor peasants. Throughout both the period of underground organization and that of open organization, the poor peasants have fought militantly all along. They accept most willingly the leadership of the Communist Party.

Overthrowing the Clan Authority of the Elders and Ancestral Temples, the Theocratic Authority and the City Gods and Local Deities, and the Masculine Authority of the Husbands

A man in China is usually subjected to the domination of three systems of authority: (1) the system of the state (political authority), ranging from the national, provincial, and country government to the township government; (2) the system of the clan (clan authority), ranging from the central and branch ancestral temples to the head of the household; and (3) the system of gods and spirits (theocratic authority), including the system of the netherworld ranging from the King of Hell to the city gods and local deities, and that of supernatural beings ranging from the Emperor of Heaven to all kinds of gods and spirits. As to women, apart from being dominated by the three systems mentioned above, they are further dominated by men (the authority of the husband). These four kinds of authority—political authority, clan authority, theocratic authority, and the authority of the husband—represent the whole ideology and institution of feudalism and patriarchy and are the four great cords that have bound the Chinese people and particularly the peasants. We have already seen the peasants are overthrowing the political authority of the landlords in the countryside. The political authority of the landlords is the backbone of all other systems of authority. Where it has already been overthrown, clan authority, theocratic authority, and the authority of the husband are all beginning to totter.

Theocratic authority begins to totter everywhere as the peasant movement develops. In many places the peasant associations have taken over the temples of the gods as their offices. Everywhere they advocate the appropriation of temple properties to maintain peasant schools and to defray association expenses, calling this "public revenue from superstition" . . . In places where the power of the peasants is predominant, only the older peasants and the women still believe in gods, while the young and middle-aged peasants no longer do so. Since it is the young and middle-aged peasants who are in control of the peasant association, the movement to overthrow theocratic authority and eradicate superstition is going on everywhere.

As to the authority of the husband, it has always been comparatively weak among the poor peasants, because the poor peasant women, compelled for financial reasons to take more part in manual work than women of the wealthier classes, have obtained more right to speak and more power to make decisions in family affairs. In recent years the rural economy has become even more bankrupt and the basic condition for men's domination over women has already been undermined. And now, with the rise of the peasant movement, women in many places have set out immediately to organize the rural women's association; the opportunity has come for them to lift up their heads, and the authority of the husband is tottering more and more every day. In a word, all feudal and patriarchal ideologies and institutions are tottering as the power of the peasants rises.

Cultural Movement

With the downfall of the power of the landlords in the rural areas, the peasants' cultural movement has begun. And so the peasants, who hitherto bitterly hated the schools, are now zealously organizing evening classes. The "foreign-style schools" were always unpopular with the peasants. In my student days I used to stand up for the "foreign-style schools" when, upon returning to my native place, I found the peasants objecting to them. I was myself identified with the "foreign-style students" and "foreign-style teachers" and always felt that the peasants were somehow wrong. It was during my six months in the countryside in 1925, when I was already a Communist and had adopted the Marxist viewpoint, that I realized I was mistaken and that the peasants' views were right. The teaching materials used in the real primary schools all dealt with city matters and were in no way adapted to the needs of the rural areas . . . As a result, the peasants wanted old-style rather than modern schools—"Chinese classes," as they call them, rather than "foreign classes"—and they preferred the masters of the old-style school to the teachers in the primary schools.

Now the peasants are energetically organizing evening classes, which they call peasant schools. The county education boards wanted to use these public funds for establishing primary schools, that is, "foreign-style schools" not adapted to the needs of the peasants, while the peasants wanted to use them for peasant schools . . . As a result of the growth of the peasant movement, the cultural level of the peasants has risen rapidly.

The Question of Land Redistribution

The Chinese Communist Party viewed relations between landlords and tenants as the main contradiction in Chinese rural areas. When Mao and his Red Army established their own government in a mountainous region in central China, they immediately tackled the issue of land distribution. The issue has concerned Chinese thinkers and officials for millennia, and the Chinese Communist Party's efforts resonate with features of earlier plans and designs for land redistribution. In the long run, the significance of the so-called land reform movement lay less in giving land to the peasants (since eventually they had to surrender it to the collectives and communes) than in the techniques of class warfare and political mobilization developed in three campaigns on the local level.

There are a few methods for distributing land. The major one is equal redistribution per capita. Only 20 percent of the land in the country was not redistributed. Of the land already redistributed, 80 percent of the land was reallotted on the basis of equal redistribution per capita, regardless of age or gender. At the beginning of the land struggle, no law existed that could be applied to this situation. The Xunwu County Revolutionary Committee (the country government) suggested the following four methods, asking that the district and township soviets summon mass meetings to discuss and choose one method:

1. Equal redistribution per capita.
2. Redistribution according to productivity. Those who have greater productivity receive more land and those who have less productivity receive less land. In other words, anyone over 4 years old and under 55 is regarded as one labor unit and receives one share; those who are under 4 or over 55 receive only one-half share.
3. Redistribution according to financial resources. Artisans get less land, and those who do not have an occupation get more.
4. Redistribution according to soil fertility. Those who receive poorer lands receive more; those who get fertile lands get less.

In the event, most places chose the first method. Later on, the Zunwu County Communist Party applied the first method to all districts and was supported by the majority of the poor peasants and the masses. At present about 80 percent of the areas that redistributed land used this method. Within these areas, regardless or age, gender, or productivity, the total amount of land was divided by the number of persons. Some villages did not redistribute the land to people under four. Among those over four years old, regardless of their productivity, some got a 50 percent share or a 70 percent share, the rest received a full share. This was the method practiced in Liuche, Fengshan, Shangqi, and Datong townships, which have a population of about 10,000.

Some areas redistributed the land equally by the number of persons and then had those who were incapable of farming return part of their share to the soviet; this land was then added to the share of those with greater productivity. (The amount of shares returned were unequal; each person decided individually.) In the end, persons capable of greater physical labor got more land and those not as capable got less. This method is similar to the second method suggested by the county government. The difference is that peasants returned some part of the land of their own accord after the land was redistributed instead of redistributing the land according to productivity from the beginning. Longtu Township followed this method. In another township, Huangsha, a similar situation occurred, except this time the land was not returned by the peasants on their own accord. When the government saw that some people could not farm the land they had received, it ordered them to return part of the land to the government. The peasants did not complain when asked to return part of the land unless the government forced them to return to the fertile part and would not let them return the poor part, then they got upset. The combined population of Longtu and Huangsha is 2,500.

CHAPTER 31

Age of Anxiety

31.1

Beyond Good and Evil, Friedrich Nietzsche

The writings of Friedrich Wilhelm Nietzsche (1844-1900), more than those of any other philosopher, foreshadow the massive intellectual and spiritual dislocations of the twentieth century. More psychologically than rationalistically attuned, Nietzsche said that the Russian novelist Dostoevsky was the only one who had taught him anything about human nature.

In the twentieth century Nietzsche became a seminal influence on existential philosophers and writers, such as Sartre and Camus, on theologians grappling with the problem of human choices in a world that seemed godless, and on Freud's school of psychoanalysis. Some scholars claim the twentieth-century Nazi doctrine of race is a manifestation of Nietzsche's "will to power," but that is clearly a distortion of Nietzsche's view; he would have regarded Nazi racism as an example of the "slave morality" of the "herd." He believed that only superior *individuals* achieved superior values. Today, Nietzsche is considered a genuinely original thinker, one of the first to recognize the absurdity of human existence as the necessary basis for creative life and to stress the importance of illusion and irrational factors in shaping human behavior.

Nietzsche was the son of a Lutheran minister who died when the boy was five years old. He grew up in a household dominated by older women. (The male desire to free himself from that female domination informs his work.) Because of doubts about religion, Nietzsche chose not to follow his father's pastoral vocation. A brilliant student, he became a professor of classical philology at the University of Basel in Switzerland at the extraordinary age of twenty-four. He held the position for ten years until failing health forced his resignation. During his Basel years he was a close friend of Richard Wagner, the German composer, although he would later break with him, rejecting what he considered Wagner's decadent late romanticism.

Nietzsche's first important work, *The Birth of Tragedy: Out of the Spirit of Music* (1872), took issue with what was then the conventional view of ancient Greek civilization as the embodiment of calm rationality and noble grandeur. He saw the dark irrationality essential to tragic drama, and pointed out its two polarities—the passionate mysteries of Dionysus (god of wine and ecstasy) and the serene clarity of Apollo (god of prophecy, light, and reason). Insightful as the book was, philological scholars attacked it for its lack of conventional scholarship and even labeled it Wagnerian propaganda. Nietzsche's thesis typifies his desire to get under the surface of conventional ideas and search for the psychological forces that he believed generated all great historical and aesthetic movements.

Nietzsche's constantly deteriorating health forced him to give up his professorial duties and become a wanderer through Switzerland, Italy, and southern France, writing constantly but beset by increasing solitude. His most popular work was *Thus Spake Zarathustra* (1883-1885). The ancient

Persian prophet, Zarathustra or Zoroaster, is the poetic incarnation of Nietzsche himself and simultaneously the imaginary companion of his solitude. The book appealed to many readers for its prophetic, almost biblical cadences and its memorably startling phrases, asserting Nietzsche's most deeply felt values in non-philosophical language: "Man is a rope stretched between the animal and the Superman—a rope over an abyss. . . . And it is the great noontide, when man is in the middle of his course between animal and Superman. . . . *Dead are all the Gods: now do we desire the Superman to live.*—Let this be our final will at noontide! . . . Only where there is life, is there also will: not, however, Will to Life, but—so I teach thee—Will to Power!"

Nietzsche's failing health and his temperament prevented him from carrying out the systematic exposition of his thoughts that he intended in a huge work titled *The Will to Power;* instead he frequently wrote aphorisms and poetry. In *The Genealogy of Morals* (1887) he traced the origins of Christian morality to a slave revolt against everything superior, and he advocated returning to an aristocratic "master morality." Nietzsche's mental breakdown came in Turin, Italy in 1889. He wrote raving notes to his friends signed "Dionysus" and "The Crucified One." He lived on in Germany until 1900, mainly under the care of his mother and sister. Some scholars have seen his fate at the dawn of the twentieth century as foreshadowing its various extreme ideologies, but this seems unfair to Nietzsche's varied individualistic perceptions. If he had a fault, it was the rhetorical extremism he sometimes adopted to make his points and the dialectical writing techniques he employed as a technique of argumentation. He developed his ideas through stating conflicting opposites, which made them easy prey for those looking for isolated quotations only to buttress their own ideas.

Nietzsche did not build a grand philosophical system. His ideas are too often unsystematic and elusive. His supercharged sayings do not always make for clarity, but they do allow him to strike off original insights into the conditions and nature of humanity. Like Dostoevsky, Nietzsche hated the ugliness and bourgeois materialism of European society in the late nineteenth century. He rejected all its "certainties"—democracy, Christianity, science, the life of reason—as diminutions of man's higher nature. Only a "transvaluation" of all traditional values could save Europe. One must understand the deepest feelings of humanity and harness them by an act of *will* to creative ends. Nietzsche's affirmative values were those of determined individuals (*Übermenschen,* "overmen" or "supermen") who, through disciplined struggle and suffering, made their lives significant and for whom the good life was rooted in the mystery of existence. His attacks on bourgeois civilization and his advocacy of relentless struggle against the "herd" who accepted its values served to inspire Social Darwinists, Fascists, and National Socialists (Nazis). However the groups that loved to quote Nietzsche often distorted his ideas. He clearly expressed his disgust with racism, nationalism, and all such collectivist perspectives. His individualistic point of view was the antithesis of any totalitarian doctrine. Most enduring in Nietzsche's thought is his fierce sincerity; his hatred of conventional falsehoods, false roles, mediocrity, and mass vulgarity; and his insight into the irrational wellsprings of human creativity. He disapproved of academic philosophy: the only true philosophy is that which one *lives.*

Beyond Good and Evil: Prelude to a Philosophy of the Future (1886), from which the following selection is taken, is among the clearest statements of Nietzsche's philosophy. It shows his distrust of reason and his rejection of the values of Christian democratic culture. Although his views cannot always be clearly understood or accepted, they do represent significant currents in human nature that should not be ignored.

SOURCE: From Beyond Good and Evil by Nietzsche, translated by Helen Zimmern, Boni and Liveright, 1917.

The will to truth which will still tempt us to many a venture, that famous truthfulness of which all philosophers so far have spoken with respect—what questions has this will to truth not laid before us! What strange, wicked, questionable questions! That is a long story even now—and yet it seems as if it had scarcely begun. Is it any wonder that we should finally become suspicious, lose patience, and turn away impatiently? that we should finally learn from this Sphinx to ask questions, too? *Who* is it really that puts questions to us here? *What* in us really wants "truth"?

Indeed we came to a long halt at the question about the cause of this will—until we finally came to a complete stop before a still more basic question. We asked about the *value* of this will. Suppose we want truth: *why not rather* untruth? and uncertainty? even ignorance?

The problem of the value of truth came before us—or was it we who came before the problem? Who of us is Oedipus here? Who the Sphinx? It is a rendezvous, it seems of questions and question marks.

And though it scarcely seems credible, it finally almost seems to us as if the problem had never even been put so far—as if we were the first to see it, fix it with our eyes, and *risk* it. For it does involve a risk, and perhaps there is none that is greater.

2

"How *could* anything originate out of its opposite? for example, truth out of error? or the will to truth out of the will to deception? or selfless deeds out of selfishness? or the pure and sunlike gaze of the sage out of lust? Such origins are impossible; whoever dreams of them is a fool, indeed worse; the things of the highest value must have another, *peculiar* origin—they cannot be derived from this transitory, seductive, deceptive, paltry world, from this turmoil of delusion and lust. Rather from the lap of Being, the intransitory, the hidden god, the 'thing-in-itself'—there must be their basis, and nowhere else."

This way of judging constitutes the typical prejudgment and prejudice which give away the metaphysicians of all ages; this kind of valuation looms in the background of all their logical procedures; it is on account of this "faith" that they trouble themselves about "knowledge," about something that is finally baptized solemnly as "the truth." The fundamental faith of the metaphysicians is *the faith in opposite values.* It has not even occurred to the most cautious among them that one might have a doubt right here at the threshold where it was surely most necessary—even if they vowed to themselves, *"de omnibus dubitandum."*

For one may doubt, first, whether there are any opposites at all, and secondly whether these popular valuations and opposite values on which the metaphysicians put their seal, are not perhaps merely foreground estimates, only provisional perspectives, perhaps even from some nook, perhaps from below, frog perspectives, as it were, to borrow an expression painters use. For all the value that the true, the truthful, the selfless may deserve, it would still be possible that a higher and more fundamental value for life might have to be ascribed to deception, selfishness, and lust. It might even be possible that what constitutes the value of these good and revered things is precisely that they are insidiously related, tied to, and involved with these wicked seemingly opposite things—maybe even one with them in essence. Maybe!

But who has the will to concern himself with such dangerous maybes? For that, one really has to wait for the advent of a new species of philosophers, such as have somehow another and converse taste and propensity from those we have known so far—philosophers of the dangerous "maybe" in every sense.

And in all seriousness: I see such new philosophers coming up.

3

After having looked long enough between the philosopher's lines and fingers, I say to myself: by far the greater part of conscious thinking must still be included among instinctive activities, and that goes even for philosophical thinking. We have to relearn here, as one has had to relearn about heredity and what is "innate." As the act of birth deserves no consideration in the whole process and procedure of heredity, so "being conscious" is not in any decisive sense the *opposite* of what is instinctive: most of the conscious thinking of a philosopher is secretly guided and forced into certain channels by his instincts.

Behind all logic and its seeming sovereignty of movement, too, there stand valuations or, more clearly, physiological demands for the preservation of a certain type of life. For example, that the definite should be worth more than the indefinite, and mere appearance worth less than "truth"—such estimates might be, in spite of their regulative importance for *us*, nevertheless mere foreground estimates, a certain kind of *niaiserie* which may be necessary for the preservation of just such beings as we are. Supposing, that is, that not just man is the "measure of things."

4

The falseness of a judgment is for us not necessarily an objection to a judgment; in this respect our new language may sound strangest. The question is to what extent it is life-promoting, life-preserving, species-preserving, perhaps even species-cultivating. And we are fundamentally inclined to claim that the falsest judgments (which include the synthetic judgments *a priori*) are the most indispensable for us; that without accepting the fictions of logic, without measuring reality against the purely invented world of the unconditional and self-identical, without a constant falsification of the world by means of numbers, man could not live—that renouncing false judgments would mean renouncing life and a denial of life. To recognize untruth as a condition of life—that certainly means resisting accustomed value feelings in a dangerous way; and a philosophy that risks this would by that token alone place itself beyond good and evil.

5

What provokes one to look at all philosophers half suspiciously, half mockingly, is not that one discovers again and again how innocent they are—how often and how easily they make mistakes and go astray; in short, their childishness and childlikeness—but that they are not honest enough in their work, although they all make a lot of virtuous noise when the problem of truthfulness is touched even remotely. They all pose as if they had discovered and reached their real opinions through the self-development of a cold, pure, divinely unconcerned dialectic (as opposed to the mystics of every rank, who are more honest and doltish—and talk of "inspiration"); while at bottom it is an assumption, a hunch, indeed a kind of "inspiration"—most often a desire of the heart that has been filtered and made abstract—that they defend with reasons they have sought after the fact.

When the *new* psychologist puts an end to the superstitions which have so far flourished with almost tropical luxuriance around the idea of the soul, he practically exiles himself into a new desert and a new suspicion—it is possible that the older psychologists had a merrier and more comfortable time of it; eventually, however, he finds that precisely thereby he also condemns himself to *invention*—and—who knows?—perhaps to discovery.

13

Physiologists should think before putting down the instinct of self-preservation as the cardinal instinct of an organic being. A living thing seeks above all to *discharge* its strength—life itself is *will to power;* self-preservation is only one of the indirect and most frequent *results.*

In short, here as everywhere else, let us beware of *superfluous* teleological principles—one of which is the instinct of self-preservation (we owe it to Spinoza's inconsistency). Thus method, which must be essentially economy of principles, demands it.

23

All psychology so far has got stuck in moral prejudices and fears; it has not dared to descend into the depths. To understand it as morphology and the *doctrine of the development of the will to power,* as I do—nobody has yet come close to doing this even in thought—insofar as it is permissible to recognize in what has been written so far a symptom of what has so far been kept silent. The power of moral prejudices has penetrated deeply into the most spiritual world, which would seem to be the coldest and most devoid of presuppositions, and has obviously operated in an injurious, inhibiting, blinding, and distorting manner. A proper physiopsychology has to contend with unconscious resistance in the heart of the investigator, it has "the heart" against it: even a doctrine of reciprocal dependence of the "good" and the "wicked" drives, causes (as refined immorality) distress and aversion in a still hale and hearty conscience—still more so, a doctrine of the derivation of all good impulses from wicked ones. If, however, a person should regard even the affects of hatred, envy, covetousness, and the lust to rule as conditions of life, as factors which, fundamentally and essentially, must be present in the general economy of life (and must, therefore, be further enhanced if life is to be further enhanced)—he will suffer from such a view of things as from seasickness. And yet even this hypothesis is far from being the strangest and most painful in this immense and almost new domain of dangerous insights; and there are in fact a hundred good reasons why everyone should keep away from it who—*can.*

On the other hand, if one has once drifted there with one's bark, well! all right! let us clench our teeth! let us open our eyes and keep our hand firm on the helm! We sail right *over* morality, we crush, we destroy perhaps the remains of our own morality by daring to make our voyage there—but what matter are *we!* Never yet did a *profounder* world of insight reveal itself to daring travelers and adventurers, and the psychologist who thus "makes a sacrifice"—it is *not* the *sacrifizio dell' intelletto,* on the contrary!—will at least be entitled to demand in return that psychology shall be recognized again as the queen of the sciences, for whose service and preparation the other sciences exist. For psychology is now again the path to the fundamental problems.

THE FREE SPIRIT

29

Independence is for the very few; it is a privilege of the strong. And whoever attempts it even with the best right but without inner constraint proves that he is probably not only strong, but also daring to the point of recklessness. He enters into a labyrinth, he multiples a thousandfold the dangers which life brings with it in any case, not the least of which is that no one can see how and where he loses his way, becomes lonely, and is torn piecemeal by some minotaur of conscience. Supposing one like that comes to grief, this happens so far from the comprehension of men that they neither feel it nor sympathize. And he cannot go back any longer. Nor can he go back to the pity of men.—

30

Our highest insights must—and should—sound like follies and sometimes like crimes when they are heard without permission by those who are not predisposed and predestined for them. The difference between the exoteric and the esoteric, formerly known to philosophers—among the Indians as among the Greeks, Persians, and Muslims, in short, wherever one believed in an order of rank and *not* in equality and equal rights—does not so much consist in this, that the exoteric approach comes from outside and sees, estimates, measures, and judges from the outside, not the inside: what is much more essential is that the exoteric approach sees things from below, the esoteric looks *down from above.* There are heights of the soul from which even tragedy ceases to look tragic; and rolling together all the woe of the world—who could dare to decide whether its sight would *necessarily* seduce us and compel us to feel pity and thus double this woe?

What serves the higher type of men as nourishment or delectation must almost be poison for a very different and inferior type. The virtues of the common man might perhaps signify vices and weaknesses in a philosopher. It could be possible that a man of a high type, when degenerating and perishing, might only at that point acquire qualities that would require those in the lower sphere into which he had sunk to begin to venerate him like a saint. There are books that have opposite values for soul and health, depending on whether the lower soul, the lower vitality, or the higher and more vigorous ones turn to them: in the former case, these books are dangerous and lead to crumbling and disintegration; in the latter, heralds' cries that call the bravest to *their* courage. Books for all the world are always foul-smelling books: the smell of small people clings to them. Where the people eat and drink, even where they venerate, it usually stinks. One should not go to church if one wants to breathe *pure* air.

31

When one is young, one venerates and despises without that art of nuances which constitutes the best gain of life, and it is only fair that one has to pay dearly for having assaulted men and things in this manner with Yes and No. Everything is arranged so that the worst of tastes, the taste of the unconditional, should be cruelly fooled and abused until a man learns to put a little art into his feelings and rather to risk trying even what is artificial—as the real artists of life do.

The wrathful and reverent attitudes characteristic of youth do not seem to permit themselves any rest until they have forged men and things in such a way that these attitudes may be vented on them—after all, youth in itself has something of forgery and deception. Later, when the young soul, tortured by all kinds of disappointments, finally turns suspiciously against itself, still hot and wild, even in its suspicion and pangs of conscience—how wroth it is with itself now! how it tears itself to pieces, impatiently! how it takes revenge for its long self-delusion, just as if it had been a deliberate blindness! In this transition one punishes oneself with mistrust against one's own feelings; one tortures one's own enthusiasm with doubts; indeed, one experiences even a good conscience as a danger, as if it were a way of wrapping oneself in veils and the exhaustion of subtler honesty—and above all one takes sides, takes sides on principle, *against* "youth."—Ten years later one comprehends that all this, too—was still youth.

32

During the longest part of human history—so-called prehistorical times—the value or disvalue of an action was derived from its consequences. The action itself was considered as little as its origin. It was rather the way a distinction or disgrace still reaches back today from a child to its parents, in China: it was the retroactive force of success or failure that led men to think well or ill of an action. Let us call this period the *pre-moral* period of mankind: the imperative "know thyself!" was as yet unknown.

In the last ten thousand years, however, one has reached the point, step by step, in a few large regions on the earth, where it is no longer the consequences but the origin of an action that one allows to decide its value. On the whole this is a great event which involves a considerable refinement of vision and standards; it is the unconscious aftereffect of the rule of aristocratic values and the faith in "descent"—the sign of a period that one may call *moral* in the narrower sense. It involves the first attempt at self-knowledge. Instead of the consequences, the origin: indeed a reversal of perspective! Surely, a reversal achieved only after long struggles and vacillations. To be sure, a calamitous new superstition, an odd narrowness of interpretation, thus became dominant: the origin of an action was interpreted in the most definite sense as origin in an *intention;* one came to agree that the value of an action lay in the value of the intention. The intention as the whole origin and prehistory of an action—almost to the present day this prejudice dominated moral praise, blame, judgment, and philosophy on earth.

But today—shouldn't we have reached the necessity of once more resolving on a reversal fundamental shift in values, owing to another self-examination of man, another growth in profundity? Don't we stand at the threshold of a period which should be designated negatively, to begin with, as *extra-moral?* After all, today at least we immoralists have the suspicion that the decisive value of an action lies precisely in what is *unintentional* in it, while everything about it that is intentional, everything about it that can be seen, known, "conscious," still belongs to its surface and skin—which, like every skin, betrays something but *conceals* even more. In short, we believe that the intention is merely a sign and symptom that still requires interpretation—moreover, a sign that means too much and therefore, taken by itself alone, almost nothing. We believe that morality in the traditional sense, the morality of intentions, was a prejudice, precipitate and perhaps provisional—something on the order of astrology and alchemy—but in any case something that must be overcome. The overcoming of morality, in a certain sense even the self-overcoming of morality—let this be the name for that long secret work which has been saved up for the finest and most honest, also the most malicious, consciences of today, as living touchstones of the soul.

There is no other way: the feelings of devotion, self-sacrifice for one's neighbor, the whole morality of self-denial must be questioned mercilessly and taken to court—no less than the aesthetics of "contemplation devoid of all interest" which is used today as a seductive guise for the emasculation of art, to give it a good conscience. There is too much charm and sugar in these feelings of "for others," "*not* for myself," for us not to need to become doubly suspicious at this point and to ask: "are these not perhaps—*seductions?*"

That they *please*—those who have them and those who enjoy their fruits, and also the mere spectator—this does not yet constitute an argument in their *favor* but rather invites caution. So let us be cautious.

34

Whatever philosophical standpoint one may adopt today, from every point of view the *erroneousness* of the world in which we think we live is the surest and firmest fact that we can lay eyes on: we find reasons upon reasons for it which would like to lure us to hypotheses concerning a deceptive principle in "the essence of things."

I could imagine that a human being who had to guard something precious and vulnerable might roll through life, rude and round as an old green wine cask with heavy hoops: the refinement of his shame would want it that way.

A man whose sense of shame has some profundity encounters his destinies and delicate decisions, too, on paths which few ever reach and of whose mere existence his closest intimates must not know: his mortal danger is concealed from their eyes, and so is his regained sureness of life. Such a concealed man who instinctively needs speech for silence and for burial in silence and who is inexhaustible in his evasion of communication, *wants* and sees to it that a mask of him roams in his place through the hearts and heads of his friends. And supposing he did not want it, he would still realize some day that in spite of that a mask of him is there—and that this is well. Every profound Spirit needs a mask: even more, around every profound spirit a mask is growing continually, owing to the constantly false, namely *shallow,* interpretation of every word, every step, every sign of life he gives.—

41

One has to test oneself to see that one is destined for independence and command—and do it at the right time. One should not dodge one's tests, though they may be the most dangerous game one could play and are tests that are taken in the end before no witness or judge but ourselves.

Not to remain stuck to a person—not even the most loved—every person is a prison, also a nook. Not to remain stuck to a fatherland—not even if it suffers most and needs help most—it is less difficult to sever one's heart from a victorious fatherland. Not to remain stuck to some pity—not even for higher men into whose rare torture and helplessness some accident allowed us to look. Not to remain stuck to a science—even if it should lure us with the most precious finds that seem to have been saved up precisely for us. Not to remain stuck to one's own detachment, to that voluptuous remoteness and strangeness of the bird who flees ever higher to see ever more below him—the danger of the flier. Not to remain stuck to our own virtues and become as a whole the victim of some detail in us, such as our hospitality, which is the danger of dangers for superior and rich souls who spend themselves lavishly, almost indifferently, and exaggerate the virtue of generosity into a vice. One must know how *to conserve oneself:* the hardest test of independence.

42

A new species of philosophers is coming up: I venture to baptize them with a name that is not free of danger. As I unriddle them, insofar as they allow themselves to be unriddled—for it belongs to their nature to *want* to remain riddles at some point—these philosophers of the future may have a right—it might also be a wrong—to be called *attempters.* This name itself is in the end a mere attempt and, if you will, a temptation.

43

Are these coming philosophers new friends of "truth"? That is probable enough, for all philosophers so far have loved their truths. But they will certainly not be dogmatists. It must offend their pride, also their taste, if their truth is supposed to be a truth for everyman—which has so far been the secret wish and hidden meaning of all dogmatic aspirations. "My judgment is *my* judgment": no one else is easily entitled to it—that is what such a philosopher of the future may perhaps say of himself.

One must shed the bad taste of wanting to agree with many. "Good" is no longer good when one's neighbor mouths it. And how should there be a "common good"! The term contradicts itself: whatever can be common always has little value. In the end it must be as it is and always has been: great things remain for the great, abysses for the profound, nuances and shudders for the refined, and, in brief, all that is rare for the rare.—

44

Need I still say expressly after all this that they, too, will be free, *very* free spirits, these philosophers of the future—though just as certainly they will not be merely free spirits but something more, higher, greater, and thoroughly different that does not want to be misunderstood and mistaken for something else.

Our Virtues

Men have so far treated women like birds who had strayed to them from some height: as something more refined and vulnerable, wilder, stranger, sweeter, and more soulful—but as something one has to lock up lest it fly away.

238

To go wrong on the fundamental problem of "man and woman," to deny the most abysmal antagonism between them and the necessity of an eternally hostile tension, to dream perhaps of equal rights, equal education, equal claims and obligations—that is a *typical* sign of shallowness, and a thinker who has proved shallow in this dangerous place—shallow in his instinct—may be considered altogether suspicious, even more—betrayed, exposed: probably he will be too "short" for all fundamental problems of life, of the life yet to come, too, and incapable of attaining *any* depth. A man, on the other hand, who has depth, in his spirit as well as in his desires, including that depth of benevolence which is capable of severity and hardness and easily mistaken for them, must always think about woman as *Orientals* do: he must conceive of woman as a possession, as property that can be locked, as something predestined for service and achieving her perfection in that. Here he must base himself on the tremendous reason of Asia, on Asia's superiority in the instincts, as the Greeks did formerly, who were Asia's best heirs and students: as is well known, from Homer's time to the age of Pericles, as their culture *increased* along with the range of their powers, they also gradually became *more severe,* in brief, more Oriental, against woman. *How* necessary, *how* logical, *how* humanely desirable even, this was—is worth pondering.

239

In no age has the weaker sex been treated with as much respect by men as in ours: that belongs to the democratic inclination and basic taste, just like disrespectfulness for old age. No wonder that this respect is immediately abused. One wants more, one learns to demand, finally one almost finds this tribute of respect insulting, one would prefer competition for rights, indeed even a genuine fight: enough, woman loses her modesty. Let us immediately add that she also loses taste. She unlearns her *fear* of man: but the woman who "unlearns fear" surrenders her most womanly instincts.

What Is Noble

257

Every enhancement of the type "man" has so far been the work of an aristocratic society—and it will be so again and again—a society that believes in the long ladder of an order of rank and differences in value between man and man, and that needs slavery in some sense or other. Without that *pathos of distance* which grows out of the ingrained difference between strata—when the ruling caste constantly looks afar and looks down upon subjects and instruments and just as constantly practices obedience and command, keeping down and keeping at a distance—that other, more mysterious pathos could not have grown up either—the craving for an ever new widening of distances within the soul itself, the development of ever higher, rarer, more remote, further-stretching, more comprehensive states—in brief, simply the enhancement of the type "man," the continual "self-overcoming of man," to use a moral formula in a supra-moral sense.

To be sure, one should not yield to humanitarian illusions about the origins of an aristocratic society (and thus of the presupposition of this enhancement of the type "man"): truth is hard. Let us admit to ourselves, without trying to be considerate, how every higher culture on earth so far has *begun.* Human beings whose nature was still natural, barbarians in every terrible sense of the word, men of prey who were still in possession of unbroken strength of will and lust for power, hurled themselves upon weaker, more civilized, more peaceful races, perhaps traders or cattle raisers, or upon mellow old cultures whose last vitality was even then flaring up in splendid fireworks of spirit and corruption. In the beginning, the noble caste was always the barbarian caste: their predominance did not lie mainly in physical strength but in strength of the soul—they were more *whole* human beings (which also means, at every level, "more whole beasts").

Corruption as the expression of a threatening anarchy among the instincts and of the fact that the foundation of the affects, which is called "life," has been shaken: corruption is something totally different depending on the organism in which it appears. When, for example, an aristocracy, like that of France at the beginning of the Revolution, throws away its privileges with a sublime disgust and sacrifices itself to an extravagance of its own moral feelings, that is corruption; it was really only the last act of that centuries-old corruption which had led them to surrender, step by step, their governmental prerogatives, demoting themselves to a mere *function* of the monarchy (finally even to a mere ornament and showpiece). The essential characteristic of a good and healthy aristocracy, however, is that it experiences itself *not* as a function (whether of the monarchy or the commonwealth) but as their *meaning* and highest justification—that it therefore accepts with a good conscience the sacrifice of untold human beings who, *for its sake,* must be reduced and lowered to incomplete human beings, to slaves, to instruments. Their fundamental faith simply has to be that society must *not* exist for society's sake but only as the foundation and scaffolding on which a choice type of being is able to raise itself to its higher task and to a higher state of *being*—comparable to those sun-seeking vines of Java—they are called *Sipo Matador*—that so long and so often enclasp an oak tree with their tendrils until eventually, high above it but supported by it, they can unfold their crowns in the open light and display their happiness.

259

Refraining mutually from injury, violence, and exploitation and placing one's will on a par with that of someone else—this may become, in a certain rough sense, good manners among individuals if the appropriate conditions are present (namely, if these men are actually similar in strength and value standards and belong together in *one* body). But as soon as this principle is extended, and possibly even accepted as the *fundamental principle of society,* it immediately proves to be what it really is—a will to the *denial* of life, a principle of disintegration and decay.

Here we must beware of superficiality and get to the bottom of the matter, resisting all sentimental weakness: life itself is *essentially* appropriation, injury, overpowering of what is alien and weaker; suppression, hardness, imposition of one's own forms, incorporation and at least, at its mildest, exploitation—but why should one always use those words in which a slanderous intent has been imprinted for ages?

Even the body within which individuals treat each other as equals, as suggested before—and this happens in every healthy aristocracy—if it is a living and not a dying body, has to do to other bodies what the individuals within it refrain from doing to each other: it will have to be an incarnate will to power, it will strive to grow, spread, seize, become predominant—not from any morality or immorality but because it is *living* and because life simply *is* will to power. But there is no point on which the ordinary consciousness of Europeans resists instruction as on this: everywhere people are now raving, even under scientific disguises, about coming conditions of society in which "the exploitative aspect" will be removed—which sounds to me as if they promised to invent a way of life that would dispense with all organic functions. "Exploitation" does not belong to a corrupt or imperfect and primitive society: it belongs to the *essence* of what lives, as a basic organic function; it is a consequence of the will to power, which is after all the will of life.

If this should be an innovation as a theory—as a reality it is the *primordial fact* of all history: people ought to be honest with themselves at least that far.

260

Wandering through the many subtler and coarser moralities which have so far been prevalent on earth, or still are prevalent, I found that certain features recurred regularly together and were closely associated—until I finally discovered two basic types and one basic difference.

There are *master morality* and *slave morality*—I add immediately that in all the higher and more missed cultures there also appear attempts at mediation between these two moralities, and yet more often the interpenetration and mutual misunderstanding of both, and at times they occur directly alongside each other—even in the same human being, within a *single* soul. The moral discrimination of values has originated either among a ruling group whose consciousness of its difference from the ruled group was accompanied by delight—or among the ruled, the slaves and dependents of every degree.

In the first case, when the ruling group determines what is "good," the exalted, proud states of the soul are experienced as conferring distinction and determining the order of rank. The noble human being separates from himself those in whom the opposite of such exalted, proud states finds expression: he despises them. It should be noted immediately that in this first type of morality the opposition of "good" and *"bad"* means approximately the same as "noble" and "contemptible." (The opposition of "good" and *"evil"* has a different origin.) One feels contempt for the cowardly, the anxious, the petty, those intent on narrow utility: also for the suspicious with their unfree glances, those who humble themselves, the doglike people who allow themselves to be maltreated, the begging flatterers, above all the liars: it is part of the fundamental faith of all aristocrats that the common people lie. "We truthful ones"—thus the nobility of ancient Greece referred to itself.

It is obvious that moral designations were everywhere first applied to *human beings* and only later, derivatively, to actions. Therefore it is a gross mistake when historians of morality start from such questions as: why was the compassionate act praised? The noble type of man experiences *itself* as determining values; it does not need approval; it judges, "what is harmful to me is harmful in itself"; it knows itself to be that which first accords honor to things: it is *value-creating.* Everything it knows as part of itself it honors: such a morality is self-glorification. In the foreground there is the feeling of fullness, of power that seeks to overflow, the happiness of high tension, the consciousness of wealth that would give and bestow: the noble human being, too, helps the unfortunate, but not, or almost not, from pity, but prompted more by an urge begotten by excess of power. The noble human being honors himself as one who is powerful, also as one who has power over himself, who knows how to speak and be silent, who delights in being severe and hard with himself and respects all severity and hardness. "A hard heart Wotan put into my breast," says an old Scandinavian saga: a fitting poetic expression, seeing that it comes from the soul of a proud Viking. Such a type of man is actually proud of the fact that he is *not* made for pity, and the hero of the saga therefore adds as a warning: "If the heart is not hard in youth it will never harden." Noble and courageous human beings who think that way are furthest removed from that morality which finds the distinction or morality precisely in pity, or in acting for others, or in *désintéressement;* faith in oneself, pride in oneself, a fundamental hostility and irony against "selflessness" belong just as definitely to noble morality as does a slight disdain and caution regarding compassionate feelings and a "warm heart."

It is the powerful who *understand* how to honor; this is their art, their realm of invention. The profound reverence for age and tradition—all law rests on this double reverence—the faith and prejudice in favor of ancestors and disfavor of those yet to come are typical of the morality of the powerful; and when the men of "modern ideas," conversely, believe almost instinctively in "progress" and "the future" and more and more lack respect for age, this in itself would sufficiently betray the ignoble origin of these "ideas."

A morality of the ruling group, however, is most alien and embarrassing to the present taste in the severity of its principle that one has duties only to one's peers; that against beings of a lower rank, against everything alien, one may behave as one pleases or "as the heart desires," and in any case "beyond good and evil"—here pity and like feelings may find their place. The capacity for, and the duty of, long gratitude and long revenge—both only among one's peers—refinement in repaying, the sophisticated concept of friendship, a certain necessity for having enemies (as it were, as drainage ditches for the affects of envy, quarrelsomeness, exuberance—at bottom, in order to be capable of being good *friends*): all these are typical characteristics of noble morality which, as suggested, is not the morality of "modern ideas" and therefore is hard to empathize with today, also hard to dig up and uncover.

It is different with the second type of morality, *slave morality.* Suppose the violated, oppressed, suffering, unfree, who are uncertain of themselves and weary, moralize: what will their moral valuations have in common? Probably, a pessimistic suspicion about the whole condition of man will find expression, perhaps a condemnation of man along with his condition. The slave's eye is not favorable to the virtues of the powerful: he is skeptical and suspicious, *subtly* suspicious, of all the "good" that is honored there—he would like to persuade himself that even their happiness is not genuine. Conversely, those qualities are brought out and flooded with light which serve to ease existence for those who suffer; here pity, the complaisant and obliging hand, the warm heart, patience, industry, humility, and friendliness are honored—for here these are the most useful qualities and almost the only means for enduring the pressure of existence. Slave morality is essentially a morality of utility.

Here is the place for the origin of that famous opposition of "good" and "evil": into evil one's feelings project power and dangerousness, a certain terribleness, subtlety, and strength that does not permit contempt to develop. According to slave morality, those who are "evil" thus inspire fear; according to master morality it is precisely those who are "good" that inspire, and wish to inspire, fear, while the "bad" are felt to be contemptible.

The opposition reaches its climax when, as a logical consequence of slave morality, a touch of disdain is associated also with the "good" of this morality—this may be slight and benevolent—because the good human being has to be *undangerous* in the slaves' way of thinking: he is good-natured, easy to deceive, a little stupid perhaps, *un bonhomme.* Wherever slave morality becomes preponderant, language tends to bring the words "good" and "stupid" closer together.

One last fundamental difference: the longing for *freedom,* the instinct for happiness and the subtleties of the feeling of freedom belong just as necessarily to slave morality and morals as artful and enthusiastic reverence and devotion are the regular symptom of an aristocratic way of thinking and evaluating.

This makes plain why love *as passion*—which is our European specialty—simply must be of noble origin: as is well known, its invention must be credited to the Provencal knight-poets, those magnificent and inventive human beings of the *"gai saber"* to whom Europe owes so many things and almost owes itself.—

Among the things that may be hardest to understand for a noble human being is vanity: he will be tempted to deny it, where another type of human being could not find it more palpable. The problem for him is to imagine people who seek to create a good opinion of themselves which they do not have of themselves—and thus also do not "deserve"—and who nevertheless end up *believing* this good opinion themselves. This strikes him half as such bad taste and lack of self-respect, and half as so baroquely irrational, that he would like to consider vanity as exceptional, and in most cases when it is spoken of he doubts it.

He will say, for example: "I may be mistaken about my value and nevertheless demand that my value, exactly as I define it, should be acknowledged by others as well—but this is no vanity (but conceit or, more frequently, what is called 'humility' or 'modesty')." Or: "For many reasons I may take pleasure in the good opinion of others: perhaps because I honor and love them and all their pleasures give me pleasure; perhaps also because their good opinion confirms and strengthens my faith in my own good opinion.

262

A *species* comes to be, a type becomes fixed and strong, through the long fight with essentially constant *unfavorable* conditions. Conversely, we know from the experience of breeders that species accorded superabundant nourishment and quite generally extra protection and care soon tend most strongly toward variations of the type and become rich in marvels and monstrosities (including monstrous vices).

Now look for once at an aristocratic commonwealth—say, an ancient Greek *polis,* or Venice—as an arrangement, whether voluntary or involuntary, for *breeding:* human beings are together there who are dependent on themselves and want their species to prevail, most often because they *have to* prevail or run the terrible risk of being exterminated. Here that boon, that excess, and that protection which favor variations are lacking; the species needs itself as a species, as something that can prevail and make itself durable by virtue of its very hardness, uniformity, and simplicity of form, in a constant fight with its neighbors or with the oppressed who are rebellious or threaten rebellion. Manifold experience teaches them to which qualities above all they owe the fact that, despite all gods and men, they are still there, that they have always triumphed: these qualities they call virtues, these virtues alone they cultivate. They do this with hardness, indeed they want hardness; every aristocratic morality is intolerant—in the education of youth, in their arrangements for women, in their marriage customs, in the relations of old and young, in their penal laws (which take into account deviants only)—they consider intolerance itself a virtue, calling it "justice."

In this way a type with few but very strong traits, a species of severe, warlike, prudently taciturn men, close-mouthed and closely linked (and as such possessed of the subtlest feeling for the charms and *nuances* of association), is fixed beyond the changing generations; the continual fight against ever constant *unfavorable* conditions is, as mentioned previously, the cause that fixes and hardens a type.

Eventually, however, a day arrives when conditions become more fortunate and the tremendous tension decreases; perhaps there are no longer any enemies among one's neighbors, and the means of life, even for the enjoyment of life, are superabundant. At one stroke the bond and constraint of the old discipline are torn: it no longer seems necessary, a condition of existence—if it persisted it would only be a form of *luxury,* an archaizing *taste.* Variation, whether as deviation (to something higher, subtler, rarer) or as degeneration and monstrosity, suddenly appears on the scene in the greatest abundance and magnificence; the individual dares to be individual and different.

At these turning points of history we behold beside one another, and often mutually involved and entangled, a splendid, manifold, junglelike growth and upward striving, a kind of *tropical* tempo in the competition to grow, and a tremendous ruin and self-ruination, as the savage egoisms that have turned, almost exploded, against one another wrestle "for sun and light" and can no longer derive any limit, restraint, or consideration from their previous morality. It was this morality itself that dammed up such enormous strength and bent the bow in such a threatening manner; now it is "outlived." The dangerous and uncanny point has been reached where the greater, more manifold, more comprehensive life transcends and *lives beyond* the old morality; the "individual" appears, obliged to give himself laws and to develop his own arts and wiles for self-preservation, self-enhancement, self-redemption.

All sorts of new what-fors and wherewithals; no shared formulas any longer; misunderstanding allied with disrespect; decay, corruption, and the highest desires gruesomely entangled; the genius of the race overflowing from all cornucopias of good and bad; a calamitous simultaneity of spring and fall, full of new charms and veils that characterize young, still unexhausted, still unwearied corruption. Again danger is there, the mother of morals, great danger, this time transposed into the individual, into the neighbor and friend, into the alley, into one's own child, into one's own heart, into the most personal and secret recesses of wish and will: what may the moral philosophers emerging in this age have to preach now?

These acute observers and loiterers discover that the end is approaching fast, that everything around them is corrupted and corrupts, that nothing will stand the day after tomorrow, except *one* type of man, the incurably *mediocre.* The mediocre alone have a chance of continuing their type and propagating—they are the men of the future, the only survivors: "Be like them! Become mediocre!" is now the only morality that still makes sense, that still gets a hearing.

But this morality of mediocrity is hard to preach: after all, it may never admit what it is and what it wants. It must speak of measure and dignity and duty and neighbor love—it will find it difficult *to conceal its irony.*—

263

There is an *instinct for rank* which, more than anything else, is a sign of a *high* rank; there is a delight in the nuances of reverence that allows us to infer noble origin and habits. The refinement, graciousness, and height of a soul is tested dangerously when something of the first rank passes by without being as yet protected by the shudders of authority against obtrusive efforts and ineptitudes—something that goes its way unmarked, undiscovered, tempting, perhaps capriciously concealed and disguised, like a living touchstone. Anyone to whose task and practice it belongs to search out souls will employ this very art in many forms in order to determine the ultimate value of a soul and the unalterable, innate order of rank to which it belongs: he will test it for its *instinct of reverence.*

Différence engender haine: the baseness of some people suddenly spurts up like dirty water when some holy vessel, some precious thing from a locked shrine, some book with the marks of a great destiny, is carried past; and on the other hand there is a reflex of silence, a hesitation of the eye, a cessation of all gestures that express how a soul *feels* the proximity of the most venerable. The way in which reverence for the *Bible* has on the whole been maintained so far in Europe is perhaps the best bit of discipline and refinement of manners that Europe owes to Christianity: such books of profundity and ultimate significance require some external tyranny of authority for their protection in order to gain those millennia of *persistence* which are necessary to exhaust them and figure them out.

Much is gained once the feeling has finally been cultivated in the masses (among the shallow and in the high-speed intestines of every kind) that they are not to touch everything; that there are holy experiences before which they have to take off their shoes and keep away their unclean hands—this is almost their greatest advance toward humanity. Conversely, perhaps there is nothing about so-called educated people and believers in "modern ideas" that is as nauseous as their lack of modesty and the comfortable insolence of their eyes and hands with which they touch, lick, and finger everything; and it is possible that even among the common people, among the less educated, especially among peasants, one finds today more *relative* nobility of taste and tactful reverence than among the newspaper-reading *demimonde* of the spirit, the educated.

264

One cannot erase from the soul of a human being what his ancestors liked most to do and did most constantly.

265

At the risk of displeasing innocent ears I propose: egoism belongs to the nature of a noble soul—I mean that unshakable faith that to a being such as "we are" other beings must be subordinate by nature and have to sacrifice themselves. The noble soul accepts this fact of its egoism without any question mark, also without any feeling that it might contain hardness, constraint, or caprice, rather as something that may be founded in the primordial law of things: if it sought a name for this fact it would say, "it is justice itself." Perhaps it admits under certain circumstances that at first make it hesitate that there are some who have rights equal to its own; as soon as this matter of rank is settled it moves among these equals with their equal privileges, showing the same sureness of modesty and delicate reverence that characterize its relations with itself—in accordance with an innate heavenly mechanism understood by all stars. It is merely another aspect of its egoism this refinement and self-limitation in its relations with its equals—every star is such an egoist—it honors *itself* in them and in the rights it cedes to them; it does not doubt that the exchange of honors and rights of the nature of social relations and thus also belongs to the natural condition of things.

The noble soul gives as it takes, from that passionate and irritable instinct of repayment that lies in its depth. The concept "grace" has no meaning or good odor *inter pares;* there may be a sublime way of letting presents from above happen to one, as it were, and to drink them up thirstily like drops—but for this art and gesture the noble soul has no aptitude. Its egoism hinders it: quite generally it does not like to look "up"—but either *ahead,* horizontally and slowly, or down: *it knows itself to be at a height.*

266

"Truly high respect one can have only for those who do not *seek* themselves."—Goethe

269

In Jesus' life there lies concealed one of the most painful cases of the martyrdom of *knowledge about love:* the martyrdom of the most innocent and desirous heart, never sated by any human love; *demanding* love, to be loved and nothing else, with hardness, with insanity, with terrible eruptions against those who denied him love; the story of a poor fellow, unsated and insatiable in love, who had to invent hell in order to send to it those who did *not* want to love him—and who finally, having gained knowledge about human love, had to invent a god who is all love, all *ability* to love—who has mercy on human love because it is utterly wretched and unknowing. Anyone who feels that way, who *knows* this about love—*seeks* death.

But why pursue such painful matters? Assuming one does not have to.—

270

The spiritual haughtiness and nausea of every man who has suffered profoundly—it almost determines the order of rank *how* profoundly human beings can suffer—his shuddering certainty, which permeates and colors him through and through, that by virtue of his suffering he *knows more* than the cleverest and wisest could possibly know, and that he knows his way and has once been "at home" in many distant, terrifying worlds of which "*you* know nothing"—this spiritual and silent haughtiness of the sufferer, this pride of the elect of knowledge, of the "initiated," of the almost sacrificed, finds all kinds of disguises necessary to protect itself against contact with obtrusive and pitying hands and altogether against everything that is not its equal in suffering. Profound suffering makes noble; it separates.

One of the most refined disguises is Epicureanism, and a certain ostentatious courage of taste which takes suffering casually and resists everything sad and profound. There are "cheerful people" who employ cheerfulness because they are misunderstood on its account—they *want* to be misunderstood. There are "scientific men" who employ science because it creates a cheerful appearance, and because being scientific suggests that a human being is superficial—they *want* to seduce others to this false inference. There are free, insolent spirits who would like to conceal and deny that they are broken, proud, incurable hearts (the cynicism of Hamlet—the case of Galiani); and occasionally even foolishness is the mask for an unblessed all-too-certain knowledge.

From which it follows that it is characteristic of more refined humanity to respect "the mask" and not to indulge in psychology and curiosity in the wrong place.

271

What separates two people most profoundly is a different sense and degree of cleanliness. What avails all decency and mutual usefulness and good will toward each other—in the end the fact remains: "They can't stand each other's smell!"

The highest instinct of cleanliness places those possessed of it in the oddest and most dangerous lonesomeness, as saints: for precisely this is saintliness—the highest spiritualization of this instinct. Whether one is privy to someone's indescribable abundance of pleasure in the bath, or whether one feels some ardor and thirst that constantly drives the soul out of the night into the morning and out of the dim and "dark moods" into what is bright, brilliant, profound, and refined—just as such a propensity *distinguishes*—it is a noble propensity—it also *separates.*

The saint's pity is pity with the *dirt* of what is human, all too human. And there are degrees and heights where he experiences even pity itself as a pollution, as dirty—

272

Signs of nobility: never thinking of degrading our duties into duties for everybody; not wanting to delegate, to share, one's own responsibility; counting one's privileges and their exercise among one's *duties.*

285

The greatest events and thoughts—but the greatest thoughts are the greatest events—are comprehended last: the generations that are contemporaneous with them do not *experience* such events—they live right past them. What happens is a little like what happens in the realm of stars. The light of the remotest stars comes last to men; and until it has arrived man *denies* that there are—stars there. "How many centuries does a spirit require to be comprehended?"—that is a standard, too; with that, too, one creates an order of rank and etiquette that is still needed—for spirit and star.

"Here the vision is free, the spirit exalted."

But there is an opposite type of man that is also on a height and also has free vision—but looks *down.*

—What is noble? What does the word "noble" still mean to us today? What betrays, what allows one to recognize the noble human being, under this heavy, overcast sky of the beginning rule of the plebes that makes everything opaque and leaden?

It is not actions that prove him—actions are always open to many interpretations, always unfathomable—nor is it "works." Among artists and scholars today one finds enough of those who betray by their works how they are impelled by a profound desire for what is noble; but just this need *for* what is noble is fundamentally different from the needs of the noble soul itself and actually the eloquent and dangerous mark of its lack. It is not the works, it is the *faith* that is decisive here, that determines the order of rank—to take up again an ancient religious formula in a new and more profound sense: some fundamental certainty that a noble soul has about itself, something that cannot be sought, nor found, nor perhaps lost.

The noble soul has reverence for itself.

There are human beings who have spirit in an inevitable way; they may turn and twist as they please and hold their hands over their giveaway eyes (as if a hand did not give away secrets!)—in the end it always will out that they have something they conceal, namely spirit. One of the subtlest means for keeping up the deception at least as long as possible and of successfully appearing more stupid than one is—which in ordinary life is often as desirable as an umbrella—is called *enthusiasm,* if we include what belongs with it; for example, virtue.

CHAPTER 32

Dictatorships and World War II

32.1

Mein Kampf (1925), Adolf Hitler

Adolf Hitler (1889-1945) was a German dictator and leader of the Nazi Party. The son of a minor customs official, he studied at Linz and Steyr, attended art school in Munich, but failed to pass into the Vienna Academy. He lived on his family subventions in Vienna (1904-13), yet inhabited hostels and did a variety of menial jobs. He emigrated to Munich in 1913, where he found employment as a drafter. In 1914 he volunteered for a Bavarian regiment, where he became a decorated corporal and suffered a wound in the last stages of World War I. He joined a small political party in 1919 that he renamed the National Socialist German Workers' Party. In 1923, with other extreme right-wing factions, he attempted to overthrow the Bavarian government as a prelude to a "March on Berlin" in imitation of Mussolini's "March on Rome." His "Beer Hall *putsch*" failed, and he was imprisoned for nine months, during which time he dictated to Rudolf Hess his political testament, *Mein Kampf* (My Struggle, 1925).

Hitler expanded his party greatly in the late 1920s, won important parliamentary election victories in 1930 and 1932 against Hindenburg, and became Chancellor in 1933. After the burning of the Reichstag building, he suspended the constitution, silenced all opposition, and brought the Nazi Party to power. In 1934, during the "Night of the Long Knives," Hitler had his personal guard, the SS (Gestapo), murder the leadership of the SA (Brownshirts) and dozens of Nazi party members who had helped bring him to power. In 1935, he openly rearmed the country, established the Rome-Berlin "axis" with Mussolini (1936) and pursued an aggressive foreign policy leading to World War II (Sept. 3, 1939). His domestic policy traded off social and economic improvements for political dictatorship enforced by the Secret State Police (Gestapo). His government established concentration camps for Jews, socialists, communists, Slavs, homosexuals, Jehovah's Witnesses, Gypsies, and political dissenters, and murdered nearly eleven million of them during World War II.

With his early war successes, he increasingly ignored the advice of military experts and wantonly extended the war with his long-desired invasion of the USSR in 1941. The tide turned in 1942 after the defeats at El Alamein and Stalingrad. He miraculously survived the explosion of the bomb placed at his feet by Colonel Stauffenberg (July 1944), and purged the army of all suspects. When the Allies invaded Germany, he retired to his *Bunker*, an air-raid shelter under the Chancellory building in Berlin. All available evidence suggests that Hitler and his wife committed suicide and had their bodies cremated (April 30, 1945).

Source: Excerpts from Mein Kampf by Adolf Hitler, translated by Ralph Manheim. Copyright © 1943, renewed 1971 by Houghton Mifflin Company. Reprinted by permission of Houghton Mifflin Company. All rights reserved.

It is idle to argue which race or races were the original representative of human culture and hence the real founders of all that we sum up under the word 'humanity.' It is simpler to raise this question with regard to the present, and here an easy, clear answer results. All the human culture, all the results of art, science, and technology that we see before us today, are almost exclusively the creative product of the Aryan. This very fact admits of the not unfounded inference that he alone was the founder of all higher humanity, therefore representing the prototype of all that we understand by the word 'man.' He is the Prometheus of mankind from whose bright forehead the divine spark of genius has sprung at all times, forever kindling anew that fire of knowledge which illumined the night of silent mysteries and thus caused man to climb the path to mastery over the other beings of this earth. Exclude him—and perhaps after a few thousand years darkness will again descend on the earth, human culture will pass, and the world turn to a desert.

If we were to divide mankind into three groups, the founders of culture, the bearers of culture, the destroyers of culture, only the Aryan could be considered as representative of the first group. From him originate the foundations and walls of all human creation, and only the outward form and color are determined by the changing traits of character of the various peoples. He provides the mightiest building stones and plans for all human progress and only the execution corresponds to the nature of the varying men and races. In a few decades, for example, the entire east of Asia will possess a culture whose ultimate foundation will be Hellenic spirit and Germanic technology, just as much as in Europe. Only the *outward* form—in part at least—will bear the features of Asiatic character. It is not true, as some people think, that Japan adds European technology to its culture; no, European science and technology are trimmed with Japanese characteristics. The foundation of actual life is no longer the special Japanese culture, although it determines the color of life—because outwardly, in consequence of its inner difference, it is more conspicuous to the European—but the gigantic scientific-technical achievements of Europe and America; that is, of Aryan peoples. Only on the basis of these achievements can the Orient follow general human progress. They furnish the basis of the struggle for daily bread, create weapons and implements for it, and only the outward form is gradually adapted to Japanese character.

If beginning today all further Aryan influence on Japan should stop, assuming that Europe and America should perish, Japan's present rise in science and technology might continue for a short time; but even in a few years the well would dry up, the Japanese special character would gain, but the present culture would freeze and sink back into the slumber from which it was awakened seven decades ago by the wave of Aryan culture. Therefore, just as the present Japanese development owes its life to Aryan origin, long ago in the gray past foreign influence and foreign spirit awakened the Japanese culture of that time. The best proof of this is furnished by the fact of its subsequent sclerosis and total petrifaction. This can occur in a people only when the original creative racial nucleus has been lost, or if the external influence which furnished the impetus and the material for the first development in the cultural field was later lacking. But if it is established that a people receives the most essential basic materials of its culture from foreign races, that it assimilates and adapts them, and that then, if further external influence is lacking, it rigidifies again and again, such a race may be designated as *'culture-bearing,'* but never as *'culture-creating.'* An examination of the various peoples from this standpoint points to the fact that practically none of them were originally *culture-founding,* but almost always *culture-bearing.*

We see this most distinctly in connection with the race which has been and is the bearer of human cultural development—the Aryans. As soon as Fate leads them toward special conditions, their latent abilities begin to develop in a more and more rapid sequence and to mold themselves into tangible forms. The cultures which they found in such cases are nearly always decisively determined by the existing soil, the given climate, and—the subjected people. This last item, to be sure, is almost the most decisive. The more primitive the technical foundation for a cultural activity, the more necessary is the presence of human helpers who, organizationally assembled and employed, must replace the force of the machine. Without this possibility of using lower human beings, the Aryan would never have been able to take his first steps toward his future culture; just as without the help of various suitable beasts which he knew how to tame, he would not have arrived at a technology which is now gradually permitting him to do without these beasts. The saying, 'The Moor has worked off his debt, the Moor can go,' unfortunately has only too deep a meaning. For thousands of years the horse had to serve man and help him lay the foundations of a development which now, in consequence of the motor car, is making the horse superfluous. In a few years his activity will have ceased, but without his previous collaboration man might have had a hard time getting where he is today.

Thus, for the formation of higher cultures the existence of lower human types was one of the most essential preconditions, since they alone were able to compensate for the lack of technical aids without which a higher development is not conceivable. It is certain that the first culture of humanity was based less on the tamed animal than on the use of lower human beings.

Only after the enslavement of subjected races did the same fate strike beasts, and not the other way around, as some people would like to think. For first the conquered warrior drew the plow—and only after him the horse. Only pacifistic fools can regard this as a sign of human depravity, failing to realize that this development had to take place in order to reach the point where today these sky-pilots could force their drivel on the world.

The progress of humanity is like climbing an endless ladder; it is impossible to climb higher without first taking the lower steps. Thus, the Aryan had to take the road to which reality directed him and not the one that would appeal to the imagination of a modern pacifist. The road of reality is hard and difficult, but in the end it leads where our friend would like to bring humanity by dreaming, but unfortunately removes more than bringing it closer.

Hence it is no accident that the first cultures arose in places where the Aryan, in his encounters with lower peoples, subjugated them and bent them to his will. They then became the first technical instrument in the service of a developing culture.

Thus, the road which the Aryan had to take was clearly marked out. As a conqueror he subjected the lower beings and regulated their practical activity under his command, according to his will and for his aims. But in directing them to a useful, through arduous activity, he not only spared the life of those he subjected; perhaps he gave them a fate that was better than their previous so-called 'freedom.' As long as he ruthlessly upheld the master attitude, not only did he really remain master, but also the preserver and increaser of culture. For culture was based exclusively on his abilities and hence on his actual survival. As soon as the subjected people began to raise themselves up and probably approached the conqueror in language, the sharp dividing wall between master and servant fell. The Aryan gave up the purity of his blood and, therefore, lost his sojourn in the paradise which he had made for himself. He became submerged in the racial mixture, and gradually, more and more, lost his cultural capacity, until at last, not only mentally but also physically, he began to resemble the subjected aborigines more than his own ancestors. For a time he could live on the existing cultural benefits, but then petrifaction set in and he fell a prey to oblivion.

Thus cultures and empires collapsed to make place for new formations.

Blood mixture and the resultant drop in the racial level is the sole cause of the dying out of old cultures; for men do not perish as a result of lost wars, but by the loss of that force of resistance which is contained only in pure blood.

All who are not of good race in this world are chaff.

And all occurrences in world history are only the expression of the races' instinct of self-preservation, in the good or bad sense.

■ ■ ■

The mightiest counterpart to the Aryan is represented by the Jew. In hardly any people in the world is the instinct of self-preservation developed more strongly than in the so-called 'chosen.' Of this, the mere fact of the survival of this race may be considered the best proof. Where is the people which in the last two thousand years has been exposed to so slight changes of inner disposition, character, etc., as the Jewish people? What people, finally, has gone through greater upheavals than this one—and nevertheless issued from the mightiest catastrophes of mankind unchanged? What an infinitely tough will to live and preserve the species speaks from these facts!

The mental qualities of the Jew have been schooled in the course of many centuries. Today he passes as 'smart,' and this in a certain sense he had been at all times. But his intelligence is not the result of his own development, but of visual instruction through foreigners. For the human mind cannot climb to the top without steps; for every step upward he needs the foundation of the past, and this in the comprehensive sense in which it can be revealed only in general culture. All thinking is based only in small part on man's own knowledge, and mostly on the experience of the time that has preceded. The general cultural level provides the individual man, without his noticing it as a rule, with such a profusion of preliminary knowledge that, thus armed, he can more easily take further steps of his own. The boy of today, for example, grows up among a truly vast number of technical acquisitions of the last centuries, so that he takes for granted and no longer pays attention to much that a hundred years ago was a riddle to even the greatest minds, although for following and understanding our progress in the field in question it is of decisive importance to him. If a very genius from the twenties of the past century should suddenly leave his grave today, it would be harder for him even intellectually to find his way in the present era than for an average boy of fifteen today. For he would lack all the infinite preliminary education which our present contemporary unconsciously, so to speak, assimilates while growing up amidst the manifestations of our present general civilization.

Since the Jew—for reasons which will at once become apparent—was never in possession of a culture of his own, the foundations of his intellectual work were always provided by others. His intellect at all times developed through the cultural world surrounding him.

The reverse process never took place.

For if the Jewish people's instinct of self-preservation is not smaller but larger than that of other peoples, if his intellectual faculties can easily arouse the impression that they are equal to the intellectual gifts of other races, he lacks completely the most essential requirement for a cultured people, the idealistic attitude.

In the Jewish people the will to self-sacrifice does not go beyond the individual's naked instinct of self-preservation. Their apparently great sense of solidarity is based on the very primitive herd instinct that is seen in many other living creatures in this world. It is a noteworthy fact that the herd instinct leads to mutual support only as long as a common danger makes this seem useful or inevitable. The same pack of wolves which has just fallen on its prey together disintegrates when hunger abates into its individual beasts. The same is true of horses which try to defend themselves against an assailant in a body, but scatter again as soon as the danger is past.

In judging the Jewish people's attitude on the question of human culture, the most essential characteristic we must always bear in mind is that there has never been a Jewish art and accordingly there is none today either; that above all the two queens of all the arts, architecture and music, owe nothing original to the Jews. What they do accomplish in the field of art is either patchwork or intellectual theft. Thus, the Jew lacks those qualities which distinguish the races that are creative and hence culturally blessed.

To what an extent the Jew takes over foreign culture, imitating or rather ruining it, can be seen from the fact that he is mostly found in the art which seems to require least original invention, the art of acting. But even here, in reality, he is only a 'juggler,' or rather an ape; for even here he lacks the last touch that is required for real greatness; even here he is not the creative genius, but a superficial imitator, and all the twists and tricks that he uses are powerless to conceal the inner lifelessness of his creative gift. Here the Jewish press most lovingly helps him along by raising such a roar of hosannahs about even the most mediocre bungler, just so long as he is a Jew, that the rest of the world actually ends up by thinking that they have an artist before them, while in truth it is only a pitiful comedian.

No, the Jew possesses no culture-creating force of any sort, since the idealism, without which there is no true higher development of man, is not present in him and never was present. Hence his intellect will never have a constructive effect, but will be destructive, and in very rare cases perhaps will at most be stimulating, but then as the prototype of the 'force which always wants evil and nevertheless creates good.' Not through him does any progress of mankind occur, but in spite of him.

CHAPTER 33

Recovery and Crisis

33.1

Truman Doctrine, Harry S. Truman

Harry S Truman (1884-1972) was a United States politician and the thirty-third President. He fought in World War I and was a presiding judge in the Jackson County Court in Missouri (1926-34). In 1934 he was elected to the United States Senate as a Democrat and became the chair of a senate committee investigating defense spending. He became the Vice President (1944) and, on Franklin D. Roosevelt's death (April 1945), President. He was reelected in 1948 in a surprise victory over Thomas E. Dewey. As president (1945-1953) he ordered the dropping of the first atomic bomb on Japan in August 1945, which led to Japan's surrender. Following World War II, he established a "containment" policy against the USSR, developed the Marshall Plan to rebuild Europe, and created NATO (1949). In 1950, Truman authorized the sending of United States troops to South Korea and promoted the Four-Point Program to give military and economic aid to countries threatened by communism. Truman established the CIA (1947) and ordered the Berlin Airlift (1948-49). At home, he introduced his "Fair Deal" program of economic reform.

Source: U.S. National Archives & Records Administration www.ourdocuments.gov

---

The peoples of a number of countries of the world have recently had totalitarian regimes forced upon them against their will. The Government of the United States has made frequent protests against coercion and intimidation, in violation of the Yalta agreement, in Poland, Rumania, and Bulgaria. I must also state that in a number of other countries there have been similar developments.

At the present moment in world history nearly every nation must choose between alternative ways of life. The choice is too often not a free one.

One way of life is based upon the will of the majority, and is distinguished by free institutions, representative government, free elections, guarantees of individual liberty, freedom of speech and religion, and freedom from political oppression.

The second way of life is based upon the will of a minority forcibly imposed upon the majority. It relies upon terror and oppression, a controlled press and radio; fixed elections, and the suppression of personal freedoms.

I believe that it must be the policy of the United States to support free peoples who are resisting attempted subjugation by armed minorities or by outside pressures.

I believe that we must assist free peoples to work out their own destinies in their own way.

I believe that our help should be primarily through economic and financial aid which is essential to economic stability and orderly political processes.

The world is not static, and the status quo is not sacred. But we cannot allow changes in the status quo in violation of the Charter of the United Nations by such methods as coercion, or by such subterfuges as political infiltration. In helping free and independent nations to maintain their freedom, the United States will be giving effect to the principles of the Charter of the United Nations.

It is necessary only to glance at a map to realize that the survival and integrity of the Greek nation are of grave importance in a much wider situation. If Greece should fall under the control of an armed minority, the effect upon its neighbor, Turkey, would be immediate and serious. Confusion and disorder might well spread throughout the entire Middle East.

Moreover, the disappearance of Greece as an independent state would have a profound effect upon those countries in Europe whose peoples are struggling against great difficulties to maintain their freedoms and their independence while they repair the damages of war.

It would be an unspeakable tragedy if these countries, which have struggled so long against overwhelming odds, should lose that victory for which they sacrificed so much. Collapse of free institutions and loss of independence would be disastrous not only for them but for the world. Discouragement and possibly failure would quickly be the lot of neighboring peoples striving to maintain their freedom and independence.

Should we fail to aid Greece and Turkey in this fateful hour, the effect will be far reaching to the West as well as to the East.

We must take immediate and resolute action.

I therefore ask the Congress to provide authority for assistance to Greece and Turkey in the amount of $400,000,000 for the period ending June 30, 1948. In requesting these funds, I have taken into consideration the maximum amount of relief assistance which would be furnished to Greece out of the $350,000,000 which I recently requested that Congress authorize for the prevention of starvation and suffering in countries devastated by war.

In addition to funds, I ask the Congress to authorize the detail of American civilian and military personnel to Greece and Turkey, at the request of those countries, to assist in the tasks of reconstruction, and for the purpose of supervising the use of such financial and material assistance as may be furnished. I recommend that authority also be provided for the instruction and training of selected Greek and Turkish personnel.

Finally, I ask that the Congress provide authority which will permit the speediest and most effective use, in terms of needed commodities, supplies, and equipment, of such funds as may be authorized.

If further funds, or further authority, should be needed for the purposes indicated in this message, I shall not hesitate to bring the situation before Congress. On this subject the Executive and Legislative branches of the Government must work together.

This is a serious course upon which we embark.

I would not recommend it except that the alternative is much more serious. The United States contributed $341,000,000,000 toward winning World War II. This is an investment in world freedom and world peace.

The assistance that I am recommending for Greece and Turkey amounts to little more than 1 tenth of 1 per cent of this investment. It is only common sense that we should safeguard this investment and make sure that it was not in vain.

The seeds of totalitarian regimes are nurtured by misery and want. They spread and grow in the evil soil of poverty and strife. They reach their full growth when the hope of the people for a better life has died. We must keep that hope alive.

The free peoples of the world look to us for support in maintaining their freedoms.

If we falter in our leadership, we may endanger the peace of the world—and we shall surely endanger the welfare of our own nation.

Great responsibilities have been placed upon us by the swift movements of events.

CHAPTER 34

Contemporary Asia and Africa

34.1

United Nations Resolution 242 (1967)

Since World War II the Middle East has been the center of violent conflict and a source of great concern for the world. The main source of conflict has been the struggle over the creation of Israel and the Palestinian problem that resulted. The roots of the Israeli-Palestinian struggle stretch back to the late nineteenth century when the Zionist movement—a nationalist movement to make Palestine the home of the Jews—began. In 1948 the struggle over the creation of Israel came to a head when the British, who controlled Palestine, left it in the hands of the United Nations. A United Nations resolution and the first Arab-Israeli war resulted in the creation of Israel, a massive number of Palestinian refugees, and decades of conflict between Arabs and Israelis.

Resolution 242 (passed by the United Nations in 1967) recognized Israel's existence and its need for security but also called on Israel to withdraw from the territories it captured in the 1967 Arab-Israeli war.

Source: From United Nations Security Council, Resolution 242, 1967.

The Security Council,

Expressing its continuing concern with the grave situation in the Middle East,

Emphasizing the inadmissibility of the acquisition of territory by war and the need to work for a just and lasting peace in which every State in the area can live in security,

Emphasizing further that all Member States in their acceptance of the Charter of the United Nations have undertaken a commitment to act in accordance with Articles of the Charter,

1. *Affirms* that the fulfillment of Charter principles requires the establishment of a just and lasting peace in the Middle East which should include the application of both the following principles:

(i) Withdrawal of Israel armed forces from territories occupied in the recent conflict:

(ii) Termination of all claims or states of belligerency and respect for and acknowledgement of the sovereignty, territorial integrity and political independence of every State in the area and their right to live in peace within secure and recognized boundaries free from threats or acts of force;

2. *Affirms further* the necessity

(a) For guaranteeing freedom of navigation through international waterways in the area;

(b) For achieving a just settlement of the refugee problem;

(c) For guaranteeing the territorial inviolability and political independence of every State in the area, through measures including the establishment of demilitarized zones.

34.2

Islamic Revival, Reform, and Nationalism (1940), Muhammad Ali Jinnah

By the 1930s, it was becoming increasingly clear, thanks to the formidable pressure mounted by the Congress Party, that an independent India was simply a matter of time. Yet, on the eve of Gandhi's triumph, a new crisis loomed. Over the years, the British had established control over an enormous collection of territories and peoples across South Asia. Plainly, some areas like those in Burma and Ceylon [Sri Lanka] were so distinctive that in case of British withdrawal, they would go their own way. Besides these cases, Gandhi and the Congress Party called for a united federation of India with broad safeguards for the religious and ethnic minorities it would contain. Largely, British officials agreed with this idea. Muhammad Ali Jinnah (1878-1948), the leader of the largest religious minority, the Muslims, did not.

Although the Congress Party promised laws to protect Muslim rights, Hindu militancy in the 1930s spawned the emergence of the Muslim League under Jinnah's leadership. Jinnah was a prominent attorney and an early leader of the Congress Party. Tirelessly, Gandhi struggled to keep Jinnah and his followers committed to the Congress Party and to the idea of a "large" India. In 1940, these efforts failed when Jinnah finally asked the Muslim League to support the notion of a separate Muslim homeland, Pakistan, "the Land of the Pure." He outlined his case in a presidential address to a session of the Muslim League, held at Lahore in March 1940.

Source: From Sources of Indian Tradition, edited by Stephen Hay, 1988. Reprinted with permission of Columbia University Press.

The British government and Parliament, and more so the British nation, have been for many decades past brought up and nurtured with settled notions about India's future, based on developments in their own country which has built up the British constitution, functioning now through the Houses of Parliament and the system of cabinet. Their concept of party government functioning on political planes has become the ideal with them as the best form of government for every country, and the one-sided and powerful propaganda, which naturally appeals to the British, has led them into a serious blunder, in producing the constitution envisaged in the Government of India Act of 1935. We find that the most leading statesmen of Great Britain, saturated with these notions, have in their pronouncements seriously asserted and expressed a hope that the passage of time will harmonize the inconsistent elements of India.

A leading journal like the London *Times,* commenting on the Government of India Act of 1935, wrote: "Undoubtedly the differences between the Hindus and Muslims are not of religion in the strict sense of the word but also of law and culture, that they may be said, indeed, to represent two entirely distinct and separate civilizations. However, in the course of time, the superstition will die out and India will be molded into a single nation." So, according to the London *Times,* the only difficulties are superstitions. These fundamental and deep-rooted differences, spiritual, economic, cultural, social, and political, have been euphemized as mere "superstitions." But surely it is a flagrant disregard of the past history of the subcontinent of India as well as the fundamental Islamic conception of society vis-à-vis that of Hinduism to characterize them as mere "superstitions." Notwithstanding a thousand years of close contact, nationalities, which are as divergent today as ever, cannot at any time be expected to transform themselves into one nation merely by means of subjecting them to a democratic constitution and holding them forcibly together by unnatural and artificial methods of British parliamentary statute. What the unitary government of India for one hundred fifty years had failed to achieve cannot be realized by the imposition of a central federal government. It is inconceivable that the fiat or the writ of a government so constituted can ever command a willing and loyal obedience throughout the subcontinent by various nationalities except by means of armed force behind it.

The problem in India is not of an intercommunal character but manifestly of an international one, and it must be treated as such. So long as this basic and fundamental truth is not realized, any constitution that may be built will result in disaster and will prove destructive and harmful not only to the Mussalmans but to the British and Hindus also. If the British government are really in earnest and sincere to secure [the] peace and happiness of the people of this subcontinent, the only course open to us all is to allow the major nations separate homelands by dividing India into "autonomous national states." There is no reason why these states should be antagonistic to each other. On the other hand, the rivalry and the natural desire and efforts on the part of one to dominate the social order and establish political supremacy over the other in the government of the country will disappear. It will lead more towards natural good will by international pacts between them, and they can live in complete harmony with their neighbors. This will lead further to a friendly settlement all the more easily with regard to minorities by reciprocal arrangements and adjustments between Muslim India and Hindu India, which will far more adequately and effectively safeguard the rights and interests of Muslims and various other minorities.

It is extremely difficult to appreciate why our Hindu friends fail to understand the real nature of Islam and Hinduism. They are not religions in the strict sense of the word, but are, in fact, different and distinct social orders, and it is a dream that the Hindus and Muslims can ever evolve a common nationality, and this misconception of one Indian nation has gone far beyond the limits and is the cause of most of your troubles and will lead India to destruction if we fail to revise our notions in time. The Hindus and Muslims belong to two different religious philosophies, social customs, literatures. They neither intermarry nor interdine together and, indeed, they belong to two different civilizations which are based mainly on conflicting ideas and conceptions. Their aspects on life and of life are different. It is quite clear that Hindus and Mussalmans derive their inspiration from different sources of history. They have different epics, different heroes, and different episodes. Very often the hero of one is a foe of the other and, likewise, their victories and defeats overlap. To yoke together two such nations under a single state, one as a numerical minority and the other as a majority, must lead to growing discontent and final destruction of any fabric that may be so built up for the government of such a state.

. . . History has also shown us many geographical tracts, much smaller than the subcontinent of India, which otherwise might have been called one country, but which have been divided into as many states as there are nations inhabiting them. [The] Balkan Peninsula comprises as many as seven or eight sovereign states. Likewise, the Portuguese and the Spanish stand divided in the Iberian Peninsula. Whereas under the plea of the unity of India and one nation, which does not exist, it is sought to pursue here the line of one central government, we know that the history of the last twelve hundred years has failed to achieve unity and has witnessed, during the ages, India always divided into Hindu India and Muslim India. The present artificial unity of India dates back only to the British conquest and is maintained by the British bayonet, but termination of the British regime, which is implicit in the recent declaration of His Majesty's government, will be the herald of the entire break-up with worse disaster than has ever taken place during the last one thousand years under Muslims. Surely that is not the legacy which Britain would bequeath to India after one hundred fifty years of her rule, nor would Hindu and Muslim India risk such a sure catastrophe.

Muslim India cannot accept any constitution which must necessarily result in a Hindu majority government. Hindus and Muslims brought together under a democratic system forced upon the minorities can only mean Hindu rāj [rule]. Democracy of the kind with which the Congress High Command is enamored would mean the complete destruction of what is most precious in Islam. We have had ample experience of the working of the provincial constitutions during the last two and a half years and any repetition of such a government must lead to civil war and raising of private armies as recommended by Mr. Gandhi to [the] Hindus of Sukkur when he said that they must defend themselves violently or nonviolently, blow for blow, and if they could not, they must emigrate.

Mussalmans are not a minority as it is commonly known and understood. One has only got to look round. Even today, according to the British map of India, four out of eleven provinces, where the Muslims dominate more or less, are functioning notwithstanding the decision of the Hindu Congress High Command to noncooperate and prepare for civil disobedience. Mussalmans are a nation according to any definition of a nation, and they must have their homelands, their territory, and their state. We wish to live in peace and harmony with our neighbors as a free and independent people. We wish our people to develop to the fullest our spiritual, cultural, economic, social, and political life in a way that we think best and in consonance with our own ideals and according to the genius of our people. Honesty demands and the vital interests of millions of our people impose a sacred duty upon us to find an honorable and peaceful solution, which would be just and fair to all. But at the same time we cannot be moved or diverted from our purpose and objective by threats or intimidations. We must be prepared to face all difficulties and consequences, make all the sacrifices that may be required of us to achieve the goal we have set in front of us.

CHAPTER 35

Developing Countries

35.1

Disease Factor in Africa, K. David Patterson and Gerald W. Hartwig

In this chapter, excerpted from *History and Disease in Africa* (1978), K. David Patterson and Gerald W. Hartwig discuss African disease in the context of postcolonization and independence problems and promises.

Although written before the current HIV/AIDS crisis (over 25 million Africans infected), it still explains the significance of disease in history and development.

Source: From Disease in African History: An Introductory Survey and Case Studies, edited by Gerald Hartwig and K. David Patterson. Copyright 1978, Duke University Press. All rights reserved. Used by permission of the publisher.

Historians of Africa have generally neglected the study of past health conditions—as well as the role of disease, health care, and medicine in history—despite the obvious importance of the disease burden on the African continent. Major epidemics, which have often accompanied ecological change, migration, or foreign contacts, have tested institutions and decimated populations. A host of endemic afflictions have restricted settlement of large areas, sapped the strength and shortened the lives of Africans, and limited their productivity. For centuries, the continent's disease environment contributed to its relative isolation from non-African civilizations.

The intrinsic importance of the subject cannot be denied, but the historical study of health and disease forces the scholar to consider a society in its total cultural and environmental setting, a detailed and demanding task. For this reason it is encouraging that Africanists as well as historians and specialists in other areas are now showing signs of interest in the significance of disease's historical role. Our intention in this book is to illustrate the importance of health-related issues in African history, to encourage scholars to examine or at least to be aware of the disease factor within their own chronological and geographical specialties, and to suggest specific problems and topics requiring significantly more research.

Most human societies normally exist in some sort of rough equilibrium with their pathogens—the specific causes of their diseases—adapting to their disease environment in a number of biological and cultural ways. They may develop genetic defenses over generations, such as sickle cell trait which provides some protection against malaria. And, since a parasite which is too virulent endangers its own survival by destroying its potential hosts, selective pressures tend to produce more moderate pathogens. Exposure to most diseases stimulates the body's immunological defenses, which provides protection of varying degree and duration. Cultural responses are equally important. Societies typically have some functionally useful standards of personal and community cleanliness. Medical techniques are developed in an attempt to control the incidence and severity of various diseases. People learn to avoid certain sources of danger, such as tsetse-infected bush, polluted water, or unnecessary contact with victims of diseases they think are contagious.

These protective mechanisms have been only partially effective. African disease environments, frequently augmented by tropical elimatic conditions, have always exacted a significant toll on human life and energy. But, unless man/parasite-vector relationships were altered by such factors as contacts with strangers and their diseases, changes in settlement patterns, movement into a new ecological zone, alteration in modes of transportation, or dramatic change in life-styles, the epidemiological and demographic situation could be expected to remain roughly stable. Epidemic outbreaks would be unusual, but endemic afflictions were common enough and, while frequently chronic in adults, caused high mortality among infants and toddlers. A long-standing cultural premium on fertility and childbearing produced birth rates sufficiently high to balance or slightly exceed Africa's seemingly high death rates before 1945. The assumption that death rates in the precolonial era, or more precisely, the era before extensive contact with aliens, were as high as those of the earlier colonial period is probably incorrect. With the apparent partial exception of West Africa, the unhealthiest period in all African history was undoubtedly between 1890 and 1930.

Conditions of relative equilibrium between man and his diseases have been broken and restored several times in the course of African history. Village agriculture, trade contacts with Europeans and Asians, and the establishment of colonial rule all created new and more complex disease environments for African peoples. These changes took place at different times in various parts of the continent, with West Africans generally experiencing them earlier than inhabitants of other areas, with the exception of North Africa. Because of this fact and because accommodation to new conditions took place at differing rates, it is likely that epidemiological conditions varied widely from region to region at any given time.

Early hunting and gathering peoples had millennia to achieve biological harmony with their microbial and helminthic parasites. The advent of settled village life broke this balance. Economies based on agriculture or intensive fishing could support larger groups of people in relatively fixed places. Concentrated populations created, for the first time in man's evolution, favorable conditions for the spread of acute viral diseases such as smallpox, measles, poliomyelitis, influenza, and the many varieties of the common cold. Infection conveys long-lasting immunity against that specific viral strain to the survivors, and, since these viruses do not persist in a latent state in their hosts and have no animal reservoir, they can survive only by continual transfer from victims to nonimmune persons. Therefore, these diseases required more hosts than a hunting and gathering economy could support and must have first afflicted man after what we refer to as the Neolithic Revolution. Village life also caused the appearance or at least a dramatic increase in enteric diseases such as amoebic and bacillary dysentery and typhoid fever. Such diseases of the alimentary system are acquired by drinking water contaminated with human wastes. Large numbers of people living in close contact thus provided a critical mass of potential hosts and enhanced the opportunities for infection with organisms transmitted by the respiratory and the fecal-oral routes. Conditions for the transmission of water-borne helminthic diseases such as guinea worm and schistosomiasis were also enhanced. In addition, new methods of food production increased exposure to a variety of pathogens. Domestic animals harbored flukes, roundworms, tapeworms, and microorganisms dangerous to man, in addition to ticks which served as vectors for relapsing fever and some rickettsial diseases. Clearing forests for agriculture created favorable breeding conditions for *Anopheles gambiae,* the mosquito which is the primary vector of falciparum malaria. Wet rice cultivation and irrigation exposed farmers to schistosomiasis, a fluke which requires certain freshwater snails as an intermediate host.

The price Africans paid for the benefits of more efficient food production and settled village life was a more complex and threatening disease environment. Quite possibly, some of these by-products of a new civilization accompanied or preceded the movements of Bantu-speaking people into central, eastern, and southern Africa. If so, alien diseases weakened the ability of the aboriginal pygmoid and Khoisan-speaking inhabitants to resist Bantu expansion. As was the case in the Western Hemisphere after 1492, disease may have been an ally of conquerors.

Most African societies experienced many centuries of relative isolation between the rise of village agriculture and their first contact with non-Africans and their diseases. During this period, which lasted well into the nineteenth century in some regions, people developed natural and cultural defenses against local strains of pathogens. Technological conservatism and manageable rates of population growth—emigration being a frequent means of adapting to an increase in numbers—minimized the likelihood of sudden ecological changes which might disturb the relationships between humans, parasites, and vectors. The extent of interaction with neighboring communities varied greatly from place to place and over time, but almost everywhere commercial and other contacts were much less frequent or intense than they have become during the last century or so. Even where long-distance trade had a substantial history, as in parts of West Africa, the impact on the disease environment might well have been more limited than normally expected. Small groups of merchants followed well-defined routes on a seasonal basis and probably had little contact with people living even a few miles off the roads. Further, some long-distance trade involved relatively little human movement because specific communities prohibited transit traffic. Instead, these communities acquired goods on one frontier and carried what they did not want to keep across their own territory to exchange with yet another neighboring community. Such practices reduced the possibility that contagious diseases would spread over large areas. It seems reasonable to postulate that traditional "precontact" Africa suffered relatively few major epidemics. Natural barriers such as oceans and deserts, combined with slow communication, prevented most epidemics from reaching sub-Saharan Africa. Endemic diseases and natural disasters such as droughts and locust invasions, however, certainly affected population growth.

Many African disease environments were extremely dangerous for outsiders. Europeans whether traders, explorers, soldiers, missionaries, or would-be "civilizers" like the participants in the Niger expedition of 1841, generally found Africa's "fevers" and "fluxes" deadly until the beginning of tropical medicine in the late nineteenth century. With the significant exception of specific climatic regions found in extreme North and South Africa, early European activity was limited by exceedingly high death rates. The claim of a French trader that parts of the Guinea Coast were so unhealthy that the slave trade there was "an exchange of whites for blacks" was a gross exaggeration, but the point made is understandable. The continent's epidemiological barriers also proved formidable for settlers of African descent who had lost their ancestors' immunity to tropical diseases while in North America and who found the disease environment very hazardous in Sierra Leone and Liberia. North African merchants suffered from local diseases in the Western Sudan, and visitors to the Swahili Coast no doubt had comparable problems. Africa's epidemiological environment has played a major role in the relative isolation of the continent throughout most of its history.

Despite these hazards, foreigners came to Africa and, by bringing their own diseases with them, disrupted the existing equilibrium. Intensifying commercial and military contacts between Africans and foreigners—be they Europeans, North Africans, Arabs, or Africans from distant places—beached previously isolated disease environments. In Africa, as in the Americas, the Pacific Islands, and elsewhere, the breakdown of isolation meant the introduction of new pathogens and new strains of familiar bacteria, protozoa, and viruses. Major epidemics resulted, with substantial population losses.

Although as we have said many regions remained relatively isolated until the nineteenth century, the introduction of cosmopolitan diseases into Africa took place over a thousand year period. Trading communities in the grasslands of western Africa and the East African coast had almost certainly been affected by 1000 A.D. Africans along the western coast encountered disease-bearing Europeans during the second half of the fifteenth century; the inhabitants of the Zambezi valley met them after 1500, and Khoisan peoples in southern Africa after the mid-seventeenth century. We know very little about the epidemiological and demographic consequences of these early contacts, but Muslim and European travelers must have introduced Africans they encountered to diseases such as smallpox, measles, and syphilis by 1600. From what is known from other world communities, it is logical to assume that there was significant depopulation in specific areas as a result of these early contacts, even if the extreme aboriginal death rates of the Caribbean were not replicated.

In western Africa, maritime and trans-Saharan commerce encouraged a steady growth of long-distance trade. Increased intercommunication, combined with political upheavals in some areas, as among the Akan states, facilitated the spread of introduced diseases into the interior. It is reasonable to assume that most communities in this region suffered the initial consequences of epidemiological change at a relatively early date. During the nineteenth and early twentieth centuries, West Africans did not experience the same catastrophic epidemics and depopulation common elsewhere in the continent, despite an expansion of trade and political unrest in many places. By 1800 West Africans had had many generations to build up defenses to cope with their more complex disease environment, though such defenses were, of course, only partial. For example, ships periodically brought in smallpox, and whenever enough time had passed between introductions for a new generation of previously unexposed and therefore nonimmune people to appear, major epidemics with high mortality reoccurred. Despite the apparent antiquity of indigenous forms of variolization, smallpox remained a serious menace well into the twentieth century.

The movement of diseases was not a one-way process. Europe and the Americas acquired deadly yellow fever epidemics from West Africa, and the slave trade was responsible for the transmission of many helminthic infections, including hookworm, filariasis, and onchocerciasis, into the New World. African strains of malaria and dysentery played a major role in early American demographic history, especially among the Indians in the lowlands of the Caribbean basin. Even in the temperate climate of Britain's North American colonies, African diseases killed thousands of the white population, partially offsetting the overall population growth resulting from the importation of Africans.

Interaction with alien disease environments took place much later in most of the interior of eastern and equatorial Africa. Here, in contrast to West Africa, recurrent and often devastating epidemics characterized the nineteenth and early twentieth centuries and, in many areas, caused substantial depopulation. The expansion of trade and the rise of secondary empires provided ideal conditions for the spread of disease. Caravans, frequently consisting of hundreds of participants, traveled hundreds of miles inland. Elephant hunters and slave-raiders operated over large areas, destroying or confiscating crops, disrupting societies, and forcing thousands to flee into tsetse-infested bush or malarial lowlands. Famine was not an uncommon threat. Even victorious groups could wind up in unhealthy places. The Kololo, a Sotho group displaced during the Mfecane, gained control over Lozi country in the Zambezi floodplain in the 1830s. By 1865, however, they had lost their dominant political position partly because malaria, an unfamiliar disease, had badly weakened them.

Psychological stress can reduce resistance to infection, and for many East Africans the collapse of familiar institutions and the dangerously fluid social and political situation must have produced tremendous stress. Uprooted, malnourished populations proved terribly vulnerable to major killers like smallpox, cholera, and later trypanosomiasis. Measles and other diseases, including the great rinderpest epizootic which decimated herds in the 1880s and 1890s, contributed to the general misery. The jigger or sand flea, *Tunga penetrans,* an annoying and potentially dangerous pest, was introduced from Brazil to Angola about 1850. Thanks to increased intercommunication, the insect had spread over most of tropical Africa by the early 1890s.

The contrasts between nineteenth-century West Africa, where some biological defenses had developed by 1800, and most of the rest of the continent are striking, but the consequences of the spread of Eurasian diseases were probably equally devastating. Calamitous "virgin soil" epidemics and the most epidemiologically destructive consequences of state formation and slaving took place earlier in West Africa and were largely beyond the ken of literate observers. European records and indigenous Islamic writings will provide some clues if the proper questions are asked, but our knowledge of the demographic and social consequences of epidemiological change will certainly be less adequate for West Africa than for areas which suffered later.

Africans dealt with the crisis of a suddenly much more complex disease environment in various ways. Certainly, they were much more successful than most American Indian, Polynesian, Melanesian, or Australian Aboriginal groups. The reasons for this are not clear, but, perhaps because of lesser isolation and hence an ancient partial overlap in disease environments, Africans had greater resistance to Eurasian diseases. Perhaps African societies responded better to the stress of widespread illness, providing better care of the sick and avoiding economic collapse. Also, the fact that many African societies had less direct European pressure at the time of epidemiological crisis may have been significant. In any case, even when decimated and displaced, most African groups showed considerable resilience. Selective pressures encouraged the development of degrees of immunity to various diseases. Indigenous therapeutic practices, including herbal medicines and variolization, were sometimes useful. Families, lineages, and ethnic groups sometimes tried to make up for population loss by incorporating outsiders in a servile capacity, or as clients, or wives. This phenomenon seems to have been widespread during the nineteenth century and probably earlier whenever conditions encouraged it. The necessity of replacing victims of epidemic diseases probably played a contributory role in the evolution of many African systems of servitude. Witchcraft, sorcery, and witchcraft eradication movements must also be examined to determine their potential and probable relationship to an altering disease environment.

The disorders caused by the colonial conquest of the late nineteenth century, a continuation of previous turmoil in some places, provided further opportunities for the spread of diseases. European troops introduced diseases, and they themselves contracted considerable sickness, despite the major advances of quinine and boiled drinking water. In any case, colonial armies employed large numbers of African soldiers, and military units, supported by long columns of porters, crisscrossed the countryside, carrying with them respiratory and intestinal diseases associated with camp life. The use of river routes helped spread virulent strains of trypanosomes, especially in equatorial Africa. Both colonial and African forces lived off the land and in some areas of heavy fighting, as in French campaigns against Samori Toure, famine and disease went hand in hand.

Colonial rule had a profound impact on the health of Africans and, indeed, has largely created the continent's present disease environment. Government policies and African responses to them often inadvertently created conditions favorable to the spread of disease. On the other hand, European colonial regimes also introduced modern preventive and curative medicine to the continent.

All colonial governments tried to improve transportation networks. Efficient movement of people and goods was essential for administrative control and economic exploitation of the newly acquired territories. Internal trade barriers were eliminated and banditry suppressed. Roads, railways, and harbors were built and greater use was made of navigable waterways. The advent of motor vehicles shortly before World War I was a major stimulus for trade and mobility. Steamships carried plague and influenza from port to port. Clearly, greater intercommunication meant a more rapid spread of disease. On a continental scale, the rapid spread of influenza in 1918-19 was made possible by the developing transportation network. Cerebrospinal meningitis periodically swept the Sahel region south of the Sahara. Short-distance mobility was often sufficient to introduce people to new strains of familiar diseases, as Good's chapter in this volume shows for tick-borne relapsing fever. Intensified interaction within regions must have disturbed the relative tolerance which many rural Africans had acquired for local strains of the parasites causing malaria, dysentery, trypanosomiasis, and perhaps other indigenous diseases.

The epidemiological importance of greater intercommunication is obvious, but it is difficult to deal with on other than a very general level. Clearly, there was more intercommunication in, say, 1930 than in 1830, but how much more and how can it be measured? Distance of movements, the ecological zones crossed, the number of people moving, the nature of their contacts with population en route and at their destination, and the previous disease exposure of the groups involved are among the variables which must be considered. Intercommunication had different effects on different occupational and ethnic groups. Traders who traveled long distances and their commercial contacts and hosts encountered a greater risk of disease than subsistence farmers dwelling some distance away from roads or major trade centers. In West Africa, where women do much of the local marketing, females would presumably have experienced increased risk. Exposure to disease would vary among ethnic as well as occupational groups in accordance with their mobility and participation in commerce.

Colonial economic policies often had serious consequences for human health, as Azevedo's investigation of the Sara indicates. Forced labor existed at various times in all colonies, and had the potential to disrupt agriculture and to move people into unfamiliar disease environments. Mark DeLancey's essay on German labor policies in Cameroon is an excellent case in point. Other flagrant and devastating examples include the French porterage system between the basins of the Ubangui and Chari rivers and forced rubber collection in equatorial forest zones controlled by France and by Leopold of Belgium.

Taxation of Africans was frequently designed to channel labor from subsistence agriculture to enterprises of interest to colonial governments. Construction, cash crop production, and mining required large numbers of unskilled workers who could be readily produced by levying head or hut taxes payable in cash. Labor migration, whether a voluntary reaction to economic opportunity or a necessary response to rural poverty and taxation, had major implications for health. The migrants, generally poor, ragged, and badly nourished, often walked or rode hundreds of miles, bringing their own diseases with them. At their destination, they encountered hostile local disease environments and faced additional hazards inherent in their marginality and in their new occupations. Migrants to urban areas frequently had to live in crowded squalor where they were vulnerable to a variety of respiratory and enteric diseases. Lumber workers were frequently exposed to harsh conditions in remote forest camps. Returning migrants brought their newly acquired afflictions back to their rural homelands. Syphilis in northern Ghana was called the 'Kumasi Sickness' for good reason; tuberculosis was spread in that country and in southern Africa by discharged miners.

Agricultural policies, especially the encouragement of cash crop production for export, influenced health conditions in a number of ways. Plantations and small African producers required seasonal migrant labor. Also colonial agriculture had an impact on nutrition, a subject requiring extensive examination. Resources devoted to commercial crops had to be diverted from food crops, and the nutritional consequences of decreased food production may or may not have been balanced by greater ability to purchase food. Monoculture of cotton or peanuts led to widespread soil exhaustion, while agricultural research was largely confined to crops raised for sale on the world market. On the other hand, colonial animal husbandry and veterinary efforts helped increase the quality and quantity of cattle, sheep, goats, swine, and poultry, thus making animal protein more readily available. Clearing forests for cocoa farms created favorable breeding conditions for *A. gambiae,* a major malaria vector. Dams and irrigation projects designed to increase agricultural productivity were often more successful in spreading diseases. Dam ponds increased exposure to mosquito-borne diseases and to guinea worm; irrigation ditches provided habitats for the snail vectors of schistosomiasis, a disease which has spread rapidly in twentieth-century Africa.

The dangers of well-intentioned but ill-informed rural development schemes is illustrated by the following tale, which describes events in Kenya between 1957 and 1961.

> Once upon a time (but not too long ago) there lived a tribe deep within the Dark Continent. These people tilled the soil to raise crops of roots and grains, for they had little meat to lend them strength. Illness often befell them, but even so, in this dry land they were not overly troubled with the fever sickness brought by the mosquito. Now in the Northern World there was a powerful republic that had compassion on these people and sent their Wise Men to relieve the mean burden of their lives. The Wise Men said, "Let them farm fish," and taught the people to make ponds and to husband a fish called tilapia.
>
> The people learned well, and within a short time they had dug 10,000 pits and ponds. The fish flourished, but soon the people could not provide the constant labors required to feed the fish and keep the ponds free of weeds. The fish became smaller and fewer, and into these ponds and pits came the fever mosquitoes, which bred and multiplied prodigiously. The people then sickened and the children died from the fever that the medicine men from the cities called malaria. The Wise Men from the North departed, thinking how unfortunate it was that these people could not profit from their teachings. The people of the village thought it strange that Wise Men should be sent them to instruct in the ways of growing mosquitoes.

Colonial governments, by accident or design, often had a major impact on settlement patterns. People increasingly chose, or were required, to live in larger villages or along roads, rather than in scattered hamlets. These conditions obviously facilitated the transmission of disease. On the other hand, population pressures and official policies often encouraged the colonization of new lands. In the bush, especially along rivers, people were frequently placed in closer contact with the vectors of *Trypanosoma gambiense* and *T. rhodesiense,* the protozoa which cause sleeping sickness.

Urbanization, a recent phenomenon in much, although certainly not all of the continent, was a vital factor in the creation of modern disease environments. Cities, magnets for migrants and the hubs of the transportation systems, were foci for the diffusion of disease. And, in Africa as elsewhere, crowded urban conditions proved ideal breeding grounds for respiratory and enteric diseases. Sewerage, water supplies, refuse collection, and housing lagged far behind the needs of the rising tide of migrants. Still, enough modern sanitary and medical technology was introduced to alleviate many of the health problems associated with rapid urbanization. In contrast to the demographic costs of early urbanization in Europe, twentieth-century African cities have had significantly lower death rates than the countryside. The medical and demographic implications of preindustrial urbanization are of general significance in world history and, as African cities have developed relatively recently and data is more abundant than, for example, seventeenth-century Europe, studies of these urban problems in Africa should be of wide interest.

Thus, the colonial period and its accompanying changes unleashed serious health problems in Africa. Plague, tuberculosis, pneumonia, dysentery, and other diseases affected urban areas; smallpox, measles, syphilis, gonorrhea, tick and louse-borne relapsing fevers, cerebrospinal meningitis, influenza, and the other infections spread more easily, and familiar diseases like malaria, schistosomiasis, and trypanosomiasis could claim more victims.

By introducing modern medical technology and by encouraging research in the developing field of tropical medicine, however, colonialism contributed to the control of the epidemiological problems it helped to create. Public health and medical measures began to counteract the outburst of communicable diseases which characterized the first decades of the colonial era. By c. 1920-30 the demographic decline experienced by many people was halted and accelerating population growth became the norm. The relative contributions of medical measures and rising standards of living to mortality reduction are still unclear, but in Africa it seems probable that preventive and curative medicine played a larger role than in industrial countries. Rapid population growth may prove to be one of the major legacies of the latter part of the colonial period.

Colonial medical services have been the subject of much more discussion than serious research. Early medical staffs were clearly inadequate in numbers and in quality, even by the meager standards of Africa today. Funding was chronically inadequate. Even in the French colonies, where serious efforts were made to serve rural areas, medical facilities were concentrated in large towns. Medical departments were often surprisingly unaware of the extent or even the existence of some major problems, as Patterson's chapter on onchocerciasis in the Gold Coast and Hartwig's discussion of relapsing fever in Sudan demonstrate. Even when diseases were recognized and their ecology understood, preventive measures were often almost impossible. Smallpox vaccination campaigns were hindered by rapid deterioration of vaccine in tropical conditions. Quarantines frequently failed to control outbreaks. Malaria, dysentery, guinea worm, hookworm, and many other chronic conditions could not be controlled without major socioeconomic changes in the countryside. Therapeutic measures were often ineffective or unknown until late in the colonial period. Arsenic and bismuth compounds were used with some success against syphilis, yaws, relapsing fever, and sleeping sickness in the 1920s, but serious side effects sometimes plagued mass treatment campaigns. Otherwise, except for quinine, used as a specific drug against malaria from the 1840s, and emetine for amoebic dysentery, drugs effective against microorganisms were almost nonexistent. Indeed, not until the development of sulpha drugs in the mid-1930s and antibiotics during World War II could physicians directly attack most pathogenic bacteria. Cheap, effective drug therapy, the only hope for the rapid alleviation of mass illness in poor tropical countries, was only possible in the last 15 or 20 years of colonial rule.

The achievements of colonial medical departments were limited by their priorities and goals, as well as by limits on staffs, funding, and knowledge. The protection of European health was the highest priority, followed by the necessity to control major epidemics, and finally a third objective—to prevent bad health conditions from disrupting the economy, a great concern in the Sudan's relapsing fever epidemic of 1926 to 1928. These three priorities largely determined the policies of medical administrators. Yellow fever, which primarily affected non-Africans, was a major fear, as were potential epidemic diseases such as smallpox and cerebrospinal meningitis. Epidemic and endemic trypanosomiasis had enormous medical and veterinary importance and rendered large tracts of territory useless; it received more attention than any other single disease. Leprosy, perhaps because of its lurid connotations for Europeans, was a much more significant target than its incidence or the state of medical knowledge could really justify. On the other hand, there was little knowledge of, or interest in, diseases of children. And with the exception of yaws, chronic afflictions of the African populations were low on the list of priorities.

Despite growing interest in medical anthropology, we still know little of indigenous efforts to restore control over the modern disease environment. Traditional techniques continued to evolve, and, by various means, many Africans incorporated aspects of western technology into their medical systems. Inexpensive but nonscientific European remedies sometimes found acceptance, as in the extensive marketing of patent medicines from the metropole. Changes in African medical ideas and practices deserve study as an important aspect of intellectual history and cultural diffusion.

Colonial medicinal efforts, or the lack thereof, often had important political effects. In Africa, as in industrializing countries during the nineteenth century, governmental concern with public health led to increasing state intervention in the daily lives of ordinary people. Quarantines, slum clearance, sanitary laws and inspections, vaccination campaigns, and the medical surveys, injections, and resettlement schemes directed against trypanosomiasis brought ruler and ruled into direct contact, and, on occasion, conflict. African desires for improved health care, urban sanitation, piped water, and employment opportunities in the medical services also played a significant role in African–European political interactions.

CHAPTER 36

One World

36.1

Charter of the United Nations (1945)

The Second World War gave birth to the United Nations, an international organization designed to preserve peace.

Planning for the United Nations began well before the end of the Second World War. The organization was founded in San Francisco in 1945 with the United States as a driving force. President Franklin Roosevelt and Democrats in the Wilsonian tradition believed that the United States' failure to join the League of Nations at the end of World War I contributed to the breakdown of world peace in the 1930s.

The organization began operations soon afterward, with its headquarters in New York City. It was organized with a Security Council including the United States, Great Britain, France, the Soviet Union, and China. Each nation had a veto power over any proposed action. It soon became apparent that the organization would be unable to intervene effectively in any dispute arising out of the conflict between the great powers. Although the United Nations and its agencies have accomplished much since its founding, its primary purpose "to maintain peace and international security" was frustrated by the Cold War. However, with the dissolution of the Soviet Union and the consequent relaxation of international tensions, the role of the United Nations in world affairs was briefly enhanced. Subsequently, the unwillingness of the United States to abide by UN Resolutions concerning Iraq has damaged the prestige of the organization. Whether its authority and its ability to maintain peace and security in the future will prove effective remains to be seen.

Source: U.S. National Archives & Records Administration www.ourdocuments.gov

---

We the peoples of the United Nations determined to save succeeding generations from the scourge of war, which twice in our lifetime has brought untold sorrow to mankind, and to reaffirm faith in fundamental human rights, in the dignity and worth of the human person, in the equal rights of men and women and of nations large and small, and to establish conditions under which justice and respect for the obligations arising from treaties and other sources of international law can be maintained, and to promote social progress and better standards of life in larger freedom, and for these ends to practice tolerance and live together in peace with one another as good neighbours, and to unite our strength to maintain international peace and security, and to ensure, by the acceptance of principles and the institution of methods, that armed force shall not be used, save in the common interest, and to employ international machinery for the promotion of the economic and social advancement of all peoples, have resolved to combine our efforts to accomplish these aims. Accordingly, our respective governments, through representatives assembled in the city of San Francisco, who have exhibited their full powers found to be in good and due form, have agreed to the present Charter of the United Nations and do hereby establish an international organization to be known as the United Nations.

CHAPTER I
PURPOSES AND PRINCIPLES

Article 1

The Purposes of the United Nations are:

1. To maintain international peace and security, and to that end: to take effective collective measures for the prevention and removal of threats to the peace, and for the suppression of acts of aggression or other breaches of the peace, and to bring about by peaceful means, and in conformity with the principles of justice and international law, adjustment or settlement of international disputes or situations which might lead to a breach of the peace;
2. To develop friendly relations among nations based on respect for the principle of equal rights and self-determination of peoples, and to take other appropriate measures to strengthen universal peace;
3. To achieve international co-operation in solving international problems of an economic, social, cultural, or humanitarian character, and in promoting and encouraging respect for human rights and for fundamental freedoms for all without distinction as to race, sex, language, or religion; and
4. To be a centre for harmonizing the actions of nations in the attainment of these common ends.

Article 2

The Organization and its Members, in pursuit of the Purposes stated in Article 1, shall act in accordance with the following Principles.

1. The Organization is based on the principle of the sovereign equality of all its Members.
2. All Members, in order to ensure to all of them the rights and benefits resulting from membership, shall fulfil in good faith the obligations assumed by them in accordance with the present Charter.
3. All Members shall settle their international disputes by peaceful means in such a manner that international peace and security, and justice, are not endangered.
4. All Members shall refrain in their international relations from the threat or use of force against the territorial integrity or political independence of any state, or in any other manner inconsistent with the Purposes of the United Nations.
5. All Members shall give the United Nations every assistance in any action it takes in accordance with the present Charter, and shall refrain from giving assistance to any state against which the United Nations is taking preventive or enforcement action.

6. The Organization shall ensure that states which are not Members of the United Nations act in accordance with these Principles so far as may be necessary for the maintenance of international peace and security.
7. Nothing contained in the present Charter shall authorize the United Nations to intervene in matters which are essentially within the domestic jurisdiction of any state or shall require the Members to submit such matters to settlement under the present Charter; but this principle shall not prejudice the application of enforcement measures under Chapter VII.

CHAPTER II
MEMBERSHIP

Article 3

The original Members of the United Nations shall be the states which, having participated in the United Nations Conference on International Organization at San Francisco, or having previously signed the Declaration by United Nations of 1 January 1942, sign the present Charter and ratify it in accordance with Article 110.

Article 4

1. Membership in the United Nations is open to all other peace-loving states which accept the obligations contained in the present Charter and, in the judgment of the Organization, are able and willing to carry out these obligations.
2. The admission of any such state to membership in the Nations will be effected by a decision of the General Assembly upon the recommendation of the Security Council.

Article 5

A Member of the United Nations against which preventive or enforcement action has been taken by the Security Council may be suspended from the exercise of the rights and privileges of membership by the General Assembly upon the recommendation of the Security Council. The exercise of these rights and privileges may be restored by the Security Council.

Article 6

A Member of the United Nations which has persistently violated the Principles contained in the present Charter may be expelled from the Organization by the General Assembly upon the recommendation of the Security Council.

CHAPTER III
ORGANS

Article 7

1. There are established as the principal organs of the United Nations: a General Assembly, a Security Council, an Economic and Social Council, a Trusteeship Council, an International Court of Justice, and a Secretariat.

2. Such subsidiary organs as may be found necessary may be established in accordance with the present Charter.

Article 8

The United Nations shall place no restrictions on the eligibility of men and women to participate in any capacity and under conditions of equality in its principal and subsidiary organs.

CHAPTER IV
THE GENERAL ASSEMBLY

Composition

Article 9

1. The General Assembly shall consist of all the Members of the United Nations.
2. Each Member shall have not more than five representatives in the General Assembly.

Functions and Powers

Article 10

The General Assembly may discuss any questions or any matters within the scope of the present Charter or relating to the powers and functions of any organs provided for in the present Charter, and, except as provided in Article 12, may make recommendations to the Members of the United Nations or to the Security Council or to both on any such questions or matters.

Article 11

1. The General Assembly may consider the general principles of co-operation in the maintenance of international peace and security, including the principles governing disarmament and the regulation of armaments, and may make recommendations with regard to such principles to the Members or to the Security Council or to both.
2. The General Assembly may discuss any questions relating to the maintenance of international peace and security brought before it by any Member of the United Nations, or by the Security Council, or by a state which is not a Member of the United Nations in accordance with Article 35, paragraph 2, and, except as provided in Article 12, may make recommendations with regard to any such questions to the state or states concerned or to the Security Council or to both. Any such question on which action is necessary shall be referred to the Security Council by the General Assembly either before or after discussion.
3. The General Assembly may call the attention of the Security Council to situations which are likely to endanger international peace and security.
4. The powers of the General Assembly set forth in this Article shall not limit the general scope of Article 10.

Article 12

1. While the Security Council is exercising in respect of any dispute or situation the functions assigned to it in the present Charter, the General Assembly shall not make any recommendation with regard to that dispute or situation unless the Security Council so requests.
2. The Secretary-General, with the consent of the Security Council, shall notify the General Assembly at each session of any matters relative to the maintenance of international peace and security which are being dealt with by the Security Council and similarly notify the General Assembly, or the Members of the United Nations if the General Assembly is not in session, immediately if the Security Council ceases to deal with such matters.

Article 13

1. The General Assembly shall initiate studies and make recommendations for the purpose of:
a. promoting international co-operation in the political field and encouraging the progressive development of international law and its codification;
b. promoting international co-operation in the economic, social, cultural, educational, and health fields, an assisting in the realization of human rights and fundamental freedoms for all without distinction as to race, sex, language, or religion.
2. The further responsibilities, functions and powers of the General Assembly with respect to matters mentioned in paragraph above are set forth in Chapters IX and X.

Article 14

Subject to the provisions of Article 12, the General Assembly may recommend measures for the peaceful adjustment of any situation, regardless of origin, which it deems likely to impair the general welfare or friendly relations among nations, including situations resulting from a violation of the provisions of the present Charter setting forth the Purposes and Principles of the United Nations.

Article 15

1. The General Assembly shall receive and consider annual and special reports from the Security Council; these reports shall include an account of the measures that the Security Council has decided upon or taken to maintain international peace and security.
2. The General Assembly shall receive and consider reports from the other organs of the United Nations.

Article 16

The General Assembly shall perform such functions with respect to the international trusteeship system as are assigned to it under Chapters XII and XIII, including the approval of the trusteeship agreements for areas not designated as strategic.

Article 17

1. The General Assembly shall consider and approve the budget of the Organization.
2. The expenses of the Organization shall be borne by the Members as apportioned by the General Assembly.

3. The Assembly shall consider and approve any financial and budgetary arrangements with specialized agencies referred to in Article 57 and shall examine the administrative budgets of such specialized agencies with a view of making recommendations to the agencies concerned.

Voting

Article 18

1. Each member of the General Assembly shall have one vote.
2. Decisions of the General Assembly on important questions shall be made by a two-thirds majority of the members present and voting. These questions shall include: recommendations with respect to the maintenance of international peace and security, the election of the non-permanent members of the Security Council, the election of the members of the Economic and Social Council, the election of members of the Trusteeship Council in accordance with paragraph 1 of Article 86, the admission of new Members to the United Nations, the suspension of the rights and privileges of membership, the expulsion of Members, questions relating to the operation of the trusteeship system, and budgetary questions.
3. Decisions on other questions, including the determination of additional categories of questions to be decided by a two-thirds majority, shall be made by a majority of the members present and voting.

Article 19

A Member of the United Nations which is in arrears in the payment of its financial contributions to the Organization shall have no vote in the General Assembly if the amount of its arrears equals or exceeds the amount of the contributions due from it for the preceding two full years. The General Assembly may, nevertheless, permit such a Member to vote if it is satisfied that the failure to pay is due to conditions beyond the control of the Member.

Procedure

Article 20

The General Assembly shall meet in regular annual sessions and in such special sessions as occasion may require. Special sessions shall be convoked by the Secretary-General at the request of the Security Council or of a majority of the Members of the United Nations.

Article 21

The General Assembly shall adopt its own rules of procedure. It shall elect its President for each session.

Article 22

The General Assembly may establish such subsidiary organs as it deems necessary for the performance of its functions.

CHAPTER V
THE SECURITY COUNCIL

Composition

Article 23

1. The Security Council shall consist of fifteen Members of the United Nations. The Republic of China, France, the Union of Soviet Socialist Republics, the United Kingdom of Great Britain and Northern Ireland, and the United States of America shall be permanent members of the Security Council. The General Assembly shall elect ten other Members of the United Nations to be non-permanent members of the Security Council, due regard being specially paid, in the first instance to the contribution of Members of the United Nations to the maintenance of international peace and security and to the other purposes of the Organization, and also to equitable geographical distribution.
2. The non-permanent members of the Security Council shall be elected for a term of two years. In the first election of the non-permanent members after the increase of the membership of the Security Council from eleven to fifteen, two of the four additional members shall be chosen for a term of one year. A retiring member shall not be eligible for immediate re-election.
3. Each member of the Security Council shall have one representative.

Functions and Powers

Article 24

1. In order to ensure prompt and effective action by the United Nations, its Members confer on the Security Council primary responsibility for the maintenance of international peace and security, and agree that in carrying out its duties under this responsibility the Security Council acts on their behalf.
2. In discharging these duties the Security Council shall act in accordance with the Purposes and Principles of the United Nations. The specific powers granted to the Security Council for the discharge of these duties are laid down in Chapters VI, VII, VIII, and XII.
3. The Security Council shall submit annual and, when necessary, special reports to the General Assembly for its consideration.

Article 25

The Members of the United Nations agree to accept and carry out the decisions of the Security Council in accordance with the present Charter.

Article 26

In order to promote the establishment and maintenance of international peace and security with the least diversion for armaments of the world's human and economic resources, the Security Council shall be responsible for formulating, with the assistance of the Military Staff

Committee referred to in Article 47, plans to be submitted to the Members of the United-Nations for the establishment of a system for the regulation of armaments.

Voting

Article 27

1. Each member of the Security Council shall have one vote.
2. Decisions of the Security Council on procedural matters shall be made by an affirmative vote of nine members.
3. Decisions of the Security Council on all other matters shall be made by an affirmative vote of nine members including the concurring votes of the permanent members; provided that, in decisions under Chapter VI, and under paragraph 3 of Article 52, a party to a dispute shall abstain from voting.

Procedure

Article 28

1. The Security Council shall be so organized as to be able to function continuously. Each member of the Security Council shall for this purpose be represented at all times at the seat of the Organization.
2. The Security Council shall hold meetings at which each of its members may, if it so desires, be represented by a member of the government or by some other specially designated representative.
3. The Security Council may hold meetings at such places other than the seat of the Organization as in its judgment will best facilitate its work.

Article 29

The Security Council may establish such subsidiary organs as it deems necessary for the performance of its functions.

Article 30

The Security Council shall adopt its own rules of procedure, including the method of selecting its President.

Article 31

Any Member of the United Nations which is not a member of the Security Council may participate, without vote, in the discussion of any question brought before the Security Council whenever the latter considers that the interests of that Member are specially affected.

Article 32

Any Member of the United Nations which is not a member of the Security Council or any state which is not a Member of the United Nations, if it is a party to a dispute under consideration by the Security Council, shall be invited to participate, without vote, in the discussion relating to the dispute. The Security Council shall lay down such conditions as it deems just for the participation of a state which is not a Member of the United Nations.

Chapter VI
Pacific Settlement of Disputes

Article 33

1. The parties to any dispute, the continuance of which is likely to endanger the maintenance of international peace and security, shall, first of all, seek a solution by negotiation, enquiry, mediation, conciliation, arbitration, judicial settlement, resort to regional agencies or arrangements, or other peaceful means of their own choice.
2. The Security Council shall, when it deems necessary, call upon the parties to settle their dispute by such means.

Article 34

The Security Council may investigate any dispute, or any situation which might lead to international friction or give rise to a dispute, in order to determine whether the continuance of the dispute or situation is likely to endanger the maintenance of international peace and security.

Article 35

1. Any Member of the United Nations may bring any dispute, or any situation of the nature referred to in Article 34, to the attention of the Security Council or of the General Assembly.
2. A state which is not a Member of the United Nations may bring to the attention of the Security Council or of the General Assembly any dispute to which it is a party if it accepts in advance, for the purposes of the dispute, the obligations of pacific settlement provided in the present Charter.
3. The proceedings of the General Assembly in respect of matters brought to its attention under this Article will be subject to the provisions of Articles 11 and 12.

Article 36

1. The Security Council may, at any stage of a dispute of the nature referred to in Article 33 or of a situation of like nature, recommend appropriate procedures or methods of adjustment.
2. The Security Council should take into consideration any procedures for the settlement of the dispute which have already been adopted by the parties.
3. In making recommendations under this Article the Security Council should also take into consideration that legal disputes should as a general rule be referred by the parties to the International Court of Justice in accordance with the provisions of the Statute of the Court.

Article 37

1. Should the parties to a dispute of the nature referred to in Article 33 fail to settle it by the means indicated in that Article, they shall refer it to the Security Council.

2. If the Security Council deems that the continuance of the dispute is in fact likely to endanger the maintenance of international peace and security, it shall decide whether to take action under Article 36 or to recommend such terms of settlement as it may consider appropriate.

Article 38

Without prejudice to the provisions of Articles 33 to 37, the Security Council may, if all the parties to any dispute so request, make recommendations to the parties with a view to a pacific settlement to the dispute.

CHAPTER VII
ACTION WITH RESPECT TO THREATS TO THE PEACE, BREACHES OF THE PEACE, AND ACTS OF AGGRESSION

Article 39

The Security Council shall determine the existence of any threat to the peace, breach of the peace, or act of aggression and shall make recommendations, or decide what measures shall be taken in accordance with Articles 4 and 42, to maintain or restore international peace and security.

Article 40

In order to prevent an aggravation of the situation, the Security Council may, before making the recommendations or deciding upon the measures provided for in Article 39, call upon the parties concerned to comply with such provisional measures as it deems necessary or desirable. Such provisional measures shall be without prejudice to the rights, claims, or position of the parties concerned. The Security Council shall duly take account of failure to comply with such provisional measures.

Article 41

The Security Council may decide what measures not involving the use of armed force are to be employed to give effect to its decisions, and it may call upon the Members of the United Nations to apply such measures. These may include complete or partial interruption of economic relations and of rail, sea, air, postal, telegraphic, radio, and other means of communication, and the severance of diplomatic relations.

Article 42

Should the Security Council consider that measures provided for in Article 41 would be inadequate or have proved to be inadequate, it may take such action by air, sea, or land forces as may be necessary to maintain or restore international peace and security. Such action may include demonstrations, blockade, and other operations by air, sea, or land forces of Members of the United Nations.

Article 43

1. All Members of the United Nations, in order to contribute to the maintenance of international peace and security, undertake to make available to the Security Council, on its request and in accordance with a special agreement or agreements, armed forces, assistance, and facilities, including rights of passage, necessary for the purpose of maintaining international peace and security.
2. Such agreement or agreements shall govern the numbers and types of forces, their degree of readiness and general location, and the nature of the facilities and assistance to be provided.
3. The agreement or agreements shall be negotiated as soon as possible on the initiative of the Security Council. They shall be concluded between the Security Council and Members or between the Security Council and groups of Members and shall be subject to ratification by the signatory states in accordance with their respective constitutional processes.

Article 44

When Security Council has decided to use force it shall, before calling upon a Member not represented on it to provide armed forces in fulfillment of the obligations assumed under Article 43, invite that Member, if the Member so desires, to participate in the decisions of the Security Council concerning the employment of contingents of that Member's armed forces.

Article 45

In order to enable the Nations to take urgent military measures, Members shall hold immediately available national air-force contingents for combined international enforcement action. The strength and degree of readiness of these contingents and plans for their combined action shall be determined, within the limits laid down in the special agreement or agreements referred to in Article 43, by the Security Council with the assistance of the Military Committee.

Article 46

Plans for the application of armed force shall be made by the Security Council with the assistance of the Military Staff Committee.

Article 47

1. There shall be established a Military Staff Committee to advise and assist the Security Council on questions relating to the Security Council's military requirements for the maintenance of international peace and security, the employment and command of forces placed at its disposal, the regulation of armaments, and possible disarmament.
2. The Military Staff Committee consists of the Chiefs of Staff of the permanent members of the Security Council or their representatives. Any Member of the United Nations not permanently represented on the Committee shall be invited by the Committee to be associated with it when the efficient discharge of the Committee's responsibilities requires the participation of that Member its work.
3. The Military Staff Committee shall be responsible under the Security Council for the strategic direction of any armed forces placed at the disposal of the Security Council. Questions relating to the command of such forces shall be worked out subsequently.

4. The Military Staff Committee, with the authorization of the security Council and after consultation with appropriate regional agencies, may establish sub-committees.

Article 48

1. The action required to carry out the decisions of the Security Council for the maintenance of international peace and security shall be taken by all the Members of the United Nations or by some of them, as the Security Council may determine.
2. Such decisions shall be carried out by the Members of the United Nations directly and through their action in the appropriate international agencies of which they are members.

Article 49

The Members of the United Nations shall join in affording mutual assistance in carrying out the measures decided upon by the Security Council.

Article 50

If preventive or enforcement measures against any state are taken by the Security Council, any other state, whether a Member of the United Nations or not, which finds itself confronted with special economic problems arising from the carrying out of those measures shall have the right to consult the Security Council with regard to a solution of those problems.

Article 51

Nothing in the present Charter shall impair the inherent right of individual or collective self-defence if an armed attack occurs against a Member of the United Nations, until the Security Council has taken measures necessary to maintain international peace and security. Measures taken by Members in the exercise of this right of self-defence shall be immediately reported to the Security Council and shall not in any way affect the authority and responsibility of the Security Council under the present Charter to take at any time such action as it deems necessary in order to maintain or restore international peace and security.

CHAPTER VIII
REGIONAL ARRANGEMENTS

Article 52

1. Nothing in the present Charter prohibits the existence of regional arrangements or agencies for dealing with such matters relating to the maintenance of international peace and security as are appropriate for regional action, provided that such arrangements or agencies and their activities are consistent with the Purposes and Principles of the United Nations.
2. The Members of the United Nations entering into such arrangements or constituting such agencies shall make every effort to achieve pacific settlement of local disputes through such regional arrangements or by such regional agencies before referring them to the Security Council.

3. The Security Council shall encourage the development of pacific settlement of local disputes through such regional arrangements or by such regional agencies either on the initiative of the states concerned or by reference from the Security Council.
4. This Article in no way the application of Articles 34 and 35.

Article 53

1. The Security Council shall, where appropriate, utilize such regional arrangements or agencies for enforcement action under its authority. But no enforcement action shall be taken under regional arrangements or by regional agencies without the authorization of the Security Council, with the exception of measures against any enemy state. . . .